HOLOCAUST CONSCIOUSNESS AND COLD WAR VIOLENCE IN LATIN AMERICA

SUNY series in Latin American and Iberian Thought and Culture
———————
Rosemary G. Feal, editor
Jorge J. E. Gracia, founding editor

HOLOCAUST CONSCIOUSNESS AND COLD WAR VIOLENCE IN LATIN AMERICA

ESTELLE TARICA

Cover image: Detail from *Ofrenda y reverberación*, by Eugene Walsh Garcia. © 2009, Eugene Walsh Garcia. Used with permission.

Published by State University of New York Press, Albany

© 2022 State University of New York

All rights reserved

Printed in the United States of America

No part of this book may be used or reproduced in any manner whatsoever without written permission. No part of this book may be stored in a retrieval system or transmitted in any form or by any means including electronic, electrostatic, magnetic tape, mechanical, photocopying, recording, or otherwise without the prior permission in writing of the publisher.

For information, contact State University of New York Press, Albany, NY
www.sunypress.edu

Library of Congress Cataloging-in-Publication Data

Name: Tarica, Estelle, author.
Title: Holocaust consciousness and Cold War violence in Latin America / Estelle Tarica.
Description: Albany : State University of New York Press, [2022] | Series: SUNY series in Latin American and Iberian thought and culture | Includes bibliographical references and index.
Identifiers: LCCN 2021032912 | ISBN 9781438487953 (hardcover : alk. paper) | ISBN 9781438487960 (ebook) | ISBN 9781438487946 (pbk. : alk. paper)
Subjects: LCSH: Holocaust, Jewish (1939–1945)—Foreign public opinion, Latin American. | Politics and culture—Latin America—History—20th century. | State-sponsored terrorism—Latin America—History—20th century. | Genocide—Latin America—History—20th century. | Latin America—Politics and government—1948–1980. | Collective memory—Argentina. | Collective memory—Guatemala. | Collective memory—Mexico.
Classification: LCC D804.45.L29 T37 2022 | DDC 940.53/18—dc23/eng/20211012
LC record available at https://lccn.loc.gov/2021032912

10 9 8 7 6 5 4 3 2 1

Contents

Acknowledgments — vii

Introduction
The "Latin Americanization" of the Holocaust — 1

Chapter One
The Demands of the Times: Jewish Holocaust Discourse in Dictatorship and Early-Transition Argentina, 1976–1985 — 31

Chapter Two
Holocaust Consciousness as Critical Consciousness in Post-dictatorship Argentina, 1995–2005 — 75

Chapter Three
José Emilio Pacheco, Tununa Mercado, and Holocaust Testimony at the Mexico-Argentina Crossroads — 109

Chapter Four
Demetrio Cojtí Cuxil's "Maya Holocaust": Victims and Vanquished in Post-genocide Guatemala — 145

Chapter Five
Holocaust Testimony and Maya Testimony between the U.S. and Guatemala — 169

Conclusion — 205

NOTES	213
BIBLIOGRAPHY	253
INDEX	289

Acknowledgments

Research for this book was assisted by the generosity, kindness, and wise counsel of a great many people. I am indebted to scholars Edna Aizenberg, Beatrice Gurwitz, Emmanuel Kahan, Laura Schenquer, Brad Prager, Mónica Szurmuk, Michael Rothberg, Yael Siman, Brett Kaplan, Adriana Brodsky, Alejandra Uslenghi, Sandra Gruner-Domic, and Debarati Sanyal for sharing sources and contacts and for the conversations that have informed my work. Tununa Mercado, Naomi Meyer, and Demetrio Cojtí Cuxil generously gave me their time and shared their perspectives. So too Alejandro Kaufman, Bernardo Kononovich, Noé Jitrik, Daniel Feierstein, Yaacov Rubel, Beatriz Gurevich, Patrice Bensimon, Rabbi Abraham Skorka, Graciela Nabel de Jinich, and the staff at the Fundación de Antropología Forense de Guatemala and the Museo del Holocausto in Guatemala. Mark Healey, Laura García-Moreno, Marilyn Miller, Mirella Affron, Carol Andrews, Ivonne del Valle, and Debarati Sanyal gave me invaluable feedback on drafts of the work. Krista Hegburg of the Mandel Center for Advanced Holocaust Studies at the United States Holocaust Memorial Museum went above and beyond to engage with and support my research. I also thank Christina Chavarria of the William Levine Family Institute for Holocaust Education at the United States Holocaust Memorial Museum, and Claudia Ramírez Wiedeman and Martha Stroud of the USC Shoah Foundation, for their interest and assistance. Judith Freidenberg, Alicia Benítez, and Ariana Huberman offered me gracious hospitality; so too did David Oubiña and Adriana Amante, who also gave me useful recommendations and leads, as did Ana Rosa Domenella and Irene Munster.

    I am immensely grateful to the librarians who made possible the archival portions of this research, especially Anita Weinstein of the Archivo Marc Turkow, Asociación Mutual Israelita Argentina (AMIA), and Rita Saccal, head librarian of the Seminario Rabínico Latinoamericano "Marshall T. Meyer," for putting so many resources at my disposal and guiding my research with their own reflections on the topics. Marisa Braylan, of the Archivo Delegación de Asociaciones Israelitas Argentinas–Centro de Estudios Sociales (DAIA-CES), and Laura Palomino, of Memoria Abierta, kindly granted me access on short notice to their holdings. Patrick Stawski, human rights archivist at the Duke University Libraries, assisted me with the Marshall T. Meyers Papers held there. Thank you also to the librarians at the U.S. Holocaust Memorial Museum Library and Archives; the Harvard College Library, Judaica Division; the New York Public Library, Dorot Jewish Division; the Library of Congress Periodical Room; and the Northwestern University Library, for their help during my visits. Closer to home, at the UC Berkeley Library, my enormous gratitude to Carlos Delgado and Liladhar Pendse, librarians of the Latin American Studies Collection; Ruth Haber, curator for Jewish Studies; and the librarians at the Bancroft Library.

Many scholars provided crucial venues for me to share my work in its early stages: Marcia Stephenson, Jorge Coronado, Debarati Sanyal, Kitty Millet, Emmanuel Kahan, Natasha Zaretsky, Marilyn Miller, Héctor Hoyos, and Ximena Briceño; Mónica Szurmuk, Maricruz Castro, and the Sitios de la Memoria group; and Adriana Brodsky, Raanan Rein, and other colleagues in the Latin American Jewish Studies Association. Thank you to George Lovell, Amy Loeserman, René Carrasco, and Víctor Goldgel, who provided me with access to key resources at key moments. My dad was an essential editor and interlocutor, as ever; his presence runs through these pages.

Colleagues and students in the Department of Spanish and Portuguese at UC Berkeley supported me during this project, through gestures big and small. Ignacio Navarrete and Michael Iarocci helped me secure time and resources. Cathie Jones worked her magic on the p's and q's. Natalia Brizuela and Francine Masiello helped make my research travel to Buenos Aires a success. Ivonne del Valle read an early chapter draft and has been a constant friend. Manuel Cuellar and Roberto Medina provided needed research assistance and served as sounding boards as the ideas emerged, as did my undergraduate research apprentices: Kendy Amaya, Ulises Atilano, Susan Cifuentes, Jeremy Costello, Claire Courtney, Swift Cullen, Socorro Galindo, Lupita Lua, Saúl Olivas, Alvaro Prieto, Maeve Sneddon, and Lili Spira. I am grateful for the funding I received from humanities research fellowships in 2009–2010 and 2017–2018 and for a five-year Mellon research grant I was generously awarded; these were crucial to the success of this research.

Portions of Chapter 1 were published as "The Holocaust Again? Dispatches from the Jewish 'Internal Front' in Dictatorship Argentina," *Journal of Jewish Identities* 5, no. 1 (2012): 89–110. An earlier version of Chapter 3 appeared in Spanish as "Pacheco, el Holocausto, y la memoria del '68," in *Sitios de la memoria: México Post 68*, eds. Mónica Szurmuk and Maricruz Castro Ricalde (Santiago: Cuarto Propio, 2014), pp. 127–60.

This book was written on unceded Ohlone land, in gratitude to the Indigenous people who live here and keep the land's history visible.

This book would not have been possible without the patience and support of my family, old and new, and without the family memory-keepers, past and future, especially my mother.

Introduction

The "Latin Americanization" of the Holocaust

My grandfather tells the following joke: "A person says to a friend: 'It's been reported that all Jews and barbers are to be rounded up and deported.' The friend asks, puzzled, 'Why the barbers?'"

What makes some kinds of violence seem normal? Holocaust consciousness in Latin America during and after the Cold War can be said to operate in a way similar to my grandfather's joke: signaling a situation of violence that needs to be "denormalized" and brought under scrutinizing judgment. We might rewrite the joke as follows in reference to Latin America during the Cold War period: "'It's been reported that all Jews and political subversives are to be rounded up and eliminated.' The friend asks, puzzled, 'Why the Jews?'" This version falls flat, of course, because we don't have the luxury of innocent perplexity with regard to the fate of the Jews, who can never realistically occupy the position that the barbers occupy in my grandfather's joke. This new, unfunny non-joke instead doubles down on memory, asking, "Because we have not forgotten the fate of the Jews, how can we let this happen to others?" This is the question that guides the Latin American instances of Holocaust consciousness that will be examined here. The question is couched rhetorically, as if it were already a settled matter, but the answer to it is far from straightforward. It presumes that Holocaust memory resonates in the present and has a moral lesson to impart, and it presumes consensus about what that lesson is or should be. These presumptions will be repeatedly tested across the stories and interpretations I offer here.

Starting in the 1970s, references to the Holocaust began to appear in order to denounce the atrocities committed by Latin American governments against their own citizens under the guise of anti-Communism. In the aftermath of these events, from the 1990s onward and in the context of polemical "memory debates" about how to remember Cold War violence and whom to hold accountable, the Holocaust has taken on an even greater significance. This book is about the Latin American conversations behind these Holocaust references. It explores the contexts that have made the Holocaust meaningful and the debates over its meaning. It focuses on Argentina, Guatemala, and to a lesser extent Mexico, three very different countries that are hardly representative of Latin America in its entirety. Across these distinct national scenarios we can perceive shared patterns and sharp divergences in how Holocaust consciousness has unfolded since the 1970s, variations on a common theme.

In the wake of the social revolutions of the 1940s and 1950s—Guatemala's in 1944, Bolivia's in 1952, Cuba's in 1959—Latin American elites undertook efforts to stabilize or regain their ascendancy. Supported by the United States, these national oligarchies deployed "national security" obsessions to defend their interests. They forged alliances with military forces in order to crush liberation and social equality movements and spread a demobilizing fear across the general population. In countries across the region, military men adopted the counterinsurgency techniques developed by their counterparts in the United States, France, and England to repress the anti-colonial rebellions in Vietnam, Algeria, and Northern Ireland.[1] Their targets included armed revolutionary organizations but did not stop there. Student activists, labor organizers, teachers and intellectuals, religious leaders, rural community groups—a host of movements for social change—became the victims of national security crusades.[2]

How did Holocaust consciousness arise in these places and during these Cold War times? What are the conversations and questions that have arisen around this process? What does this "Latin Americanized" Holocaust consciousness look like, compared to its counterparts in other parts of the world, and what does it do in this region? That the Holocaust would be evoked in order to think about Cold War violence is far from given. Indeed, the historical differences between these two events create a vast field of disparities in the scale of the atrocities, the methods used to carry them out, the contexts in which they took place, and the ideological reasons that motivated them. These differences pose immense challenges to comparative thinking. Yet as I will describe in this book, such thinking can be found across the Latin American archive. When we delve into sources such as newspapers, personal memoirs and testimonies, literature, essays, and scholarly works of the past fifty years, we find repeated use of references to the Holocaust to talk about the terrifying realities of state repression.³ We also find dialogue and debate about the validity of those references and about the nature and strength of the connection between such disparate histories.

Conversations within local Jewish communities and interventions by local Jewish thinkers, activists, and survivors were key drivers of Latin America's Holocaust consciousness in this era. So too were the outreach and protest work of political exiles, human rights groups, and victim-aid organizations—Jewish and non-Jewish. Each of these was shaped in turn by global developments in Holocaust consciousness across the 1960s. Holocaust testimony by Jewish survivors began to reach a larger transnational audience during this period, due especially to legal proceedings against Nazi perpetrators in Israel and Germany, when the voices of Jewish victim-witnesses took center stage. Latin American authors and activists linked those testimonial practices to projects of political solidarity and national self-determination. This in turn sparked a connection between Holocaust testimony, human rights testimony, and revolutionary *testimonio*. The growth of Holocaust denialism in the late 1960s also had an impact. From the perspective of Latin America, this form of undermining or silencing the voices of the victims converged with the censorship policies of antidemocratic regimes. It lent urgency to a memory work that was increasingly inspired by Holocaust memoirs and, eventually, by mass-media representations such as the television miniseries *Holocaust*. Meanwhile, the presence in Latin America of Nazi perpetrators and of an active Nazi-inspired right-wing anti-Semitism brought the connections home more forcefully. Following these various pathways, across which global and in-country developments are so deeply intertwined that it is practically impossible to tease them apart, the Holocaust threaded into conversations about places and events otherwise distant from it.

My term of choice, "Holocaust consciousness," is a capacious one. The consciousness whose presence is signaled by diverse sources should be taken in the sense of knowledge or awareness. I use the term purposefully to avoid specifying whether that knowledge has been gleaned from memory or history or personal experience or something else. The idea of Holocaust consciousness is similar to the idea of collective memory of the Holocaust, but without the implied methodological preference for memory over history, and without the problem of having to define or name the collectivity whose memory is being examined. Holocaust consciousness may be vaguer, more fragmentary, and less defined than a discourse; and it may not be a memory or be historical in any meaningful sense of these terms. But Holocaust consciousness should be taken to imply that, regardless of whether it is based on history or on memory or on vague ideas or images about the past, an awareness of the Nazis' industrial extermination of the Jews has been internalized to some degree and thereby rendered available for reflection on the killing zones of Cold War violence.[4]

What happens to our understanding of global Holocaust awareness once we put Latin America on the map? Holocaust consciousness has spread across the globe to places far distant from its original setting to shape the thinking of people whose experiences are different from those of the Jewish victims of Nazism. But it is not everywhere the same. Although the Holocaust is now almost universally known as a symbol for genocide, its universalization has been accompanied by particularization and localization in different situations, as Andreas Huyssen notes.[5] This means that, although there may be an established or conventional set of pregiven meanings that shape how we approach the Holocaust, it is by no means a fixed template. Its legacy is multifaceted and has evolved in complex ways over the years. "The stories and meanings it entails can vary," note Alejandro Baer and Natan Sznaider.[6]

Thanks to the work of scholars in the field of Latin American Jewish studies, our understanding of how Latin Americans think and talk about the Holocaust has grown tremendously in recent years. We know how Latin American governments and Jewish communities reacted to the rise of Nazism and responded—or failed to respond, in the case of most governments—to the needs of Jews fleeing persecution in the 1930s and 1940s.[7] It is estimated that over 110,000 European Jews made their way to Latin American countries in the period 1933–1945.[8] We know more about Latin American intellectuals, Jewish and non-Jewish, who mobilized in defense of Jews and to call attention to events in Europe.[9] There is a growing body of work on the experience of Jewish Holocaust escapees and survivors who emigrated to Latin America[10] and on the memorial efforts undertaken by Jews in Latin America whose families perished in the Shoah and who waited for "the letters that never arrived" from Eastern Europe.[11] Creative writings by Jewish Latin American authors such as Marjorie Agosín, Sergio Chejfec, Eduardo Halfon, Liliana Heker, Michel Laub, Mauricio Rosencof, and Moacyr Scliar, to name just a few, provide insight on Holocaust memory.[12]

Scholars have spoken of the "Americanization" of the Holocaust, by which they mean that Holocaust consciousness has become a feature of U.S. life and taken on particularly U.S. forms, for better or worse, that distinguish it from the Holocaust consciousness of other countries.[13] Can one speak in turn of the "Latin Americanization" of the Holocaust resulting from the region's experience of the Cold War? Perhaps not. The term excludes those facets of Holocaust awareness in Latin America that have no anchor in Cold War experiences and no "Latin American" frame of reference. It also overstates the commonalities across and within a diversity of national contexts. Yet there is something to be said for holding on to the idea of a "Latin Americanized" Holocaust consciousness. It captures an essential element of the period after the Cuban Revolution of 1959, namely, the revitalization of a nineteenth-century idea about the unity of the region in its difference from "Anglo America," the United States. The revolutionary, anti-colonial aspirations of the moment converged in this other America, shaped the cosmopolitan educations of the voices that will be heard in this book, and left an imprint on their notions of what makes the Holocaust meaningful to future generations.

When we step back to observe patterns across the sources I examine here, three core features stand out. One, this Holocaust consciousness is comparative; it compares Holocaust violence to Latin American state violence. Two, the comparisons it wields are not very historical, tending rather to involve parables and paradigms rather than historical analysis, although not exclusively so.[14] Three, this Holocaust consciousness is deeply politicized. It consciously takes itself to be a form of political critique and grapples with the legacy of the national liberation struggles that were defeated in the Cold War. Let us examine each of these features more closely, before moving on to situate them with respect to global trends in Holocaust consciousness and then to address the dilemmas and controversies to which they give rise.

Latin American Holocaust Consciousness— Comparative, Paradigmatic, Political

Perhaps the most noticeable feature of the Holocaust consciousness described here is that it is comparative—the Holocaust is compared to other events—and instrumentalist—"used" to make a point about something unrelated to the historical events of the Holocaust. Consider some brief examples. In 1979, Argentine journalist and Peronist militant Jorge Luis Bernetti, from his exile in Mexico, wrote of "the holocaust of thousands of Argentines" and of "the justice for them and for the millions of survivors" that was surely to come.[15] This use is similar to the one we see a few years later in 1984, when Rabbi Marshall T. Meyer, an American who worked in Argentina for many years as the head of a Jewish congregation and founded Latin America's first rabbinical seminary, declared in a public speech in Buenos Aires, "We Argentines lived through a mini-holocaust during the dictatorship years."[16] There is also this one, from 1982: a group of Native American activists from the United States, Mexico, Canada, and Guatemala denounced the atrocities against Maya in highland Guatemala, noting:

> Remember that when neighbors of the death camps of the Nazi holocaust were asked how they were able to deal with horror so close, many replied, "We shut the windows." We urge all who read these words to read all the rest. No one can say, "We didn't know what was happening."[17]

We can see a reference to the Holocaust regarding Chile in 1974, when Hernán Valdés published his "Diary of a Chilean Concentration Camp," describing his detention in a camp just outside Santiago in the months following Pinochet's coup and accusing his fellow Chileans of the same false innocence claimed by German citizens under Nazi rule.[18] All of these examples use the Nazi machinery of genocide in Europe to help us understand state terror in Latin America in the era of anti-Communist counterinsurgency campaigns, and do so in order to highlight an element of that situation rather than to inform us about the historical events of the Holocaust. These references intend for the key word "Holocaust" and associated phrases to bring us closer to the visceral horrors of the torture centers, detention camps, and extermination sites and to the shameful indifference of the surrounding world.

The sound-bite style of these particular references hides the layers of history that make comparisons such as these possible and meaningful. We would need to delve into their contexts to perceive them as multifaceted utterances. Most of the materials I will address in this book involve more complex and extended interweavings of the Holocaust and Cold War violence than these rhetorically simple ones. These are useful, however, because they illustrate the extent to which the Holocaust operates as what Tzvetan Todorov calls "exemplary" memory. Exemplary memory works as follows: "Without denying the singularity of the event itself, I decide to use it . . . as one instance among others in a more general category, and I use it as a model to understand new situations."[19] The past event then becomes a "key" to understanding the present or the future. He contrasts it to "literal" memory, which tends to view past events as "absolutely singular, perfectly unique."[20] In Latin America, the Holocaust has been interwoven as an "exemplary" story that helps us pay attention to other stories.

It bears noting that, although Todorov's distinction between literal and exemplary memory is a useful one, in practice the lines between the two kinds of memory are far less defined than he implies. He argues that these two kinds of memory do not go together, that "it is impossible to affirm at the same time that the past should serve as a lesson and that it is absolutely incomparable with the present."[21] However, much Holocaust memory involves literal and exemplary forms together in a kind of unresolved dialogue.

We can see this in the work of two Auschwitz survivors, Elie Wiesel and Primo Levi. In 1976, in a short essay about the genocide of the Aché people in Paraguay, Wiesel wrote:

> I always forbade myself to compare the Holocaust of European Judaism to events which are foreign to it. Auschwitz was something else, and more, than the Vietnam war; the Warsaw ghetto had no relation of substance with Harlem—deplorable and misplaced comparisons which often reveal the ignorance, the arrogance of those who formulate them. I found these offensive, revolting. The universe of concentration camps, by its dimensions and its design, lies outside, if not beyond, history. Its vocabulary belongs to it alone.[22]

But he has changed his mind, he writes, in view of the extermination of the Aché: "I am compelled to this comparison, even though reluctantly." He continues:

> I read the stories of the suffering and death of the Aché tribe in Paraguay and recognize familiar signs. These men, hunted, humiliated, murdered for the sake of pleasure; these young girls, raped and sold; these children, killed in front of their parents reduced to silence by pain. Yes, the world impregnated with deliberate violence, raw brutality, seems to belong to my own memory. . . . There are here indications, facts which cannot be denied: it is indeed a matter of a Final Solution. It simply aims at exterminating the tribe.[23]

The parallels with the Holocaust, created by flashes of personal memory as well as a more factual assessment of genocide, were further cemented for Wiesel by the fact that Josef Mengele had fled to Paraguay and was living there "as an honored guest."

In *The Drowned and the Saved*, Primo Levi made this observation: "Up to the moment of this writing, and notwithstanding the horror of Hiroshima and Nagasaki, the shame of the Gulags, the useless and bloody Vietnam war, the Cambodian self-genocide, the *desaparecidos* in Argentina, and the many atrocious and stupid wars we have seen since, the Nazi concentration camp still remains an *unicum*, both in its extent and its quality."[24] It is a strong statement for the Holocaust as "absolute" crime, existing in its own category. Yet almost in the same breath Levi communicates his fear that the concentration camp may come back, if it has not come back already, and wonders, "What can each of us do, so that in this world pregnant with threats, at least this threat is nullified?"[25] His testimony will be offered, at least in part, as an instruction against the repetition of that which logically cannot be considered absolutely unique. Almost unwillingly, he returns to an understanding of the Holocaust as exemplary and, therefore, as a lens through which to see other events.

The second feature of the Latin American Holocaust consciousness described in this book is its paradigmatic nature. By this I mean that it tends not to be anchored in deep or rigorous historical knowledge of the Holocaust. Many of the Holocaust references to be discussed here operate at the level of paradigm, offering models that help us understand other events, or at the level of parable, as highly condensed tales of moral instruction. The Holocaust references used by Jorge Luis Bernetti and Rabbi Marshall Meyer to describe the "dirty war" in Argentina, or by Four Arrows Press and Elie Wiesel to describe the genocide of Indigenous peoples, call on emblematic scenes or images from the past: the neighbors who shut their eyes to the death camps, the justice eventually meted out to Nazi perpetrators, the destruction of a people. Brief, allusive, rhetorical, these invoke the Holocaust on a symbolic plane. Such a gesture is not at all uncommon. David Roskies notes that symbolization has been a core feature of Jewish collective memory of the event: "When Jews now mourn in public . . . they preserve the collective memory of the collective disaster, but in so doing fall back on symbolic constructs and ritual acts that necessarily blur the specificity and implacable contradictions of the event."[26] Latin American Holocaust consciousness is constituted by such paradigms, parables, symbols, and icons, that is, by historical events of the Holocaust that have gained an abstract meaning "applicable" to other historical events. This process of transposition inevitably involves a degree of blurring of the specificities of the Holocaust, as Roskies notes, and also of historical and semantic dispute as terms deeply associated with the Holocaust are brought to bear on other situations and events.

If we go back to my grandfather's joke, we note that it relies on a knowledge of history in order to work as a joke. Knowledge of the Nazi Holocaust prompts the question "Why the barbers?" instead of "Why the Jews?" But the joke shows us the limits of this knowledge of history, which has tricked us into normalizing a past that should not be normalized. We know about the Jews already, but what's this about barbers? It is for this reason that, as the joke would have it, historical knowledge is not sufficient; it must be shattered by irony and then cede to a moral awareness, which ultimately has the last word. The Holocaust consciousness that will be discussed here works on this double level. It is the result of a historical awareness of the Holocaust, an awareness of it as a specific event: the Nazi crimes that constitute the Shoah. Yet it also takes leave of that history when it brings the Holocaust to a new situation in a new place to draw attention to a different history.

The third feature of the Latin American Holocaust consciousness described in this book is its political nature. This Holocaust consciousness emerges among the vanquished of Latin America's brutal Cold War scenarios and develops out of the shattered cultures of left-wing mobilization. It is borne by militants and former militants, by their allies and sympathizers, by those who were not self-professed militants but were deemed "subversive" by the state. In some cases, this Holocaust consciousness manifested initially during the period of state terror in order to denounce it. This was the case, for example, for the clandestine news agencies, led by militant Peronists, who published underground during the first years of the Argentine dictatorship and used terms like "concentration camps" and "final solution" to describe the actions of the military junta.[27] But Latin American Holocaust consciousness is more common in the aftermath of state terror, carried by those who remember the dead and disappeared. It is a piece of the memory debates that shape the stories we tell about the political violence of the past.

The memory and human rights work of this period is sometimes examined under the aegis of trauma, or of mourning and loss of the certainties of an earlier age that were guided by the heroic project of realizing a modern, liberated Latin America.[28] Indeed, it is often to those elements of post-Holocaust art and philosophy that speak to the trauma of the Jewish catastrophe and the destruction of faith in modernity that Latin American thinkers turn in grappling with the past, as I will demonstrate in this study.

But trauma and mourning tell only part of the story of Latin America's Holocaust consciousness during the late-period Cold War and beyond. The other part of the story centers on anger and the activism it galvanizes, on the memory of the Holocaust wielded as a rallying cry that echoes through the emblematic "Nunca más" and beyond it toward the horizon of justice.[29] The Holocaust consciousness described here belongs to witnesses and survivors, family members of the dead or disappeared, solidarity and human rights activists, artists and intellectuals. It marks a critical, hostile approach to attempts to close the book on the past. It takes up questions of moral and criminal responsibility for state crimes, confronts enduring structures of impunity and social inequality, and endows acts of memory and testimony with political force.

Latin American Holocaust Consciousness in Global Perspective

To apprehend Latin American Holocaust consciousness, we must be open to a field dominated by comparative, paradigmatic, and political approaches. We must also address its complex position in a global field. Latin American Holocaust consciousness develops its own shapes and forms out of disparate national histories, but it also fits into and participates in global patterns of Holocaust consciousness. It dialogues with cosmopolitan intellectuals from other parts of the world for whom the Holocaust sparks a profound critique of Western modernity. Recent years have seen pioneering scholarly work on the circulation of this kind of Holocaust memory around the globe. Many scholars now recognize that the trend has been toward a "dislocated" and "decontextualized" understanding of the Holocaust, terms used by sociologists Daniel Levy and Natan Sznaider to describe how the Holocaust "is dislodged from its historical framework and thereby rendered more 'accessible.'"[30] Critic Debarati Sanyal refers to this as the Holocaust's "unmooring from its historical occurrence," which is "the condition of its relevance for other histories of violation and victimization."[31]

Michael Rothberg has proposed the term "multidirectional memory" to describe this aspect of globalized Holocaust memory; his concept provides an alternative to the model of "competitive memory" characteristic of memory cultures in the United States, which operates on the principal that "the remembrance of one history erase[s] others from view" in a kind of "zero-sum struggle for preeminence."[32] "Multidirectional memory," in contrast, emerges through "ongoing negotiation, cross-referencing, and borrowing."[33] Rather than seeing one group's memories cancel out or infringe on another's, Rothberg suggests that a dialogue can emerge when different histories of violence are brought into proximity. This is particularly true of the Holocaust: "Far from blocking other historical memories from view in a competitive struggle for recognition, the emergence of Holocaust memory on a global scale has contributed to the articulation of other histories."[34] Rothberg has demonstrated that this has been a feature of Holocaust memory practically since the end of war. He shows that a host of writers, including Frantz Fanon and Aimé Césaire, brought the Holocaust into the intellectual archive of the "age of decolonization," a period during which the "emergence of collective memory of the Nazi genocide in the 1950s and 1960s takes place in a punctual dialogue with ongoing processes of decolonization and civil rights struggle and their modes of coming to terms with colonialism, slavery, and racism."[35]

Other cosmopolitan intellectuals have also facilitated these processes of decontextualizing the Holocaust and recontextualizing it elsewhere. Levy and Sznaider identify the work of thinkers Hannah Arendt and Zygmunt Bauman as especially important because of their focus on "structures of modernity" as the origin for Nazi violence rather than on its emergence in a particular country or culture.[36] They note that Arendt, in her famous chronicle of the 1961 Eichmann trial, opened an avenue for universalization through her concept of "the banality of evil," which focused on the impersonal bureaucratic structures that allowed Eichmann to implement the Final Solution; this "allows one to remove the perpetrators of the Holocaust from their original cultural and national contexts . . . This is one more step in decontextualizing the Holocaust."[37] Martin Jay points, in a similar vein, to the philosophical work of Theodor Adorno, Giorgio Agamben, and Jean-François Lyotard, whose accounts of history and language in the post-Holocaust West turn Auschwitz into "a kind of symbol of historical unintelligibility and radical unrepresentability. . . . The Holocaust became a kind of rebuff to the very belief in historical meaningfulness or the ability of contextualization to make sense of traumatic events."[38] For these thinkers, Jay explains, "the lesson is not 'never again' but 'always already.'"[39]

Many of these globalizing-universalizing intellectual endeavors have played a role in the Holocaust consciousness developed in Latin America to reflect on Cold War violence, as will be seen throughout this book. Arendt is a frequent point of reference for Argentine thinkers who examine the bureaucratic and social-structural elements of state violence. Latin

American authors have likewise taken up Lyotard and Adorno but have also questioned and repurposed them with a view to rethinking or rebuilding the shattered cultures of the left, rather than holding them over the abyss of meaninglessness. The thinking of Frantz Fanon was influential to the anti-colonial rewriting of national history in 1970s Guatemala and reappears two decades later in Demetrio Cojtí Cuxil's condemnation of the "third Maya holocaust." More to the point, however, beyond the influence of individual post-Holocaust thinkers, is that the Latin American authors and activists to be discussed here, who decontextualize and recontextualize the Holocaust, are participating in an established comparative and cosmopolitan tradition.

This "unmooring" of the Holocaust, in Sanyal's suggestive words, its transformation from a historical event that affected particular people and places into a symbol and idea that speaks to the experience of people in so many other places—does it mean that the significance of the Holocaust has become variable? Yes and no. Levy and Sznaider follow the work of sociologist Jeffrey Alexander, who has argued that the Holocaust has become "the master symbol of evil," one that works as a "powerful bridging metaphor to make sense of social life."[40] The Holocaust as "evil" suggests an underlying bedrock stability to its significance, since no matter where it appears, the Holocaust symbolizes "the abstract nature of 'good and evil.' "[41] To name something a "holocaust"—or "Holocaust"—builds on a shared global awareness that the Nazi genocide of the Jews happened and that it has been universally condemned.[42] "The Holocaust is always in the background," note Baer and Sznaider.[43] The word "holocaust" presupposes a common language of history and addresses a global audience. To use this word is to enter into conversation with a world perceived as shamefully indifferent to local reality and to consciously evoke the idea of a crime of global proportions, one that concerns all of us.[44] Unmoored from its original history and dislocated from its original geographies, the Holocaust is not an empty signifier; it is used to point to evil in the world.

Yet scholars also remind us that "the Holocaust does not become one totalizing signifier containing the same meanings for everyone" and that the globalization of the Holocaust should not be taken to mean its homogenization.[45] Rothberg warns of the risks of centering Holocaust memory on a vague idea of evil that is "too singular and abstractly universal," ignoring "the active role [of] other histories and memories."[46] We need to know more about these other histories and memories, to speak about a recontextualized Holocaust consciousness rather than simply a decontextualized one and study the complex patterns of light and shadow that result.

Seen from a global perspective and with respect to global trends in Holocaust consciousness, Latin America is not an outlier. Nevertheless, its comparative, paradigmatic, and political approach to the Holocaust raises a series of interpretive problems. As an object of study, Latin American Holocaust consciousness lies somewhere between two fields that rarely speak to one another: Holocaust studies and Latin American studies. As a result, its features are apt to be misrecognized by one side or the other and taken for something they are not. The cultural codes of Holocaust memory can easily be misread. From the perspective of scholars of the Holocaust, Latin American forms of Holocaust consciousness may look like Holocaust trivialization or mild forms of denialism. From the perspective of Latin Americanist scholars, the use of Holocaust paradigms may look like a depoliticizing revision of the Cold War past, one that places victims at the center of history and in so doing marginalizes or "forgets" the role of leftist political activists. My argument throughout this book is that these concerns are largely though not entirely misplaced. Holocaust consciousness in Latin America is primarily an anti-denialist discourse, and it contains a political force that carries something of the ethos and aims of prior liberation struggles.

Holocaust Comparisons and the Shadow of Denialism

Comparative historical and sociological analysis of the Holocaust has grown exponentially in the past two decades.[47] Yet comparative approaches remain polemical. Holocaust comparisons in the United States have been perceived—and sometimes misperceived—as a form of minimizing the Holocaust, and in Western Europe since the 1970s, comparisons have furthered the aims of Holocaust denialism. It is important, therefore, to explain how and why Latin American comparative approaches are not inherently denialist.

In the United States the nonexemplary form of Holocaust consciousness has been fiercely defended in public discourse. The existence of polemical debates about the "uniqueness" of the Holocaust, which came to a head in the late 1990s, testifies to the fear that a comparative approach will diminish the enormity of the event, profane the suffering of its victims, or negate the determining role of anti-Semitism in Nazi ideology.[48] These debates in the United States were particularly inflamed around the question of the United States' own "Native American Holocaust."[49] The predominant approach has been to treat analogies with great suspicion, even hostility, as expressions of partisan self-interest or careless historical reasoning,[50] or as a form of theft from the Jewish people, as in Edward Alexander's essay "Stealing the Holocaust" and Yehuda Bauer's early work on the Holocaust.[51] According to historian Kirsten Fermaglich, the U.S. anxiety about comparison was not always as strong as it is today. In her study of American social scientists working in the late 1950s and early 1960s, she demonstrates that the use of Holocaust images to create analogies between Nazi Germany and American society was generally perceived by readers in this period as "thrilling and instructive."[52] Roughly speaking, it is only in the late 1960s that analogies linking the Holocaust to disparate experiences of oppression and to other genocidal events came to be seen, by many U.S. Jews and by scholars of the Holocaust, as illegitimate, trivializing, and false. Polemical debate on this point has diminished since the 1990s, yet the issue continues to be contentious.[53]

In Europe there have also been criticisms of a comparative approach to the Holocaust, primarily because these have been linked to efforts to minimize or deny the existence of Nazi crimes. More so than in the United States, the Holocaust comparisons that have circulated in Europe since the 1970s and 1980s are tainted by "historical revisionism," that is, Holocaust denialism. The Holocaust analogies that appeared in public discourse in France and Germany provoked enormous debate because they sought to lessen, if not outright evade, the criminal responsibility of Nazi perpetrators and the moral responsibility of collaborationist societies. Critiques of comparative, paradigmatic, and political uses of the Holocaust have therefore rested, in part, on the connection between such uses and Holocaust denialism.

Two events from the 1980s in Europe, the "historians' debate" in Germany and the trial of Klaus Barbie in France for crimes against humanity, gave rise to strong concerns about how comparisons can be used for the purpose of relativizing Nazi crimes in order to exonerate Germans morally or acquit Nazi perpetrators of their crimes. During the historians' debate in 1986, German historians offered new interpretations of World War II that focused on Soviet atrocities and therefore seemed to relativize or ignore Nazi crimes; they were accused of "apologetic tendencies" toward Nazism.[54] U.S. historian Dominick LaCapra explains that the German historians' comparisons of the Holocaust to other crimes, such as Stalinism, serve as "mechanisms of denial" through normalization, especially those that "evenhandedly show the distribution of horror in history."[55] That is, when Germans place the Holocaust as one on a long list of historical atrocities, they run the risk of normalizing it or of evading a confrontation with it.[56]

Something similar occurred in France during the 1987 trial of Klaus Barbie, the notorious "Butcher of Lyon," when lawyer Jacques Vergès defended Barbie by comparing Nazi crimes in occupied France to the actions of the French in colonial Algeria.[57] The analogy was intended to acquit Barbie and relativize his crimes. In this case, the comparison offered by Barbie's defenders may in fact have been illuminating; many French intellectuals, including Jews, had thought the comparison was correct for the Algerian war. French historian Pierre Vidal-Naquet, in his extended analysis of the Barbie trial, was highly critical of Vergès's comparative strategy and rebutted most of the analogies on historical grounds, yet recognized that the visibility given French colonial atrocities in the context of the trial gave rise to "some unbearable contradictions from which no one quite managed to extricate himself."[58]

It is important to stress that these reservations about Holocaust comparisons by LaCapra and Vidal-Naquet are based on the fact that the comparisons lack historical rigor, not on the fact of comparison itself. Most historians refute the "uniqueness theory" of the Holocaust as antithetical to the discipline of history. "A historian, by definition, works in relative terms," writes Vidal-Naquet.[59] The position is not one to which it is easy for him to commit, given that at the time of his writing, revisionist historians were offering comparisons between Nazi crimes and the crimes of other states like France and the United States in order to relativize Nazi crimes in an exculpatory vein. He considered these comparisons odious, yet even so, he reiterates the fundamentally comparative nature of historical inquiry and dismisses what he calls an "absolutist" approach to specificity that would remove the Holocaust entirely from "the movement and trends of history," even if he recognizes that such an integration into history "is not always a matter of course."[60] He notes that to insist on the specificity of the Holocaust "does not mean that . . . the genocide of the Jews should not be inserted into a history that would be simultaneously German, European, and worldwide, and thus compared, confronted and even, if possible, explained."[61] LaCapra says of Nazi crimes: "They will be compared to other events insofar as comparison is essential for any attempt to understand."[62]

Vidal-Naquet found the Holocaust comparisons offered in Barbie's defense to be historically indefensible. This is also the argument he advanced against Holocaust uses in contemporary Israel, where Holocaust memory has been especially politicized. He noted that the Holocaust had become a "commonplace tool of political legitimacy" rather than "a historical reality," and in regard to how the Nazi years have been "used" in Israel, he wrote:

"Their permanent exploitation toward extremely pragmatic ends deprives them of their historical density, strips them of their reality, and thus offers the folly and lies of the revisionists their most fearsome and effective collaboration."[63] We can see here the historian's attempt to counteract revisionist history on the grounds of historical inquiry itself. He does not say that the instrumentalization of the Holocaust in Israel is itself revisionist, but he does charge it with unwittingly providing revisionism with ammunition because it normalizes an approach to the past that is not based on historiographical understanding.

The "use" of the Holocaust in Latin America necessarily raises similar questions. How does Holocaust discourse here compare to the examples that Vidal-Naquet and LaCapra deplore from France, Germany, and Israel in the 1970s and 1980s? Are these Latin American uses of the Holocaust pragmatic? Do they thereby strip it of its historical density and reality? Yes, undoubtedly. The Latin American examples are highly instrumental. They are rhetorical tools used to make a point about something else: to stake moral claims, advance arguments, identify political positions. As such, they have an air of expediency. They teach us little about the Holocaust as a historical event.

Yet is this paradigmatic approach to the past truly the problem? We remember that, as demonstrated by the historians' debate in Germany, even rigorous historical analysis of the past risks normalizing and relativizing Nazi atrocities. In contrast, the not-very-historical use of the Holocaust in Latin America is neither revisionist nor relativizing. It is true that these analogies are not necessarily good tools for instructing students about Holocaust history. But such uses do not minimize or deny it and should not be simply dismissed as false. These Holocaust analogies are wielded to provoke a moral, political, and eventually legal confrontation with state violence. In this regard, they operate very differently in Latin America from how Holocaust analogies operated in Europe in the 1980s, where the point was to exonerate, morally or criminally, German perpetrators and their collaborators.

When an Argentine intellectual refers to an infamous Buenos Aires detention center as "our Auschwitz," he does so to lend added weight to the past, not to lighten its load on the present.[64] When Native American activists denounce the genocide of the Maya as similar to Nazi crimes, they do so to highlight its horror, not to turn away from it. Whereas in Germany claims for the Holocaust's uniqueness aim to force Germans to confront their own responsibility, in the United States the same talk, notes Novick, "performs the opposite function: it promotes *evasion* of moral and historical responsibility. The repeated assertion that whatever the United States has done to blacks, Native Americans, Vietnamese, or others pales in comparison to the Holocaust is true—and evasive."[65] Evasive, Novick argues, because the denial of comparison seeks to free Americans from the burden of confronting the violence of their national past. The same might plausibly be said for some of the Holocaust references that circulated in Guatemala during the 2013 trial for genocide of General Efraín Ríos Montt, the military dictator who oversaw the most brutal phase of the counterinsurgency war. Such Holocaust references were intended to show that the extermination of Maya in the early 1980s by the Guatemalan army was not like the extermination of the Jews by the Nazis and therefore not a criminal offense. "Would They Vote for Hitler?" asked one Guatemalan commentator in reference to the Jews, implying that Mayas, many of whom had indeed voted for Ríos Montt when he ran for president in 2003, would not have done so if he had committed genocide against them.[66] In this instance, the author denies comparison to the Holocaust in order to deny a confrontation with Guatemala's own grim past—that is, to relativize the violence committed against the Maya as "not that bad."

The Holocaust analogies discussed in this book work in precisely the opposite direction. They are attempts to confront Cold War violence, to lend it due weight and magnitude, and they do so by presupposing the due weight and magnitude of the Holocaust as a settled question. Whether or not that presupposition is a correct one, and whether or not these comparisons work on a historical level or even on a rhetorical and emotional level, are debatable—certainly Latin American thinkers and their U.S. interlocutors have subjected these analogies to debate, at times polemically, as this book intends to demonstrate. But the question of historical analysis should be separated from the question of denialism. Whatever their shortcomings, most Latin American uses of Holocaust paradigms, parables, and symbols are not denialist.

Latin Americanism after Eichmann: Cold War Victims and Holocaust Victims

French historian Annette Wieviorka calls our age "the era of the witness."[67] It began its global reach after the trial of the Nazi Adolf Eichmann in 1961, which drew increased global attention to the survivors of the Holocaust and their testimonies. Eichmann had escaped capture immediately after the war and settled in Argentina in 1950. Israeli special forces kidnapped him there in 1960 and brought him to Israel to stand trial. These events had an immediate and direct impact in Argentina because his extrajudicial kidnapping by Israeli special forces constituted a violation of Argentine national sovereignty, creating a political crisis in the country and setting off a wave of serious anti-Semitic attacks against Argentine Jews. The Eichmann kidnapping drew heightened attention to their complex identity positioning along an Argentine-Jewish hyphen, rendering Argentine Jews newly vulnerable to nationalist pressures and forcing them into defensive postures.[68]

The legal proceedings against Eichmann, meanwhile, had a broader and longer-term impact on developments in Holocaust consciousness. Eichmann was tried in a national court and for crimes against a particular group ("the Jewish people"), yet the event was decisive in terms of globalizing and universalizing the Holocaust. Coverage of the trial made it accessible to a wide public. Novick writes about its impact in the United States, noting that "it was the first time that what we now call the Holocaust was presented to the American public as an entity in its own right, distinct from Nazi barbarism."[69] Wieviorka deems it "a pivotal moment in the history of the memory of the genocide," and she points to several features of the trial that were to have global repercussions. One, the Holocaust became linked for the first time "to the themes of pedagogy and transmission," because the Israeli prosecutor used the trial to provide the world with a history lesson.[70] Two, through the trial, "the genocide came to be defined as a succession of individual experiences with which the public was supposed to identify," meaning that the Holocaust's victims became available as models for victims of other atrocities but also for victims of very different kinds of suffering.[71] Three, Holocaust survivors were given a central role in teaching history. The prosecutor placed the survivors' testimony at the heart of the trial, such that for the first time their words "attained a social dimension"; the truth they spoke was acknowledged by the state and "relayed to the world media as a whole."[72] Wieviorka credits the trial with "creat[ing] a social demand for testimonies" and granting the survivor-witness a "new function" as "the bearer of history" and the bearer of "a memory rich in lessons for the present and the future."[73]

However, in the post-Eichmann period, the acquisition of an ever more central role played by the Jewish victims and their testimonies in narrating Holocaust history is not without its problems. The increased dominance of a historical narrative structured by victims and perpetrators was initially greeted with ambivalence by Jews. If we look to Jewish ideas in the 1960s about the figure of the Holocaust victim, we see how strongly Jews tried to escape this connotation and expressed an aversion to victim-centric interpretations of the catastrophe. Wieviorka cites Wiesel's words from 1967: "I do not like to think of the Jew as suffering. I prefer thinking of him as someone who can defeat suffering—his own and others."[74] Novick reminds us that among U.S. Jews during the Eichmann trial, "there was widespread reluctance to seeing Jews portrayed as victims."[75] Historian Raanan Rein describes Argentine Jews' refusal of a victim identification in their responses to the surge in anti-Semitic attacks in Argentina after Eichmann's kidnapping and trial; Jews formed self-defense groups and organized a strike.[76]

Scholars of the Holocaust have also expressed ambivalence about a victim-centric, testimony-based view of history, for several reasons: that it may lead to an overly simplistic view of complex and multivalent historical events; that in privileging direct witness testimony, it may lose some of the benefits of more distanced historical analysis; and that in centering national history on the figure of the victim, it may contribute to a depoliticized understanding of a conflict that had an ideological dimension. Novick criticizes "the cult of survivor as secular saint," and A. Dirk Moses, in a similar vein, points to the problems that arise if victim narratives are not subjected to the same critical scrutiny as other narratives about the past.[77] Wieviorka worries about the "power struggle" between the role of the victim-witness and the role of the historian: "Each person has an absolute right to her memory, which is nothing other than her identity, her very being. But this right can come into conflict with an imperative of the historian's profession, the imperative of an obstinate quest for the truth."[78] Historian Enzo Traverso has also greeted this development with ambivalence, fearing that the figure of the victim-witness has displaced the figure of the anti-fascist militant in the stories we tell about Europe's past. He argues that in Europe since the 1980s, the memory of the Holocaust has erased "the legacy of liberation struggles," and notes: "The victims of violence and genocide occupy the stage of public memory, while the revolutionary experiences haunt our representation of the twentieth century as 'larval' specters. Their vanquished actors lie in wait of redemption."[79]

Latin America, too, has seen a marked turn toward victim-centric and testimonial accounts of the past, and as in the case of Holocaust memory in Europe and the United States, this development has been the subject of sustained critique. This book focuses on the era of defeat and rally, meaning the period when popular movements for social equality and national liberation were decisively defeated by U.S.-backed governments in the region and solidarity and human rights activism emerged to denounce state violence. Across the region this activism has focused on the victims of state atrocities and the criminality of state violence. It has attempted to center national Cold War histories on the victim-witnesses and on their testimonies about their experiences of victimization, testimonies it has endowed with moral, legal, and political authority. These efforts have been criticized by a range of thinkers in ways that closely parallel criticisms of Holocaust memory.

Sociologist Elizabeth Jelin holds that in Argentina in the immediate post-dictatorship period, the trials of military perpetrators "strengthened the figure of 'victim' of state repression as the central figure of the period, regardless of his or her ideology or actions," and that the victim figure acquired an utterly depoliticized connotation: "A victim is a passive being, harmed by the actions of others. The victim is never an agent, never productive. He or she receives blows but is construed as incapable of provoking or responding."[80] Historians Steve Stern and Scott Strauss, writing about contemporary human rights discourses, point to the stories of political commitment that tend to get left out of human rights narratives once these circulate on the global stage; these stories of "class and ideological fractures" become a silent trace that a casual observer cannot perceive behind the more conventional portrayal of "innocent victims."[81] Anthropologist Carlota McAllister's arguments about testimonial genres in post-genocide Guatemala express similar concerns. She tracks the demise of testimonial forms that looked forward to a future that would have made suffering meaningful in favor of therapeutic forms of testimony that search for collective healing but do not speak of struggle against social oppression.[82] In view of these reflections, we might say that Latin America has its own post-Eichmann debates, extending beyond Latin American Jewish concerns, and venture to postulate a "Latinamericanism after Eichmann," so strong have been the lines of concern about the status accorded to the figure of the victim and to victim testimony in contemporary memories of the Cold War past.[83]

This concern about creating a depoliticized understanding of Cold War violence extends to Latin America's Holocaust consciousness, the predominant tendency of which is to establish parallels between Cold War victims and Holocaust victims. The prevailing view is that this will lead to a collective forgetting of the ideological stakes of state terror in Latin America, which was implemented to eliminate those who held political ideas deemed to be subversive. Many thinkers fear that Holocaust testimony and the figure of the Holocaust victim should not be taken as models for the Latin American context, because these will displace narratives that grant agency to those vanquished by the state. I use Traverso's distinction here between two possible frames for interpreting the historical contexts of twentieth-century atrocities: a century of revolutionary struggles against oppression versus a century of genocide. One frame focuses on "the vanquished," the other on "the victims." He writes: "The memory of the Holocaust replaced that of antifascism, and the memory of slavery eclipsed that of anti-colonialism: the remembrance of the victims seems unable to coexist with the recollection of their hopes, of their struggles, of their conquests and defeats."[84]

I consider these fears to be overstated when it comes to Latin America, for two reasons. First, Latin American history provides evidence for a more flexible and capacious understanding of "victim" that does not exclusively connote "passivity" and "political innocence." We can look, for example, to the actions of the official Jewish community in Argentina, the DAIA, in the wake of the Eichmann kidnapping. The DAIA led efforts to defend a young Jewish Communist who had been kidnapped and tortured by a right-wing group; her captors had told her, "This is in revenge for Eichmann."[85] Rein notes that critics disagreed with the DAIA's role on the grounds that "the DAIA did not have to defend Communists,"[86] but it did anyway, resisting the idea that, being a Communist, she was not a true victim (although it did not defend her Communism, it bears noting). If we look at the more recent past, Jelin reminds us that the Argentine trials of military perpetrators conducted in 1995, in contrast to those conducted in 1985, "do not hide the political conflicts of the 1970s or the political agency of the victims," and she points out that in other Southern Cone countries, the figure of the victim and the figure of the militant are not mutually exclusive.[87] In Guatemala, Demetrio Cojtí Cuxil's understanding of Maya victims as holocaust victims takes shape in the context of 1992, the five hundredth anniversary of the Conquest; it is inspired by decolonizing and national liberationist thought and seeks to honor Maya resistance over the centuries. His usage would be a case of what Geoffrey Robinson calls human rights "from the ground up," an effort that is "inextricably linked to the struggle for self-determination."[88]

Second, Latin Americans tend to read Holocaust victim testimony somewhat differently than it is read in the U.S. and Europe—they attribute to it a political force that it has largely lost elsewhere. Sociologist Pilar Calveiro, a political militant in Argentina who survived detention and torture during the dictatorship, demonstrates this in her use of Tzvetan Todorov's analysis of Holocaust testimonies in his book *Facing the Extreme*. She uses Holocaust victim testimony to buttress her arguments against her former militant comrades, who insisted on too heroic an interpretation of the fallen and denied the experience of traumatic victimization that they had endured at the hands of government security forces. This move would seem to confirm fears about the drawbacks of the human rights frame—that is, that it substitutes the "victims" for the "vanquished." But Calveiro also reads these testimonies in order to argue against the official *Nunca más* report on the disappeared, which insisted on their innocence and thereby, in her view, reinforced the idea that one should not resist power.[89] She offers the possibility of a politicized reading of victim testimony when she uses it to denounce the idea, quite prevalent in Argentina, that "some people deserve the concentration camp or at least deserve it more than others."[90] Calveiro speaks here of militants who were both victim and vanquished. Mexican poet and novelist José Emilio Pacheco achieves a similar double valencing, as I will show later in this book. He works with verbatim accounts by Jewish survivors of Auschwitz that give us a sense of the horrors they witnessed and drag us toward an unbearable abyss of cruelty and suffering; but he links this to the pursuit of bringing the perpetrators to justice after the war and to a redemptive memory of the atrocities, implicitly offering this as a path to follow for Latin Americans under dictatorship. These and other post-Eichmann encounters with Holocaust victim testimony show that it has acquired a critical and political force in Latin America.

One explanation for the existence of these political readings of Jewish victim accounts is that developments in Holocaust testimony coincide historically with the rise of testimony as a genre in its own right in Latin America. Between the Eichmann trial of 1961 and the *Holocaust* television miniseries of 1978, during which time the global demand for Holocaust testimony reached a new peak, the Cuban state launched official celebrations of the revolutionary potential of testimony. Cuba's Casa de las Américas, the most influential hemispheric cultural institution of the day in Latin America, created a special prize for *testimonio* in 1970 and granted it state recognition as a distinct literary genre, with prizes going primarily to *testimonios* about revolutionary armed struggle. Meanwhile, in Peru, Colombia, Brazil, El Salvador, Nicaragua, and Guatemala, Catholic liberation theologians were pioneering a process of what McAllister calls "testimonial reflection" as a political consciousness-raising tool among the poor; they "used the prophetic and testimonial logic of biblical texts as a tool of reflection" and to inspire grassroots mobilization. These Latin American testimonial forms—the Cuban and the liberation-theological—are oriented toward "revolutionary futurity" and depict a suffering made meaningful in the struggle against oppression.[91] Most Jewish Holocaust testimony does not attribute any purpose to the suffering experienced by the victims of the Nazi genocide. Yet it elevates testimony to an imperative, one that intends a positive effect on the world. "The story of the death-camps should be understood by everyone as a sinister alarm-signal," writes Primo Levi on the first page of his first written testimony, and he continues: "The need to tell our story to 'the rest,' to make 'the rest' participate in it, had taken for us, before our liberation and after, the character of an immediate and violent impulse, to the point of competing with our other elementary needs."[92] Latin American survivors have recast this commitment in political terms and in reference to Cold War Latin America, creating a convergence between Holocaust testimony and revolutionary *testimonio*.

Therefore, just as the history of Holocaust comparisons in Europe and United States should not be used as a singular template to understand Latin American Holocaust comparisons, so too Europe's post-Holocaust focus on the victim does not match up consistently with Latin America's. In reality, victims and vanquished cannot easily be untangled in Latin America's human rights cultures of memory. These are nearly always carriers of a demand for social justice that takes up some of the language and aspirations of the era of national liberation and of anti-colonial struggles dating back centuries, that thinks with but also beyond the horizon of criminal justice. Revolutionary futurity like the one that inspired mass mobilizations in the 1960s and 1970s? No. But those who confront the impunity enjoyed by the perpetrators of state atrocities can and do activate their historical debt to the vanquished of the past.[93]

Much in the way that Rothberg speaks of "the Holocaust in the age of decolonization," we can speak of the Holocaust in the age of national liberation or "the age of revolt," in the words of Beatrice Gurwitz.[94] Traverso reminds us that in the 1960s, "the comparison between Nazi violence and U.S. imperialism was a commonplace of the antiwar movement," and that during the 1967 Russell Tribunal, which convicted the United States of committing genocide in Vietnam, "memory was mobilized to fight the executioners of the present, not to commemorate the victims of the past."[95] When the concept of genocide was adopted by the United Nations in 1948 in response to the Nazi crimes of the Holocaust, it established a new means to criminalize state violence. Its use by the Russell Tribunal extended that legal-moral condemnation to include situations in which the victims of state violence constitute an insurgent political opposition. The concept of genocide was a vector of globalized Holocaust consciousness with a significant impact in Latin America.[96] Elements of that legacy continued to be felt across the

1970s and into the 1980s and continue into the present day. In other words, as will be seen in this book, Holocaust consciousness in Latin America has contributed to, rather than detracted from, a politicized approach to Cold War violence. We can say that Holocaust consciousness in Latin America has often operated as "a place to work out a critical subjectivity," as Guatemalan thinker Sergio Tischler Visquerra might put it.[97] It animates the spirit of what Jewish liberation thinker Marc Ellis refers to as "the command of the ghetto scribes: the Holocaust event critiques all unjust use of power."[98]

Structure of the Book

I have spoken here of a "Latin American" Holocaust consciousness, but the extent to which the historical and conceptual framework I offer works across the myriad Cold War and post–Cold War scenarios of this vast region remains to be tested. In the following chapters I opt for a focus on three places: Argentina, Guatemala, and Mexico, though this last to a much lesser extent. Argentina was a predictable choice because of the depth and density of Holocaust discourses there. Also inevitable was the need to move beyond Argentina, and beyond the Southern Cone more generally, to bring out new facets of the topic. Guatemalan Indigenous and other thinkers and activists who respond to the Maya genocide in the early 1980s open up other timescapes for Holocaust references by adapting these to the anti-colonial memory work of the Maya movement. Guatemala also provides a view on the transnational impact of U.S. Holocaust consciousness. In between these two cases, I offer up a vision of Mexico City in the 1970s as a meeting point for Argentine exiles, Jewish Holocaust survivors, and Mexican intellectuals grappling with the grief and fear created by Cold War state repression. We can use these stories from Argentina, Mexico, and Guatemala to begin tracing the Cold War histories of Latin American Holocaust awareness. Whether these echo the Holocaust consciousness of other countries—Brazil, Chile, Colombia, El Salvador, and others—remains to be seen.

Chapters 1 and 2 take a deep dive into Argentina in the dictatorship and post-dictatorship periods. In 1976 in Argentina the armed forces had taken over the government in a coup d'état and initiated their "Process of National Reorganization." The "Proceso" was a top-down effort by the military to impose on Argentine society, by use of force, its vision of political and economic order. That vision was antidemocratic, patriarchal, pro-oligarchy, and free-trade oriented. As critic Idelber Avelar notes about the Southern

Cone military regimes, "the dictatorships' raison d'être was the physical and symbolic elimination of all resistance to the implementation of market logic."⁹⁹ The method used by the military government was terror, with which it infected Argentine society as a whole, even those who supported the coup, who were many.¹⁰⁰ But above all it sowed terror on those citizens whom it suspected of holding an opposing vision of society. The Argentine state set out to round them up and then detain, torture, and "disappear" them. The vast majority of these victims, who number thirty thousand by human rights estimates, were unarmed.¹⁰¹

Chapter 1 examines the circulation of Holocaust references during the dictatorship and early post-dictatorship periods (1976–1985). Use of the Holocaust to mark the intensity of state brutality was at first limited to clandestine oppositional writings. Soon, however, it became a feature of the Argentine Jewish community's mixed response to authoritarian rule, sparking intense debates about whether the experience of political repression and the military regime's anti-Semitic practices engendered a situation similar to the Holocaust. At the time, about 280,000 Jews lived in Argentina and were prominent across all fields of life.¹⁰² Between 35,000 and 39,000 Holocaust escapees and survivors had arrived there in the years 1933–1945, with a vibrant memorial culture.¹⁰³ During the dictatorship, Jews were disproportionately targeted for repression by the military junta. Debates about Holocaust legacies deepened the political rifts within the Argentine Jewish community, as can be seen in Jewish newspapers, testimonies by Jewish political prisoners and by Jewish families of the disappeared, and the actions of Jewish community leaders and activists. Despite some resistance, Holocaust analogies found a resonance both nationally and internationally and expanded outward beyond Argentine Jews to other sectors, such that when the dictatorship officially ended, in 1983, the Holocaust as a point of reference had become fairly commonplace. This was due in part to the work of Jewish human rights activists and in part to the increasing mass media circulation of Holocaust representations on a global scale, such as the airing in 1981 of the television miniseries *Holocaust*, which had previously been censored by the junta.

Chapter 2 picks up the thread in the subsequent decade, focusing on the years 1995–2005, from the start of a new "memory boom" to the start of the Kirchner presidencies and the greater institutionalization of human rights. The Argentine memory politics of the post-dictatorship period have been deeply saturated by the Holocaust, particularly among Argentine intellectuals, for whom Holocaust testimonies, and philosophical and scholarly works about how and why the Holocaust happened and about its troubling legacy in the modern West, serve as a touchstone for critical approaches to political violence in Argentina and animate debates about the shape of memory. This chapter looks at three distinct intellectual projects in which Holocaust consciousness is determinative: one, in the field of human rights activism; two, among thinkers associated with the journal *Punto de Vista*, especially Beatriz Sarlo and Hugo Vezzetti; three, among those associated with the journal *Confines*, particularly Héctor Schmucler and Nicolás Casullo.

Many Argentines escaped into political exile to avoid death, as they had begun to do already in the years prior to the 1976 coup, when rightwing death squads had labeled political and labor activists "subversives" and targeted them for murder. Mexico was a major destination, accepting several thousand exiles from Argentina, more than any other single country. Ironically, at the same time the Mexican government was giving left-wing exiles legal permission to settle in Mexico, it was in the midst of waging its own war against political dissidents, most visibly with the repression of the student movement. On October 2, 1968, government security forces massacred unarmed student protestors in the plaza at Tlatelolco in Mexico City. In those years the conversations between Mexican authors and Argentine exiles—the latter had integrated, not without difficulties, into the fabric of Mexico City's cosmopolitan cultural and intellectual life—created a complex mirroring between the two countries. Although with markedly less frequency and density than in Argentina, here too, against the backdrop of 1970s Mexico, the Holocaust appears as a point of reference to create linkages between the Latin American victims of state terror and the Jewish victims of Nazism.

Chapter 3 turns to this circulation of Holocaust testimony at the interface between Mexico and Argentina. In post-1968 Mexico, testimony and memory are fragile, embattled endeavors, lacking state recognition and with limited media circulation. Their value has to be constructed, laboriously, by writers working with materials taken from other places and other times. One of these is the Conquest of Mexico; the other is the Jewish Holocaust. Mexico's Jewish community in the 1970s numbered about thirty-five thousand, with fewer than two thousand Holocaust escapees and survivors.[104] These play a small yet crucial role in the stories I tell here. This chapter examines the work of two writers who contributed to the endeavor of constructing a memory culture for the present out of the fragments of past genocides: José Emilio Pacheco, whose experimental novel *Morirás lejos* (You Will Die Far Away) incorporates Jewish Holocaust testimony from documentary sources, and Tununa Mercado, whose formative encounters with Jewish Holocaust survivors in 1970s Mexico nurtured her commitment to what Wieviorka calls "the testimonial situation," the scene in which a testimony comes into being as such.[105] Both writers demonstrate that Holocaust testimony became relevant in 1970s Mexico as a model for Latin American testimony against state terror.

Chapters 4 and 5 turn to Guatemala in order to explore the connections between two genocides, Indigenous and Jewish. The Guatemalan military—trained, financed, and armed by the United States, Israel, and other countries—had been waging war since 1960 against armed guerrilla groups and unarmed activists such as peasant and labor organizers. In 1981 it intensified what had already been a brutal counterinsurgency campaign and focused its attention on the Maya highlands. Army officials categorized Maya villagers as a base of support for the guerrillas—or a *potential* base of support—one that had to be eliminated all the way down to its cultural roots.[106] They ordered the wholesale massacre of entire villages to implement this strategy. Infants and children were killed alongside adults; the material signs of Maya life were systematically destroyed; Maya civilians were relocated to "model villages," organized into squads, and forced to participate in the destruction of their neighbors. In 1982 Guatemala's military junta unveiled its "National Plan for Security and Development" to rationalize the violence, which over the course of the thirty-six-year war claimed an estimated two hundred thousand lives, 83 percent of them Maya.[107]

Although state atrocities against the Maya have been increasingly recognized as "genocidal," the term remains hotly contested, especially in the wake of the 2013 trial against Efraín Ríos Montt, whose conviction on charges of genocide was almost immediately overturned by a higher court and provoked intense debate in the public sphere. The term has been in circulation since the early 1980s to condemn the atrocities in Guatemala and to this day retains an ideological charge in a country whose military and business elites, among others, still routinely justify the army's massacres of Mayas as a necessary tool against Communist subversion. Meanwhile, the term "holocaust" to describe these same events has not occupied a large role in public consciousness. Guatemala's small Jewish community, for its part, has never promoted the connections between the two histories.[108] Yet the Holocaust is there nevertheless, paratextually, as a point of intensification and debate, among those who have denounced the army's violence.

Chapter 4 tackles the semantics of "holocaust" in post-genocide Guatemala. It focuses on the 1990s and particularly on the symbolic year 1992, the five hundredth anniversary of the "conquest," another term of intense debate. These separate events and their loaded terms—the conquest of the Indies; the genocide of highland Mayas; the Jewish Holocaust—make contact in the phrase "the Maya holocaust," proposed by Maya author Demetrio Cojtí Cuxil and sparking a semantic dispute among scholars about how we name and remember the victims of Guatemala's long civil war. Why name it a "holocaust" instead of a "genocide," and why does the term "conquest" play such an important role in his choice? What vision of the victims did Cojtí intend to put forward when he chose this loaded word, and what vision of the victims did this word communicate to others?

Chapter 5 returns to the question of testimony, this time to examine two distinct moments of convergence between Holocaust testimony and Maya testimony in post-genocide Guatemala. The first concerns the debates centering on Rigoberta Menchú's 1983 *testimonio—I, Rigoberta Menchú: An Indian Woman in Guatemala*—that were provoked in the 1990s by anthropologist David Stoll's accusations that she had fabricated parts of her story. Holocaust testimony became a feature of the ensuing debate, when some of the U.S. academics who came to Menchú's defense turned to scholarship about Holocaust survivor testimony to support their arguments and pointed to the parallels between this case and Holocaust denialism. The second, a more recent moment, concerns the partnership inaugurated in 2015 between the Shoah Foundation Institute for Visual History and Education at the University of Southern California and the Guatemalan Forensic Anthropology Foundation (Fundación de Antropología Forense de Guatemala, FAFG) to produce video testimony by Maya survivors of army massacres in the 1980s. Both of these instances—the Stoll-Menchú debate and the Shoah Foundation–FAFG partnership—involve attempts to place Maya voices at the center of national narratives of the past and to do so in dialogue with Holocaust survivor testimony.

The Holocaust consciousness described in these various instances can be found in works by both Jewish and non-Jewish thinkers. It is sometimes the direct result of Latin American Jewish Holocaust memories, sometimes not. There is a link between the fact that Argentina has the largest Jewish community in Latin America and the fact that a Cold War–inflected Holocaust consciousness there has become an element of public discourse.[109] But the quantitative link should not be overemphasized. More significant is the fact that many Argentine Jews have actively participated in fostering the comparative and integrative approach to the Holocaust that concerns me here. One can speculate that this has to do with the fact that the Holocaust has played a smaller role for Latin American Jews in defining their diasporic identity than it has for U.S. Jews.[110] Because it is not a pillar of identity for Latin American Jews—or at least has not been historically—the memory of it takes a more protean shape than it does in the United States.

The past decade has seen rapid changes in the field of Holocaust education and commemoration in Latin America. International organizations such as the United States Holocaust Memorial Museum, Yad Vashem, UNESCO, Yahad–In Unum, the Auschwitz Institute for Peace and Reconciliation, the International Holocaust Remembrance Alliance, and the USC Shoah Foundation have developed diverse initiatives and partnerships with Latin American ministries of education and with nongovernmental organizations and local communities, Jewish and non-Jewish, to promote Holocaust awareness in the region and support the inclusion of Holocaust content in primary and secondary school curricula. The landscape of Holocaust consciousness in Latin America is thus in the process of undergoing a profound transformation. What will it look like as it continues to develop in coming years?

As I hope this book demonstrates, such efforts are but the newest phase in Latin America's Holocaust consciousness, where the Holocaust legacy has been a living discourse, an active, shaping force in the world. Will new initiatives in Holocaust awareness keep open the door to Latin American histories and experiences and enable a confrontation with the region's past, as the cases described in this book have done? Or will a more "competitive memory" framework evolve as resources are funneled toward Holocaust education in societies that have invested little in education about their own histories of atrocity? My hope is that these new efforts will build on the Holocaust consciousness examined here, which, in its own unsystematic and at times oblique way, has made connections between the fascist extermination of the European Jews and the extermination of progressive social movements in Latin America, and has seen in the Jewish commitment to memory and testimony about the Holocaust a model for struggles against oppression and impunity.

Chapter One

The Demands of the Times

Jewish Holocaust Discourse in Dictatorship and Early-Transition Argentina, 1976–1985

Since the mid-1990s in Argentina, comparisons between the Holocaust and the military dictatorship of 1976–1983 have become common. Recent debates about how to remember the period—about the severity of state violence, the experiences of its victims, and the responsibility of the perpetrators and of civil society—are often couched in language that expressly recalls the Holocaust and in terms that have been influenced by Holocaust discussions on similar topics. This somewhat controversial phenomenon has become the focus of increasing though still fragmentary scholarly attention and will be the subject of my next chapter. But what about *during* the period of military dictatorship itself, the years 1976–1983?

This chapter examines the use of Holocaust references in Argentina during the military junta's "Proceso de Re-organización Nacional." Comparison of the military government to the Nazis and its repression to the Holocaust was a not-infrequent way to express opposition to the regime. This was especially true in the latter years of the dictatorship and after the return to democracy, when the Holocaust became a common reference point, but it was a feature of earlier years as well. These comparisons were wielded primarily but not exclusively by Jews and are found primarily but not exclusively in Jewish writings. My goal here is to identify and examine some of the major lines and features of these comparisons. Structured in roughly chronological order, the chapter starts with a consideration of the dictatorship's earliest and most harshly repressive years, 1976–1979, drawing on lesser-known sources like clandestine news-service reports, poetry, and unpublished letters to demonstrate that Holocaust comparisons in this climate of censorship intended to sound an alarm about the scale of the violence.

The chapter then turns to examine debates within the Jewish "internal front," as it was often ironically called, using the Jewish newspaper *Nueva Presencia* as a key source. *Nueva Presencia* was a weekly supplement in Spanish of the Yiddish paper *Die Presse*. It had no official political affiliation but was decidedly progressive in most of its positions—openly left-Zionist in its coverage of Israel and increasingly vocal about its pro–human rights stance against the Argentine dictatorship. Its editor, Herman Schiller, became the cofounder, along with Rabbi Marshall T. Meyer, of the Jewish Movement for Human Rights (Movimiento Judío de Derechos Humanos) in 1983.

Nueva Presencia was inaugurated in July 1977 and published continually during the dictatorship, whereas other progressive Jewish publications, such as the monthlies *Fraie Schtime* (in Yiddish and Spanish, also known as *Voz Libre* or *La Voz*) and *Nueva Sión*, both of which will also appear here, published only sporadically during this period or were forced to cease publication altogether due to censorship. One of *Nueva Presencia*'s goals since its inception was to present a venue that included a plurality of Jewish voices, including those from the more conservative end of the community. Thus, although Schiller's recognizably progressive voice left its stamp on the paper's editorial line, its contributors represented a broader political spectrum. *Nueva Presencia* is also a useful source because it provides a vantage point from which to appreciate the development of the Holocaust as a global media phenomenon; the paper covered the spate of Holocaust-related films and telefilms that appeared in the United States, Europe, and Israel during the dictatorship period and published translations, reviews, and analyses of works by Holocaust historians, survivors, and perpetrators, including Yehuda Bauer, Viktor Frankl, Henry Bulawko, Léon Poliakov, and Rudolf Hoess. *Nueva Presencia* was hardly representative of the Jewish community during the dictatorship, yet even so it serves as a valuable compendium of the range of Jewish discussions during the period.

One of the most significant controversies within the Jewish community during the dictatorship revolved around the case of Jacobo Timerman, a well-known journalist and newspaper publisher detained and tortured by the military. In various public statements as well as in his testimony, *Prisoner without a Name, Cell without a Number*, published in 1981 less than two years after his release, he not only compares the regime to the Nazis and the violence it perpetrated to the Holocaust but also Argentine

Jewish leaders to the Jewish Councils of the Nazi period, a feature of his discourse to be extensively analyzed here. The Jewish Councils of the 1930s and 1940s, "Judenrat" or "Judenräte" in German, were composed of Jewish leaders appointed by the Nazis for administrative purposes in Nazi-controlled territories, especially the ghettos. The Judenrat was responsible for organizing Jewish labor production and, most controversially, for delivering Jews to the Nazis for "resettlement" transports—that is, extermination.[1] Timerman's charged accusations comparing Argentine Jewish leaders to the Judenrat provoked a fierce debate that revealed the deep ideological fissures dividing the community. These divisions have been the subject of a respectable body of scholarship already.[2] The extent and impact of Timerman's polemical use of Holocaust references, however, have not. As will be shown below, these Holocaust references, though strongly resisted, ended up framing how Jews experienced the ethical dilemmas of complicity and resistance under dictatorship.

The chapter then examines how Jewish authorities, particularly the Delegación de Asociaciones Israelitas Argentinas, commonly known by its acronym DAIA, responded to Timerman's accusations. They sought to appropriate the Holocaust for their own ends to advance a view of the "normalcy" of Jewish life during that period and of their own continued effectiveness. Curiously, the American television miniseries *Holocaust: The Story of the Family Weiss*, broadcast in December 1981 after years of having been banned by the government, had a role to play in this effort. The chapter also examines progressive Jewish voices in these debates about anti-Semitism, especially *Nueva Presencia*'s editor Herman Schiller and Rabbi Marshall T. Meyer, and explores their attempts to link specifically Jewish concerns to the broader current of human rights advocacy. It then turns to the use of Holocaust references in the last years of the dictatorship and the early years of the return to democracy, 1982–1985, when Holocaust metaphors became commonplace and were taken up even by those who had earlier resisted them. The chapter concludes in an evaluative mode by assessing the aptness of these various Holocaust invocations. In analyzing their power as rhetorical tools, much can be learned about the legacy of the Holocaust for Argentine Jews. To have carried the Holocaust over, like a metaphor, to the Jews' own situation in Argentina; to have been unable to restrict the Holocaust to its own historical time and place; to have it burst beyond those bounds or to not be certain exactly where those bounds lie—these are both inescapable features of its legacy and a matter that has received insufficient critical attention. Here I give special consideration to the influence of post-Holocaust reflections on Jewish complicity and victimization in framing the demands of the times.

The presence of fugitive Nazis in Argentina raises its own set of questions. Like Bolivia, Chile, Paraguay, and Brazil but to a far greater degree, Argentina welcomed the perpetrators of the Holocaust to its territory and often shielded them from prosecution.[3] Holocaust comparisons might then be inevitable for those for whom, like the post-WWII generation of Argentine Jews, Nazis and Nazi ideology were a real and living presence wielding some not inconsiderable, if perhaps ultimately immeasurable, degree of influence on national politics and culture—especially among the armed forces.[4] The literal presence of Holocaust perpetrators in Argentina leads to the question of whether we are in the presence of truly metaphoric uses of the Holocaust or rather in a blurry zone where literal and metaphoric uses cannot be distinguished from one another.

The issue of Holocaust instrumentalization in Argentina is further complicated by the fact that this question became itself a bone of contention among prominent Jews during the dictatorship, who argued over whether or not the Argentina of that time could properly be compared to a Holocaust situation. These arguments were not just about the Holocaust; rather, they became a way to rehearse debates among Jews—or "the Jewish community," in scare quotes, given that whether such a unified body could be said to exist and how best to characterize and represent it were questions that these debates tended to inflame—about how to respond to the demands of the times. The question of instrumentality was thus already folded into Holocaust representation during the Argentine dictatorship and became, as it were, instrumentalized itself, placed in the service of other pressing debates about the contemporary moment. These disagreements about the legitimacy of comparisons between the Holocaust and Argentina under dictatorship were a symptom—not the only one—of the fissures within the Jewish community, which lacked consensus on the most important issues of the day: the political legitimacy of state repression, its magnitude and scale, the moral status of its victims, and the role of individual Jews and of the Jewish communal leadership in responding to it. Notably, the debate was directed entirely inward and became a forum for accusation and recrimination among various Jewish voices. It was thus difficult to assess whether or not Holocaust comparisons were justified without entering into a discussion about other, often unresolved or unresolvable issues and ideas with which the Holocaust became inextricably entwined in dictatorship Argentina and to which it lent a particular flavor and frame.

Particularly contentious was the role of the DAIA. A federation of Jewish institutions formed in the 1930s, its role was to serve as a spokesperson for the Jewish community on a national scale in defending against anti-Semitism; its elected leaders met directly with government authorities to that end. The DAIA was considered an "official" representative of the Jewish community, and along with the Asociación Mutual Israelita Argentina (AMIA), originally a *chevra kadisha*—a Jewish benevolent burial society—that had grown into a multipurpose communal organization, it provided Jews with an organized leadership. The DAIA was widely respected as an important bulwark against anti-Semitic extremism, but by the 1960s both it and the AMIA had come to be associated with conservative political tendencies, and the ability of these groups to represent a pluralist Jewish community was often called into question, especially by younger Jews.[5] Indeed, ever since the 1940s, from within a few years of its inception, the DAIA's mandate to represent the Jewish community had been contested during times of heated political debate over Zionism and Peronism within the Jewish "internal front."[6] This state of affairs extends to the present day, sharpened most recently in the wake of the 1994 bombing of the AMIA, the Buenos Aires *kehilla*—Jewish community center—when the DAIA leadership's unsavory links to the government of President Carlos Menem created a conflict of interest that hindered a full investigation of the attack and provoked a storm of criticism from the Jewish community. Since the days of the first Peronist regime, the DAIA has negotiated an at times self-contradictory stance regarding its relationship to Argentine politics—professing its autonomy from the government and seeking to remain as "detached" as possible from national politics, as Lawrence Bell describes, yet at the same time involved in highly politicized engagements with both Peronist and anti-Peronist governments.[7] In reality, its legitimacy, effectiveness, and survival have always rested on a measure of both apolitical detachment and political engagement. Bell has written of Peronism that it "highlighted the long-standing ambivalence within the Jewish community concerning its proper place within Argentine national politics."[8] The same can be said of the DAIA during the military dictatorship of 1976–1983, which brought these contradictions once again to the fore. Existing fractures between the leadership and other Jews were deepened during the dictatorship when critics accused the DAIA of not advocating for Jewish detainees and for the Jewish families of the disappeared, a situation that will be amply discussed below.

Returning to the question of Holocaust comparison, the story I seek to recount here must grapple with the substance of the ideas with which the

Holocaust becomes entwined during the dictatorship and with the ethical dilemmas that Holocaust references reveal and perhaps seek to negotiate—dilemmas that Holocaust memory sometimes serves to illuminate, and sometimes not. If the Holocaust might seem insubstantial or merely expedient in this context, the matters to which it becomes rhetorically connected are not. These matters concern the situation of Argentine military dictatorship and state terror: the physical elimination and silencing of political opposition through kidnapping, disappearance, torture, exile, and censorship, and the imposition by force of a new social contract and new economic policies.

It must be noted that although anti-Semitic actions and ideologies circulated throughout this period, with varying degrees of intensity, Jews were not the principal targets of Argentine state terror during the Proceso de Re-organización Nacional. Unlike the Nazis, the military junta was not centrally concerned with Jews, did not systematically persecute them, and did not view the destruction of the Jews as an end in itself. Rather, Jews were caught up, like so many others, in the "war against subversion" that the government waged against its own citizens. Although it is undeniable that there were some commonalities between Argentine state security forces and the Nazis in terms of their methods of repression—including the infamous "Nacht und Nebel" technique, originating in Occupied France, which made the victims totally disappear—Argentina's military rulers shared no goals in common with the Nazis when it came to the Jews.

Even so, Holocaust images resonate deeply, both in Argentina and abroad, to describe Argentina under dictatorship. If Jews evoke and debate the Holocaust in this context—and as I said above, it is primarily but not exclusively Jews who do so—it is in part because it frames for them a situation that makes demands of them "as Jews" to which they do not know how to respond properly. The image of the "Jews of silence" who passively accepted their fate in the Holocaust returns here as a troubling reference point for questions of complicity and resistance under dictatorship.

The discord among these diverse voices reflects several features that do not pertain exclusively to Jews but were common to Argentine society in general, such as the ideological divisions between right and left or the state of great uncertainty and fear that characterized life under dictatorship, when it was both difficult to know for certain the scope of state violence and when there were serious incentives to not want to know, to look the other way, ask no questions, keep out of it. But it also reflects an uncertainty of particular relevance to the Jewish community, namely, the extent to which the violence targeted Jews. The Jewish population in

1970s Argentina is estimated to have been about 250,000 to 300,000, or 1 percent of a population of about 26 million.⁹ Yet by all accounts, Jews were detained and disappeared at a rate far exceeding that proportion; of the total number of disappeared, Jews constituted between 10 percent and 20 percent, depending on the source.¹⁰ It is difficult to pin down the exact number of Jewish disappeared because there is still no definitive agreement about the total number of the disappeared, but in a 1999 report on this topic, COSOFAM (the Comisión de Solidaridad con Familiares de Presos y Detenidos en la Argentina) estimates that between 1,900 and 3,700 Jews were disappeared.¹¹

But were Jews targeted "as Jews"? Does the detention of Jews by military authorities constitute an act of anti-Semitism? The picture is much clearer now than it was then. Now it is widely believed that Jews were not detained "as Jews" but for other reasons—that is, for presumed "subversive" activity. Jews were amply represented among the sectors that bore the brunt of the repression: students, social activists, political militants, union leaders, intellectuals, professionals. But, once detained, Jews were given "special" treatment—portraits of Hitler in the torture rooms, swastikas carved on Jewish bodies, jeering references to Auschwitz and the gas chambers, heightened sadistic pleasure among the guards—and they had a greater likelihood of being killed.¹² Thus, by the end of the dictatorship, a general consensus had formed that anti-Semitism was an entrenched, pervasive aspect of the Argentine military's ideology. The 1984 *Nunca más* report by the National Commission on the Disappeared (CONADEP) contained a section devoted specifically to this topic.

But during the dictatorship, and despite some knowledge of the specific abuses suffered by Jewish detainees, no such consensus existed.¹³ This not only was due to the lack of definitive information in a climate of censorship and fear but also reflected the fact that recurring high levels of anti-Semitism had been a feature of Argentine life for decades, making it difficult to appreciate the distinctiveness of this political period.¹⁴ The question became, "Is it 'official'?" The anti-Semitic ideology of the government during the Proceso, which has now been recognized, was rarely if ever officially proclaimed. On the contrary, junta leaders publicly denied being anti-Semitic.¹⁵ Amid the wave of anti-Semitic activities that accompanied the military regime's consolidation of power in 1976, the government responded to pressure from the DAIA to put some limits on the open circulation of Nazi literature—a belated and ineffective response, to be sure, but an "official" one nonetheless.¹⁶

But despite these public denials, the regime's underlying anti-Semitism was clearly manifested through the operations of its security forces and thus wrapped up with the broader question of human rights violations. Emmanuel Kahan usefully distinguishes between "public" and "clandestine" modes of anti-Semitism during this period; the former includes the commercial distribution of anti-Semitic literature, imputations that Jews were not true Argentines, and physical assaults and other attacks, including threats thereof; the last refers to the treatment of Jews in the clandestine torture centers.[17] "Official" anti-Semitism during the dictatorship was primarily of the clandestine sort: the clearest evidence of state-sponsored anti-Semitism occurred in the torture rooms of the prisons and detention centers—a fact that the DAIA was generally unwilling to confront. It did not like to get involved in what it termed "political" matters; thus, if a Jew was detained but not "as a Jew," then the DAIA did not necessarily consider it within its purview to respond. When Jewish families, including Jewish members of the Mothers of the Plaza de Mayo, appealed to the institution for help in locating detained relatives, its representatives often would either call their Jewishness into question or suggest that the detention was justified. This latter attitude was widespread during the dictatorship and constituted an implicit political endorsement of the junta. The question of "official" anti-Semitism thus became particularly politicized. The DAIA's denials of its existence were often repeated by junta officials as proof that international concerns were misplaced. The DAIA's stance therefore gave the government legitimacy and contributed to the smoke screen concealing the state's extrajudicial repressive apparatus—even if, as may have often been the case, such denials, like all public utterances during the period, were instances of doublespeak, the protective self-censoring of speech under dictatorship that Marguerite Feitlowitz calls "double discourse."[18]

Within the Jewish community, the DAIA's approach was considered by many to be a betrayal—of Jewish principles, of Jewish parents and youth—and an abdication of its leadership role, further evidence that it was out of touch with its constituency. As will be seen, Rabbi Marshall Meyer and the Jewish members of the Mothers of the Plaza de Mayo were especially vocal in disputing the DAIA's approach, which also led it to downplay the extent of anti-Semitism and insist on the "normalcy" of Jewish life under dictatorship.

Thus the answer to the question "Is this a Holocaust?" in part depends on whether one thinks Jews are being victimized "as Jews" or for other reasons and in part depends on whether one thinks Jewish victimization is the outgrowth of an official government policy of anti-Semitism or the work of isolated, if widespread, extremists. And the answer also depends on a number of other, quite ideological considerations about what role Jews should play, if any, in Argentine politics, and about the nature of politics itself, especially as concerns the legitimacy of militant activism by government opponents, the turn to violence by some of them, and hence the relative innocence or moral standing of the victims. These are issues that apply equally to Jewish and non-Jewish victims and remain unsettled to this day, as the process of reckoning with the legacy of violence as a political tool is ongoing in Argentina. Finally, the answer depends on one's understanding of the Holocaust, particularly as regards two issues of long-standing concern that recur among Jewish discussions in Argentina: the status of the Holocaust as an exclusively Jewish event and the legacy of Jewish complicity and victimization during the Holocaust.

The fear that the Holocaust will be "de-Judaized" is at the heart of the so-called "uniqueness debate" in Holocaust scholarship and, at least in the United States, serves to justify taboos against comparison.[19] Similar concerns animated responses to Holocaust comparisons in Argentina. Is the comparison to the dictatorship one that de-Judaizes the Holocaust by extending it to a non-Jewish context or rather one that correctly emphasizes the anti-Jewish nature of the Argentine repression? The answers by Argentine Jews reflect a number of permutations that I will delve into below.

Regarding the question of Jewish passivity in the face of their aggressors and complicity with the extermination, these issues have lost much of their urgency in recent years and are no longer at the center of Holocaust scholarship. But they were burning questions in the years immediately following the war, when they were placed at the center of Israeli national identity and debates about Holocaust memorialization, and through the 1960s, when the heroic aspects of Jewish Holocaust experience, condensed as "Shoah uGevurah" (Holocaust and Heroism), began to be integrated into progressive movements for national liberation and anti-imperialist politics.[20] This is why the Warsaw ghetto uprising of April 1943 dominated practices of Holocaust memorialization, in Argentina and elsewhere, leading Peter Novick to comment ironically that "the event most atypical of the Holocaust was made emblematic of it."[21] *Nueva Presencia* and other progressive Jewish newspapers, which sometimes sponsored commemorative events in April and always highlighted the anniversary on their front pages, often presented the Warsaw ghetto uprising as a model for practices of resistance and liberation in the present.[22] Meanwhile, 1970s research by Israeli historian Yehuda

Bauer returned again to the question of whether Jews "went like sheep to the slaughter"—referencing a slogan from the ghetto uprisings that urged Jews to take up arms and resist; his work was discussed in Argentina in the pages of *Nueva Presencia* and *Fraie Schtime* and reprinted by the DAIA.[23]

The most polemical Holocaust references during this period fall under the "Shoah uGevurah" line of commemoration. Timerman's "Judenrat" accusation against the DAIA, and the DAIA's own response, which will be discussed below, cannot be understood apart from this paradigm of heroic resistance, which forced all those who participated in the debate to assert, anxiously, their commitment to a combative stance, to not being "sheep"—even as there was disagreement about whether the situation warranted it or not. Regardless of whether the metaphor comparing Argentine Jewish leaders to the Judenrat had an element of historical accuracy—it did so only in a very limited sense and certainly not as regards the main accusation against the Nazi-era Jewish Councils, namely, that they delivered Jews to their deaths—it activated a piece of the collective memory that saw in the Judenrat a symbol for complicity. The Argentine dictatorship thus brought these issues of the Holocaust legacy into new relief while also framing in a particular way the situation of the contemporary moment. In other words, far from being alien to the Holocaust, these references very often reflect its ongoing hold over Jews of the 1970s.

But this brings us back to our primary questions: Are Holocaust metaphors apt comparisons to the Argentina of that period? What, if anything, can they tell us about the Holocaust and about Argentina under dictatorship? The problem of instrumentality that I wish to discuss has to do not with the fact that the Holocaust is being linked to an otherwise distant event and called on to legitimate ideas in an otherwise distant context, but with the consequences of that linkage and with the substance of those ideas. In addition to documenting the presence of Holocaust references during the dictatorship, the following discussion therefore seeks to explore the kind of awareness of the Holocaust, and of Argentina under dictatorship, that such linkages promote.

1976–1979: Sounding the Alarm

In an article published in 1985, soon after Argentina's return to democracy, Ignacio Klich offers the view that comparing Argentina during the Proceso to the Nazi genocide runs the risk of "banalizing" the Holocaust.[24] But in order to sustain that view, would we not have to find the Argentine situation banal? In fact, it is precisely against this sense of normalcy, of life as usual, that most Holocaust comparisons occurring during the dictatorship are made. They intend, first and foremost, a "debanalization" and "detrivialization" of the violence in Argentina. One of the most important features of Holocaust references is thus their use in an attempt to put the world on alert as to the scale of the violence and to draw fellow citizens into an awareness of their proximity and civic responsibility in regard to it.

In Argentina during the Proceso, the use of Holocaust comparisons was intended to provoke a confrontation with the violence of the period and call attention to its magnitude. This is especially true of the clandestine news agencies that sprang up in the first year of the dictatorship, whose reports stressed the similarities in aims and tactics between the Nazis and the Argentine armed forces. These dispatches referred to torture centers as "concentration camps" (a term that gained widespread usage), to government policies toward Bolivian and Paraguayan immigrants in Buenos Aires as a "final solution," and, in Rodolfo Walsh's famous "Open Letter from a Writer to the Military Junta," to the secret massacres conducted by the armed forces as "genocidal."[25] These same clandestine press agencies identified the Nazi-tainted anti-Semitism of the Argentine military, reporting on special commando forces that venerated Hitler and engaged in for-profit activities such as extra-official kidnappings of wealthy Jews.[26]

The clandestine press was also one of the first sources to identify the military government's vulnerability to imputations of Nazi-like behavior. One police action that was reported in the clandestine press involved the temporary closure in 1976 of a TV station that was in the midst of broadcasting an episode of the documentary series *The World at War*, part of the station's official programming that had been going on for several months. The particular episode that led to the closure included documentary footage from the Nazi occupation of the Netherlands, which showed the brutality of the Germans toward the Dutch and particularly toward the Jews. The episode also included testimony from a Dutch Communist who had been a resistance fighter. The whole thing was deemed "subversive propaganda" by the Argentine authorities, leading the clandestine press agency ANCLA to speculate that the military feared their repressive methods might be identified with Hitler's.[27] According to ANCLA, elites in both the armed forces and business circles were nervous about being perceived in Europe as similar to the Nazis.[28] If these speculations are correct, then we take note of the ironic hold of the Holocaust in the minds of military leaders, who were capable of being embarrassed by their association with Nazism yet also repeatedly defended Nazis and held Nazi Germany up as a model. One notorious case of the regime's defense of Nazism occurred during a trial concerning the censorship of the 1979 U.S. film *The House on Garibaldi Street*, about the kidnapping of Eichmann from Argentina by Israeli special forces in 1960. Those who argued in favor of government censorship of the film referred to Eichmann as "a peaceful worker" and denied that he had committed any crimes.[29] In other venues of the political opposition in Argentina, references to the Holocaust are much scarcer than they are in these clandestine news reports, although a great deal of investigation still remains to be done on this front.[30]

However, outside Argentina, allusions to the Holocaust were more frequent. Argentine exile groups in Mexico and Spain used Holocaust references to denounce the regime.[31] In the international community, allusions to Argentina as a potential Holocaust state were also frequent, and not only in those news reports that expressed particular fears for the safety of the Jewish community. A 1979 newsletter produced by a Latin American organization of Social Democrats carried the title "The Disappeared: 'New Holocaust.' "[32] In the United States the matter came up several times before Congress. In 1976, Father James Weeks testified before the House of Representatives on his detention in Argentina, saying, "The kidnappers were like Nazis."[33] In 1978, Representative Henry Waxman asked, "Is Argentina Becoming like Nazi Germany?" He expressed strong fears that Argentine Jews might face the same fate as European Jews: "The parallels between the situation of Argentina's Jews now and the predicament of Eastern European Jewry in the 1930s leads me to view the Argentinian situation with alarm. History has taught us the bitter lesson that frequently by the time it becomes crystal clear that Jews must flee, it is too late to do so."[34] In 1979, Senator Edward Kennedy put a number of materials into the *Congressional Record*, including a piece by Rabbi Morton Rosenthal, the Latin American affairs director of the B'nai Brith's Anti-Defamation League (ADL), who quotes U.S. Representative Silvio Conte as saying, on his return from Argentina and a visit to Jacobo Timerman, then under house arrest, "It reminds me of nazi Germany."[35] In France, meanwhile, in 1978 a widely circulated article by Marek Halter in *Le Monde* also sounded the alarm, asking, "Must we wait until a night of broken glass before we cry out?"[36] The article was very badly received by Argentine authorities and set in motion an international counterpropaganda campaign involving Jewish leaders from Argentina and abroad.[37]

When we look at the first few years of the dictatorship, the harshest in terms of repression and terror, we find relatively few Jewish voices openly using Holocaust comparisons in this "debanalizing" or "detrivializing" way. One exception is the newspaper *Nueva Sión*, already threatened by censorship, its publication and distribution becoming more sporadic before ceasing entirely in 1977. Yet it continued to provide coverage of the wave of anti-Semitic activities that accompanied the military regime's consolidation of power in 1976 and called attention to the government's tepid and belated response to the open circulation of Nazi literature. The paper also brought home the comparison between the Nazi era and the Argentine present by featuring a photograph of Nazis rounding up Jews with the caption "Nazi-fascist sectors seek Jewish blood like in Hitler's Germany."[38]

Two lesser-known examples of Jewish Holocaust discourse also merit some attention. One, by the poet and Yiddishist Eliahu Toker, dates to 1980; the other is from 1977 and is contained in an unpublished letter by Bernardo Rus, whose son Daniel was disappeared. Toker's 1980 poem "Buenos Aires in the Seventies" meditates on parallel experiences of torture, political repression, and anti-Semitism and, like the ANCLA, seeks to draw attention to the unacknowledged magnitude of the situation. Early in the poem we encounter the following lines:

> Berlín de los años treinta.
> Varsovia de los años cuarenta.
> Buenos Aires de los años setenta.
> No resultan comparables, claro.[39]
>
> [Berlin in the thirties.
> Warsaw in the forties.
> Buenos Aires in the seventies.
> They're not comparable, of course]

Despite the poet's assertion of the incomparability between these three places and times, everything in the poem's narrative content, its structure, syntax, and rhythm, affirms the opposite. The anaphora of the lines I just quoted serves as one example. The repetition of certain key themes serves as another. Toker links together the description of the three cities and the events that marked these crucial decades by focusing in each case on the complicit silence of the bystanders, on the arrogance and apparent omnipotence of the perpetrators, and on the culpability and subhuman status assigned to the victims. Anti-Semitism and the persecution of artists and politicians—features common to all of these times and places—are presented as analogous instances involving the same dehumanizing and authoritarian practices on the part of the perpetrators. As a result of these analogies, the line "They're not comparable, of course" must ultimately be read as an ironic statement.

But the poet's approach to the question is not limited to irony. The poem's first lines, which later serve as a kind of refrain, use the phrase "campos de concentración":

> Los campos de concentración andaban por las calles.
> Se habían desatado y vestidos de civil, repartiendo muerte
> a manos llenas, andaban en falcon por las calles.
>
> [The concentration camps moved through the streets.
> They had cut themselves loose and dressed in civilian clothes,
>   distributing death
> with their hands full, they moved like falcons through the streets.]

Toker is referring here to the infamous "Falcon"-model cars that the Argentine security forces used in order to detain, torture, and "disappear" presumed subversives. These cars were literally mobile concentration camps, working in tandem with what we might call the "stationary" camps such as the one housed in the Naval Mechanics School (ESMA). The phrase "campos de concentración" had already become something of a commonplace by 1980 but becomes newly charged with historical resonances to the Holocaust by virtue of its proximity, in the poem, to Toker's references to World War II.

For many Argentine Jews, the situation could not help but bring to mind the Holocaust in personal ways that spoke directly to their experience of vulnerability. Circumstances forced them to examine anew their integration into Argentine life and confront, again, their status as victims. This was the case for Bernardo Rus, the father of a young man who had been disappeared by the military. In 1977 Rus sent a letter to Admiral Emilio Massera, the head of the navy and member of the governing military junta; his letter responded to Massera's public statement of good wishes to the Jewish people on the occasion of the Jewish New Year, an act of monstrous hypocrisy under the circumstances.[40] Massera's statement alluded repeatedly to the millennial suffering of the Jewish people and, in a self-congratulatory mode, recognized that many Jews had found in Argentina a haven from hunger and injustice. For the parents of Daniel Lázaro Rus, the disappeared man, this statement provided an opening to make a direct and personal plea for compassion from the military leader. As proof of the suffering to which Massera himself had alluded and appended to other documents containing proof of their son's whereabouts in the hands of state forces, Bernardo Rus attached several pages containing reproductions of photographs from the Nazi occupation of Poland. These appear to have been taken from one of a series of books published by an organization of militant Polish ex-combatants.[41] Rus avoided the photos that depict the Nazi executions of Polish partisans, which are common in these books. Instead, he selected from the many examples of suffering children and from the iconic images of the so-called "living corpses" rescued from the camps at the time of the liberation. The status of these photos as historical witnesses to a time of iniquity and their placement in this letter to Massera by Daniel Lázaro Rus's father underscore one of the most painful aspects of Argentine state terrorism, namely, the lack of documentary evidence of the fate of most victims. They also tell us something about Daniel's parents: although nowhere stated in the letter, both of them were Auschwitz survivors.[42]

The photographs establish a powerful link between present and past suffering, but to quite disparate ends. On the one hand, the images serve as a veiled accusation of the Argentine government because they suggest a continuity between the Argentine present and the Nazi past. Certainly that was how Daniel's parents experienced it; his sister would later recount that these two situations had become conjoined in her parents' minds.[43] On the other hand, the author of this letter, by identifying his son with these pictures of helpless victims of Nazism, perhaps hoped to remind Massera that Jews were not a threat to his power. Obviating the question of Massera's criminality, Bernardo Rus appealed to him as a benevolent ruler. The theme recurs in another letter he wrote in 1977, this time addressed to General Videla, which recounts the story of his successful immigrant experience, expresses his gratitude to Argentina for having taken him in after his ordeals in the Holocaust, and asks for merciful intervention in Daniel's case.[44] In both letters, Bernardo Rus felt compelled to take on the role of millennial victim into which he had been cast by Massera in his High Holidays address, with the military leaders and Argentine society playing savior—a role they refused to enact in the case of Daniel Rus, who remains disappeared to this day. Beyond the frame of these letters to the junta, however, both Rus parents refused to play the part of grateful victims in searching for their son. Notably, Sara Laskier de Rus joined the Mothers of the Plaza de Mayo, lobbied the U.S. State Department and the Israeli embassy for assistance, and was a signatory to the "Réplica al 'Informe especial' sobre detenidos y desaparecidos judíos 1976–1983" (Reply to the "Special Report" on Jewish Detainees and Disappeared Persons) published in 1984 by a group of Jewish parents of the disappeared who were critical of the DAIA's actions in this arena and disputed its version of events.[45]

The letters by Rus and the poem by Toker are notable for their use of what Feitlowitz calls the "double discourse" characteristic of speech under dictatorship, whereby denial and knowledge coexist in the same enunciation. This was a consequence of the regime's distorting use of language, she argues, which induced a kind of schizophrenic awareness of the relationship between words and reality and became in turn a protective self-censoring mechanism for those who engaged in public or semipublic speech. Toker uses irony, Rus excessive deference. Both are instances of the "skillful wielding of contradiction," as Feitlowitz says of such patterns, that was crucial to speech under dictatorship.[46] Both Toker's poem and the letter from Bernardo Rus, with its accompanying Holocaust photographs, suggest, without stating so directly, that there might be a connection between the Argentine military regime and Nazism and between its victims and Holocaust victims.

Jacobo Timerman and "Anti-Semitism without Soap"

> The ghetto was ruled by neither German nor Jew; it was ruled by delusion.
>
> —Elie Wiesel, *Night*[47]

Jacobo Timerman was not so circumspect. He represents a case of Holocaust speech unfettered by Feitlowitz's "double discourse." Timerman was a well-respected career journalist and newspaper editor who had worked in both the national and Jewish Argentine press for decades. In the 1970s he founded and became the editor of the liberal-moderate *La Opinión*, a highly regarded newspaper in the mold of France's *Le Monde*. In April 1977 he was detained and tortured by the military on charges of subversion. Originally accused of being connected to the Montoneros, a left-wing guerrilla organization, and arrested as part of the broader investigation against the family of David Graiver, an Argentine banker and significant investor in *La Opinión*, Timerman continued to be detained by security forces long after he had been cleared of those charges by Argentine courts. It is important to note that *La Opinión* had initially supported the coup in March 1976 and collaborated with military authorities. Indeed, Timerman vaunted his inside knowledge of military politics and his role as informal adviser to prominent members of the military hierarchy.[48] However, *La Opinión*'s decision to publish the names of the disappeared on its pages angered the junta. Timerman claims he was also targeted because he was a Jew and a Zionist. His *testimonio*—*Prisoner without a Name, Cell without a Number*—was written in Israel immediately following his release from prison (the military had revoked his Argentine citizenship and deported him to Israel as a condition of his freedom). In the book, which appeared first in English in 1981, he compared Argentina's military rulers to Hitler, Stalin, Mussolini, and Castro, but he focused predominantly on Hitler in his analysis of the years 1976–1979 in Argentina, which he considered to be a repetition of Nazi Germany: "It's curious, the extent to which the recent years in Argentina have repeated—in a different geographical context, another culture, another period, another calendar moment—the world of terror, hatred, madness, and delirium that governed the Hitlerian epoch in Germany."[49] He was outraged by how the Nazi past could be repeated in Argentina, asking: "How can a nation reproduce in every detail, though employing other forms, the same monstrous crimes explicitly condemned and clearly expounded so many years before?"[50]

But what angered him most and provoked his most controversial statements was the attitude of Argentina's Jewish leaders. He criticized them for failing to respond to the violence and deplored their silence in the face of atrocities—a silence that, for him, ultimately signaled their complicity with the repression. Embracing a combative Judaism, he framed the legacy of the Holocaust as one of overcoming Jews' shameful silence and passivity in the face of destruction:

> After the war, we began to fathom the magnitude of the Holocaust. And we promised ourselves that never again would this silent, methodical destruction of our people be repeated. We also promised ourselves, and swore repeatedly through the years, that never again would our own silence, passivity, confusion and paralysis be repeated. We promised ourselves that never would horror paralyze us, intimidate us, allow us to develop theories of survival, of compromise with reality, of delaying our public indignation.[51]

He wrote that the most important lesson of the Holocaust was not the horrors committed by the Nazis and the number of victims but the silence of the Jews and their inability to defend themselves against aggression.[52] In fact, he blamed the Jews' "voluntary acceptance" of a destiny imposed on them from outside for the Nazi horrors,[53] calling this a "common denominator" between 1930s Germany and 1970s Argentina and issuing a dire warning about the risks of Jewish silence: "Because only the repetition of silence would make a new Holocaust possible."[54]

Timerman argued that one of the most dangerous mistakes committed by Argentine Jewish leaders was to use only the most extreme, most horrifying elements of Holocaust violence, such as the gas chambers, as the measure for determining how to respond to present-day anti-Semitism. Because they took these as their only points of reference, Jewish leaders forgot their own responsibility in determining the course of history: "The point of reference is Jewish action; the Jewish silence of the Hitler years toward Hitler's acts."[55] The result of this mistaken approach to the Holocaust was that Jewish leaders distorted the reality of the contemporary situation. Thus, he writes:

> I was never able to understand how the horrors of the Holocaust could diminish the significance of the rape of Jewish girls in clandestine Argentine prisons. I was never able to accept how the act of remembering, the remembrance industry of the Holocaust, could render it seemingly unnecessary to confront openly the publication of anti-Semitic literature in Argentina. . . . To my mind, always, the incorporation of the Holocaust into my life meant never to allow the Argentine police to feel that they were authorized to humiliate Jewish prisoners. I never imagined that there would be Jewish leaders who would utilize the horrors of the Holocaust to maintain that the most advantageous response to certain anti-Semitic aggressions of a much less brutal nature was silence.[56]

In unpublished declarations written while he was still under house arrest, in July 1979, Timerman had launched the same blunt accusation: "Argentine Jews are consoled within their own misfortunes with a very simple argument every time that someone suggests a battle: 'Don't exaggerate, nobody is taking us to the gas chambers.'"[57] A few months after his liberation, in an article published in the Israeli newspaper *Ma'ariv* in January 1980, Timerman's accusations became even more rhetorically loaded: he claimed that the DAIA's failure to recognize that there could be "anti-Semitism without soap" made it no different from "the Judenrat of Hitler's ghettos."[58] Timerman's reference to "anti-Semitism without soap" would have been transparent to his Argentine readers, because in Argentina the word "soap" (*jabón*) is a common anti-Semitic epithet, shorthand for the (mythical) Nazi fabrication of soap out of Jewish bodies during the Holocaust. Chants of "Jabón, jabón" can be heard at public events, and the word is also used to insult individual Jews, often to their face. Timerman's "anti-Semitism without soap" thus refers to anti-Semitism that is not identical to the Nazis'—but that even so must be confronted directly by Jews.

For Timerman, the silence of Jewish leaders and their unwillingness to protest state crimes against Jews were both the most troubling reminder of the Holocaust and the greatest betrayal of its legacy. Here we can see Timerman writing against the notion of the Holocaust as an "absolute crime," that is, one compared to which all other crimes appear trivial or nonexistent. Like Timerman, historian Peter Novick writes about the deleterious effects of presenting the Holocaust in such a way: "To make it the benchmark of oppression and atrocity works in precisely the opposite direction, trivializing crimes of lesser magnitude. It does this not just in principle, but in practice."[59] Historian Pierre Vidal-Naquet has also criticized this tendency: "The notion of an absolute crime, alas, functions in Israel and even elsewhere to justify relative crimes."[60]

Although Timerman's stance against the "absolute" nature of Holocaust crimes goes against the dominant tendency in Israel, his Judenrat accusation and his focus on the Argentine Jewish community's victim-like behavior demonstrate that his understanding of the Holocaust legacy was shaped by Israeli discourses. The use of the Judenrat as a synonym for cowardice, treachery, and complicity dates to post–World War II debates in the Israeli Knesset on the Law of Remembrance of Shoah and Heroism, which authorized the founding of Yad Vashem in 1953. As Dalia Ofer records, Benzion Dinur, who was the Israeli minister of education and culture (under whose auspices Yad Vashem would be established), maintained in his speech to the Knesset that "the real beginning of the Shoah was when Jews accepted appointment to a group [i.e., the Judenrat] clearly aimed at breaking the spirit of their own people."[61] Ofer describes how the leftist parties of the Knesset took up this characterization—despite disagreeing with some other aspects of Dinur's account of resistance in the ghettos because it did not sufficiently stress the leadership of the left—and used it "to establish the dichotomy between the youth movement socialist fighters . . . and the rest of Europe's Jews, including those who had betrayed their brethren by co-operating with the Nazis as members of the Judenrat."[62] By this thinking, there were only two kinds of Jews during the Holocaust: heroes (those who rebelled against the Nazis) and victim-traitors (those who did not rebel), effectively erasing the differences between the Judenrat and the majority of nonrebelling Jews; all were tarred with the same brush of victimhood-cowardice-treachery. The view of the Judenrat as accomplices to the Nazis, and of Jewish "passivity" as partly responsible for the extermination, was not limited to left-nationalist ideology; it had been further reinforced, though in more tempered language, by Raul Hilberg in his monumental and groundbreaking *The Destruction of the European Jews*, which devoted a section to analyzing and condemning the Jews' "almost complete lack of resistance" and said of the Jewish councils, "Playing into German hands, they speeded the process of destruction."[63] Timerman's reference to the Judenrat during the dictatorship was cut in the same mold.

Note that the Law of Remembrance of Shoah and Heroism did not end up condemning Jewish victims, despite the tenor of the debates leading up to its passage. Even as it distinguishes the heroism of Jewish fighters in the ghettos, the law commemorates all the six million as "martyrs" who struggled for their dignity.[64] Furthermore, Yad Vashem's "Monument of Heroism" offers a vision of the hero that encompasses ordinary Jews in the daily battle for survival.[65] Nevertheless, the "dramatic demarcation" that Ofer exposes in the earlier debates, between "the Jewish public, who went 'as sheep to the slaughter' and those who had stood up to fight the nazi oppressors," remains a constant theme in Holocaust remembrance in Israel. James Young notes ironically that during the official commemorative events on Yom Hashoah, "The Day of Remembrance of the Holocaust and Heroism," the "heroes" are foregrounded while the "martyrs" are "barely visible" in the last row.[66] The linkage of the Holocaust to heroism in "Shoah uGevurah"—encapsulated in the seemingly innocuous "and" between the two terms—is thus a site of tension and contradiction.

Timerman's criticisms of the DAIA received a great deal of press in the United States, generating some controversy but also fairly wide acceptance.[67] His Holocaust analogies were if anything amplified in the wake of the publication of his testimony: the *New York Times* review of *Prisoner without a Name, Cell without a Number*, by Anthony Lewis, was titled "Final Solution in Argentina."[68] Well before the book appeared, while Timerman was still in captivity, he had become an international figure as a prominent symbol of the Argentine government's repression of human rights. His case crystallized fears about anti-Semitism and his cause was championed in the United States by high officials, including Cyrus Vance and Edward Kennedy, and by the ADL, which awarded Timerman its Hubert Humphrey Freedom Prize in 1979 while he was under house arrest.

But in Argentina he was a polarizing and controversial figure, especially in the Jewish community. While he was still imprisoned, the DAIA was constantly forced to defend itself against accusations of inaction in his case. Rabbi Meyer was especially direct in his criticisms of the DAIA, and *Nueva Presencia* often served as a venue to question Timerman's imprisonment and pressure Jewish authorities to do more for him. But after his release, his public statements and then his book provoked indignation among some of those who had been openly supportive of him during his imprisonment.[69] DAIA officials, meanwhile, had to ramp up their efforts at damage control once he left Argentina and especially after *Prisoner without a Name* appeared. At home and abroad, the DAIA sought to minimize the threat to the organization's reputation provoked by "the Timerman case" by disputing Timerman's view of the situation of Jews in Argentina.

The DAIA's Response: Never Again "Jews of Silence"

In a number of declarations issued in the months surrounding the publication of Timerman's book, the DAIA insisted that he was exaggerating and refused the Holocaust metaphor. Mario Gorenstein, president of the DAIA during 1980–1983 (and president of the AMIA prior to that) responded to Timerman's accusations by saying, "Not all anti-Semitism leads inexorably to the gas chamber."[70] The group defended its record of speaking out on behalf of Jews and called the book false.[71] Its position on anti-Semitism was that it existed but was "not as spectacular as those outside of the country infer," nor did it have official support. The DAIA insisted on the "normalcy that also surrounds us" and cast suspicions on the motives of those who would argue otherwise.[72] While traveling in Europe and the United States, Gorenstein found himself having to calm fears for Jews' safety in Argentina while also seeking allies in his attempts to discredit Timerman. At a meeting of the Memorial Foundation for Jewish Culture in Zurich, he enlisted historian Lucy Dawidowicz to his cause. According to Gorenstein, "[Dawidowicz] told him that she didn't share the view of those who 'bring up to date' certain words proper to the Holocaust ('judenrat' among them) to refer to this situation and that she thought these were being used inappropriately."[73]

The DAIA's claims for the "normalcy" of the situation had been a refrain of their public statements for several years already, well before the Timerman controversy. Nehemías Resnizky was the DAIA president for the period 1970–1980; he continued to make public statements after being succeeded by Gorenstein, often in order to defend himself against complaints about his term as DAIA president. During that time he had repeatedly insisted on the "absolute normalcy and calm" of Jewish life, alluding in euphemistic fashion, if at all, to "difficult moments."[74] In fact, recent scholarship has confirmed that Jewish organizations flourished during the dictatorship.[75] The claims about "normalcy" by the DAIA and others were thus not exactly false, yet this rhetoric clashed with the state of urgency experienced by those who were more directly touched by state terror, and Resnizky used it in a censoring fashion, to silence certain kinds of discussion about the current political situation. His main concern was that "interests alien to the Jews may try to use the [Jewish] community for their own benefit."[76] In the process he promoted so narrow a concept of "Jewish interests" that it did not even extend to Jews in other countries, whose international efforts on behalf of human rights in Argentina, like those of Rabbi Rosenthal of the ADL, he continuously sought to undermine. Although Resnizky did bring complaints to the government about anti-Semitic activities, during the dictatorship he was also intent on downplaying their scope, a marked change from his more dispassionate evaluation of the Argentine armed forces before the coup, in 1975, when he had recognized their tendency toward anti-Semitism.[77]

As regards the tendency to see events in Argentina through the lens of the Holocaust, Resnizky offered contradictory statements. In 1975, he invoked the legacy of the Holocaust in ways quite similar to Timerman, stressing the need for a combative Judaism that refused to be silent and whose actions in its own defense would transcend its past as victim:

> To those sectors who are fighting each other in Argentina, know that a proud and dignified Jewish community will never permit the repetition of Auschwitz or Maidenek. Know too, as Sartre pointed out, that fearful Jews, cowardly Jews, Jews with no dignity, know that the victims' passivity only inflames the aggressive rage of the anti-Semite.[78]

In 1977 and again in 1978, he repeated the sentiments, declaring: "Our enemies should know that never again will we be the 'Jews of Silence.' "[79] Yet in 1979, he warned against the pitfalls of being "dragged along by history" and "overestimating" anti-Semitism in Argentina, and he declared his refusal to "mechanically transfer" past events to the present.[80] But paradoxically, even as he denied the prevalence of anti-Semitism, he invoked the "nunca más" of the Warsaw ghetto and returned to the theme of Jewish self-defense, proclaiming, "Never again will Jews be silent and passive when faced with the outbursts of their enemies," a claim he continued to repeat against his critics in Argentina and abroad even after he had stepped down.[81]

Gorenstein proceeded in a similar self-contradictory vein once he assumed leadership, invoking the Holocaust to justify the DAIA's minimization of anti-Semitism *and* its heroic stance against it. In his view, the situation in Argentina was nothing like the Holocaust: he told the *Boston Globe*, "We are not in a pre-holocaust situation."[82] As for Timerman, Gorenstein said: "'Timerman lies in important ways. He was not arrested for being a Jew, we know that. His comments not only hurt Argentina, but they hurt Argentine Jews.'"[83] Yet he also shared Timerman's view that Jewish silence was one of the greatest tragedies of the Holocaust, serving as a lesson that Jews should vigorously protest even the most innocent-seeming anti-Semitism.[84] The resulting position was oddly contorted: *There is no serious anti-Semitism here*, the DAIA insisted, *but if there were, we'd vigorously protest it.* It is difficult to determine, ultimately, whether this is an instance of Feitlowitz's "double discourse," a self-protective measure of self-censorship, or whether the DAIA's shielding of the government stemmed from its genuine political support of it.

As these debates about Timerman were happening in 1981, after the publication of his book in the United States, they became entwined with another Holocaust question in Argentina: the censorship of the *Holocaust* television miniseries by the Argentine government. The miniseries had been produced in 1978 for U.S. television in the wake of the success of *Roots*. It proceeded to become an international media event, shown in many different countries to acclaim and controversy, at times associated with an upswing in anti-Semitism.[85] The show had been prohibited from airing on Argentine television, but the junta finally agreed to lift the ban in December 1981, three years after it appeared in the United States and two years after it had aired in other Latin American countries.[86] To defend itself against charges of inaction on the Timerman case, the DAIA repeatedly drew attention to its campaign with the government to have the miniseries shown on television in Argentina.[87] The timing of its remarks on this issue suggests an attempt to deflect attention from the Timerman case. Once the show aired, in December 1981, the DAIA took credit for having convinced the government to lift the prohibition.[88] Several months later Gorenstein went so far as to incorporate the miniseries into his comments at the annual Warsaw ghetto uprising commemoration, holding up Rudy, a character from the film, as a model of heroic resistance and Zionist commitment.[89] The importance the DAIA accorded to the airing of the show, while vaunting its own role, might seem contradictory, given its desire to silence Holocaust comparisons to Argentina. In fact, it was of a piece with its earlier statements, because the DAIA in this instance used the Holocaust as an evasive tactic in the way described by Peter Novick: to divert attention from present-day crimes and vexed questions of complicity.[90] As one exasperated Jewish critic pointed out, showing the miniseries was not a solution to anti-Semitism[91]—which ironically the DAIA had downplayed as a problem in the first place.

From the perspective of Jews in other countries, the DAIA's reluctance to treat anti-Semitism as more serious, and especially its minimal defense of Timerman, were seen as confounding at best, dangerous at worst. The DAIA had an ally in the influential World Jewish Congress and the American Jewish Committee (AJC); the latter echoed the DAIA's "normalcy" line even though its representative in Argentina, Jacobo Kovadloff, had been forced to flee Argentina in June 1977 after receiving death threats, and its own publication, *Present Tense*, highlighted the case and the seriousness of the anti-Semitism.[92] Even as the AJC publicized the case, Kovadloff was careful to avoid the appearance of criticizing the government, and the organization defended Videla as a moderate.[93] But other Jewish publications and organizations, especially the ADL, remained suspicious and openly criticized the Jewish leadership in Argentina.[94] Allusions to the naivete of German Jews and to the Judenrat were not infrequent, generally echoing Timerman, though in some cases the implication was floated well before Timerman made his accusations.[95] One publication pointed to the DAIA's apparent hypocrisy in documenting anti-Semitism yet refusing to publicly denounce it; another commentator thought Argentine Jews were deluding themselves in downplaying anti-Semitism.[96] Aryeh Neier, writing in *The Nation*, provided perhaps the most lucid examination of the DAIA's position, comparing it to that of the Judenrat of Germany with some telling historical analogies. He quoted a headline from the right-wing Argentine Jewish newspaper *La Luz*—"ADL Go Home! No One Needs You Here"—then showed it to be nearly identical to the Berlin Jüdische Gemeinde's response to the American Jewish Committee in the 1930s. Like the DAIA and others in Argentina, the Berlin Jewish Community had downplayed anti-Semitism, ostensibly to protect the German national reputation. Neier did not offer this illuminating comparison in order to condemn the DAIA but rather to point out that organized Jewish communities, whether Germany's of yore or Argentina's of today, face particular dilemmas in that they are forced to negotiate with hostile governments; vulnerability and compromise are the inevitable price.[97]

Since the return to democracy in 1983, the DAIA's shortcomings during the dictatorship period have been amply documented and described. Writing in 1985, Ignacio Klich sets forth the controversial and morally compromised choices of the Jewish leadership. He disputes Timerman's "Judenrat" metaphor, considering it exaggerated, but in other respects does not pull his punches in describing the DAIA's serious faults. These include its poor treatment of the family members of detainees and the disappeared, victims who were often deemed "not sufficiently Jewish" to warrant attention by the DAIA and implicitly blamed for their predicament.[98] This was in line with what Klich terms the DAIA's "ideological cooptation by the Junta" and its refusal to admit the anti-Semitism of the armed forces, despite clear evidence to the contrary. It distanced itself from human rights groups and actively tried to prevent international Jewish organizations from campaigning on behalf of detainees unless they did so under the DAIA's auspices and agreed with its version of the situation, which minimized anti-Semitism. Finally, Klich claims that it falsified its record of actions.[99]

Progressive Jewish Voices—"Isms" beyond Judaism

Returning again to Timerman's Holocaust analogies, we can see that he exposed a particularly sensitive and unresolved issue, namely, the "normalcy" of Jewish life under dictatorship. Despite numerous anti-Semitic incidents, many Jews still considered life to be "normal" because Jewish institutions were able to function unimpeded; they thus refused the Holocaust analogies to Argentina. From Timerman's perspective, as well as that of Jews in other parts of the world, such an attitude was dangerously defeatist, because it suggested that a degree of anti-Semitism was simply a normal feature of everyday life. The DAIA, meanwhile, insisted that Timerman had not been arrested "as a Jew," that is, for the sole reason of being Jewish—as had obviously been the case with the Nazis—and used that reasoning to exonerate itself for its lethargic efforts on his behalf and to deny the legitimacy of the Holocaust analogy.

It is important to point out, however, that on the question of the extent and nature of anti-Semitism during the dictatorship period, particularly the existence of an "official" component, the debate did not divide along clean ideological lines. Many prominent progressive voices matched the DAIA's stance that anti-Semitism was being exaggerated outside Argentina. Naomi Meyer, author of the yearly "Argentina" report in the *American Jewish Yearbook*, initially agreed with the DAIA; her dispatches concerning the years 1976–1978 reported on the increase in anti-Semitic incidents but sought to allay concern about their seriousness, especially as regards 1976–1977, and gave voice to those who denied there was any connection to the government. In her 1979 and 1980 reports (about 1978 and 1979, respectively), however, Meyer provided evidence that justified greater concern.[100] Her husband, Rabbi Marshall Meyer, who was at the time active in human rights work in Argentina, echoed the DAIA's line about the normalcy of Jewish life—though in most other respects, such as its treatment of the Timerman case, he was one of the DAIA's most vocal critics.[101] Herman Schiller, editor of *Nueva Presencia*, also stressed that Jewish life "functions here without interruption" and disputed Timerman's claims to the contrary.[102]

Nevertheless, unlike the DAIA's claims, statements on anti-Semitism by Rabbi Meyer and by Schiller had an important strategic dimension that aimed to strengthen the case *against* the military government, not defend it. Meyer would later say, in 1983, that what made Argentina different from other places was not that anti-Semitic attacks occurred but that the government never prosecuted them.[103] Meanwhile, Schiller, speaking to Stephen Kinzer of the *Boston Globe*, said, "When [Timerman] accuses the government of unleashing an anti-Semitic terror campaign, the government can easily refute that. Our newspaper, for example, has had its share of threats, but we are allowed to publish freely. It is better to speak the pure truth—such as denouncing the 'disappearances' which the government cannot possibly refute.'"[104] Perhaps this explains why *Nueva Presencia* was consistently equivocal in its assessments of the magnitude of anti-Semitism. Along with other Jewish papers and organizations, it consistently reported on and protested against anti-Semitic activities—including bombings, desecrations, physical assaults, and the fomenting of hatred against Jews in extreme-right-wing publications. But it did not associate these directly with the state or link them to the abuses perpetrated by state security forces against Jewish detainees. Schiller's editorial in a July 1980 edition of the paper sums up its position when he writes about the necessity of avoiding both "complicit silence" and "paranoid exaggeration," painting these two options as a kind of "Scylla and Charybdis" of Jewish responses to anti-Semitism.[105] It is thus fair to say that until the final years of the dictatorship, *Nueva Presencia* treated the question of the normalcy or not of Jewish life as practically undecidable.

Attempts to determine the question were also hampered by the ideological effects of the military regime's "dirty war" against "subversion," which permeated political language across the spectrum and led to a distorted analysis of the situation that favored the regime. *Nueva Presencia*, a progressive publication that supported oppositional human rights groups, was not immune to these effects. Especially in the first three years of publication, 1977–1980, its editorials constantly invoked what would later come to be called the "dos demonios" or "two demons" theory, which was enshrined in the CONADEP's *Nunca más* report in 1984. The "dos demonios" approach conflated "terrorism from the left and the right" and presented them as equally pernicious. In the name of promoting moderation, it lumped together all forms of political violence by non-state actors under the rubric of "terrorist extremism." *Nueva Presencia* was often a forum for prominent oppositional voices like Adolfo Pérez Esquivel and Ernesto Sábato, who were key in setting forth this political vision.[106] This rhetoric had an important tactical aim: to clear a space for independent critical voices who could defend themselves against being considered sympathetic to the left and tarred with the brush of subversion and extremism—"We repudiate the right *and* the left" was the standard response. Furthermore, as Hugo Vezzetti has discussed, it established the grounds for a moral repudiation of political violence, regardless of ideology, one that would eventually become key to delegitimizing the dictatorship's pursuit of war against its political enemies and set the stage for a prosecution of its crimes.[107] Yet during the dictatorship it also had the problematic effect of shielding the government from any responsibility for the violence, which by being labeled "terrorist" was attributed exclusively to non-state forces; the fact that the state had become itself a perpetrator of terror could not be addressed directly. The "dos demonios" approach thus initially served to ratify the junta's self-image as the solution to the problem of extremism, one that obscured the fact that they were themselves extremists and that most of their victims, however politically engaged they might have been, were not. All of this had consequences when it came to the question of "official" anti-Semitism: since *Nueva Presencia* and other progressive voices consistently differentiated the state from extremism, it was difficult then to link it to the anti-Semitic activities carried out by extremist groups.

One important exception to this tendency was the presence of the Mothers of the Plaza de Mayo in *Nueva Presencia*. They were frequent contributors to the paper but espoused a more overt oppositional view than the paper's own editorial line. Schiller was particularly sympathetic to their aims, at times placing their "letters to the editor" on the paper's front page, in the space generally occupied by editorials, suggesting an ideological convergence between the paper and the Mothers. But although Schiller seems to have shared their political views, he did not state so directly until the last year of the dictatorship, when he openly supported them in the pages of the newspaper through interviews and articles about their activities.[108] The earlier reticence was due in part to the paper's commitment to pluralism, itself a kind of "double discourse" (though not in the precise sense meant by Feitlowitz). On the one hand, it served as an earnest injunction to the community to be more accepting of ideological diversity, and on the other, it offered ideological cover for a progressive agenda in a context where left-progressive Jewish publications were in peril and conservative voices were in ascendancy. The mantle of pluralism thus allowed Schiller great latitude but may also have constrained the paper's ability to adopt a forthright progressive stance on politically sensitive issues. By printing the Mothers' letters and featuring them prominently, *Nueva Presencia* found a way to bring their openly critical voices to its readership and thus circumvent some of its self-imposed constraints.

But the presence of the Mothers of the Plaza de Mayo in the pages of the paper also reveals the extent to which Jewish concerns about anti-Semitism did not converge cleanly with the work of activist human rights groups and in fact often stymied it. On the question of the culpability of the government in human rights violations, the Mothers were absolutely clear. On the question of the culpability of the government in anti-Semitism, the Jewish community was not at all clear. The divergence can be starkly appreciated around the moral meaning of silence. For the Mothers and other human rights activists, silence was complicity, that is, a failure to speak out against human rights abuses equaled an endorsement of the perpetrators. Thus Pérez Esquivel, in a speech he gave after learning he had been awarded the Nobel Peace Prize, cited Martin Luther King Jr.'s words condemning "the silence of good people."[109] The same vision of silence, when carried over into the realm of anti-Semitism in Argentina, held true for some leading Jewish voices, such as Timerman, but not for others, such as the DAIA, for whom silence was reasonable, and Schiller, for whom the meaning of silence in this context remained unclear.

Figures like Schiller and Meyer were conscious of the lack of convergence between the human rights struggle and the question of anti-Semitism. They warned of the dangers of stressing anti-Semitism without due attention to human rights violations. Thus Schiller, in his comments above, criticized

Timerman for making accusations against the regime that were difficult to prove. He sought instead to draw attention to the more fundamental problem of the disappearances and to align Jewish interests with a concern for human rights in such a way as to circumvent the unanswerables of anti-Semitism. We might say that he sought to shift the question of silence and complicity away from anti-Semitism and the Holocaust frame provided by Timerman and toward human rights and the frame provided by the Mothers. Unlike the DAIA, whose refusal of the Holocaust metaphor had the effect of shielding the junta from criticism and normalizing the state of repression, Schiller and many of *Nueva Presencia*'s contributors sidestepped the entire debate of whether the regime was anti-Semitic. They did so to create a broader, more inclusive basis for opposing the regime—its violations of human rights rather than its degree of anti-Semitism. Schiller's aim was to promote a vision of Jewish interests that went beyond anti-Semitism, that did not limit itself to concern for Jewish lives exclusively.

This was also true of the Yiddish-Spanish newspaper *Fraie Schtime*. Like *Nueva Presencia* it covered a controversial event, the meeting of the Latin American section of the World Jewish Congress in Brazil in November 1980, and used it as an opportunity not only to expose the profound differences of opinion within the Jewish community about how Jews had become integrated into national politics but also to question the decisions of the Jewish leadership. The Argentine delegation at the conference was composed of AMIA leaders and others who engaged in an open dispute about how to represent the Argentine situation to the Congress. AMIA members protested against the "alarmist" vision promoted by other members of the delegation, insisted that only they constituted a legitimate representation of the community before the Congress, and apparently tried to suppress the circulation of a resolution asking the World Jewish Congress to publicly support democracy, freedom, and human rights. Gregorio Lerner, writing in *Fraie Schtime/La Voz* a few months after the event, criticized the vision of Judaism put forward by the AMIA leaders and offered an alternative concept emphasizing the humanist, historicist, and pluralist values of Judaism.[110] *Nueva Presencia*, meanwhile, dedicated an entire "separata" to the event and made sure to highlight the fact that it itself had become a target of the AMIA leadership, which claimed that *Nueva Presencia*, as one representative put it, "serves an -ism that is not Judaism."[111]

The debate on "normalcy" and "anti-Semitism without soap" thus exposed differing conceptions about the role of Jews in Argentine society and about Jewish-Argentine identity "on the hyphen"—Was normalcy to be measured solely in terms of Jewish life, or also in terms of Argentina or Latin America as a whole? Would other "isms" be allowed to blend with Judaism? For Schiller and other progressive figures, the goal was to link Jewish concerns with the broader struggle for human rights led by outspoken groups such as the Mothers of the Plaza de Mayo, the Servicio Paz y Justicia, and the Asociación Pro-Derechos Humanos. The 1983 founding of the Movimiento Judío de Derechos Humanos made that goal explicit, and indeed, many of its public acts combined Holocaust commemoration with human rights advocacy featuring figures like the Mothers, who used the accusatory language they normally reserved for the dictatorship to describe the Holocaust, thus transposing the two: "What has allowed these tragedies to occur is the fragility of memory, the not-wanting-to-know-about-it, the lack of solidarity, the cowardice hiding behind comfortable attitudes."[112] Schiller was even more explicit, stating: "Because we suffered the world's indifference when the Nazis massacred six million Jews, we could not nor should not have been indifferent when the holocaust—here and now—was right under our noses."[113] This melding of Holocaust commemoration with contemporary issues became a trend that would continue into the post-dictatorship period.[114] In contrast, Timerman's form of Holocaust memory engendered accusations that, although he was instrumental in calling attention to a serious problem, he had framed it in such a way as to obscure some important elements of the Argentine situation in that he did not link anti-Semitism to the wider problem of human rights.

Marshall Meyer and Jewish Human Rights

The leader in this effort to incorporate a specifically Jewish presence to human rights work under dictatorship was Rabbi Marshall T. Meyer, a U.S. Conservative rabbi who had lived in Buenos Aires since the late 1950s and had founded a synagogue there as well as the first rabbinical seminary in Latin America. Meyer used his pulpit and the pages of *Nueva Presencia* to shift the debate within the Jewish community onto new ground. Whereas the disagreements between the DAIA and Timerman often boiled down to disputes about whether Jews were being persecuted as Jews or for other reasons, that is, alleged subversion, Meyer took the view that this was ultimately irrelevant. Of greater importance was the fact that human rights violations had occurred, which Jews should always condemn regardless of whether Jews were the victims or not. Meyer was thus a strong voice for an expansive view of "Jewish interests" under the banner of a pluralist Judaism that taught sociopolitical activism. This vision resonated with many progressives who since the 1960s had been contemplating the contradictions of life on the Argentine-Jewish hyphen and sought to transform the accusatory framing of "doble lealtad" (dual loyalty) from a negative to a positive light. Their goal was an integrated experience bringing together a commitment to Judaism with support of Latin American liberation movements.[115] This was the editorial line of the newspaper *Nueva Sión*, which had ceased publication during most of the dictatorship due to censorship, and whose editor I. Iudain (the pseudonym of Julio Adín) declared in 1962: "We do not accept that division . . . which condemns us to having to choose between two conditions that we consider indivisible."[116] The discussion had been reactivated in the 1970s around the question of "la doble militancia," double militancy, regarding Jewish participation in non-Jewish political organizations.[117] It was the more narrow view of Jewish identity, which advocated against "double militancy," that predominated in the organized leadership of the DAIA and the AMIA. Schiller and *Nueva Presencia* took the opposite stance; the paper's inaugural issue in July 1977 featured a front-page editorial titled "Ser argentinos, ser judíos" (To Be Argentine, to Be Jewish), which laid out its two guiding principles of reconciling Argentine and Jewish identities and including the plural voices of the Jewish community.[118] Schiller, in 1981, wrote of the need to teach young Jews how to stay true to the fight against injustice without abandoning their Jewish identity.[119]

For Rabbi Meyer, Judaism "is synonymous with justice and the struggle for human dignity," as one of Meyer's graduates from the rabbinical seminary put it.[120] Meyer advanced a Jewish liberation theology that promoted the defense of human rights as intrinsic to Judaism and that, via Isaiah and the biblical concept of "brother's keeper," placed compassion for others' suffering at its core.[121] During the dictatorship he allied himself with human rights groups like the Mothers of the Plaza de Mayo, the Grandmothers of the Plaza de Mayo, the Asociación Pro-Derechos Humanos, and the Servicio Paz y Justicia. In 1983 he cofounded, with Herman Schiller, the Movimiento Judío de Derechos Humanos, against the vocal opposition of Resnizky and other DAIA officials, and he was appointed by President Raúl Alfonsín to serve on the National Commission on the Disappeared (CONADEP), where he helped to produce and then promote its report *Nunca más*.[122]

However, on the question of whether the situation in Argentina could be compared to the Holocaust, Meyer took a contradictory stance. In a couple of public statements, he presented a view of the Holocaust as incomparable and refused to accept any parallels. In 1980 he wrote: "Eichmann and the Nazi hordes were responsible for the worst and only holocaust in history. I refuse to compare it to other persecutions, it simply has no parallel."[123] In 1983, in an interview published by the group Servicio Paz y Justicia, he repeated the sentiment: "I don't think that we can compare what happened here to the Holocaust of the 6,000,000. . . . I think the Holocaust of our brethren in the Second World War was a frighteningly unique event."[124] In 1984, in a piece in the New York Yiddish newspaper *Morning Freiheit* about his service to CONADEP, Meyer stated: "I never believed in a pogrom or a holocaust. No one was arrested because he was a Jew."[125] Yet in an article published in the *Washington Post* on the same day, he deliberately used Holocaust imagery to describe the dictatorship period—"Nobody can doubt that there were crematoria in Argentina. . . . I'm talking about crematoria, I'm talking about concentration camps, I'm talking about violent torture that makes one vomit when one hears the details"—and told of how, after living through those years in Argentina, he had finally come to understand how it was that people living near Auschwitz never bothered to ask about the smoke.[126]

In fact, despite his reluctance to explicitly compare the two events, Meyer seems to have kept the Holocaust in mind throughout his experience of the dictatorship. It is significant, for instance, that Meyer invited Elie Wiesel to visit Argentina in September 1979 in the hope of drawing more attention to Jacobo Timerman's continuing imprisonment. Wiesel at the time was the head of the U.S. President's Commission on the Holocaust. He was not permitted by the authorities to visit Timerman but gave interviews and speeches, and the visit received some limited coverage in the national press. At no point in these public statements did he refer directly to the political situation in Argentina, to human rights violations, or to Timerman.[127] In that sense, the visit might be said to have failed in its original purpose. Yet it demonstrates that for Meyer, the Holocaust—Wiesel being a "symbol" for the Holocaust, as Timerman described him during the visit—could be used by association to draw attention to the Argentine situation.[128]

Furthermore, Meyer frequently invoked the Holocaust when speaking about Argentine state terror. He referred to the military authorities as "Nazis who repressed, starved and tortured the Argentine people,"[129] a metaphorical usage that he would later be told was inappropriate in the United States.[130] Like Resnizky and Timerman, he also frequently reflected on the troubling legacy of silence bequeathed by the Holocaust and saw the same pattern repeated in Argentina. In a 1978 interview, he stated, "Judaism cannot survive in a society where human rights are not the rule," then continued later, "As a rabbi, I wouldn't be able to forgive myself if I repeated the silence of the rabbis in 1930s Europe."[131] This theme recurs for him throughout the dictatorship and later, when after his return to the United States in 1984 he wrote a memoir of his experiences (unpublished) and frequently lectured to Jewish audiences in the U.S. about the Argentine "dirty war." In the prologue to the memoir, he wrote: "I had never understood how one could live so close to Treblinka, or Bergen-Belsen, or Dachau, or Auschwitz and claim that he didn't know what was going on. I learned how this was possible in Argentina after March 24th, 1976."[132] In the same memoir, and regarding the fears of alienating the regime expressed by Jews in response to his efforts to raise money for the Asociación Pro-Derechos Humanos during the dictatorship, he wrote: "It seems to me I've read that argument many times in Jewish history. Not too long ago as a matter of fact. Was that not the attitude of the Jewish establishment to the Nazis and the Hitler government in the Second World War? To what did it lead? Isn't there a word for that event? Isn't it called the Holocaust? Haven't we learned that silence, apathy, and inactivity lead to acquiescence?"[133] He used the same argument to protest against the more conservative elements in the community who disliked *Nueva Presencia* and tried to muzzle it. Meyer speculated that had there been a diversity of Jewish voices in Nazi-occupied territories, the Nazis would not have been able to liquidate the Jews so easily.[134]

In 1984 Meyer returned to the United States, first in his capacity as representative of the CONADEP and tasked with interviewing exiled ex-detainees still living abroad, then more permanently, as a rabbi in Los Angeles and New York. That year he was interviewed frequently by the U.S. press and repeatedly used Holocaust imagery to describe the Argentine dictatorship. Back in Buenos Aires, at a speech on April 25, 1984, for Yom Hashoah, he conjoined the Holocaust and the years of dictatorship: "We are here tonight, Argentines in silent or not so silent pain, because here in Argentina we have lived through our own long night of horror and crime. . . . We Argentines lived through a mini-holocaust during the dictatorship years."[135]

1981–1985: The Holocaust in the Early Transitional Years

Rabbi Meyer is representative of a general trend in the usage of Holocaust imagery, which increased enormously in the period 1982–1985, the years spanning the end of the dictatorship, the publication of the CONADEP report *Nunca más*, and the first judicial trial against the members of the junta. As discussed above, during the early years of the dictatorship the clandestine Argentine press and international public opinion were forthright in making accusations and establishing analogies between the Holocaust and the current Argentine situation, but the Jewish press in Argentina was not. In the case of *Nueva Presencia*, it was not until the final years of the dictatorship that it began to publish editorials and articles containing the comparison, at which point there was a veritable explosion in analogies to the Holocaust across its pages. Comparisons to the Holocaust became almost commonplace. Perhaps this is due in part to the relaxing of government censorship of the press and of the need for self-censorship, which had prevented too critical a view of the government from appearing earlier. But it may also be linked to an event that occurred in December 1981, which seems to have played a role in sparking this new trend: the belated airing of the *Holocaust* television miniseries.

Reaction to the show in Argentina was mixed, as it had been wherever it was shown. The non-Jewish press hyped the event with splashy ads and multiple stories before, during, and after the broadcast. *La Nación* ran a story on how the miniseries had been received in the U.S. and Europe and printed interviews with two Argentine Holocaust survivors, Elsa Rosner and Eugenia Unger; significantly, Unger's statement ends with the words "Nunca más."[136] *La Nación*'s reviews were uniformly positive.[137] Regarding the question of why it had taken so long for the show to appear, *La Nación* made no mention of censorship, attributing the delay to technical problems of dubbing and distribution.[138] Coverage in the newspaper *Clarín* was somewhat more critical; its reviewer found fault with the show's melodrama and lack of subtlety but praised it overall as a valuable endeavor. Interestingly, it took on the question of censorship directly, naming it as such and wondering why it had been necessary.[139] In contrast, and not unexpectedly, the coverage by the newspaper *La Prensa*, further to the right than *La Nación* or *Clarín* and considered a mouthpiece for the regime, functioned as a classic "mechanism of denial" in the sense described by Dominick LaCapra.[140] The paper dismissed as irrelevant the question of why the broadcast had been so long delayed, compared Perón to Hitler, and proffered two negative reviews that sought to relativize the crimes by "de-Judaizing" them.[141]

Turning to the coverage in *Nueva Presencia*, some in the Jewish community dismissed it as too commercial, melodramatic, and mystifying. Leonard Senkman, a historian and frequent contributor to *Nueva Presencia*, found the show too "escapist" in its desire to provide viewers with an easy parable against genocide and cited warnings by historian Lucy Dawidowicz that a universalist and "humanist" approach to the Holocaust risked dissolving the specifically Jewish character of the tragedy and obscuring the importance of anti-Semitism in causing it.[142] Juan José Sebrelli, who had written a history of anti-Semitism in Argentina, found the show "forgettable" and recommended that people skip television and read about the Holocaust instead.[143] Ex-DAIA president Resnizky contributed his thoughts as well, deriving from the show the lesson that—in an ironic and unacknowledged citation of Timerman—even small-time anti-Semites were "potential installers of crematoria ovens."[144] Comments in the paper by Simón Fainland, ex-president of Sheerit Hapleitá (Organization of Holocaust Survivors), summed up the mixed feelings, expressing both appreciation for the lesson of "no callar" (speak out, do not be silent) that the miniseries sought to convey and an awareness that the show was utterly unequal to the reality of the Holocaust: "Nothing shown [on the show] can be equalled to what we had to endure."[145]

Of particular interest is the fact that *Nueva Presencia* solicited opinions about *Holocaust* by prominent figures, Jewish and non-Jewish, from human rights groups and oppositional political organizations, many of whom pointed to the analogies between contemporary Argentina and the events depicted on the television.[146] Federico Westerkamp, physicist and member of the human rights group Centro de Estudios Legales y Sociales, remarked that what happened "there, during the Holocaust, looks similar to what happened in Argentina." He was echoed by Alfredo Bravo, an ex-detainee and torture victim, a human rights and labor leader, who said: "We are very close to that miniseries, but 'live' and in reality." Bravo established a connection that he would later make even more explicit when, at a 1983 event commemorating the Warsaw ghetto uprising and the importance of human rights in Argentina, he ended his speech with a version of Anne Frank's famous line: "In spite of everything, I still believe in man."[147] In a separate article, Hector Polino of the Confederación Socialista Argentina also emphasized the connection: "What the country suffered in these last interminable years has a lot to do with the methods used by Nazism."[148] And as in the case of *The World at War*, the censorship of the *Holocaust* miniseries led to the suggestion that it was precisely the existence of these parallels that explained the government's refusal to let the show air.[149] Mario Gorenstein, then the president of the DAIA, confirmed this perspective in an interview conducted by Marguerite Feitlowitz some ten years later:

he claimed that the "generals were worried that the scenes of the Warsaw Ghetto Uprising would incite the guerrillas."[150]

While the impact of the media event of the *Holocaust* miniseries on the development of human rights discourses cannot be precisely measured—the appearance of the "Nunca más" slogan on the pages of *La Nación* is certainly suggestive—it inaugurated a veritable avalanche of Holocaust comparisons in *Nueva Presencia*, all of them aimed at delegitimizing the government. In the years 1982 and 1983, references to the Holocaust, to genocide, and to the coming "Nuremberg trials" of Argentina are too numerous to cite. One notable example can be found in a letter to the editor using Elie Wiesel's *And the World Was Silent*—as the original version of *Night*, first published in Argentina, was known—as a reference point to condemn the indifference of the Argentine people to "the holocaust our country experienced in the past seven years." The writer had earlier likened his state, as the father of a disappeared child, to that of an Auschwitz survivor whose child has been murdered by Nazis.[151] Another example is Rabbi Baruj Plavnik, who in a speech at an event to commemorate the Warsaw ghetto uprising took up the common theme of complicitous silence and established rhetorically, by repeating the phrase "Nothing was done," the parallels between then and now.[152] Antonio Elio Brailovsky compared not only Argentina's recent murderous policies but also its nineteenth-century extermination of Indigenous people to the Nazi atrocities, and concluded that the only difference between Eichmann and the Argentine generals was one of scale.[153] The following week, Schiller also took up the analogy and insisted that Jews who spoke exclusively of the Jewish Holocaust but omitted "the one produced in these latitudes" adopted an "unjust and incorrect attitude."[154] Another piece, by Nobel Peace Prize winner Adolfo Pérez Esquivel, compared Argentines to the Jewish people in terms of the suffering they had experienced.[155] Gregorio Lerner, in a letter to the editor in honor of his son, who had been assassinated in 1977, referred to a "solución final" in Argentina.[156]

Victims and Heroes

Let us return now to the questions raised at the start of this chapter: What do comparisons between the Holocaust and dictatorship Argentina reveal about these two disparate catastrophes? The answers vary depending on the case. As regards the use of Holocaust references in the early years of the dictatorship by the clandestine news agencies and others, they were highly rhetorical, of a brief and allusive nature. As such, they have little to say about the Holocaust except insofar as to demonstrate the extent to which it had become by then a shorthand for state-sponsored extermination whose terminologies had gone global. Despite their expediency, these references resist cliché because of the circumstances in which they appear. Furthermore, by highlighting the corruption and criminality of state forces and the climate of fear that the Proceso inaugurated, they may have infused some elements of the Holocaust past with a renewed sense of reality. Their limited audience notwithstanding, these analogies sought to break through the junta's ideological screen, which at the time was still effective in shielding the public from an awareness of the extent and nature of the violence the state was committing. Of course we can say, with hindsight, that the junta's extermination program was utterly incomparable to the Nazis' in terms of scale, yet this was not as clear at the time as it is now. This is a point that Jacobo Timerman kept reiterating by reminding his readers that German Jews in the 1930s did not know what was coming either. All the more reason, he argued, to sound the alarm early and attempt to stop the course of events while one still can.

But the equation "silence = complicity" or "silence = passivity," which Timerman was instrumental in publicizing when he used the loaded "Judenrat" term and which crystallized debates within the Jewish "internal front," generates thornier lines of comparison whose effects are harder to measure. The apparently straightforward equation was never that simple. It exposed some unresolved issues concerning the Holocaust legacy as it was brought to bear on this contemporary instance of state terror—issues concerning the victimization and complicity of Jews—but in such a way as to prohibit a full reckoning with either the present or the past.

As regards the situation of dictatorship, the focus on whether the DAIA was complicit like the Judenrat established that the organization had a special role to play as appointed leader of the Jewish community, but it also served to hide the fact that if some Jews sought to defend the government against Timerman's charges of anti-Semitism, it was not only because, as in the case of the German Judenrat of the 1930s, they were forced to negotiate with a hostile state. It was also because the junta enjoyed political support among the Jewish community, just as it did more broadly in Argentina, where there was no shortage of people sympathetic to its aims and tactics beyond its first year (when many leftists and liberals had also welcomed the junta's promise to stabilize the country). Thus the Judenrat accusation covered over the existence of very real political differences among Jews and perhaps contributed to the censoring of true ideological debate that was already a feature of the repression.

Furthermore, the use of Holocaust language to code questions of passivity and complicity, via references to the Judenrat and the "Jews of Silence," reinforced a black-and-white image of situations that involved many shades of gray. It obscured the fact that silence in such circumstances may not be simply an act of cowardice or moral abdication. Such usage thus also tells us something about the legacy of the Holocaust as it developed in Argentina. In hindsight, it is troubling to see the extent to which the dictatorship period activated Jewish anxieties about being weak, complicitous victims, the result of post-Holocaust discussions about Jewish identity. This absorption of a particular Holocaust code cut across the fissures that divided Timerman from the DAIA. Each of these participants in the debate understood the legacy of the Holocaust primarily through the prism of silence as shame—but focused predominantly on the silence of the Jewish victims, which Timerman and the DAIA frequently invoked, rather than the silence of the bystanders (the meaning implied by Wiesel's title *And the World Was Silent*). The Holocaust legacy thus understood presents a clear-cut ethical obligation to speak—speech as action. Yet on the part of Timerman and the DAIA presidents, this moral clarity became attached to a particularly harsh interpretation of silence as the manifestation of an internalized Jewish willingness toward victimhood. The debate was therefore guided by the unstated pressure not to be perceived as a victim.

Resnizky, in a 1979 speech that responded implicitly to accusations about the DAIA's inaction on the matter of Timerman and other Jewish detainees, cited Amos Oz's 1967 essay "The Meaning of Homeland," which discusses the two anti-Semitic archetypes of the Jew in the shadow of Auschwitz: the vampire and the victim.[157] Resnizky used it to deflect attention onto his heroic refusal of the victim role, declaring: "The world does not forgive the Jew who abandons the role of victim."[158] This desired abandonment of the victim role, however, had consequences for how Jews interpreted the situation in Argentina. Ironically and tragically, because it was such a missed opportunity, this repudiation of Jewish victimhood had nothing to say about the disappeared. Note, in this regard, the difference between Timerman's moral discourse on silence and that of Meyer or the Mothers, who reserved their judgment not for the victims but for the bystanders—whether living in Argentina or in sight of Auschwitz's chimneys.

The discussions generated by Timerman's Judenrat accusations took on a circular quality, shadowboxing with the ghosts of the Holocaust but not able truly to respond to the circumstances at hand. Thus, for all the speech that this "victim versus hero" use of the Holocaust generated in the Jewish "internal front," there was much that it condemned to silence. This included, strangely enough, the abduction of Resnizky's son Marcos in August 1977 by security forces, a fact that was reported in the international press but that in Argentina was covered only by the virulently anti-Semitic journal *Cabildo* and by the clandestine news agency.[159] Marcos was returned several days later, after U.S. secretary of state Cyrus Vance had intervened and after having reportedly suffered torture. To what extent was Resnizky's stance throughout the dictatorship determined by his refusal to publicize his own victim status and that of his son? *Cabildo* suggested that Marcos was freed in exchange for his father's guarantee of silence on the matter of anti-Semitism; *Cabildo* is hardly a reliable source, yet others wondered about this possibility as well. In the "frente interno" the event was not really aired until 1984, when the DAIA discussed it in its special report on Jewish detainees and disappeared.[160] But in their response to the DAIA's report, the Jewish families of the disappeared rightly questioned why Marcos's abduction had not been made public earlier, and why Resnizky, having been made especially vulnerable to the junta through this despicable extortion, had not resigned his post.[161]

Resnizky's reference to Amos Oz suggests the extent to which Argentine Jews interpreted their situation according to Israeli paradigms of Jewish identity. Certainly, as I suggested earlier, the Israeli concept of "Shoah uGevurah" structured their debates in a fundamental way. But by the 1970s and 1980s this concept was undergoing substantial revision in Israel, where "the public ha[d] also come to appreciate that resistance can consist in moral courage, not just armed force" and "the tragedy of the Holocaust evoke[d] greater sympathy" than it used to, as Charles S. Liebman and Eliezer Don-Yehiya show.[162] This changing Israeli consciousness of the Holocaust was reported on in Argentina through Leonardo Senkman's contributions to *Nueva Presencia*.[163] In April 1981 he published a news story about an Israeli television documentary on the Holocaust that involved a discussion about the national tendency to glorify suicidal resistance over survival. According to Senkman, during the televised discussion a child of Holocaust survivors forcefully spoke out against the tendency to treat with contempt those who "went willingly" to their deaths in the camps.[164] A month later he reported on the work of Israeli intelligence officer–turned–historian Yehoshafat Harkabi, who criticized what he called the "Bar Kochba" syndrome, that is, the Israeli inclination to see in the second-century warrior's irrational military sacrifice a model of heroism.¹⁶⁵ A year earlier, in May 1980, Senkman had written on new research by historian Yehuda Bauer, who aimed both to disprove the myth of Jews marching "like sheep to the slaughter" by focusing on the number of rebellions led by Jews in the camps, and also to remind his readers that their expectations of rebellion were entirely misplaced, based on a gross underestimation of the terrible challenges faced by most Jews in those circumstances.¹⁶⁶ Bauer and these other figures thus sought a more nuanced approach to the question of Jewish passivity and heroism, one that was not so tightly bound to a victim-hero dichotomy.

Turning to representations of the Holocaust in Argentina along these lines, especially as regards commemorative events for the Warsaw ghetto uprising, we see a decidedly mixed picture: an expansive notion of resistance that includes a more generous account of the experience of Jewish victimization competes with the more limited and narrower version of resistance embodied in the figure of the ghetto fighter that stigmatizes those who did not rise up. In April 1977, at a speech given in Yiddish to commemorate the Warsaw ghetto uprising, Nachmann Dreschler offered one of the few expansive accounts of resistance under oppression that can be found in the Argentine Jewish discourse of the era. Dreschler considered witnessing and testimony as acts of resistance, and asked that the audience remember "not just the warriors who with weapons in hand rose up against the Nazi assassins, but also all those heroes, silent and anonymous heroes of the Jewish resistance, manifested in the most diverse forms. Because all was resistance in the ghettos and the concentration camps of occupied Poland. When the martyr Dr. Emanuel Ringelblum buries, under cover of the night, cans and milk jugs in which he's hidden important documents for history, he realizes an act of resistance."¹⁶⁷ The same issue of *Fraie Schtime* that contained Dreschler's speech also contained a positive review of a short-story collection by Simja Sneh, *El pan y la sangre*, a book that includes a story about the gruesome end befalling a leader of the Judenrat yet nevertheless manages to present the character as a tragic figure rather than an apathetic coward.¹⁶⁸ In 1981, Gustavo Perednik, a frequent contributor to *Nueva Presencia* (and also at times a critic of the paper), offered a long reflection on Holocaust suffering, separating out the innocent victims, "sin culpa, sin defensa, sin lucha" (without guilt, defenseless, without struggle), from the other dead and placing them at the center of Holocaust remembrance.¹⁶⁹

But these more nuanced images of the destruction of Jewish lives in the Holocaust competed with depictions of armed heroism as the most interesting and legitimate form of resistance, a tendency that could not help but be reinforced by the fact that the Warsaw ghetto uprising was the centerpiece of Holocaust commemoration. The focus of these depictions is "the salvation of honor" achieved by the ghetto fighters—the phrase is that of Dov Schmorak, the Israeli ambassador to Argentina, from a speech he gave in La Plata in 1982, and it is as representative of how the Holocaust was depicted as the examples mentioned above, or perhaps even more so.[170] Also in this vein is a story by the poet and partisan resister Abba Kovner, reprinted in *Fraie Schtime* in 1980, which describes the transport from Vilna to Auschwitz. It ends with an image of Jews with their heads bowed, quietly awaiting orders from the Nazi guards.[171] Kovner himself had been an active participant in the debates about the shape and scope of Yad Vashem in the late 1940s, and his short story is consonant with his position in these debates, namely, that commemoration should honor those heroic few who distinguished themselves from the mass of Jews to grasp the reality of their predicament and fight against it.[172] Following the story, and as if to drive home the point, the editors of *Fraie Schtime* reprinted the call to arms of the Vilna ghetto, which Kovner himself had authored and which concludes with the phrase: "Judíos, no vayamos como rebaño al degollador" (Jews, do not go like sheep to the slaughter).[173]

Holocaust remembrance in *Nueva Presencia*, meanwhile, also focused on the Warsaw ghetto uprising. The paper sometimes reprinted the same piece (or slightly altered versions thereof) in its yearly commemoration, which described various forms of struggle and resistance yet nevertheless, in a manner already formulaic, glorified the heroism of the fighters and placed it at the center of the story. It liked to reprint a letter by Mordejai Anilevich, the leader of the Warsaw ghetto rebellion and embodiment of heroic sacrifice and combative Judaism. This depiction, it should be noted, was intended primarily as a political act in the newspaper's interpretive battle with right-wing Jews over the past. It meant to underscore the leadership of leftist militants in the ghetto and recapture the universal aims of their struggle "for a better future for all," not just for the Jews.[174]

With respect to these "victim-hero" tensions in Holocaust commemoration, the eventual melding of Holocaust remembrance with the Argentine discourse on human rights—exemplified in the Jewish Movement for Human Rights and its ally the Mothers of the Plaza de Mayo—takes on a special significance, because it tipped the balance dramatically in favor of a compassionate attitude toward the victims and a more expansive account of resistance. It is true that Schiller attempted, at one point, to incorporate the heroic aspects of the Warsaw ghetto uprising, expressing his desire to "unite . . . the rebellion led by Anilevich and the issue of human rights in our country." In his article he appealed to the figure of the "guerrilla" to describe the Jewish resisters in the ghetto rather than the more traditional "partisan," knowing full well that the term would be controversial because of its association with left-wing liberation movements and the figure of Che Guevara. He defended his usage of the word in a telling parenthesis about the uprising: "It was a guerrilla war (and let's not be afraid of this phrase nor cloak it with the less sonorous word 'partisan,' because the word 'guerrilla' was used by Anilevich himself and to extend it to that case is not incorrect)."[175] Schiller had consciously stepped into the debate about the aptness of Holocaust analogies.

But the bulk of Holocaust references that flourish while human rights discourse takes center stage on the cusp of Argentina's democratic transition do not include the hero figure, much less overt praise for guerrillas. On the contrary, as Hugo Vezzetti has noted, the tendency was to "de-ideologize" the junta's victims and forget that many of them were activists and militants pursuing ideological goals, sometimes through violent means. Vezzetti suggests that, through the CONADEP report and the first judicial proceedings against military leaders, Holocaust memory had a role to play in this process, because it enabled the public to frame the criminality of the regime's leaders and the innocence of its victims—a process of "purifying the victims" that Vezzetti likens to the "sanctification" of Anne Frank and that he criticizes, in the Argentine instance, because it served to depoliticize the past.[176]

Yet if we think specifically about Jewish practices of Holocaust remembrance rather than broader trends in Argentina, we notice a different history and context for this turn to the innocent victim; what was true for Argentine society at large was not entirely true for the Jews who had been caught up in the Judenrat debates inaugurated by Timerman's polemical statements, where to be a victim, to let oneself be victimized by the state, was to be morally complicit in one's own destruction. It is only by way of the human rights idea of the victim as morally innocent that Jews were able to cast off the self-castigating image of Jewish victimhood—of victimhood as a complicitous rather than innocent state—that the references to the "Jews of Silence" had served to reinforce. Even Meyer, who seems to have kept the Holocaust in mind throughout the period yet resisted overt comparisons to it, began to use Holocaust terminology in this highly rhetorical manner during the latter years of the dictatorship and through the transition to democracy. By that point, use of the Holocaust to describe the Proceso was common enough that it became a kind of shorthand for stating one's opposition to the regime and what had been done in its name.

Conclusion

The unifying function of Holocaust remembrance in the Jewish community of Argentina was already questionable in the decades before the dictatorship. During the dictatorship, Holocaust memory worked actively to deepen the fissures in the Jewish community. It was not until the late-dictatorship period and afterward that it took on a unifying role, and then not for particularist Jewish identifications. In both cases, during the Argentine dictatorship and immediately after, the use of the Holocaust is a clear case of the politicization of Holocaust memory. Should it be deplored as such? Novick suggests not; on the contrary, he finds to be more troubling the U.S. situation of a "banal" and "inconsequential" Holocaust memory, "unrelated to the real divisions in American society." He argues instead that "collective memory, when it is consequential, when it is worthy of the name, is characteristically an arena of political contestation in which competing narratives about central symbols in the collective past, and the collectivity's relationship to that past, are disputed and negotiated in the interests of redefining the collective present."[177] Extending his reflections to Argentina, we can say that use of the Holocaust, and the debates about such use, "redefined the present" for Jews under dictatorship and became "consequential" to them in a new way. Though wielded as a tool for purposes having little to do with the events of the Holocaust and at times seemingly facile and empty, these references nevertheless involve a return to some of the more difficult elements of the Holocaust legacy, but it is a return that illuminates both present and past only partially.

The victim-hero dichotomy, so clearly instrumental to the Israeli nationalist tendency to repudiate Jewish passivity, returned with a vengeance for Argentine Jews under dictatorship. Timerman's highly political interpretation of the Holocaust enabled Jews to frame their sense of outrage at the complicitous silence of the Jewish authorities. In this sense, it was a response to the demands of the times, yet it involved significant missed connections and unacknowledged silences about other pressing issues of the day. It also made manifest a fundamental confusion produced by some tendencies in post-Holocaust discussions of Jewish identity, in which the Jewish victims are poorly differentiated from their perpetrators when it comes to assigning historical responsibility.[178] The full-fledged entry of the Holocaust into human rights discourses, meanwhile, involved a new emphasis in Holocaust remembrance—displacing heroes in favor of victims—a move that perhaps, in keeping with contemporary scholars, would later prohibit a full reckoning with the reality of the Argentine past.[179] The Holocaust was therefore both an inevitable backdrop but also a questionable model under the circumstances, which worked to expose the political fissures among Argentine Jews and to dissolve the certainties and clichés that had characterized Shoah uGevurah. Questions about the innocence of the junta's victims and the guilt of bystanders and civilian leaders, and about the relevance of the Holocaust in making these determinations, are a feature of debates in contemporary Argentina. The use of the Holocaust throughout the Proceso to frame ethical dilemmas of complicity and resistance under dictatorship demonstrates the extent to which these issues were already on the table well before the transition to democracy.

Chapter Two

Holocaust Consciousness as Critical Consciousness in Post-dictatorship Argentina, 1995–2005[1]

We know that analogies are deceptive and should be avoided. Jewish history, its drama, is a singular event. . . . But there are texts that, although they refer to particular events, help to trigger other memories.[2]

The Shoah and the massacre of the 1970s in Argentina are different events. Yet for many of us, both tragedies are intertwined.[3]

It's not that Auschwitz and the ESMA . . . are "the same." An infinite number of historians have taken on the task of showing the specificities of each historical experience. . . . But to speak these events "together"— Auschwitz and the ESMA, the Nazi genocide and the Argentine genocide—carries a different meaning than to speak them separately.[4]

This chapter examines the years 1995–2005 in Argentina. The decade begins with a "memory boom" amid new revelations about the state's crimes against humanity during the dictatorship period (1976–1983) and a renewed push by civil society for criminal prosecutions of the perpetrators.[5] This period culminates with the inauguration of state-sponsored public spaces to remember state crimes and the greater institutionalization of human rights under the presidency of Néstor Kirchner. In contrast to the debates within the Argentine Jewish community during the dictatorship, discussed in Chapter 1, in the post-dictatorship period there was little actual debate in Argentina on "the meaning of the Holocaust" as such. But as literary scholar Florinda

Goldberg has noted, the Holocaust constitutes a "semantic field" through which to discuss the dictatorship and the "dirty war."[6] The epigraphs for this chapter are but three examples of many that illustrate how the Holocaust and the Argentine "Proceso" have become intertwined for many Argentines. The three authors cited above are all Jewish, evidence that this intertwining is perhaps most strongly felt by Jews in Argentina. But it is far from limited to Jewish thinkers. Throughout the decade examined here, human rights activists, scholars, and intellectuals turned to Holocaust memory to model Argentine memory practices.

My interest here lies in a Holocaust consciousness in Argentina that speaks politically and critically. For the thinkers examined in this chapter, Holocaust consciousness serves as a wedge that opens a critical distance between Argentine society and the stories it tells about its past. The Holocaust is not "compared" to Argentine history so much as used to keep it electrically and intellectually charged, a living counterpoint to narratives that seek closure and might lead to political complacency. Of particular importance to the Argentine authors that I will examine here are European authors, including Holocaust survivors, whose work deals directly with the legacy of the Holocaust and comes to constitute, in post-dictatorship Argentina, a repository of critical thinking on which to draw in seeking to understand the legacy of the "dirty war." Holocaust consciousness calls attention to and denormalizes the state violence of the recent past, casting it as monstrous and as having permeated Argentine society. It helps frame this past as one that holds such terrible implications for the nation that it cannot yet be put to rest without doing an injustice to its victims; one that requires serious, collective mental effort to comprehend who were its victims and perpetrators and who its complicitous participants.

In short, this chapter emphasizes that Holocaust consciousness in post-dictatorship Argentina is tied to critique, to a critical understanding of the past that animates a critical consciousness in the present. But critical of what, and on what grounds? This is where fault lines appear in post-dictatorship Holocaust consciousness. This chapter looks at how the Holocaust becomes meaningful in Argentina's "politics of memory," that is, in the tendentious and polemical conversation about why the atrocities of the "dirty war" happened and how to speak about them, about which currents of Argentine political life led to these atrocities and who is criminally or morally responsible for them. It will illustrate these fault lines by looking at Holocaust consciousness among those affiliated with the human rights movement and among those critical of that movement.[7]

The human rights approach to memory in Argentina is thoroughly infused with Holocaust consciousness. "Never Again," "Never Forget," and "Never Be Silent" are calls to arms for those working to bring the perpetrators to justice. Most human rights work regarding the dictatorship starts with the premise that more needs to be said; that speech is a necessary counterweight to the censorship of the dictatorship period itself, when the junta promoted the slogan "El silencio es salud" (Silence is health),[8] and to the censoring effects of prevailing political winds in the post-dictatorship period. Indeed, as historian Emilio Crenzel explains, the human rights movement succeeded in counteracting these currents of denialism and silencing.[9] The Holocaust legacy had already been an important reference point for human rights struggles during the dictatorship itself. In the post-dictatorship period, human rights activists in Argentina who focused on bringing criminal charges against military perpetrators turned to the vast field of Holocaust memory to forge the link between memory and justice and to inspire and validate their critical memory practices in Argentina.

The human rights modalities of memory activists and scholars represent the most visible and arguably influential kind of Holocaust consciousness in the post-dictatorship. But this modality is not the only one. The intellectuals I will focus on here—two figures associated with the journal *Punto de Vista*, Beatriz Sarlo and Hugo Vezzetti, and two associated with the journal *Confines*, Nicolás Casullo and Héctor Schmucler—all start from the opposite view regarding how best to make the past a concern of the present, a view that also draws from the Holocaust legacy. They hold that it is possible, indeed likely, that representations of past atrocities, instead of communicating the enormity of the violence, will trivialize them, whether through media oversaturation, oversimplification, or sentimentalization. They consequently advocate various modes of skepticism toward the memory work of human rights activists. That skepticism rests largely on questions of language and cultural representation, on how we speak, write, and make art about the violence of the nation's collective past.

One angle of critique concerns the role of the culture industry in the construction of memory. Claudia Feld notes that in the mid-1990s the mass media took on "el deber de la memoria," memory as a moral duty, and contributed to framing the debate about the legacy of the past in terms of a simple opposition between memory and forgetting rather than in terms of a more complex interaction among "rival" memories.[10] The thinkers I discuss here charge that memory discourses have been coopted by a mass media that generates trivializing, morbid, and anesthetizing understandings of past violence. This is the question of "the *market* for social memory," as Francine Masiello writes, anchoring Argentina's politics of memory in the context of neoliberalism and pointing to a concern about whether memory "functions as an impetus for future social action" or leads rather to quietism and complacency.[11]

Another point of critique concerns language—the language of memory in post-dictatorship Argentina. This view holds that some contemporary memory discourses reproduce elements of the authoritarian discourse of the military junta or of its political opponents and thereby do not constitute a strong enough break with the social worlds that made the "dirty war" possible.[12] An important effect of this focus on the power of language to generate a shared field of complicity is that it dilutes the distinction between victims and perpetrators that is central to the human rights framework. It draws attention away from the individual whose rights have been violated in order to focus on an underlying web of complicity, one that both the military and its opponents participated in together because both used violence—physical or discursive or both—to advance political ends. However, the thinkers whom I'll examine here do not dispute the idea that the actions of the military in the "dirty war" constitute crimes for which the perpetrators should be held criminally responsible. All of them believe that the judicial sphere is an important arena for reckoning with the past. But they also insist, as do many of those involved in human rights struggles, that the legal arena is not the only one in which to pursue justice and that, in addition to the element of criminal responsibility, Argentina must also address the element of moral and social responsibility for past atrocities by contemplating deeper patterns of Argentine modernity.

Hannah Arendt is a key thinker in this respect. As early as 1946 she proposed that there were as yet no legal categories adequate to describe Nazi crimes.[13] Alejandro Kaufman, in *Confines*, had Arendt in mind when he wrote against "the punitive paradigm" and for a broader, deeper understanding of justice that was not solely focused on discipline and on determining criminal culpability.[14] Neither Arendt nor Kaufman would argue against the criminal prosecution of the perpetrators. Rather, they point to those elements of the violence that exceed criminal definitions and that must be approached through other frameworks of analysis. Human rights activists have made similar points. Estela Carlotto, one of the leaders of the Grandmothers of the Plaza de Mayo, reminds us that in addition to fighting to learn *what* happened during the dictatorship, we must also fight to learn *why* it happened, a question that a legal proceeding cannot answer on its own.[15]

The thinkers I discuss here, however, consistently intervene outside the legal framework to interrupt activist strategy by questioning the truth-telling capacity of the dictatorship's victims—not on primarily partisan political grounds (though a partisan subtext may also be present) but by insisting on the protagonism of language rather than its speakers and on the social machineries that displace individual acts. Miguel Dalmaroni, in his insightful analysis of similarities and differences between *Punto de Vista* and *Confines* when it comes to memory politics, shows that both look to aesthetic, nonrhetorical, recursive narrative forms over "prosaic" and rhetorical ones, thereby marking a big gap between their work and that of political activists.[16] These points of critique largely derive from their readings of post-Auschwitz philosophy, sociology, history, and testimony. Sarlo turns to Claude Lanzman's film *Shoah* and Primo Levi's *Survival in Auschwitz* (*If This Be a Man*); Vezzetti turns to Norbert Elias and Karl Jaspers as well as to numerous historians of the Holocaust; the authors of *Confines* grapple with Jean-François Lyotard, Hannah Arendt, and Elias Canetti. In this way, and despite the fact that the Holocaust has been an important reference point for thinking about the dictatorship in terms of a violation of human rights, it also emerges as a reference point for a critique of human rights–centered approaches to memory.

In what follows, I will examine the importance of Holocaust consciousness among human rights activists and survivors of the Argentine detention centers, then turn to analysis of the writings of authors associated with the journals *Punto de Vista* and *Confines*. Both journals were voices of cosmopolitan cultural analysis that flourished in the post-dictatorship period. More recently their founding members became political opponents, taking opposite sides with respect to the cultural and economic policies of the Kirchner presidencies and the legacies of Peronism.[17] Yet despite these ideological differences, the journals had much in common: both brought European philosophy and critical theory to bear on memory debates in Argentina, and both advanced a critique of human rights and testimonial practices derived from their readings of Holocaust texts. The intellectuals I examine here delve into the Holocaust archive in making their claims against the memory practices of groups like the Mothers and Grandmothers of the Plaza de Mayo, which they cast as a "forgetting" and which they charge with mystifying the past rather than illuminating it. Alejandro Baer and Natan Sznaider analyze the presence of Holocaust discourses in post-dictatorship Argentina as evidence for the global spread of an "ethics of 'never again.' "[18] But the intellectuals discussed here cut against the grain of global trends in

Holocaust consciousness. They use their readings on the Holocaust to cast suspicion on, if not outright disable, the testimony and memory developed by human rights activists, seeing them as at best sentimental and complacent, at worst a continuation of the discursive practices that made political violence possible. These thinkers view Holocaust testimonies as models that Argentine testimonies largely fail to live up to, thus simultaneously invoking and rejecting parallels between the two situations. How is it that the victims' voices in Argentina came to be compared to the voices of Primo Levi or the survivors in Lanzmann's *Shoah* or European Jewish escapee intellectuals, and found wanting? Came to be, indeed, accused of complicity with the violence against which they protest now and may have protested, militantly, before?

Human Rights and the Holocaust in Argentina

Human rights activism emerged as a political force in Argentina during the dictatorship to denounce state crimes, led by several key human rights organizations.[19] After the dictatorship and during the transition to democracy, it was in part thanks to pressure from human rights groups that the new democratic state took up the twin demands for truth and justice, first through the creation of the National Commission on Disappeared Persons (Comisión Nacional sobre la Desaparición de Personas, CONADEP), which issued its groundbreaking *Nunca más* report in 1984, then through the 1985 Trial of the Juntas (Juicio a las Juntas), which successfully prosecuted the highest-ranking military officers for criminal acts.[20] In the years following the Juicio a las Juntas, criminal prosecution of military perpetrators suffered a reversal of fortune with the promulgation of acts and laws guaranteeing impunity for past crimes.[21] Ten years later, in March 1995, the human rights movement gained new impetus when ex–military officer Adolfo Scilingo appeared on television and confessed to having tossed living people into the sea from an airplane during the state's "war against subversives."

Scilingo's appearance decisively reinstated the topic of dictatorship and repression at the center of the public eye after a decade of relative silence.[22] It mobilized a younger generation of activist citizens, prominent among them the group HIJOS (Hijos por la Identidad y la Justicia y contra el Olvido y el Silencio [Children for Identity and Justice and Against Forgetting and Silence]), which brings together the adult children of those who were disappeared by the military and was founded immediately after the Scilingo revelations.[23] The group, along with other established human rights groups, such as the Madres de Plaza de Mayo and the Abuelas de Plaza de Mayo, inaugurated a new era of creative public protest denouncing the state's crimes during the dictatorship. Human rights at that point also saw greater institutionalization by the state. In Buenos Aires middle schools, the CONADEP's best-selling book *Nunca más* became a part of the official curriculum and was reissued twice in 1995.[24] At the university level, "memory studies" took hold as an academic subdiscipline, thanks in large measure to the pioneering work of sociologist Elizabeth Jelin.[25] The state designated public spaces for remembering state crimes: a memory park was approved in 1998 by the city of Buenos Aires, and the military's most infamous detention center, the Navy Mechanics' School in Buenos Aires (Escuela Superior Mecánica de la Armada, ESMA), became a museum dedicated to memory and human rights in 2004 under President Néstor Kirchner.[26]

In the midst of these changes, Holocaust consciousness has come to permeate discourse about the dictatorship. When the CONADEP's *Nunca más* report was reissued in 1995, it contained artwork that explicitly linked the Nazi genocide to the "dirty war."[27] In 2004, the minister of human rights, Eduardo Luis Duhalde, declared the ESMA to be "the Argentine Auschwitz" when the site was officially designated a memory museum.[28] The phrase had been in circulation for a decade or more before Duhalde's public statement and resonates with a 1985 statement by Víctor Melchor Basterra, an ESMA survivor.[29] These examples demonstrate the idea that there are parallels between the victims of the Nazis and the victims of the military dictatorship, and between the Nazis and the Argentine perpetrators. Highly rhetorical, they function as a code that identifies the criminal nature of the dictatorship and the enormity of its crimes.

But these emblematic phrases and images, however codified, should not be taken as mere cliché. To do so would be to ignore the work that Holocaust consciousness accomplished for human rights organizations and survivors in the post-dictatorship period. In the first place, Holocaust consciousness helped to project state terror as criminal. Second, it centered national history on witness testimony and memory. Third, it provided a meaningful narrative and conceptual framework for survivors and family members of the disappeared.

First, Hugo Vezzetti argues that it was through the figure of the Holocaust that Argentines came to appreciate the criminal nature of state violence and to differentiate this particular instance of dictatorship from the many prior instances of it. A fundamental shift occurred in how Argentines viewed the dictatorship: "Videla and Pinochet are no longer simply Latin

American dictators but rather have acquired a more general quality as part of the series that starts with the Holocaust and the condemnation—not just judicial but also political and moral—of crimes against groups, races and communities."[30] An important consequence was a change in how Argentines viewed the protagonists of the violence: they were now labeled either "victims" or "perpetrators" of criminal acts rather than "heroes" in a revolutionary or anti-subversive war.[31] The trial against the junta leaders in 1985 was key to establishing this new "scene" of victims-perpetrators to replace the older scene of war. "The figure of the Holocaust" thus enabled a "projection of the Argentine experience onto a universal dimension."[32]

In the second place, Argentine human rights activists saw in the Holocaust a model for placing individual memory at the center of history. The Holocaust had inaugurated what historian Annette Wieviorka calls "the era of the witness."[33] In Argentina, official testimony by survivors and by the families of the disappeared first played a crucial role in the "transition to democracy" of 1984–1985, with the CONADEP report and the Trial of the Juntas, both of which echoed the Eichmann trial because it was surviving witnesses who made the wider society appreciate the horror and enormity of the violence. Ten years later, survivors and family members reoccupied center stage in debates about the past and spearheaded new legal battles to prosecute perpetrators. Legal activism by the Grandmothers of the Plaza de Mayo led the state to initiate criminal proceedings in 1998 against former members of the military junta for child abduction, that is, for having "stolen" or "appropriated" children born in the junta's torture centers or kidnapped with their parents. These charges had not been covered by the "impunity laws" and provided a new opening for criminal prosecutions. In 2000, international criminal proceedings were launched in two countries against several Argentine perpetrators, and in 2001 an Argentine judge nullified the most important impunity laws, a decision that survived several appeals and was definitively ratified by Argentine lawmakers in 2004.[34]

Third, as early as 1986, psychotherapists working with the Mothers of the Plaza de Mayo were reading Bruno Bettelheim's analysis of the psychological defense mechanisms developed by prisoners in the Nazi concentration camps.[35] A decade later, numerous otherwise disparate works by survivors and by victims' families demonstrated the extent to which the Holocaust as reference point had become embedded in the Argentine testimonial tradition and understood as key to processes of psychological healing. Historian David Sheinin points out that survivors of the Argentine camps "stress that the perpetrators explicitly made reference to the Holocaust as both something to be emulated and as a frame of reference that should be surpassed."³⁶ Their focus is generally less on the historical similarities between the two regimes and more on the fact that "the victims cannot tell whether they are in the concentration camps of the Nazis or the Argentines. They cannot tell the difference between past and present."³⁷ Sheinin continues: "Although several genocides repeat certain elements of the Holocaust, only in Argentina did perpetrators present their actions of abduction and extermination as a reenactment of the Holocaust."³⁸ Sociologist Daniel Feierstein reports that for members of the Association of Formerly Detained and Disappeared Persons (Asociación de Ex-Detenidos y Desaparecidos), works by Levi and Bettelheim were crucial for their understanding of their own experience.³⁹ He notes that when he organized an encounter in 2001 between an Auschwitz survivor and three survivors of the Argentine camps, it generated intense feelings of mutual recognition.⁴⁰

Other significant examples that demonstrate that Holocaust consciousness has permeated the survivor testimony tradition in Argentina include Pilar Calveiro's *Poder y desaparición: Los campos de concentración en Argentina*, one of the best reflections about the "gray zone" inside the Argentine camps. A survivor-turned-scholar, she refuses to tell her story in the first person yet listens attentively to the first-person voices of Primo Levi and Jorge Semprún.⁴¹ Ludmila da Silva Catela's study of family members of the disappeared and how they coped with their loss was inspired by Michael Pollak's book *L'expérience concentrationaire*, based on his work with women survivors of the Shoah.⁴² The testimonies gathered in the book *Ese infierno* (That Hell), by women ex-detainees, provide another example. In their conversations about their experiences in Argentine camps, they refer to the writings of Jean Améry on Auschwitz and devote an entire chapter to reflecting on "the Jewish Holocaust."⁴³ Nora Strejilevich's beautiful defense of testimony "beyond the language of truth," and Alicia Partnoy's defense of "poetry as a strategy for resistance"—both of these authors are Argentine camp survivors—find validation and inspiration in writings by Holocaust survivors, which have come to be woven into the texture of memory of the Argentine concentration camps.⁴⁴

Undoubtedly the "memory boom" that began in 1995 marks a particularly active moment of Holocaust consciousness in Argentina. But even in the previous decade, from the mid-1980s to the mid-1990s, referred to as the "years of national reconciliation" or years of forgetting because of the promulgation of the impunity laws, one can find examples of Holocaust consciousness.⁴⁵ The work of writer Osvaldo Bayer, who had been in exile in West Germany during the dictatorship, is especially notable in this regard. His essays examine the dictatorship from a historical awareness of Argentina's structures of political and economic injustice. Because he had been living in Germany, the Nazi past is especially present in his political critique. Bayer wrote often about the scandalous "business as usual" mentality that linked the Nazi past with the West German present. In 1977, he pointed to the parallels between the Nazi suppression of political dissent in the 1930s and the Argentine situation under dictatorship, and was promptly disinvited from a seminar hosted by the German Institute of Foreign Relations.[46] He also criticized the West German ambassador in Argentina for refusing to condemn the Argentine dictatorship, and he ironized about the West German businessmen who were happy to conduct business with the Argentine military.[47] Siemens and other industries complicit with the Holocaust thrived and entered into business deals with the Argentine junta, he noted. Meanwhile, auto workers at the Mercedes-Benz plant in Argentina numbered among the disappeared.[48] In a 1985 piece he echoed Margaret Bourke-White's words at the liberation of Bergen-Belsen in 1945. She had condemned the "passive tolerance" of the society that had given its implicit consent to Nazi crimes, and she would have said the same had she seen Argentina thirty-five years later, writes Bayer.[49] In 1986, before his return from exile, he criticized Argentine intellectuals who rejected the visible violence of the military and of leftist militants but did not acknowledge the existence of embedded structural violence.[50] Bayer was an active supporter of the Mothers during and after the dictatorship, and when, in the period after the promulgation of the Obediencia Debida and Punto Final laws, their continued strident insistence on the scandal of impunity merited for them the epithet "crazy," Bayer defended them, arguing that their memory work constituted a bulwark against the trivialization of "our Auschwitz."[51] In the 1990s, he continued to support survivors and family members by establishing connections to Holocaust testimony.[52]

The group Comisión Provincial de la Memoria has been one of the most active in promoting Holocaust consciousness as part of its human rights work. Founded in 2000, the Comisión is a highly effective group of memory activists that includes respected human rights leaders and prominent jurists.[53] They support a wide spectrum of artistic, educational, and legal actions that use memory in their fight against impunity for the crimes committed during the dictatorship. In their journal, *Puentes*, the Holocaust has served as a key reference point from the very beginning. Consider the first lines of the first issue of *Puentes*: "An earthquake so strong that it broke the instruments of measurement. That is how a French thinker defined the Holocaust. This is how we might also describe the consequences of authoritarianism and state terror in our country."[54] The metaphor of "bridges," from the journal's title, signals its reparative approach to this traumatic past—reparative not in the sense of laying the past to rest, but in the opposite sense of laying down pathways of memory and testimony so that the past may speak in the present.

In *Puentes* the focus is on the redemptive and political meaning of memory, particularly of victim testimony, notwithstanding the fact that it published Jelin's work on memory. Jelin advocates for a pluralist, constructivist approach to memory, one that presupposes the existence of "rival memories" in conflict whose ultimate significance will be decided in the field of democratic politics without reference to any stable moral or empirical grounds.[55] Personal testimony by family members of the disappeared who are active in the human rights movement is a constant feature of the journal, as is scholarly work on the topic of Holocaust memory by authors such as Zygmunt Bauman, Tzvetan Todorov, Andreas Huyssen, Enzo Traverso, and James Young. In the first issue, articles about the Shoah Foundation's Visual History Archive and about the moral imperative to remember the Shoah intermingle with Argentine testimonies about the Proceso and Argentine debates about memory. In sum, in the period 1995–2005, these and other human rights activists and survivors promoted Holocaust consciousness as part of legal and political efforts to combat impunity and center Argentine history on the victims of state terror.

Sarlo, *Shoah*, and the Critique of the Testimonial "I"

Beatriz Sarlo represents a dissident voice to these efforts. Since the mid-1980s, she has been a strong critic of those who, like the Mothers and Grandmothers, focus on holding the military perpetrators to account without also addressing the responsibility of the armed left, whom she considers morally complicit in creating the climate of political violence of the late 1960s and early 1970s.[56] Hers is an intellectually nuanced version of the "dos demonios" theory advanced by the Alfonsín presidency and expressed in the first edition of the *Nunca más* report in 1984, whose very first lines portrayed Argentine society as the victim of violence from both the left and the right—omitting the fact that right-wing violence was sponsored by the state in order to maintain an unjust social order.[57] Sarlo and other members of the *Punto de Vista* editorial group hold that although the crimes of the military government and the militant left are not equivalent in terms of scale or criminal liability, the individuals in these groups who committed violent acts are equally suspect on moral grounds, regardless of their ideological affiliations.⁵⁸ This view dilutes the distinction between the victims and perpetrators of state violence that is fundamental to post-dictatorship human rights discourse. Although Sarlo credits human rights organizations with breaking through the censorship imposed by the military during the dictatorship, she finds their approach to memory too linear and limited; it is not up to the task of confronting a "complex" and "contradictory" past, one that encompasses a view of the violence committed by both the left and right.⁵⁹

Sarlo is also antagonistic toward human rights activists on another front: she holds a far more limited view on the value of memory and witness testimony than do the proponents of human rights. Sarlo's critique of witness testimony takes aim at the fact that testimony and memory are important features of the political public sphere in Argentina.⁶⁰ Though taken up by the state at various moments, as in the *Nunca más* report and the Trial of the Junta, human rights testimony has not been contained by these government spheres. Especially in the mid-1980s and then again in the mid-1990s and beyond, it continued to circulate beyond the legal realm, amplified by the mass media, and continued to voice a demand for justice to which Argentina's government institutions could not or would not respond.

Sarlo is suspicious of this demand for justice because it is couched in sentimental and personal terms that focus on individual human suffering. She makes her distaste for this kind of discourse plain in her analysis of the televised *Nunca más* program that aired in July 1984, on Argentina's Channel 13, a few months before the CONADEP had completed its written Report and presented it to President Alfonsín. Members of the commission made presentations on camera during the program, as did some of the people who had testified before the commission.⁶¹ Reflecting on the show shortly after it aired, Sarlo writes that she was impressed by the "ordinary tone" ("medio tono") and "modest reserve" ("pudor") with which the televised victims delivered their testimonies about atrocity.⁶² She contrasts this middle-range tone to the high-tone sensationalism of the mass media's coverage of the exhumation of clandestine grave sites that had occurred earlier that year.⁶³ But her critique is not targeted at just the media. It also encompasses other kinds of high-pitched expression then circulating about the disappeared, such as those by the human rights movement, especially the Mothers of the Plaza de Mayo, who had taken to the streets in huge marches at the same time as the media propagated its "horror show."⁶⁴ Sarlo does not perceive a difference between mass mobilization and mass-media sensationalism. She values the voice of the witness-survivor or family member, but not if it is strident or emotional, and not if it attracts undue attention to the victim's suffering and exceeds the bounds of reasonable discourse. She finds these more intense tones too reminiscent of populist politics, which she considers to be fundamentally antidemocratic because it constructs citizenship through emotion and moralism rather than reason—that is, it relies on narratives of the self whose truths, by their inherently subjective nature or their reliance on received notions of good and evil, are not open to reasoned debate. For Sarlo the problem is further compounded by the fact that these narratives of personal suffering are vastly more media friendly than other forms of citizen expression. Their circulation in the mass media, she argues, threatens to reify a simplified account of Argentina's past and supplant more complex or unsettling kinds of knowledge about it. All reification is a forgetting, she notes, quoting Adorno.⁶⁵

These are her accusations against personal, testimonial forms of memory, and quite paradoxically, Sarlo turns to Claude Lanzmann's *Shoah* and, to a lesser extent, writings by Primo Levi to buttress her criticisms—two emblematic instances of personal Holocaust testimony. Sarlo's treatment of Levi's testimony aims to validate how Holocaust testimony has been used to forge a distanced view of the past and a skeptical view on the healing power of memory. She does not like how Argentine testimony tends to refer to the personal truth of the witnesses, to their suffering and healing, which cannot be debated. She writes: "Testimony [in Argentina] asks that the rules of other referential discourses not apply to it."⁶⁶ She insists that this demand is baseless, as testimony cannot be exempted from critical discourse, and finds in Primo Levi grounds for her critique of the subject and the moralizing approach to the victims. Levi's perspective on testimony, she writes, "is dubitative and finally skeptical of its power to restore the witnessing subject and heal wounds."⁶⁷ She concludes that if his Auschwitz testimony can convey skepticism about his own subject position, then so too should Argentine testimony.⁶⁸

It is in her treatment of Lanzmann's *Shoah* that we can best perceive Sarlo's Holocaust refractions. She first discussed Lanzmann's film in 1989, when it was first shown in Buenos Aires, praising the film for its treatment of memory. The timing of her analysis of *Shoah* is important: it occurred after President Menem's famous pardons and after the "historians' debate" about Holocaust historiography in West Germany, which the journal *Punto de Vista* had covered.⁶⁹ Sarlo makes clear that she is using her analysis of the film to protest against the pardons and the politics of forgetting that Menem promoted, and that she is drawing lessons from the historians' debate and the German context about what is at stake in Menem's actions.⁷⁰

However, Sarlo's positioning is more complex, because she is using *Shoah* to differentiate herself not only from Menem's official politics of memory but also from the approach to memory adopted by human rights groups. Sarlo couches the film's approach to the past, which she praises, in terms that are hostile to how human rights activists deal with the past. Sarlo's main idea is that history, by which she means historiography and an objective, critical approach to the past, is more powerful against forgetting than memory is. The idea is a surprising one with respect to Lanzmann's film, because *Shoah* consciously avoids the use of historical documents and images and includes only one historian among its many voices; almost the entirety of the film is dedicated to filming the witnesses and their testimony.⁷¹ Sarlo locates that distanced, objective approach in Lanzmann's use of the camera, particularly the camera's obsessive attention to "apparently trivial details." She proposes that these details serve to deepen our understanding of the Final Solution: "[Lanzmann] knows that we know, but he also believes that we don't know enough. Or, better said, that we know the horror of the Final Solution, but we haven't sufficiently understood its workings and administration."⁷² For Sarlo, the memory of the witnesses whom Lanzmann interviews in his film is significant, but not because it tells us something about their suffering and how they survived. Their memory is important, Sarlo says, because Lanzmann constructs memory with a camera that goes "beyond emotion" and therefore contributes to our understanding of the administration of mass death.⁷³

Key to Sarlo's simultaneous invocation and marginalization of the witness in this essay is her decision to include a citation by Josef Hayim Yerushalmi, a historian known for his description of the clash between memory and history as two divergent and mutually hostile approaches to narrating the past. Yossi Goldstein has shown that Yerushalmi's work had a tremendous impact in Argentina, where it was translated and published less than a year after it appeared in France.⁷⁴ Sarlo quotes the following words from Yerushalmi: "For the historian, God lives in the details. But memory rebels and denounces the transformation of details into gods."⁷⁵ What Sarlo appreciates about Lanzmann's work is precisely that affront to memory that historical detail provides: "Lanzmann runs the risk of this rebellion [of memory], which he defends himself against by his definition of detail: it is that which we least understood."⁷⁶ Behind Sarlo's obvious critique of

Menem and the government's official policy of forgetting or distorting the past lies a buried critique of certain kinds of memory work that she fears have become complacent because they think they know everything about the past. She suggests that to arrive at a deeper and fuller understanding of the past, it is necessary to employ techniques against which memory rebels.

Sarlo returned to *Shoah* in 1997. Once again, her praise for the film constitutes an attack against contemporary memory practices in Argentina, now focusing on the media's sensationalist approach to the dictatorship past. She critiques the media's desire "to show and tell all," its fondness for narratives containing an abundance of visual details at the expense of providing an overarching meaning. In contrast, she argues, *Shoah* strengthens our understanding of the past, yet without using "either a single photograph or a single documentary shot of the millions and millions of corpses that lay in heaps in the concentration camps, in the mass graves, at the doors to the ovens."[77] She writes: "Very slowly, with the slowness that thinking requires, an image of the Holocaust's material and ideological design is drawn out."[78] There may seem to be a contradiction between Sarlo's 1989 and her 1997 analysis of *Shoah*, because the first praises the film's unveiling of historical detail, the second its reticence with respect to showing it. In both cases, however, the object of Sarlo's criticism is the same: a public discourse that creates an environment hostile to critical thought because of its excessive focus on personal suffering. Whatever details Lanzmann may or may not have included, none of them, according to Sarlo, are designed to make suffering sensational.

Sarlo's third analysis of *Shoah* appeared in 2005 in *Tiempo pasado*, similarly cutting against the grain of most appreciations of the film. Here Sarlo writes about how the film decenters and deauthorizes witnesses despite the fact that it is composed almost entirely of witness testimony. She proposes that this is so because Lanzmann exercises a subtle violence against his witnesses by forcing them to talk much more than they wish to. In other words, he imposes memory on them:

> Holocaust memory is decentered [in *Shoah*] . . . because it goes to [the scene of massacre] in spite of those who give their testimony, pressing down on conventional memory. Lanzmann's knowledge of the camps pushes on the memory of the victims or witnesses to make them say more than they would say if they were free to be spontaneous. The intervention is a forcing of the spontaneous memory of that past and its codification in a conventional narrative.[79]

It is "an imposition of memory . . . memory is compelled to go beyond where the subjects thought it could go, beyond their interests or desires."[80] Beyond the witnesses, in spite of the witnesses: these phrases are key to understanding Sarlo's intervention in Argentina's memory debates. She is criticizing our faith in the "I" of testimony, in the truth of its speech. She is concerned that the culture industry will make testimony into "an icon of the Truth," an icon of suffering as truth that cannot tolerate reasoned criticism.[81]

In summarizing Sarlo's analysis of *Shoah* in these essays from 1989, 1997, and 2005, three points stand out: that the film communicates a critical consciousness through its camerawork rather than through the voices of the witnesses; that it avoids a sensationalist account of the atrocities; and that the film, although it might seem to put the witnesses and their speech front and center, in reality marginalizes them by imposing on them a duty to remember so strong that it surpasses their own will and desire.

As I stated at the outset of this section, Sarlo's main impetus in turning to these works about the Holocaust is to dispute a version of Argentina's recent past that holds only the military perpetrators responsible for the violence of the 1970s. From the earliest moments of the return to democracy, she has argued in her work that the political opponents targeted by the government were also perpetrators of violence and should be held to account, morally if not criminally. This applies, in Sarlo's view, not just to the government's armed opponents but also to its unarmed opponents, including herself, whose fervent embrace of ideas and willingness to participate in hierarchical or dogmatic political groups, she argues, generated a climate of totalitarian absolutism.[82] Any victim testimony that refuses to acknowledge some element of the victims' complicity in creating the circumstances that led to their victimization is repugnant to her.

Sarlo eschews a psychological account of trauma and thereby renders moot the possibility of a "politics of memory" that would be linked to a process of individual or collective reconstruction. She does not deny the existence of trauma or the wounded subject, but for her, trauma is not the place from which to think about the collective past. Across her work she holds that memory work and witness testimony should not be used to empower the victims, insisting that reparation is not the point of memory. Memory is political, she suggests, to the extent that it destabilizes identity rather than secures it, and that it unsettles our ideas about ourselves and the world.[83] However, her suspicion of discourses that adopt a moral perspective on personal suffering causes her to miss the larger moral context that animates both the Holocaust works she praises and the Argentine works she criticizes. If Levi and Lanzmann decenter Holocaust victims in their works, it is in order to arrive at an even greater appreciation of the enormity of the atrocities the Nazis committed, the violence done to the psyche, an appreciation that clarifies even further the difference between victims and perpetrators. Sarlo's decentering of the dictatorship's victims, however, attempts to work in the opposite direction, to diminish the enormity of the dictatorship's crimes by linking them to those of their political opponents and thereby to dilute the distinction between victims and perpetrators in Argentina. Indeed, at its most severe, her critique finds certain testimonial and memorial practices on a continuum with authoritarianism because of their nondebatable status.[84]

Though she correctly perceives that Levi and the *Shoah* victims do not consider themselves to have been ennobled by their suffering in the Nazi camps, she misses the point in holding this up as a standard for Argentine witnesses: it is not just the suffering of the Argentine witnesses that their public may find ennobling, but also their courage to speak out against the politics of business as usual. In a sense her aim is to limit their authority exclusively to the legal realm, where their testimony is subject to formal, rational procedures of evaluation. It seems that Sarlo, in her negative assessment of Argentine testimonial practices during the memory boom, does not sufficiently appreciate how narratives of suffering can convey a political critique of the status quo. Critic Silvia Tandeciarz writes regarding Sarlo's skepticism that "the assumptions underlying it—namely, that expressions derived from personal proximity to trauma stymie thoughtful engagement or critique—in hindsight prove problematic," because so often these expressions have indeed provoked "the kind of deep reflection and response" that Sarlo seeks.[85]

Vezzetti and the Problem of the Victim in Argentina

Appearing in 2002, *Pasado y presente* is Hugo Vezzetti's pointedly "intellectual" critique of the memory boom, one that sees itself as competing with melodrama, media sensationalism, and ideological cliché for control over how Argentines understand the recent past. The book's critique of memory discourses coincides in many respects with Sarlo's (the two were long-time colleagues at the journal *Punto de Vista*). Both use Holocaust materials to refract the Argentine situation, but Vezzetti is far more steeped in Holocaust historiography than Sarlo. His book offers a sustained analysis of post-Holocaust debates, especially as regards Germans' noncriminal complicity with Nazism, and Vezzetti uses these as a constant backdrop to his analysis of contemporary Argentina. The book situates itself within a renewed, richly contentious field of contemporary publications about the dictatorship, comprising scholarly, journalistic, and autobiographical and testimonial approaches. *Pasado y presente* focuses on the spate of recent books about the military, the state prosecutions of military perpetrators, the families of the disappeared, and former guerrillas and other survivors of the Argentine concentration camps. Vezzetti's intervention is in large part an extended and critical "literature review" of the state of the field. His assessment of the contemporary memory boom is overwhelmingly negative, and that negative assessment is buttressed, time and again, by his use of Holocaust historiography.

Pasado y presente appeared in the midst of the economic crisis sparked by Argentina's default on international loans in 2001, which coincided with the twenty-five-year anniversary of the military coup of 1976. The book responds directly to the political convergence between the human rights movement and the protest movement against the government's neoliberal economic policies. The two causes created a shared language of critique that brought terms like "genocide" to bear on economic suffering, a development of which Vezzetti is critical.[86] As happens in Sarlo's work, Vezzetti finds it useful to analyze Argentina through the lens of the Holocaust and indeed to draw comparisons between Nazi Germany and Argentina during the Proceso, as we will see, yet balks at comparisons between Argentine victims of state terror and Holocaust victims.

The book's publication date is also significant because it comes shortly on the heels of the historic March 2001 decision by an Argentine judge to overturn the Punto Final and Obediencia Debida laws, thus opening the way for new criminal prosecutions of military perpetrators. This means that the question of criminal responsibility, though far from settled in 2002 when *Pasado y presente* appeared, had at last found another path forward and been made newly actionable. With the judicial sphere once again empowered to tackle the past and to address the dictatorship in criminal terms, Vezzetti sees an opening to explore other forms of addressing the past that had previously taken a back seat to the more immediate and tangible question of criminal responsibility. Here too the Holocaust legacy in Germany is significant: he turns to German philosopher Karl Jaspers, who in 1945 had insisted on distinguishing among three different kinds of culpability: "there exists a *criminal culpability*, a *political culpability*, and a *moral culpability*."[87] On the matter of criminal culpability, the courts had finally been able to assert themselves. But on the matter of political and moral culpability, Vezzetti argues, Argentine society had failed to come to grips with its past.

His main point, after he had surveyed the field, was that Argentine society was more culpable than it liked to admit in regard to the violence perpetrated during the last dictatorship. Vezzetti holds that just as the Holocaust must be understood in terms of deep patterns of violence embedded in the social order and the moral complicity of the broader society, so too must the case of Argentina. Vezzetti launches his challenge to Argentine self-complacency through his readings on the intellectual and political legacies provided by Holocaust survivors and other postwar European thinkers, who developed explanatory frameworks to comprehend how such a mass-scale atrocity could have taken place and who defended a reasoned, pluralist environment in which to debate them. He particularly engages with those thinkers who address the question of the complicity of everyday Germans in allowing the mass extermination of the Jews to happen, thinkers who might therefore shed light on the "weave of less visible conditions" that made the Argentine dictatorship possible[88]—thus his treatment of Daniel Goldhagen's *Hitler's Willing Executioners*, Arendt's *Eichmann in Jerusalem*, and Erich Fromm's *Escape from Freedom* to shed light on the question of the "normalcy" of authoritarianism and atrocity and the complicity of everyday people in perpetrating state crimes.[89] Vezzetti also addresses the world of the Argentine concentration camps and their status *within* the broader society, not apart from it. He refers to Zygmunt Bauman's *Modernity and the Holocaust* on the machinery of terror, and to Giorgio Agamben's *Remnants of Auschwitz* and Primo Levi's *The Drowned and the Saved* and *Survival in Auschwitz* (*If This Be a Man*) on life in the concentration camps, to demonstrate that the Argentine camps, far from representing a perverse or exceptional "hell space," in fact were embedded in the existing social fabric and representative of the existing social order.[90] Just as the enormity of the Holocaust—the how and the why of it—cannot be appreciated by a focus solely on its Nazi perpetrators, so too the how and why of Argentina's political violence cannot be appreciated by a focus solely on its military perpetrators; a deeper, broader understanding of violence and complicity is required.

Vezzetti uses the analogy between post-Holocaust Germany and post-dictatorship Argentina to criticize "the usual memory of the Argentine massacre," which is divided three ways into "perverse perpetrators, innocent and defenseless victims, and an even more innocent society that is alien to evil."⁹¹ He believes that the stories Argentines tell about the recent past are deeply flawed because they demarcate too clear a line separating the innocent from the guilty and thereby diminish the enormity of the event and exonerate themselves, and Argentine society as a whole, from responsibility for the violence of the past. He argues that the kinds of social memory that have been forged in the post-dictatorship period and achieved the greatest circulation in Argentine society are clichés, and therefore constitute forms of forgetting, not memory.⁹² *Pasado y presente* indicts what he considers to be the dominant trends in contemporary memory discourses because of their failure to adequately grasp deeper or more complex patterns of complicity with state violence—patterns that Holocaust historiography helps to expose.

Vezzetti does not deny the importance and necessity of human rights work in Argentina and the concomitant focus on victims and perpetrators. On the contrary, he spends a significant amount of time explaining why human rights activism was crucial in providing a needed sea change in Argentine political thinking, especially once it was taken up by the Alfonsín government during the early years of the transition to democracy. Yet Vezzetti is profoundly critical of the broader influence that human rights organizations have exercised on Argentine memory discourses. He dislikes their focus on sentimental and melodramatic "family stories" centered on the experience of personal suffering. He also dislikes the fact that some human rights activists, such as the Mothers, Grandmothers, and HIJOS, have adopted militant political causes as their own and now celebrate the heroism and political idealism of the dictatorship's victims. He argues that these various and at times combined forces have had pernicious effects. He believes that a sentimental and idealistic approach to the past has blocked a more complex historical, political, and sociological understanding of the nature of the violence and of the many factors that made it possible. He seeks instead an approach that avoids "the risks of media trivialization, which insists on personal drama and on the primary affective bonds of mothers, grandmothers."⁹³ He holds that the idealism of HIJOS and the Mothers has allowed those who were not in the armed forces yet were still, in his view, complicit in the violence to escape historical responsibility for it. He is referring here in particular to armed leftist militants, especially former Montoneros, whose voices are reaching new audiences in the new millennium yet who, according to Vezzetti, lack sufficient critical distance from their own past actions. He notes that their memory discourses too easily take up the banner of past ideologies and identities and remain self-complacent about the roles they played in the past.⁹⁴ The result, for Vezzetti, is an ideological blindness that hinders self-critique on the part of ex-militants of the armed left and other social sectors.⁹⁵

Vezzetti holds that Argentina's political violence was a case of reason temporarily defeated by unreason. The best defense against this legacy, he maintains, is to promote reasoned perspectives and pluralist debate about the past instead of subjective and emotional perspectives that are felt rather than argued. This is especially relevant for Vezzetti's analysis of how the left contributed to the violence. He uses the figure of "barbarism" to identify the surge in "revolutionary thinking" of the 1960s as an underlying cause of the violence and thereby to inculpate the armed opposition in the atrocities of the period.⁹⁶ The reference to "barbarity" might appear to directly cite Domingo Sarmiento's famous nineteenth-century nation-building paradigm of a war between "civilización y barbarie," as if to suggest a genealogy of violence that stretches back to the Argentine state's nineteenth-century genocidal campaigns against the hinterlands.⁹⁷ But in fact the reference is to German philosopher Norbert Elias, who speculated that the Nazi genocide was possible because of the "breakdown in civilization" in German society, driven by the Nazis' "professed irrational beliefs"; therefore, it cannot be understood from the standpoint of rational interests.⁹⁸ The Nazis were more like a "sect" than a political party, Elias proposes, and Hitler's message was "messianic."⁹⁹

Vezzetti transposes Elias's idea to Argentina, arguing that the mass violence of the 1970s is best understood as an instance of "barbarity," one that can be explained in terms of strongly held irrational beliefs.¹⁰⁰ Vezzetti proposes that the revolutionary politics of the 1960s and 1970s in Argentina, whether of the left or the right, were a form of messianism, echoing Elias's language about Hitler and Nazism. Both the left and right were captivated by this "messianic vision," he argues, noting the "exaltation of violence" that state terror and what he calls "subversive terror" had in common; both engaged in a "common militaristic reduction of social and political conflicts to a sacred war of annihilation that knew no limits and placed itself above the law."¹⁰¹ This shared vision, he believes, was directly responsible for the violence of the dictatorship.¹⁰² His indictment of the armed left for its responsibility for the violence repeats the core tenets of the "dos demonios" theory put forward in the original *Nunca más* report.

Vezzetti's critique of the Mothers and Grandmothers is likewise undergirded by a broad narrative of embattled reason that takes its cues from his analyses of Nazi Germany. In Vezzetti's account, the Mothers and Grandmothers seek the fulfillment of irrational beliefs structured by a sentimental family drama that centers on maternal emotion. He argues that, because their framing of the past is melodramatic and familial, these human rights groups have trivialized and simplified the violence, shielding Argentine society from a more complex and difficult awareness of what really happened, including its own complicity.[103] His aim: "to break with that fiction of *innocence* that society associates with the family drama monopolized by Mothers and Grandmothers."[104] This narrative is easily commodified by the mass media, he notes, leading to representational practices that exploit atrocity for commercial or political gain while "sanctifying" the victims.[105]

Furthermore, Vezzetti, like Sarlo, is deeply critical of the authority granted to survivor testimony and its power to shape collective memory. Here too Holocaust scholarship shapes his intervention. References to Dominick LaCapra, Eric Santner, Peter Novick, and Giorgio Agamben buttress his claims that survivor testimony is not a good basis from which to develop a complex and accurate historical account or from which to confront the true extent of the horror.[106] To provide an alternative to the Mothers and Grandmothers in the popular imaginary, Vezzetti evokes the model provided by two authors of survivor testimony—Primo Levi on Auschwitz and Pilar Calveiro on ESMA—whose approaches to their traumatic experience are distanced and intellectual rather than sentimental and subjective, going beyond their own personal suffering. Their testimonies, he continues, contain both personal testimony *and* historical knowledge, and thereby, unlike the "clichéd" and "conventional" memory that the Mothers and Grandmothers of the Plaza de Mayo practice, these works by Levi and Calveiro expand our understanding of the past rather than freeze it ideologically.[107]

If Vezzetti does not like how human rights organizations have been able to take and keep center stage and thereby be decisive in framing national understandings of the past, it is in part because he finds the image of innocent victims that they advance to be misleading if not totally false. Most uses of the Holocaust in post-dictatorship Argentina work on the implied analogy between the dictatorship's victims and the Jewish victims of the Nazis. Vezzetti outright refuses that analogy and seeks to correct it by reminding us that the dictatorship's victims were political opponents, often *armed* political opponents, of the government that tortured and killed them. Vezzetti insists that because some of the dictatorship's victims were active agents of destruction, they were complicitous in the violence, morally culpable for it, and therefore radically unlike Holocaust victims.

If he believes in differentiating Holocaust victims from the dictatorship's victims, how then does Vezzetti continue to work through the Holocaust in seeking to understand Argentina? The question is similar to the one I posed for Sarlo. Given each author's refusal of analogies between Holocaust victims and the victims of the Proceso, why bother with a Holocaust frame of reference at all? The answer is that, ultimately, the Holocaust readings he chooses support Vezzetti's anti-ideological approach to Argentine history, his refusal to assign validity to any of the political beliefs that animated the violence. He dismisses the question of what people were fighting for and against—Peronism, Communism, imperialism, a whole host of political ideas about what constitutes a just society—to focus on the "revolutionary messianism" that the right-wing military government shared with its left-wing opponents. Thus, although on one level he recognizes that the conflict between the two drove the violence, on another level he renders that conflict meaningless. The meaningful site of conflict, for Vezzetti, is between reason and unreason. Instead of an analysis of the Argentine past centered on historical and ideological conflicts about or within modernity, he prefers to view this as a case of modernity's conflicts with its nonmodern or antimodern Others.

Beyond providing us with valuable analysis of deeper patterns of social complicity, Vezzetti's turn to the Holocaust is wielded to buttress his own clear sense of intellectual superiority at the expense of the Mothers and Grandmothers, who appear in his text as incapable of lucid critique. The whole point of his critique is to minimize, if not entirely displace, the value of the broadly human rights–centered frames of memory that involve testimony by victims and their families and that are concerned with justice in the name of the victims. This explains why so many of the authors and texts he discusses are concerned primarily with Germany and address the question of the German people: Vezzetti focuses on perpetrators and complicit bystanders, not victims. Like Sarlo, Vezzetti uses the Holocaust to cancel the authority of those who speak about the dictatorship's victims.

Confines 1995–1998: Do Not Forget the Forgotten

The journal *Confines* ("Limits" or "Boundaries") was founded in 1995 by Nicolás Casullo.[108] Casullo had been a Peronist militant, eventually joining the Montoneros. He spent nearly a decade in exile, starting in 1974, after receiving threats from right-wing death squads.[109] In the 1990s and until his death in 2008, he was a professor at the Universidad de Buenos Aires and an influential voice on the intellectual left. Other well-known public intellectuals, such as Héctor Schmucler, Ricardo Forster, Oscar del Barco, Gregorio Kaminsky, and Alejandro Kaufman, participated as members of the journal's editorial board and as contributing writers and lent the endeavor a distinctive philosophical, ex-Peronist edge. From its inaugural issue in 1995 to its last print version in 2009, the journal was centrally concerned with memory debates in the post-dictatorship period.

Confines' intellectual approach to these debates is anchored in critical theory and post-WWII philosophy and criticism. It dedicates substantial portions of each issue to translations of European and American authors and is particularly concerned with a critical analysis of the "culture industry" and its capacity to anesthetize the public and create a passive, self-complacent citizenry. Like Sarlo and Vezzetti, *Confines* was centrally animated by fears about the trivialization of memory through media oversaturation and oversimplification. It offered a skeptical approach to memory with the idea that this would prevent it from becoming its opposite, "desmemoria," un- or anti-memory. A big difference from Sarlo and Vezzetti, however, is that *Confines* authors affirmed a left-wing, anti-capitalist perspective on memory. This meant that the journal's relationship to the memory discourses of human rights groups in Argentina in the mid to late 1990s, such as the Mothers of the Plaza de Mayo, was far more ambivalent than that of *Punto de Vista*.

These tensions appear in Casullo's essay in the inaugural issue of *Confines*, which explains that one of the journal's main concerns is to develop a practice of critical memory about Argentina's recent past. Casullo's essay positions the journal against the climate of indifference that characterized the Menem presidency. As if anticipating that this project in favor of memory might be labeled "mere nostalgia" by critics on the right, Casullo defends memory as a form of political resistance, one that combats the presentism of Menem's "politics of forgetting." He refers to Walter Benjamin's seminal essay "On the Concept of History," advocating that memory be understood as "a continuous resistance to the cancellation of human experience."[110] But Casullo also positions the journal against would-be allies on the left in the struggle for memory. As if to differentiate this journal's memory practice from the pamphleteering practices of contemporary human rights groups or the militant left of the pre-dictatorship past, Casullo adopts a modernist, deconstructive skepticism of language, affirming that his will be a memory practice attuned to the fragility and nontransparency of language, a feature exemplified in the dense, heavy style of philosophical writing adopted by most contributors, prizing allusion and opacity. Throughout its career, *Confines* will attempt to marry these competing demands—committed to remembering but suspicious of how we speak and write about the past; committed to anti-capitalist critique but also to criticizing the practices of the Argentine left in the 1960s and 1970s and the Argentine human rights movement of the 1980s and 1990s.

Another important feature of this journal that differentiates it from other journals devoted to cultural criticism in the post-dictatorship period is its concern with Jewish philosophy. *Confines* is not a self-professed Jewish publication, but there is an unmistakably Jewish thread running through it. Like the works by intellectuals associated with *Punto de Vista*, *Confines* approaches Argentina's recent past through a post-Auschwitz lens. Unlike *Punto de Vista*, however, its contributors occasionally speak on these topics "as Jews" and explore questions related to Jewish literature and theology.

In the first issue of *Confines*, half of the articles touch directly on the Holocaust. These include an excerpt from Jean-François Lyotard's 1988 *Heidegger and "the Jews"*; a response by Héctor Schmucler to Lyotard's work; an analysis of Paul Celan's poetry; a dossier reproducing key texts from the German debate initiated in 1993 by playwright Botho Strauss's controversial comments on the politics of memory in contemporary Germany; and Ricardo Forster's review of Tzvetan Todorov's 1991 book *Facing the Extreme*.[111] Most of these make scant reference to Argentina. In this first issue of the journal the laborious work of refracting Argentina's field of memory through the field of Holocaust memory is barely emergent. Ricardo Forster's review of Todorov's book contains only a brief parenthetical reference to the book's relevance for post-dictatorship Argentina.[112] The editorial comments prefacing the Botho Strauss debate pose the question of whether Germany's confrontation with its traumatic past is close to Argentina's, but they do not pursue it.[113] The article on Celan makes no reference to Argentina.

The one exception, in this inaugural issue, is Schmucler's essay, which does develop the connection between Argentina's situation and post-Auschwitz Europe. Schmucler is responding to Lyotard's 1988 book *Heidegger and "the Jews,"* of which *Confines* published a lengthy excerpt. The book had been written in response to the "Heidegger affair" surrounding the publication of Victor Farias's 1987 book, which substantiated claims about Heidegger's Nazi sympathies.[114] In *Heidegger and "the Jews,"* Lyotard offers a series of complex, paradoxical arguments about memory and forgetting that center on the difficulties of representing the Holocaust in a manner that does not betray the suffering of its victims. Lyotard's decision to put the term "the Jews" in scare quotes is an important component of his ideas. Lyotard's "the Jews" is meant to be different from "real Jews," even if it also encompasses them.[115] His "the Jews" refers to a *general* problem of representation in the West, namely, its tendency to forget what he calls "the Forgotten," which is "what every representation misses," that which cannot be represented.[116] But "the Jews" also refers to a *specific* problem of representation in the West, namely, the tendency to dismiss real Jews from the West. With "the Jews," Lyotard is thus also referring to the "non-place" of real Jews in Heidegger's thought, to their absence from his vision of Europe, to his having "forgotten" them even though Heidegger's main contribution to European philosophy had been to remember the forgetting of Being. In other words, Heidegger forgot this forgetting of the Jews. Lyotard takes this vision, from which Jews are absent and forgotten, as representative of the worldview that contributed to the Holocaust. Lyotard's "the Jews" restates the post-Auschwitz ethical demand with a twist: do not forget the forgetting that led to these crimes. The injunction, as Lyotard formulates it, casts suspicion on the work of those who attempt simply to make real Jews present in words or images.

These paradoxes form the basis for Lyotard's critique of how most representations of the Holocaust, seemingly devoted to preserving the memory of the event, in fact contribute to its forgetting. The appeal to human rights, the cry "Nunca más"—never again—he continues, constitutes a facile easing of our collective conscience because it suggests that the Holocaust was a horror of repairable proportions, that humanity can move beyond it.[117] Lyotard advocates a memory practice that conveys the West's silence, its forgetting, of real Jews, and he comes close to proposing that silence is more effective than words when it comes to the Holocaust.

Schmucler's response to Lyotard in *Confines* starts in a personal vein, by confessing his attachment to memory: memory has become trivialized in our time, he notes, yet "I think that I am nothing other than irresistible fragments of memory."[118] He then refuses Lyotard's scare quotes around "the Jews." Lyotard put them there to mark the Jews' position of negativity in Heidegger and Europe at large; Schmucler insists on a positive inscription of Jewish identity that claims memory at its core. Schmucler's is not a misreading of Lyotard. It is, rather, a Jewish reading of Lyotard, a refusal of the scare quotes and, ultimately, of the silence that Lyotard places at the heart of ethical memory. Sometimes silence really is forgetting, Schmucler notes, rather than the paradoxical gesture of remembering that Lyotard propounds, and sometimes that which has been forgotten really has been forgotten rather than rendered absent. Schmucler's own silence about his Jewishness illustrates the point. He writes: "I write 'the Jews' and I perceive that I can't think of it as a category, as Lyotard proposes. For me, 'the Jews' is nothing other than myself; I belong in the flesh to *that*. I am, indissociably, that memory act, and yet as I look back over my life, I observe the forgetting of this condition in me."[119] Lyotard removed memory and forgetting from the logic of inscription, identity, and moral responsibility; Schmucler returns them to it.

Only after this critique of Lyotard, offered in the name of Jewish identity, does Schmucler proceed to the question of "memory and forgetting" in Argentina in 1995, as if to say this is a question that Lyotard cannot fully answer. For Schmucler, the current silence about the disappeared, and about the defeat in the Malvinas War, really is silence; it really is an attempt to forget these events and how they came about. But Schmucler's critique of Lyotard, though it rejects the more radical propositions about the originary forgettings at the heart of all language, is not total. He takes up Lyotard's paradoxical accusation that Heidegger "forgot the forgetting" of the real Jews and extends it to the question of the disappeared in Argentina. He notes that Argentina is in danger of forgetting its earlier forgetting, the one that allowed the disappearances to happen. Schmucler writes: "Disappearance tries to suppress all traces, even the trace of the will to suppress traces. Argentina tries to forget that a space of disappearance was possible."[120] Menem's amnesty of the military perpetrators is a part of the problem, he continues, but there is more to it than that, because it is not just a question of an individual's criminal responsibility but also a question of society's moral responsibility, which a criminal judgment alone cannot address. Argentine society as a whole, he proposes, must find a way to confront the fact that it has forgotten that it made disappearance possible.

Lyotard's suspicion of most Holocaust representations, and his advocacy for a recursive memory practice that does not presume to make the forgotten present, will become a hallmark of *Confines* in its writings about the memory of the disappeared in Argentina. Its critical work will center on counteracting the tendency to "forget what has been forgotten," "olvidar el olvido." But so too is it guided by Schmucler's concern with the question of collective identity and one's allegiance to it, with the question of how to be honest with oneself about one's past and who one is. *Confines* approaches this as a problem for Argentina as a whole, and even more so for those Argentine intellectuals on the left, like Casullo and Schmucler, who had participated in militant Peronist organizations before the dictatorship.

In 1996, the journal published a lengthy dossier to commemorate the twentieth anniversary of the military coup of 1976.[121] The essays collected in this volume had been presented originally at a symposium on the topic of the Mothers of the Plaza de Mayo, which the authors had organized in order to discuss their views about a speech given the year before by Hebe de Bonafini, one of the founders of the Mothers.[122] Their meeting was *about* the Mothers but did not include them; the intention was to define a properly intellectual voice about the *desaparecidos* in contradistinction to the activist speech of the Mothers—similar, we note, to Vezzetti's aims. These intellectuals grappled in particular with the significance of Bonafini's militant approach to human rights work concerning the disappeared, such as her refusal to accept forensic remains of the disappeared and her insistence that the disappeared be returned alive ("aparición con vida").[123] The nine articles that appear in this issue of *Confines* adopt a range of positions vis-à-vis the Mothers. One of these, by Ricardo Forster, is outright dismissive of the Mothers; Forster says of Hebe de Bonafini that her speech "silences" memory rather than activates it.[124] Others, such as Alejandro Kaufman, are directly supportive of the Mothers and defend them against those who see them as "crazy."[125] Most authors in the dossier, however, are more circumspect in their approach to the Mothers and offer more ambiguous statements about the significance of the Mothers' contributions to memory debates. Over half of the articles refer to Holocaust memory to develop their arguments about the Argentine memory of the disappeared. Let us look here at the two notable contributions by Schmucler and Casullo.

In contrast to Sarlo and Vezzetti, Schmucler establishes a direct parallel between those killed in the Nazi death camps and Argentina's disappeared. His essay builds on a 1946 essay by Hannah Arendt, "The Image of Hell"—a line from Arendt's essay provides the title for his piece: "not even a face upon which death could stamp its seal."[126] His aim is to foreground one element of the Nazi atrocity that for him rings especially true for Argentina: the Nazi murder of the Jews, like the junta's practice of disappearing its detainees, produces a "generic" death, one that erases the individual identity of the dead. He writes: "The Shoah implemented by the Nazis and the technique of disappearance practiced in Argentina during the dictatorship . . . have in common the fact of not permitting the individual death of each person."[127] This mass death is "worse than death," he explains, following Arendt, because it reduces the individual to mere organic matter. Arendt had written, regarding the Nazi "death factories":

> They all died together, the young and the old, the weak and the strong, the sick and the healthy; not as people, not as men and women, children and adults, boys and girls, not as good

and bad, beautiful and ugly—but brought down to the lowest common denominator of organic life itself, plunged into the darkest and deepest abyss of primal equality, like cattle, like matter, like things that had neither body nor soul, nor even a physiognomy upon which death could stamp its seal.[128]

Arendt had been making a point about how the facts of the Holocaust, this "monstrous equality" of mass death, surpass ready-made ideas about justice, innocence, and guilt.

Schmucler, meanwhile, seeing in it an image of the disappeared in Argentina, finds a lesson for memory and develops his thoughts about the devastating consequences for those who seek to remember these dead. Denied his or her own death, Schmucler notes, the individual is not really dead, and therefore cannot be properly remembered. It is these specific forms of administering death, he continues, that mark these two regimes as particularly evil, and that bring them together despite their vast historical differences: "I'm aware that between the Shoah and the disappeared there is so much distance that, historically, they are not comparable. Except on one point: in that incomprehensible presence of evil."[129] Schmucler's essay, though conscious of their differences, reinforces grammatically the parallels between the two events, using phrases like "the Shoah and the disappeared . . ." and "just as the disappeared, so too the gas chambers . . ." The article does not directly mention the Mothers of the Plaza de Mayo, yet one senses that its goal is to justify their continued relevance, to explain how and why the generic death of the disappeared, like the generic death of the Jews in the Nazi camps, produces an inexhaustible, inconsolable need to understand their deaths in those who remember them.[130]

Casullo's contribution to this dossier, in contrast, is ambivalent in its assessment of the Mothers. His focus is on the speech used by the left and by human rights groups when they talk about the victims of state violence. He offers exemplary episodes from the past that illustrate his critique of the language the Montoneros used to describe the fate of their comrades at the hands of the state. One of these episodes concerns events from 1980, when an important Peronist journal, *Controversia*, produced by Argentine exiles in Mexico, published an essay by Lilia Walsh about the death of her husband, the writer and Montonero militant Rodolfo Walsh. Rodolfo had been killed by state security forces in March 1977. Lilia's article described his work for the Montonero organization prior to his death and also eloquently spoke about his decision not to go into exile even though he knew he would be a target of state repression, about his resolve to die fighting.[131] Her article incensed high-ranking Montoneros, Casullo reports, because she identified Walsh as a Montonero militant and because she spoke of his death. These facts were highly inconvenient for the organization because it was waging an international campaign to free Walsh, part of the broader effort to call attention to the military junta's violations of human rights. To make public that Walsh was a member of an armed group rather than simply a journalist, and to speak of his death rather than his detention and disappearance, seriously compromised their efforts and, in their words, "benefitted the military junta."[132] They insisted that Walsh be spoken of exclusively as a political prisoner and torture victim.

Casullo's point is that the memory of Walsh and other Montonero militants that was then in the process of being forged was utterly false, a betrayal and a forgetting of who they had been. The human rights campaign waged by the Montoneros and others during the dictatorship shattered the language that had made sense of their struggle. Using a highly significant turn of phrase, Casullos writes that as a result of the Montoneros decision to obfuscate the facts of Walsh's life and death, "we were deported from ourselves" ("habíamos pasado a estar deportados de nosotros mismos").[133]

Let us dwell on the word "deport" in this utterance. We start by noting that the use of "deport" to describe the actions of the Argentine military is uncommon. The Argentine state "detained" and "disappeared" its victims, or forced them into exile. The word "deport," meanwhile, clearly evokes the Nazi era. Its linguistic transposition to Argentina therefore establishes an implicit parallel between the two situations. Other words, such as "concentration camp" and "genocidal," had already become second nature by the 1990s in Argentina. *Confines* referred to the Argentine dictatorship as "genocidal" constantly and matter-of-factly, as if there existed a consensus around this description, even though it is also clear that the word was precisely chosen by *Confines* authors, that it carried a sharp accusation and remained polemical, not consensual.[134] The word "deport," however, lacks any established symbolic purchase when it comes to the Argentine context; it is a novel transposition.

One effect of Casullo's decision to bring the word into the Argentine context is to blur the distinctions that we rely on to make sense of the violence in Argentina, distinctions between victims and perpetrators that the words "genocidal" and "concentration camp" had been crucial in establishing. The state was genocidal. The state administered death in concentration camps. The state is criminal; its victims are innocent. To say that the revolutionary left "deported" its militants by negating the truth of their identity, as Casullo does in this essay, confuses these certainties by placing the left in the position of both victim and perpetrator. Obviously Casullo's use is metaphorical, referring to a sense of self-alienation, not literal transport to death. Yet even so his use of the word signals that his moral compass for judging the crimes of the past will be different from that of human rights discourse.

Casullo brings the revolutionary left into affinity with the military junta and, by extension, the Nazis—not on the question of literal violence, the genocide, because the Montoneros, whatever their faults, were neither literally nor metaphorically genocidal, but certainly on the question of their cynical use of language, the violence done to the memory of their dead and the identity of the survivors. Casullo names that violence "a calamity."[135] In an extraordinary passage, he writes of the Montoneros' discourse: "The victims' identity, their biographical language, got lost, became unrecognizable, which seemed to go along with the genocidal strategy of the military dictatorship, which in making the bodies disappear, made all identity, all names, all history disappear. . . . Both sides, for different reasons, seemed to coincide in liquidating identity and memory."[136] Various distinct calamities—the deportation of the Jews in the Holocaust, the genocidal disappearances committed by the Argentine junta, the deportation of memory by Argentine's armed vanguards—merge here into a single calamity of language and memory.

The "debacle of language in Argentine society" that he accuses the memory discourses of the left of perpetrating rests on his readings of Elias Canetti and Karl Kraus, Canetti's mentor in 1930s Vienna.[137] Casullo stresses how these thinkers understood their own language to have been irremediably "unhinged" and "undone" by Nazism and the Holocaust. He paraphrases Kraus, writing: "To name the world I use the same words that served, harmoniously as ever, the machinery of death."[138] Casullo insists that a similar reserve regarding language—what he calls "the aesthetics of the impossible word"—must likewise take hold in Argentina, where language has similarly been "shipwrecked" by a recent history of barbarity, for us to do justice to the disaster. He calls for a Krausian recognition that cliché and common sense, the need for information and for labels, render language a site of forgetting. The languages of human rights in Argentina are guilty in this regard.

Casullo proposes that the calamity of language for which the left is just as responsible as the right has had catastrophic consequences for Argentine intellectuals, that it has led to the "retreat, distancing or extinction" of a properly intellectual consciousness. The Mothers have stepped into the void created by the absence of intellectual thought and "replaced" it, he writes, but inadequately so. For Casullo, the strength of the Mothers lies on a symbolic and mythic plane, not an intellectual-critical one; their "tragic" voice should not be confused with an intellectual voice.[139] He celebrates the Mothers yet insists that their speech is insufficient; it requires intellectuals to interpret it, to think critically about it, for it to become an authentic site of memory.[140] Although he does not censor the speech of the Mothers, Casullo's demand for a nontransparent, nonexpressive language comes close to a demand for outright silence. Citing Canetti, he writes: "What is needed from an intellectual, reflexive point of view, for Canetti, is 'to stop speaking, to place words one next to the other and look at them.'"[141] He will refer to this as an "ethical silence" in the face of an evil that threatens to "ensnare" language and turn it into an agent of forgetting.[142] Silence is a form of critique, Casullo explains, and he asks intellectuals to search for a paradox, for "a word that doesn't 'speak,' that has fallen mute," where "that which cannot be seen" is seen.[143] Like Sarlo and Vezzetti, then, Casullo draws on post-Holocaust reflections to question the value of Argentine victims' speech.

Conclusion

An interesting poll conducted in 2000 by Gallup Argentina on behalf of the American Jewish Committee and the AMIA shows a large majority of Argentines agreeing that the memory of the Holocaust should be kept alive and should be taught in schools but an even larger majority not knowing what Auschwitz was.[144] Would the answers be different if the poll were to be conducted today?

The fact of Holocaust consciousness in the post-dictatorship is easy to perceive, but its story arc and ultimate significance are not. This is true in part because the "post-dictatorship period" is still very much our own and, as such, cannot yet be assigned a beginning, middle, and end; in part because use of the Holocaust as a sign for collective historical trauma and human rights violations has become both more prevalent and more diffuse in post-dictatorship Argentina, in tandem with global trends; and in part because it has been taken up in order to offer different and competing lessons for the present. This chapter has identified a Holocaust consciousness that serves the work of human rights in its criticisms of the state and also serves to criticize the work of human rights. These two tendencies are unified in that both show that Holocaust memory serves as a vital repository for critical thinking during the post-dictatorship period. This enormous intellectual engagement with post-Auschwitz thought has turned it into a mirror for a society that is grappling with the violence it allowed to happen and refusing to normalize that violence. But does this Holocaust mirror provoke a confrontation with the difficult truths of the past, or an evasion?

With regard to the work of Sarlo, Vezzetti, and Casullo in the decade 1995–2005, and notwithstanding the brilliance of each one of these thinkers, I believe the Holocaust mirror they hold up to Argentina runs the risk of relativizing the violence of the "dirty war." The Holocaust consciousness pioneered by these thinkers has been used to blame the left for its own annihilation and to discredit victim and activist voices. They have used Holocaust reflections to tar ideological rhetoric with the brush of dogmatism. By this perspective, ideological differences between the state and its opponents (and within the ranks of opponents, who were diverse) cease to be of great importance. In other words, the fact that each militantly pursued ideological ends is ultimately more important, for many of the thinkers discussed here, than the vast differences between the military's ideological ends and those of its victims. Thus, whereas human rights activists look to the Holocaust legacy for lessons about holding the perpetrators criminally responsible and attaining a measure of dignity for the victims, these other thinkers look to the Holocaust legacy to advocate less speech or more circumspect speech and consistently undermine the distinction between victims and perpetrators. At first glance it would seem that the thinkers discussed here advocate a more ideological or political account of the violence than human rights activists do, because they refuse to think of the victims as politically or morally "innocent." Most of the junta's victims, they stress, were involved in some kind of oppositional political activity. In fact, by downplaying the ideological stakes of the conflict, they contribute to a depoliticized account of the past.

Chapter Three

José Emilio Pacheco, Tununa Mercado, and Holocaust Testimony at the Mexico-Argentina Crossroads

> In the conditions of the camp
> it was sufficient resistance
> to remain vigilant
> and never forget
> that a time would come
> when we would be able
> to relate our experiences.[1]

> The will to bear witness had to be cultivated. It did not arise in mystical fashion out of the Holocaust and its aftermath.[2]

Let's turn now to consider the case of Mexico in the 1970s, a scenario of Holocaust consciousness that took shape in direct connection to the Argentine dictatorship. This chapter will discuss two interrelated stories from that time and place that demonstrate the power of Holocaust testimony to shape Latin American confrontations with state terror. The first story is about Mexican author José Emilio Pacheco and his groundbreaking Holocaust novel *Morirás lejos* (You Will Die Far Away).[3] First published in 1967, it was revised and reissued a decade later with significant changes that are key to the story I want to tell here. The novel is a challenging and compelling experimental work. It depicts two millennia of Jewish persecution while tracking a character who appears to be an escaped Nazi in present-day Mexico. Pacheco included graphic testimony about the Nazi death camps drawn from Jewish survivors and other witnesses. *Morirás lejos* is also a work that speaks obliquely to Pacheco's own moment in Mexico in the wake of the Tlatelolco massacre of October 2, 1968, and during the wave of authoritarian repression moving across Latin America, when witness testimony about these events became crucial in resisting state terror.

The second story recounted in this chapter takes up similar themes. It concerns Argentine writer Tununa Mercado, a left-wing political exile who moved to Mexico to escape death threats from right-wing paramilitaries in Argentina. She lived in Mexico City in the years 1974–1987. Not long after her arrival, she was offered a chance to interview four Jewish Holocaust survivors for a weekly glossy. This event led her to new thinking about the importance of victim-witness testimony for Argentine solidarity struggles taking place across the terrain of exile in Mexico and elsewhere.

The work of these two authors is instructive because it shows us how Latin American authors participated in a post-1968 global environment where Holocaust testimony circulated more frequently and widely than before. Yet Holocaust consciousness in 1970s Mexico remained limited. Fewer than two thousand Jewish Holocaust escapees and survivors had settled in Mexico, and as Yael Siman notes, there were few interlocutors in Mexico for their testimonies until the 1990s, despite the fact that Holocaust commemorations had been a feature of Jewish communal life since the 1950s.[4] A history of Mexican Holocaust consciousness is still in the making, but evidence from this chapter will make clear, if only in fragmentary form, that spaces for Holocaust awareness were beginning to be more actively cultivated in the 1960s, from both inside and outside the Jewish community. The work of Pacheco and Mercado contributed to this small yet growing Holocaust consciousness. These authors helped put Holocaust testimony into greater circulation in Mexico through their journalism, essays, and fiction.

Pacheco and Mercado also demonstrate that Holocaust testimony became relevant in 1970s Mexico as a model for Latin American testimony against state terror. At that time, Latin American thinkers were responding to a political climate of fear, censorship, and military repression that generated new conditions for witness testimony and new ideas about its significance. Testimony by the surviving victims of repression provided invaluable information about the workings of state violence and the fate of its victims as well as evidence of specific criminal acts committed by state security forces. It also accrued a positive symbolic value because it signaled resistance against military-imposed silence and conformity.

Nevertheless, as the two stories recounted in this chapter will make clear, it was not always easy to take up victim testimony for purposes of political solidarity and resistance. Pacheco's *Morirás lejos* explores how difficult it is to find an audience willing to listen to more stories about the genocide, and how difficult it is for any narrative to do justice to it. The novel also reveals how a critique of the structural criminality of the West, popularized in the1960s and derived in no small part from post-Holocaust reflections about the violence at the heart of modernity, threatens to displace the individual experiences of suffering to which survivors testify. Mercado's experiences with first-person testimony by women who had escaped Argentine detention centers likewise illuminate the difficulties of putting survivor testimony at the center of history. Leftist detractors considered these victim-witnesses to be lacking in moral or epistemological authority, either because the victim's perspective was too limited or because the victim, by virtue of having survived the exterminatory environment, was suspected of having been complicit with the perpetrator and therefore less of a victim. How far could this kind of first-person testimony be trusted? Could it be manipulated by political enemies and by collaborators trying to prove their innocence? Did its message conform to the political messages that activists had worked hard to craft in their strategies against repressive states? Pacheco's *Morirás lejos* and Mercado's work in exile show us that the positive symbolic, political, and evidentiary value of survivor testimony had to be created, nurtured, and defended. Holocaust testimony, having itself survived against tremendous odds, was important in helping these Latin American authors achieve that purpose.

German playwright Peter Weiss, in his play *The Investigation*, based on testimony given at the 1963–1965 Frankfurt "Auschwitz" trials and serving as an intertext of sorts for the works discussed here, records the following words by a camp survivor:

> The main duty of the Resistance
> was to maintain
> solidarity
> To do this we documented
> events in the camp
> and buried our documents
> in metal boxes.[5]

Taking up that ethos to excavate buried first-person histories, Pacheco and Mercado create intricate "memory knots" of solidarity from the threads of Holocaust testimony they encounter in Mexico, bringing together distinct histories to confront a moment of crisis.[6]

Pacheco, the Holocaust, and the Memory of 1968

Pacheco's novel *Morirás lejos* was published twice, first in 1967, then in 1977 in a revised edition. Between these two versions of the novel, we can perceive, obliquely, the time and space of what Jorge Luis Borges would call the author's invisible and "subterranean" work: the work of literary creation whose textual presence remains elusive.[7] Here I propose that Mexico's Tlatelolco massacre of 1968 and the Argentine dictatorship of 1976–1983 form a part of this novel's invisible work. Let me be clear from the outset: neither Tlatelolco nor the Southern Cone dictatorships appear in this novel, not even by allusion. Its principal theme is the millennial persecution of the Jews, centered on the Nazi Holocaust and on the crisis of reason and representation that this catastrophe provoked in the West and that has been one of its enduring legacies. But the Holocaust and its legacy come to be subtly interwoven with Latin American state terror of the late twentieth century through Pacheco's process of revision from 1967 to 1977, which endows the ten-year lapse between the two editions with a particular significance.

Morirás lejos is a difficult novel. It presents a confusing collage of fictional narration, metafictional self-reflection, and documentary sources such as first-person testimony, letters, political speeches, reports, and historical accounts. There is a great deal of self-deconstructing narrative trickery as these various sections alternate across the novel. In the present of narration, we are in contemporary Mexico City—1967 or 1977. In the past, we look back over centuries of Jewish persecution, starting with the expulsion of the Jews from Jerusalem by the Romans in 70 CE, then moving to the Inquisition and the expulsion of the Jews from Spain in 1492, then on to the Warsaw ghetto uprising in 1943 and the death camps of the Shoah. Pacheco recounts these events by using recognizable historical sources, including victim-witness testimony. In the present, meanwhile, we are faced with persecution and inquisition of an epistemological kind, on the terrain of reason and its limits: an enigma about the identity of the protagonist, known only by the letter "em" ("eme"). He is looking out his window at another character, known only as "Someone" ("Alguien"), and "em" is afraid that "Someone" is out to get him. Who are "em" and "Someone"? Pacheco playfully avoids answers. Em may be an ex-Nazi hiding out in Mexico; maybe not. His fear may be legitimate; maybe he is paranoid. Someone may be a Jewish survivor, come to claim vengeance; maybe not. Pacheco poses but refuses to answer these questions; in fact, he turns them into a kind of game, one composed of endless speculations: maybe em is a former

Nazi, or maybe he's a Jew; maybe Someone is persecuting em; or maybe Someone is just an unemployed stranger who happens to be sitting on a bench in the park outside em's house; and so forth.

Gazing out at the park from his window, em becomes a kind of detective, guided by reason. And yet at every turn, reason finds itself undone by the ludic and ultimately arbitrary nature of his search, which converts the past into a series of unproven hypotheses, drowns rational inquiry in a sea of doubts, and disconnects the search for truth from any empirical and moral groundings. The only stable element of this present time in the novel is the pestilential urban landscape that Pacheco constructs, a vision of modernity in ruins. In the foreground, Mexico City: crumbling, smog ridden, toxic, apocalyptically polluted. In the background, Auschwitz, Vietnam, the atomic bomb.

Both editions of the novel, the 1967 and the 1977, received critical acclaim in the Mexican cultural press and among some scholars, even though by any standard the 1967 edition was a publishing flop.[8] Many of those who commented on *Morirás lejos*, for both editions, agreed that it was a highly relevant portrait of contemporary society. The novel's critical vision of industrial society was a popular one at the time, a hallmark of the student movements of 1968 in Europe and the United States that had erupted a few months after the novel's first publication. The student movements criticized technological society and the bureaucratic state and held them responsible for Auschwitz and Vietnam, Dachau and consumerism, for a global machinery of misery and horror. As we will see, a repeated theme in the novel is that these disparate problems and events are held together by the same industrial excess.[9]

If we look at the second edition of the novel, from 1977, these concerns remain intact, even if the cultural moment is no longer the same as ten years before. But in other respects this new edition of the novel contains significant changes. Most notably, Pacheco expanded some sections of the novel while cutting others, and in particular, he granted more space to Holocaust testimonies and less space to metafictional disquisitions about the identity of "em" and the present-day industrial apocalypse. Certainly the testimonial and documentary portions of the novel were already present in the 1967 edition, but in the later version they take up more space. To what can we attribute this greater emphasis on testimony? The shift tells us something about Pacheco's changing sense of literary priorities over the ten-year gap, namely, that testimony had acquired for him more importance in the years since 1967. Why?

My argument is that through this change in emphasis, it is possible to trace the rise of two distinct historical phenomena: one, repressive authoritarianism in Latin America; two, Holocaust denialism in the scholarly world.[10] Censorship and the intensification of political violence characteristic of this post-1968 phase of the Cold War contributed to the increasing importance of testimony as a genre and gave acts of memory a new moral and political weight. So too did the pernicious use of Jewish survivor testimony to question the facts of the Holocaust or whether it happened at all. The changes that Pacheco made to the novel before its republication in 1977 textualize those events. By examining the differences between the first and second editions of the novel, we see how Pacheco takes up their legacy without once representing them directly. *Morirás lejos* responds to denialism and censorship and carries the memory of the Tlatelolco massacre and the Argentine "dirty war," even though it contains no reference to these histories.

Metafictional Destabilizations in *Morirás lejos*

Pacheco's novel is similar to other prominent novels of the 1960s in its use of avant-garde techniques to question the distinctions between truth and fiction. Carlos Fuentes's *The Death of Artemio Cruz* (1962), Julio Cortázar's *Rayuela* (1963), Salvador Elizondo's *Farabeuf* (1965)—all involve a strong metafictional element that destabilizes our epistemological certainties about our ability to distinguish reality from fantasy. They tell a story that feels truthful, but interrupt that story with ironic commentaries about its arbitrary or constructed nature. Ostensibly these are distancing techniques that help us develop our critical faculties and make us feel like coparticipants of the writing rather than passive consumers of a good story. Yet these works can also undermine and block our critical faculties with Escher-like narrative structures or with false leads that toy with us and confound our expectations. These writers take a page from Borges in building stories around detectives and scholars who get lost in mirrors or crazy labyrinths of their own making and never arrive at the truth. These Borgesian characters experience a humbling of their rational and intellectual powers, which trap them in contradictions from which they cannot break free.

Metafictional elements abound throughout Pacheco's novel but concentrate especially in those parts of the novel under the heading "Salónica," which alternate with other sections of the novel. "Salónica" employs an omniscient narrative voice to describe em, the presumed ex-Nazi who is the novel's main character. But the narrator, despite the pretense of seeing all, sows only doubts about the main character's real identity. Em is never definitively identified, and his pursuer always remains Someone. Em may be Eichmann or may be Mengele—both men fled to Latin America to escape justice, and the novel contains elaborate allusions to both. Yet the Nazi identity of em remains hypothetical. Meanwhile, em is searching for the truth of his presumed pursuer. The narrative develops around his detective-like search, one guided by "lucidity, the spirit of inquiry, the deductive capacity," yet the aims of the search remain constantly frustrated.[11] Each "fact" becomes a mere hypothesis or possibility, including the possibility that em's deductions are delirious, nothing more than paranoid fantasies. The detective structure of the novel comes apart under the weight of these doubts.

Doubts about the identities and life histories of em and Someone bring up many reflections about our tenuous grasp of the past and about the powerlessness of language to communicate the facts beyond a reasonable doubt. These epistemological and linguistic doubts nourish a salutary philosophical skepticism about the limits of human reason. But they have more problematic consequences when brought into the realm of morality and justice, consequences that the novel tackles head on. It confronts the fact that the epistemological uncertainty that clouds our ability to correctly identify the characters makes it impossible to differentiate between the innocent and the guilty, between victims and perpetrators, and thus by extension, to locate responsibility for the crimes that em or Someone might have committed. This plays right into the hands of the presumed Nazi, who uses the lists of hypotheses as a "delay tactic."[12] Em, we suspect, is manipulating the epistemological doubts so as to hide the facts and get out from having to face charges of Nazi crimes. Philosophical skepticism becomes a tool of moral evasion and criminal exculpation. This is buttressed by the fact that one of the hypotheticals considered in "Salónica" completely confuses innocence and guilt: "Em and a seated man—one is guilty, the other innocent; both guilty; both innocent—they see each other, they scrutinize each other."[13] Thus the self-questioning thrust of "Salónica" generates tremendous moral problems. These come to constitute the heart of the novel in the form of an internal dialogue as to whether one can arrive at an accurate judgment about historical truth and moral or criminal responsibility for past actions.

Pacheco on Industrial Modernity and Global Complicity in the Vietnam Era

The difficulty in determining who are the victims and who the perpetrators, a difficulty produced by reasonable self-questioning that escalates into all-consuming doubt, is connected to another theme of the novel, namely, the complicity of modern society in its own destruction. Pacheco permeates *Morirás lejos* with a critical vision about modern industrial society, in keeping with much of his other writing from the 1960s and 1970s. The Nazi concentration camps play an important role in that critical vision. For Pacheco, as for so many other thinkers of the time, Auschwitz and other Nazi camps represent an instructive and representative evil, not a unique one. Such a view gained a widespread audience in 1968 with the European and U.S. student movements and was broadcast among Mexican students and thinkers during that time. Carlos Fuentes, who wrote several journalistic articles about the student movements, synthesizes this view when he declares that consumer society "is the most sublimated form of genocide," a true "Dachau of the spirit."[14] While living in Europe, Fuentes met up with Pacheco in England, where Pacheco held a post as a visiting professor. Both authors took note of the student demonstrations in the UK against companies that manufactured chemical weapons for the United States. Referencing Zyklon B and napalm, Pacheco writes, "The students no longer see science as the light of the future."[15]

Pacheco was a direct witness to the revolutionary wave across Europe and an indirect witness to protests in the United States against the Vietnam war. He produced a series of passionate articles for *La Cultura en México*, cultural supplement to the weekly glossy *¡Siempre!*, directed by Fernando Benítez. These articles reveal the extent to which the themes of *Morirás lejos* were inspired by the same political and philosophical concerns that animated the student protesters, especially those concerns to which philosophers like Herbert Marcuse, Hannah Arendt, and Jean-Paul Sartre had already given voice.[16] With clear allusions to Arendt and Eichmann, Pacheco explains to his Mexican readers that the student movements are an attack on "the system that seems to have adapted teaching to the mass production of docile technocrats."[17] Regarding the work of Marcuse, he reflects on the idea that the United States in the era of Vietnam is a monster similar to Nazi Germany: "Does what is about to happen in the world look like what happened in Germany between 1933 and 1945, or what is happening right now in the United States? Marcuse lived inside both monsters and knows their innards."[18]

Meanwhile, Carlos Fuentes reported on how the Italian student protesters shared similar thoughts: "Does not each European or North American capitalist practice a mass extermination comparable to the Nazis?"[19] *Morirás lejos* shares a clear affiliation with these ideas. In the words of writer Margo Glantz, it offers "a new allegory about technological society that makes the whole world into a 'concentrationary' space."[20] Glantz's use of the phrase "concentrationary space" ("espacio concentracionario") alludes to David Rousset's 1947 book *L'univers concentrationnaire* (The Concentration Camp Universe or Concentrationary Universe) about his experience in Buchenwald, where he was deported by the Nazis for his activities in the French Resistance.[21] Pacheco used Rousset's phrase himself in *Morirás lejos*.[22] In line with these views, the Holocaust was but the most extreme expression of the evil created by industrial society. For Pacheco, the Vietnam war served to confirm and deepen this perspective. His articles on Vietnam for *La Cultura en México* recur to images of the Holocaust to describe the magnitude of the violence. He says of Saigon in 1968 that "it ominously evokes the destruction of the Warsaw Ghetto just twenty-five years ago."[23] Faced with this scene, he wrote in the article, "Willingly or not each of us is victim, perpetrator, arena and trial of the horror all at the same time."[24] Other Mexican writers also saw similarities between Vietnam and the Holocaust.[25]

Mexico, too, provides a mirror for this apocalyptic view of industrial society under the shadow of Auschwitz. In Pacheco's writings on Mexico, he speaks of "genocide" to refer to deaths by poverty and starvation.[26] His comments about the ever more lamentable condition of Mexico City, a theme reiterated across much of his work, constantly evoke the catastrophic destruction wrought by the Nazis. Surveying the demolition of Mexico City that was undertaken for a massive traffic-improvement project, he sees a bleak reminder of the bombing of Warsaw by the Nazis; the ruins of Warsaw are "an advance model of Mexico in 1980."[27] The city's pollution reminds him of the gas chambers: "Before the Nazi scientists perfected Zyklon B, the gas of the chambers, the technicians of genocide had deemed executions by way of diesel engine exhaust fumes to be too cruel, incapable of imagining the Mexico City of 1989."[28] These hyperbolic comparisons should be taken in the spirit of the moment, as evidence for the fact that a view of the Holocaust as emblematic of the dark side of modern progress had come to permeate Mexican intellectual life, and as evidence for how seriously Pacheco worried about the human costs of the changes he saw happening around him.

Mexico City in all its perverse grandeur features prominently in the "Salónica" sections of *Morirás lejos*, becoming the locus for his reflections on the sense of complicity that settles over industrial modernity like a toxic gas. Mexico exemplifies what Pacheco refers to as "the guilty cities" ("las ciudades culpables") in his prose poem "Transparency of the Enigmas" ("Transparencias de las enigmas"). The poem is from 1966, around the time he was completing the first version of *Morirás lejos*: "The combustion, the age of fire that now hangs over the guilty cities, guilty because as they ate their fill they let poverty prosper around them."[29] The poverty and pollution of Mexico City make it complicit with global industrial and bureaucratic systems and reveal that progress is an illusion. In the novel, the shadow of Nazism contaminates every human achievement, every effort at reason and critique. Critic Noé Jitrik has said of this element of the novel: "We are not safe from any crime, not even the ones we have not committed."[30] Just as the British students protesting biological arms factories had observed, the gases and smells that circulate in *Morirás lejos* are concrete examples of a symbolic universe of evil composed of Zyklon B, napalm, the bitter smell of vinegar, and the smog that pervades Mexico City. As Ricardo Aguilar Melantzón and Mimi Gladstein point out in their analysis of the novel, it is as if the dust, fire, and toxic air created by those technological experiments have penetrated the lines that separate distinct spaces, trapping everyone in a global web of ethical and environmental pollution.[31]

But if we are all guilty, no one is, because the categories of victims and perpetrators, innocent and guilty, lose their validity. The fact that genocidal acts have since been perpetrated by the same powers who liberated the Nazi camps makes the problem even worse. It is as if the normalcy of genocide would absolve the genocidal perpetrator of his crimes. Pacheco incorporates this view into the novel with a strong dose of narrative irony. In one of the many hypothetical story lines proposed in the novel, a chorus of anti-Semitic, anti-Communist voices in *Morirás lejos* refuse to contemplate a Mexican book about the Holocaust:

> I assure you that not even one percent of what you say is true—The thing is, Germany lost the war—You fell for all the Communist propaganda against Hitler—Anyway if you're not Jewish why the devil would you take this on—Don't believe for a second that you'll be thanked for this—Why not write about Mexico's Indians—Why not take advantage of your materials to write about the bombing by Churchill the crimes of Stalin (Hitler got the short end I assure you Stalin invented the concentration camps) the purges in China the brainwashing in Korea and Vietnam of course mentioning Hiroshima and Nagasaki.[32]

The last lines quoted here, regarding the Allied bombing of Germany, Stalin's crimes, and so forth, are tainted by their proximity to the Holocaust denialism of the earlier lines. Yet even so Pacheco does not allow us to dismiss these thoughts as so much pernicious relativizing. They resonate too closely with the novel's depiction of shared complicity and a fallen humanity. He shows us that, although this depiction is useful as a lens through which to view global industrial modernity, it has perverse effects when used to think about justice for particular acts of atrocity. It is a known alibi for atrocity, identified by Primo Levi in his "Letters from Germans"—Germans who seek to absolve themselves by appealing to the eternal existence of human evil. Levi responds to them by saying: "One must answer personally for sins and errors, otherwise all trace of civilization would vanish from the face of the earth, as in fact it had vanished from the Third Reich."[33]

The general sense of widespread complicity is not the only obstacle to moral clarity we encounter in the novel. The narrative voice must also confront doubts expressed by Holocaust survivors who question whether the narrator is up to the task of representing so terrible a reality. No testimony can communicate that horror, says a survivor—"Nothing can come even close to the frightening reality of memory"—before shutting the narrator down: "Better that you keep silent. Nothing, I repeat, nothing can express what the camps were."[34] One can understand why the witness-survivor would question the narrator's ability to do justice to history. But as with the justifiable critique of industrial modernity, here too the moral foundation of that position slides into the abyss once it is echoed by publishers who find the whole topic boring: "No one is interested in this anymore—We've read about it a million times. . . . It's been done already—It's been said already."[35] Ironically, these words echo at least one of the real-life criticisms received by the novel.[36] But the imaginary critics represented in the novel are not just bored by the Holocaust; they are anti-Semites: "Well Hitler did some very good things—You can't deny or condemn him outright," and so forth.[37] The narrator of "Salónica" is trapped between the Holocaust survivor, who questions whether any attempt to represent that past is destined to falsify and betray it, and the anti-Semite, who questions the truth of the genocide or its status as a criminal act.

The task of narrating genocide becomes impossibly enormous and leads the narrator to question his own abilities.[38] Toward the end of the novel, the narrator openly despairs:

> Because everything in this story is unreal. Nothing happened as was suggested. The effort to touch the truth through fiction,

through a lie, deforms the places and events. All unreal, nothing happened as it has been referred to here. It was only an attempt to help that the great crime not be repeated.[39]

The narrative wants to be an instrument for memory. But between the delay tactics of the presumed ex-Nazi, the skepticism of the Holocaust survivor, and the cynicism and anti-Semitism of the publisher, it runs the risk of becoming its opposite: an accomplice to forgetting.

Testimony Insists: The Changes from 1967 to 1977

These doubts about the reliability of testimony and history, about their ability to capture the truth, constitute only one part of the novel. Other sections of the novel consist precisely in testimonies and historical narrations that are free of such metafictional murk. In these sections, we can clearly distinguish between victims and perpetrators. The section titled "Diaspora" is based on the testimony written by Flavius Josephus, a participant and witness to the events who described the Jewish uprising against Rome leading to the destruction of the Second Temple and the expulsion of the Jews from Israel in 70 CE.[40] The section titled "Grossaktion," on the Warsaw ghetto uprising of 1943, is based on testimony by direct witnesses—Jewish resisters and Nazi officials—who describe the events that culminated in the total destruction of the ghetto and the deportation and murder of its Jewish inhabitants.[41] The section "Totenbuch," about the Nazi extermination camps, provides a historical synthesis of what we know about how these functioned. Pacheco alludes here to documents held in British and North American archives and in the Auschwitz Museum.[42] Furthermore, although not stated explicitly, it is clear that he is using Holocaust survivor testimony from the Frankfurt "Auschwitz" trial of 1965. This can be seen in his descriptions of the *Sonderkommando*, the Jewish prisoners charged with the Auschwitz crematoria, almost all of whom were exterminated in turn. *Morirás lejos* uses language that corresponds closely to the language used by a *Sonderkommando* survivor who testified at the Frankfurt trial.[43]

What is the connection between the part of the novel that offers testimonies and is based on historical documents and the part that questions testimony and the truth of all narratives of history, that transforms the documented past into an imagination game played on the edge of a moral abyss? Although doubts about the reliability of narrative permeate the novel and extend to the historical and testimonial sections, the novel never cancels out the internal tension between its two debating elements, the testimonial/historical and the "literary" or skeptical/metafictional.[44] But although a line of uncertainty runs through all the spaces of the novel, there is a noticeable difference between those sections that encourage self-deconstruction and those that do not. In the former, the weave of the past never coalesces into a single text or around a single person. Its threads continuously loosen and disperse, touching everyone with their violence and spreading complicity for that violence. In the latter, the novel constructs a coherent and chronological account of the past, identifies people and gives them voice, describes their actions based on empirical evidence, and establishes the difference between oppressors and oppressed.[45] Margo Glantz affirms the novel's internal tension by speaking of an encounter between two "insistences," one of which is characterized by "the signal" and "the mark"—the side I have been calling testimonial and historical—the other of which insists on hypothesis, which "instead of fixing, defining, marking, blurs, branches off, renders indeterminate."[46]

It is important to recognize the presence of this internal debate between two "insistences" within the novel because without it we cannot appreciate the significance of the changes between the first and second editions of *Morirás lejos*. Pacheco was a reviser; he revised all the works he published more than once (e.g., compare poems published in an original collection and then republished in an anthology). The same can be said of this novel: he revised the second edition from start to finish, to such a degree that there is hardly a sentence that remained identical to the original.[47] In many respects, the two versions are the same: the same epistemological doubts and ambiguities lodged within its historical narratives; the same playful metafictions; the same universalization of the Holocaust as part of Pacheco's vision of modernity in ruins. Nevertheless, we notice an evident change regarding the novel's testimonial, memorial, and documentary "insistence": it is longer than before, especially those sections relating to the Shoah, while the metafictional sections of "Salónica" are shorter. Testimony, therefore, is granted more importance, more space, more authority in the 1977 version than in the 1967 version.

Specifically as regards its depictions of the Holocaust, the second edition contains more historical information and more images of horror. The first edition includes images of horror too, but in the second edition the depiction becomes more intense, with more details. It provides more information about Jewish resistance in the Warsaw ghetto and more information about the death camps, especially as concerns the industrialization of death. It names the companies that worked with the Nazis to implement the genocide, driven by the profit motive, such as Siemens, Krupp, and Farben.[48] It reveals that Farben has a factory in Mexico.[49] The second edition spends more time on depictions of human suffering. The images of the gas chambers are longer and more detailed. So too are the description of the *Einsatzgruppen*, the SS groups operating in the East who massacred Jews with machine guns and left them in mass graves.[50] Sections about the tortures practiced by the Gestapo involve more elaborate descriptions than in the first.[51] The second edition describes the sadistic pleasures experienced by camp guards; the first edition does not.[52] The second edition describes the children on the death camp transports—"Dying of thirst the little children licked the sweat off their mothers' faces"—the first edition does not.[53] The second edition holds the Allies responsible for not bombing the gas chambers, which would have saved thousands of Jews; the first edition does not.[54] Overall, in the second edition Pacheco's description of the genocide is more detailed, more extensive, more graphic, and more outraged. This change toward a more precise and documented vision of the Holocaust generates an even greater tension with the metafictional elements of the novel. It is not that these have lessened in the second edition; it is that the testimonial-historical insistence is that much stronger. It has been buttressed by more research and demonstrates a greater commitment, on the part of the author, to documenting the extremities of cruelty and indifference perpetrated on the Jews.

The Memory Imperative Post-1968

To what can we attribute the renewed importance granted to testimony in the 1977 *Morirás lejos*? Two factors that intervened between the first and second edition undoubtedly play a role: one, the growth of scholarly research promoting denial of the Holocaust, a phenomenon that Pacheco followed closely and with great alarm; two, the growth of testimonial memory as resistance against state repression in Latin America, especially the Mexican government's massacre of peaceful protestors on October 2, 1968, in the Plaza at Tlatelolco and the "dirty war" in Argentina. These two events receive constant attention in Pacheco's poetry and prose. We therefore have grounds to argue that the revisions he made to *Morirás lejos* respond, at least in part, to the need to amplify the voices of the survivors and defend the memory of the victims against oblivion.

Regarding the first factor, Holocaust denialism, in August 1977 Pacheco published a brief note in the Mexican weekly *Proceso* about David Irving, the British historian notorious for his anti-Semitic statements and his affiliation with groups that denied the Holocaust. Irving's book about Hitler had become a best seller; it tried to exonerate Hitler from responsibility for the Holocaust by showing the lack of documentary evidence that would establish, once and for all, that Hitler knew the genocide was happening.[55] Pacheco, in his article "Hitler Vindicated?," refutes this argument by referring to numerous historical sources, including testimonies collected by left-wing Jewish resisters in the Polish ghettos and sent to the Allies in a vain attempt to convince them of the need to bomb the death camps. Elements of these testimonies can be found in the second edition of *Morirás lejos*, which appeared three months later.[56] His article also lamented the fact that Irving's book had already had harmful effects in the legal realm: "It has served the defense to exonerate fourteen criminals from the Maidenek camp who were tried in July in Düsseldorf."[57] Clearly, then, a short time before the second edition appeared, Pacheco wanted his readers to understand that victim testimony is a key piece of history.

That concern for the testimony of Holocaust victims resonated in the age of state repression in Latin America, a period symbolically inaugurated, from the perspective of Mexico, on October 2, 1968. The novel's second edition responds to the post-Tlatelolco era, when activists discovered that victim testimony could be a powerful way to denounce state repression. The phenomenon crystallized around the work of Elena Poniatowska, especially *La noche de Tlatelolco*, which appeared in 1971 and became the most influential and widely read book about the student movement and October 2 massacre.[58] Like *Morirás lejos*, it uses witness testimony as a weapon against a politics of denial that actively promotes forgetting. In Argentina as well, during the years of the military dictatorship and in the midst of a brutal campaign of silencing, testimonial voices of the survivors and their families began to acquire a new political and moral authority by those who worked to denounce the junta's brutal regime.

The situation in Argentina was a constant source of concern for Pacheco during the era of state repression. This concern can be felt in *Morirás lejos*, which incorporates Argentina of the "Proceso" years into its "invisible work." It is no coincidence that the second edition includes a dedication to Argentine literary critic Noé Jitrik in addition to the dedication to Mexican editor and author Fernando Benítez already present in the first edition. Jitrik had been instrumental in making the first edition of the novel accessible to an audience in Argentina. Jitrik taught a course on *Morirás lejos* in 1973, in the process training a generation of Argentine literary critics around it. In 1974, Jitrik was forced into political exile with Tununa Mercado, his wife, because of death threats from right-wing paramilitary groups; they went to Mexico. When the 1977 edition of Pacheco's novel appeared, Jitrik, in Mexico, wrote a review that gave this earlier Argentine context a renewed significance. He writes that Pacheco's novel had a special resonance for his students, that he had been teaching it "to an audience that deserved to know it, because they were in some ways taking their very lives into their hands, as the cursed years starting in 1974 would make evident."[59] Many of his students from that time, Jitrik continues, "have now disappeared off the face of the earth, swallowed by the night of terror." But, with this new edition of Pacheco's novel, the ones remaining "can begin to establish a connection between this book, which we attempted to decipher and which tells of the destruction of the temple, and what was happening to them, the destruction of other temples, from writing to life itself."[60] He concludes: "All of us were connected to this book as a result."[61] He saw in Argentine state repression the shadow of the destruction of the Jewish people, as did so many other Argentine thinkers—and Pacheco himself. In 1977 Pacheco wrote a bitter, anguished piece about the disappearance of Argentine author Rodolfo Walsh. He highlighted the similarity between the Argentina of his day and Nazi Germany: "The garrisons have become concentration and extermination camps, where they practice torture without limits and summary executions."[62] His words echo Walsh's own words in his famous "Open Letter to the Military Junta," which compared the junta to the Nazi SS, and was written in Buenos Aires on March 24, 1977, a day before the junta disappeared him.[63]

Regarding the October 2 massacre at Tlatelolco, the Mexican government's response to the event in the days immediately following instantly empowered testimony as a resistant literary genre. The government imposed a campaign of near total silence about the event via direct censorship of the media as well as through a disinformation campaign, a push to discredit its critics nationally and abroad, and the violent repression of Mexican student leaders by imprisonment, disappearance, and assassination. The government sought popular support for its actions by appealing to the need to preserve Mexico's image before the world's eyes, which were turned to Mexico for the 1968 Olympic Games. Jorge Volpi writes:

> During ten days [the government] accomplished the impossible such that, starting on October 2, Mexico and the world became convinced that *nothing had happened*. Nothing. Ten days that,

together with the extreme act of Tlatelolco, were sufficient for the government to erase the student movement from history. . . . An urgent manipulation of the media, a repression that intensified underground, and a skillful public image operation almost succeeded in convincing everyone that freedom prevailed in the republic.[64]

In what came to be known as "the Olympic truce," the press postponed any comments about the student movement and the events of October 2 until after the Olympics were over. Even left-wing intellectuals, who were horrified by the event and had been allies of the student movement, postponed discussing it in the press in order to allow the 1968 Mexico City Olympic Games to proceed smoothly. The cultural supplement *La Cultura en México*, an open sympathizer of the student movement, waited until its October 16 edition to publish its first pieces about what had happened.

In the midst of this silence, poetry became one of the most important spaces of protest about the event. It began with a poem by Octavio Paz, "México: Olimpiada de 1968," published on October 30, 1968, in *La Cultura en México* and accompanied by a letter in which Paz announced his refusal to participate in the World Encounter of Poets that was supposed to take place as part of the Olympic games.[65] Then followed a veritable avalanche of poems about October 2.[66] Many of them evoked the Conquest of Mexico, an event that offered itself as a parallel to the Tlatelolco massacre. The coincidence of locales was striking: In 1521 in Tlatelolco, the residents of the Aztec capital had suffered a devastating military defeat at the hands of the Spanish and their allies. Mexican poets in the 1960s had been given unprecedented access to native accounts of the Conquest thanks to the 1959 publication of the poetry anthology *Vision of the Vanquished*, compiled by Miguel León-Portilla, containing sixteenth-century Nahuatl poetry about the Conquest.[67] Its appearance in a mass pocket edition gave a general audience access to an archive of haunting poems about the Aztecs' defeat through their own eyes and in their own words. These testimonial poems offered a model anchored in the figure of the witness-survivor and inspired a post–October 2 poetry testifying to anger, fear, and sadness about the Tlatelolco massacre and expressing a commitment to remember it.[68]

Innumerable poems about 1968 allude to the defeated Indigenous peoples of the Conquest. Among the earliest to appear after the massacre were Pacheco's own "Reading of the 'Songs of the Aztecs'" (Lectura de los "Cantares Mexicanos"), published on November 6, 1968; a long poem by Juan Bañuelos, "Acts Not Registered" ("No consta en actas"), a fragment of which was published on November 13, 1968; and "Altar of the Dead" ("El altar de los muertos"), by Marcos Antonio Montes de Oca, published on December 11, 1968.[69] Each is a testimonial poem that positions the poet in the role of the witness and uses the poem as a site of memory. The poem by Montes de Oca begins:

> The poet remembers what the people forget.[70]

Bañuelos writes:

> I the remainder, the survivor, I speak.[71]

In Pacheco's poem, the poetic voice says:

> I see the desolation that hangs over the temple.[72]

These works convey the need for the direct witness to relate their experience.

Memory as urgent, as a moral and political need, came to be felt even more forcefully in the months and years after the event. This was due in part to the sinister repetition of events on June 10, 1971, the date of the Corpus Christi festival, when a paramilitary group associated with the Mexican government massacred student demonstrators (the "Halconazo," so named for the "Halcones" paramilitaries). It was also because the passage of time threatened to work in favor of a state engaged in a campaign of forgetting. In 1970, on the second anniversary of the Tlatelolco massacre, José Revueltas wrote the following: "Neither historical justice nor anyone or anything can erase this memory: it will always be an accusation and a condemnation."[73] In 1971, in Poniatowska's *La noche de Tlatelolco*, Rosario Castellanos published her "Memorial de Tlatelolco," devoted entirely to the theme of remembrance. Its final verse reads: " I remember, we remember / until justice be established among us."[74] In 1978, on the tenth anniversary of the massacre, Pacheco wrote a new poem about it, "Las voces de Tlatelolco" (The Voices of Tlatelolco). He composed the poem entirely of witness testimony drawn from press accounts of the event. A brief "author's note" explains:

> All of us, in one way or another, are survivors of Tlatelolco. But today in the tenth year since the event, nothing can replace the testimony of those who lived it. This is a collective and involun-

tary poem, made with sentences taken from oral narratives, and to a much lesser degree newspaper articles, collected by Elena Poniatowska in *La noche de Tlatelolco*.[75]

All the texts about Tlatelolco reviewed here reveal the presence of a moral and protolegal discourse of memory and testimony. They use testimony as a tool in the struggle to criminalize the repressive state and to endow a special prestige on witnesses and survivors and on those who remember the victims. This is what Hugo Vezzetti has called, with reference to post-dictatorship Argentina, "the memory imperative," in which "the value and the duty of memory responded to the aim of confronting the silence and falsification surrounding the events."[76] This duty to remember takes on reparative and protolegal meanings: we remember in order to accuse and condemn, so that one day there will be justice.

Returning to *Morirás lejos*, the transformation of testimony into a tool against censorship and to criminalize the perpetrators also occurs in the novel. We can see it particularly in how the second edition treats the question of complicity: it has adopted a more conventional moral and legal approach in which victims are clearly distinguished from perpetrators. In the second edition, there exists the possibility that "Nazism is an absolute evil: no one can be Nazi and innocent," a prospect not in evidence in the first edition.[77] The perpetrators are, in a sense, guiltier in the second edition than in the first. The second edition puts greater emphasis than the first on the imbalance between Jewish resisters and imperial armies. For example, in the first edition, the Jewish resistance in first-century Jerusalem is "poorly armed" ("mal armada"), while in the second edition this same resistance is "without arms" ("sin armas").[78] Another example: in the first edition, the Jewish resisters in Warsaw fight in hopes of preventing mass deportation to Treblinka, while in the second edition this hope has been omitted; the Jews fight only to kill the greatest number of Germans before being killed themselves.[79] In other words, the second edition underlines that the Jewish forces are much weaker than the Nazis, whose victory looks more like a crime against humanity than a military triumph. In the same vein, the second edition depicts the Jewish children who perished in the Nazi camps; the first edition does not.

Furthermore, in the second edition, more space is given to the testimony and memory of the direct witnesses and survivors, in part by expanding the sections that contain testimony about the ghettos and the extermination camps, in part through subtle word changes. In the first edition, a war "correspondent" narrates the battle of Warsaw ("corresponsal"); in the second edition, it is a "direct witness" ("testigo presencial").[80] In the first edition, the evidence for Gestapo atrocities "lies in legal folios" ("consta en folios legales"); in the second edition, "it lies in legal folios *and in the memory of the victims*" (my emphasis).[81]

These are small changes, certainly, but taken together they contribute to strengthening the victims' perspective and distinguishing it from that of the perpetrators. They demonstrate a transformation in how the author approaches the question of innocence and guilt for modern industrial atrocities. Again, this is not to say that the second edition has eliminated its discourse on generalized social complicity for such crimes; in the "Salónica" line, the moral abyss threatens to engulf everyone, as if there were no victims, only perpetrators. But in the second edition the novel's other sections—Jewish testimony about the Roman destruction of the temple, the German destruction of the Warsaw ghetto, and the German destruction of European Jewry in the killing fields and death camps of the East—the evidence against specific, identifiable perpetrators is stronger, their crimes are greater, the moral and legal authority of the victims and survivors is more secure, their memory more transmissible. By way of these differences, the 1968 Tlatelolco massacre and the crimes of the Argentine Proceso become a part of this novel even though they never visibly appear in it.

Tununa Mercado: Solidarity and the Testimonial Situation

Tununa Mercado is part of Pacheco's story insofar as Pacheco supported her and other Argentine exiles when they lived in Mexico. She also has her own story of Holocaust consciousness in 1970s Mexico because of the role played by Holocaust testimony in her work. An Argentine essayist and novelist, she went into political exile in Mexico in 1974 with her husband Noé Jitrik to escape the actions of the "Alianza Anticomunista Argentina," or "Triple A," paramilitary forces who had embarked on a campaign of terror to advance their right-wing political agenda. Mercado was part of a wave of leftist intellectuals and prominent figures from the political and cultural scene who were forced to leave Argentina because of state terror in the years surrounding the military coup of 1976; she returned to Argentina in the 1980s after the dictatorship had ended. There exists a scattering of writings about this particular situation of Argentine exile, but none as consistent, deep, and personal as Mercado's.

That the Holocaust would figure prominently in her work is practically an accident of history. In 1975, the year after her arrival in Mexico, an editor sympathetic to the precarious economics of exile life assigned her to interview four Jewish Holocaust survivors for his paper. Since then, she has turned to the words of Holocaust victim witnesses—those who survived and those who did not—in order to reflect on the transformative effects of testimony and solidarity.[82] Here I will focus on a group of paraliterary texts. These include her 1975 interviews in Mexico as well as her later writings about these and other Holocaust testimonies and on testimonies by survivors of Argentina's concentration camps.[83]

My interest here will be in bringing out what we can call, following historian Annette Wieviorka's model, the "testimonial situation" in Mercado. Wieviorka writes: "The witness is the bearer of an experience that, albeit unique, does not exist on its own, but only in the testimonial situation in which it takes place."[84] Wieviorka refers here to the historical situation in which a testimony is enunciated, and consequently the ideas and expectations that shape it. She gives as an example the differences between the testimony given by a Holocaust survivor in Claude Lanzmann's film *Shoah* (1985) and the testimony given by the same survivor years earlier during the Eichmann trial (1961).

Looking at the various "testimonial situations" in Mercado's work, we notice how thoroughly they have been colored by a commitment to solidarity—solidarity understood in the historical sense as international fellowship amid political repression, a practice of material and political accompaniment and support. Notably, these ideas about solidarity go beyond the idealistic into the idealized, such that her depictions of the past occasionally strike me as being historically evasive. Such is the case with Mercado's emphasis on the Mexican government's solidarity with Argentine and other Southern Cone leftists during the 1970s, which does not acknowledge Mexico's own terrible "dirty war" during that time, and her depictions of its generosity to immigrants, which does not acknowledge that Mexico placed severe restrictions on Jewish immigration during the Nazi period. But the same evasion of history in the name of solidarity, when seen in the testimonial situations she creates with Jewish survivors of the Holocaust and with Argentine survivors of torture and disappearance, takes on a different significance. It stems from a drive to see in the situation of testimony a moment of opening, a moment of contingency not overdetermined by the past or the present, even if the words disclosed in that moment depict a horror so overwhelming that it shuts the future down. Idelber Avelar has said of Mercado's texts and others' from the post-dictatorship period in the Southern Cone that they "carry the seeds of a messianic energy," and regarding Mercado's writing in specific, he notes that it contains "a gesture toward what is yet to come that refuses to confine it into a predetermined content."[85] This temporal feature of Mercado's testimonial situation, its life within and outside history, links her to a powerfully heterodox Latin American leftist tradition.[86]

When she collected testimonies by Auschwitz survivors while she was in exile in Mexico, she focused on their depictions of solidarity in the camps in order to activate their positive value within a broad horizon of socialist ethics, which meant "unmooring" them, as Debarati Sanyal might say, from the events of the Holocaust so as to "moor" them to the demands of the times.[87] Thanks to what the Auschwitz survivors told her, to what she heard them say, the Holocaust became relevant in a new way in 1970s Mexico. But the question of testimony also became ideologically slippery during that period, hardly a solid ground on which to rest one's expectations of solidarity. As she recounts, Argentine exiles in Mexico and human rights activists in Argentina debated the validity of testimonies by survivors of the dictatorship's concentration camps, which contained truths that could not be easily assimilated into the immediate strategic goals of the human rights movements and were therefore silenced. Mercado refused to view them solely through that lens of political expediency. Years after the fact, Mercado would compare these testimonies to Holocaust testimonies and thereby in turn "unmoor" Argentine testimonies from the political impasses of their original moment to project them back onto a utopian horizon.

Mexico as Political Refuge

Mercado inscribed the Auschwitz testimonies under the theme of solidarity, as we will see in more detail below. The theme derived much of its contemporary importance from the Mexican government's decision to welcome the political exiles fleeing the dictatorships of the Southern Cone. That decision was itself the mirror, as Mercado and others saw it, of an earlier decision of world-historical significance: Mexico's role as a haven for Republican exiles from Spain and other Europeans fleeing fascism in the 1930s. She writes of the "halo" surrounding Mexican foreign policy ever since it opened its doors to Spanish exiles, which was "an ethical decision without precedent in the century."⁸⁸ For the Argentine exiles of her generation, she continues,

> Spain in Mexico was one of the backdrops that predated us in that landscape. Heroism, death, uprooting were referents for a political consciousness that aspired to be liberating and universal: the Latin Americans were the children of that Spain which had arrived in Mexico, but also of other refugees from World War II, or of victims of Stalinism like Trotsky, who had the same spirit and were marked by the same breaks, and who from Lázaro Cárdenas onward would be children of Mexico. Mexico then was mother and father, and in so being, and so unequivocally, for refugees of all types, it restructured the political consciousness of an entire continent.⁸⁹

Mexican history in this regard provides a stark contrast to Argentina, "where all the Nazis went," at least in the popular imagination.⁹⁰ Mexico's 1943 *Black Book of Nazi Terror in Europe* is a model of anti-fascist solidarity, with a prologue by Mexican president Manuel Ávila Camacho and distinguished contributors from the worlds of Mexican and European art and letters.⁹¹ In her writings on her Mexican exile, Mercado focuses on the gestures of solidarity that she encountered at every level of Mexican society. She points out that it was President of the Republic Luis Echeverría himself who sponsored the two rival exile organizations that Argentines established in Mexico on their arrival.⁹² For Mercado, the relationship between Argentine exiles and the PRI, the political party that had been in power for decades, was "idyllic," and she uses metaphors of family and home in her depictions of Mexico's welcoming stance.⁹³

Mercado makes an important point about the symbolic role of Mexico's revolutionary legacy in the twentieth century. She frames her own experience of exile within that broader history of anti-fascist struggles. But just as it is necessary to grasp the importance of this image of Mexico as a standard bearer in the struggle against fascism and dictatorship, so too should we confront its illusory elements and try to understand why these illusions are crucial to Mercado's work. Mercado's work confronts the harsh lessons of history—she herself lived some of them. Yet her writing does not rest there. Unlike many other contemporary Argentine thinkers who were committed leftists in the 1970s, Mercado evokes that time without repudiating it, as if refusing to let hindsight guide her recollections about her political passions.

For instance, we note that in her portrait of President Echeverría, Mercado evades the historical ironies surrounding a government that simultaneously repressed domestic opposition and supported the leftist consciousness of Argentine exiles. Echeverría's sinister legacy in domestic affairs remains an unfinished chapter in Mexican history. In 1968, at the time of the Tlatelolco massacre, Echeverría was secretary of the interior and as such was considered directly responsible for the events that occurred. Surviving members of the student movement have charged him with committing genocide for his role in Tlatelolco. His term as president (1970–1976), meanwhile, saw the expansion of Mexico's own "dirty war" against activists, which led to serious cases of state terror, including the Corpus Christi Massacre of 1971, in which students were gunned down by the paramilitary group Los Halcones; Echeverría refused to investigate the massacre.

Mercado's account of Mexican immigration policies is also noticeably romanticized. In the case of Jewish refugees from Europe, the historical record paints a grim picture, since "throughout the period of Nazi persecution (1933–45) Mexico accepted only 1,850 Jews."[94] Jewish immigrants without refugee status had been prohibited entry since 1934.[95] In contrast, more than twenty thousand Spanish Republicans gained entry during the 1930s, and an estimated six thousand to ten thousand Argentines were welcomed during the 1970s.[96] Judit Bokser Liwerant, Daniela Gleizer, and Yael Siman document Mexico's repeated refusals to seriously consider accepting Jews over the course of the 1930s and point out that its acceptance of Spanish Republicans was used at one point as an argument *against* accepting Jews.[97]

Meanwhile, back in the 1970s, other Argentine writers, in contrast to Mercado, stressed how difficult it was to make a life in Mexico. This was not just because of the cultural dislocations that Argentines experienced there but also because Mexico, in their view, enforced a set of particularly ungenerous immigration laws that sent the exiles into a frustrating bureaucratic limbo, a process that Jorge Luis Bernetti and Mempo Giardinelli recount in their book on the Argentine experience of exile in Mexico.[98] Both lived in Mexico during Argentina's last military dictatorship, and their view of the official welcome they received is decidedly less rosy than Mercado's. They describe the bureaucracy imposed by the Mexican secretary of the interior as "interminable" and "Kafka-esque."[99] The process of regularizing one's status as a legal immigrant was "extraordinarily complex" because of "Mexico's meticulous and discriminatory legislation towards foreigners."[100]

It is not that Mercado did not also experience the many hardships of exile. Indeed, she reflects on the difficulty of maintaining "bridges or ties of solidarity" in an environment so highly charged with cultural difference and notes that the "internationalism" so dear to "socialist ethics" was constantly being tested in exile by the differences that separated Argentines from Mexicans and splintered the exile community into factions.[101] Yet those differences were not absolute, and in Mercado's telling the threshold between them was constantly being crossed by the gestures of solidarity that Mexicans extended to her and her compatriots. These included offers of gainful employment, such as the one extended to Mercado by Vicente Leñero, Mexican novelist, critic, and screenwriter, who in the 1970s worked as an editor at the journal *Revista de Revistas*, a supplement to the daily newspaper *Excélsior*. He hired Mercado to write a few pieces for the journal on topics that had little or nothing to do with her particular areas of interest or expertise, including a piece on industrial design and, significantly, a piece on Holocaust survivors living in Mexico City.

1975: Four Holocaust Testimonies

The article appeared in June 1975 and bore the title "Cuatro historias del terror nazi." It is a short article, six pages largely taken up by photographs of life in the concentration camps, and it also contains brief testimonies—a few paragraphs each—of four Jewish survivors whom Mercado had interviewed. The first testimony was from Dunia Wasserstrom, founder and president of the Mexican Union of Resistance Members, Deportees and Victims of the Second World War. She was an Auschwitz survivor who been deported as a Jew and as a member of the French Resistance. The second came from Salomón Schlosser, a member of the same organization as Dunia, a survivor of the Lodz ghetto and Auschwitz.[102] The third was from Simón Rubinstein, a Belgian Jew who had evaded capture by Belgian and French police and escaped ahead of German forces to Spain. The fourth person to offer testimony was Eva Alexandra Uchmany, born in Czechoslovakia. Also an Auschwitz survivor, as an eight-year-old she had escaped selection to the gas chamber by hiding under a stranger's nightshirt. In Mexico, Uchmany became a historian of colonial Mexico.

Mercado's prefatory words to the article draw attention to themes of solidarity and human dignity. She says of the experience of listening to the survivors:

> Many times the survivor's voice would break with pain, indignation or rebellion. Other times they would be moved by the memory of solidarity and comradeship. Thirty years after the

end of the war and the liberation of the prisoners who escaped extermination, to know about and mark these events is a human obligation. Looking into the eyes of these survivors—implacable mirror; opening one's ears to their words and letting one's skin shudder with each tremor that passes through them, we and the men and women of new generations extol man's dignity.[103]

The survivors, too, emphasize the theme of solidarity, and each speaks of its importance in the death camps. Dunia Wasserstrom remembers how she would try to give hope to other inmates, saying, "I am with you. . . . Be strong, comrade!"[104] Salomón Schlosser tells an anecdote about a prisoner who stole into the infirmary at Auschwitz to give water to a sick friend. He reflects: "Solidarity would have saved many people."[105] Eva Alexandra Uchmany also emphasizes this point in the description of her experiences. She says: "There was an incredible spirit of comradery and solidarity. . . . I was able to survive only because of [the bread] my comrades gave me. Everybody helped out."[106] Her parents had perished in the camps early on, yet she was able to receive a final message from her father thanks to another inmate. The message said: "You must endure."[107] Simón Rubinstein, finally, recalls his decision while in hiding not to leave behind a group of Jews who relied on him as a leader even though doing so meant he lost an opportunity to save his mother.[108]

The survivors are speaking here about what Tzvetan Todorov, in *Facing the Extreme*, his study of testimonies by survivors of the Nazi camps and the Soviet gulags, refers to as "ordinary virtues," including "dignity, caring, the life of the mind," as distinct from the "traditional heroic virtues," such as "strength, courage, loyalty."[109] "Acts of ordinary virtue benefit individuals," he explains, while acts of heroism can be undertaken for abstract concepts ("Poland" is the abstraction he mentions).[110] Both kinds of virtue make themselves present in the "limit situations" he examines, but it is on the examples of ordinary virtue, including in the Nazi death camps and death transports, that he dwells most, so as to understand the existence, shockingly, of "a moral life" in the camps: "Alongside examples illustrating the disappearance of all moral sensibilities, one finds examples that have a different lesson to teach," he notes, and shows how these examples are brought forward by survivors almost in spite of themselves, for their main themes remain the pitilessness and moral corruption of the places in which they found themselves.[111]

Pilar Calveiro draws on Todorov's discussion of ordinary virtues in her study of the Argentine concentrationary universe, of which she herself is a survivor. She notes that there is less testimony about these acts because they went largely "unobserved" and highlights the "serious commitment" ("compromiso grave") they required because of the dangers involved for those who practiced them.[112] But ordinary virtues were absolutely necessary for survival in the camps: "These were practiced constantly and formed the basis of subsistence for the majority of survivors, greatly increasing their physical, psychological and spiritual strength. Without the circulation of these daily virtues, survival would have been simply impossible."[113] Calveiro's language is strikingly similar to the language of Mercado's interviewees.

Do Mercado's interviews of Holocaust survivors in Mexico 1975 paint too rosy a picture of the Nazi camps? Her approach is uncomfortably close to that of the 1977 NBC miniseries *Holocaust*, which drew outraged commentary from survivors who found its depiction of solidarity in the camps utterly false. Wieviorka notes that Simone Veil, an Auschwitz survivor, "rejected the miniseries vision of the relationship among prisoners, portrayed as attentive to one another and acting in solidarity. Prisoners might have stolen the blanket of someone who died, as the series shows, but, she points out, they could also take the blanket from another living prisoner, which is not shown [in the miniseries]."[114] To focus on solidarity would from this perspective evade confrontation with Primo Levi's "grey zone" of the camp, by which everyone, inmates and guards alike, became an active participant in carrying out the violence and was thereby made morally complicit in it, a situation that made companionship among inmates a rare occurrence.[115]

But if Mercado's intervention in *Revista de Revistas* evades the gray zone, it is not because of the lofty tones of virtuous idealism in her opening lines, which might seem to cloak, to hide, the grim truths described by the survivors. If we listen carefully to these tones, carried within the abstract nouns, we hear other voices. She is making a statement about the importance of hearing difficult stories, and of being heard as one tells them; this is where the question of dignity and obligation comes in, abstractions made concrete in that moment of encounter. For Mercado, this testimonial situation is a visceral experience. It generates solidarity because of the physical closeness of speaker and listener. This is the Holocaust "unmoored" from its original time and place by the energies of the sympathetic nervous system that the testimonial situation has released.

It appears that Eva Alexandra Uchmany was especially sensitive to the testimonial situation, and that for this reason Mercado's relationship with her was the most formative. In 2002, at an event on memory and history for the Comisión Provincial de la Memoria in La Plata, Argentina, Mercado tells Eva's story again, this time explaining more about the interview's immediate context.¹¹⁶ She says that Eva was known to others in Mexico's small survivor community as someone who did not like to talk about her experience. Dunia Wasserstrom had said of herself in the *Revista de Revistas* interview that she wanted "to write, to speak . . . to shout out in the name of those who are gone."¹¹⁷ In contrast, Eva, or so Mercado was told, was not the kind who liked to shout about it. Mercado recalls that when she arrived at Eva's door, she did not expect to be let in: "I had been told ahead of time that she didn't give interviews and not once in the past thirty years had anyone managed to get her to talk about her history. But she let me in when she found out I was Argentine and in exile, as if, barring the differences, she thought of me as an equal, someone she could talk to, a foreigner."¹¹⁸ Eva's perception of their shared situation of exile rendered Mercado "equal to her" yet also "a stranger" or "foreigner" ("una extranjera"). The phrase evokes what Bruce Robbins refers to as the "old cosmopolitan ideal of transcending the distinction between strangers and friends."¹¹⁹ Mercado explains that she and Eva were "fellows" or "neighbors" to one another ("Fuimos prójima una de la otra"). She notes: "[Eva] was immediately interested because of the theme of Argentina—she became interested because I came from a situation of dictatorship."¹²⁰ Eva's notions of solidarity extended to include Mercado and other Argentine exiles, and she became a supporter of the Comisión Argentina de Solidaridad, the exile solidarity group in Mexico that Mercado had cofounded.

Uchmany's testimonial situation was also distinct from that of the others because Mercado was, apparently, the first person to have created it for her. Wasserstrom had provided her testimony before, first in France after the war in a book and in newspaper articles, later at the 1964 Frankfurt "Auschwitz" trial.¹²¹ Her words were then included by playwright Peter Weiss in his 1965 play *The Investigation*, which drew directly from the Frankfurt trial transcripts.¹²² Schlosser, as a fellow member with Wasserstrom of the Union of Resistance Members, Deportees and Victims of the Second World War, had already participated in an established circle of shared experiences. For his part, Simón Rubinstein was the author of a lengthy novel based on his Holocaust experience, titled *Sobrevivir* and self-published in Mexico in 1970.¹²³ Their stories were already in circulation in one form or another, and had been shaped by demands that had little to do with their encounter with Mercado. Uchmany's testimony, in contrast, came about through her interpersonal encounter with an Argentine socialist in exile, who was its very particular initial destinatee. Again we see a contrast with other modes of Holocaust testimony from the period, with other *situations* of testimony.

It was shaped not by a state-sponsored legal proceeding, nor by a survivors' association, nor by a commercial television show, but, improbably, by the idea of political solidarity shared by two women and hosted, also improbably, by Mexico, a revolutionary state but also a perpetrator state responsible for Cold War horrors of its own.

The Politics of Survivor Testimonies

A time came during the Mexican exile when the demands of political solidarity clashed with and ultimately silenced the testimony of Argentine survivors of torture and disappearance. The political commitments of Argentine exilees in the 1970s, their principled disagreements over political tactics, and their complex relation with activists in Argentina made for a fractious community. Bernetti and Giardinelli treat us to a list of no fewer than nineteen political groups operating in Mexico within the Argentine exile community.[124] These divisions were particularly apparent during a painful episode involving testimonies by former detainees of Argentina's clandestine concentration camps. The testimonies had begun to circulate in 1979 thanks to the work of Argentine exilees in Spain (via the Comisión Argentina por los Derechos Humanos, CADHU) and then in 1980 in reports by Amnesty International.[125] Some of these survivors had escaped; others had been released. Mercado was directly involved in helping to circulate these testimonies at the time and would later turn to Holocaust testimony to reflect on their significance.

The debate over "los testimonios de los sobrevivientes," as it came to be called, was especially acute in Mexico. It unfolded against the backdrop of the human rights movement's increasing visibility in Argentina itself and reflected some of the tensions between intellectuals who had gone into exile and intellectuals who had remained in Argentina. The debate had been instigated by Héctor Schmucler in December 1980 in the journal *Controversia*, published by a heterogeneous group of Peronist exilees in Mexico (some of these, like Nicolás Casullo and Schmucler, would go on to start the journal *Confines* in 1995, discussed in Chapter 2). Schmucler accepted as true the junta's statements that the concentration camps had largely ceased functioning and that the detainees were dead.[126] At the time, this was a highly polemical statement. In 1979 the junta had declared that most of the "subversives" it had detained were either dead or living underground, a view that it circulated in an attempt to defuse the forthcoming report of the Interamerican

Commission of Human Rights (CIDH, sponsored by the Organization of American States), which was expected to be severely critical of the human rights situation in Argentina.[127] The Madres de Plaza de Mayo, increasingly the center around which human rights activism mobilized in Argentina, became more active in responding to these declarations, demanding proof of death and eventually rallying around the slogan "Aparición con vida de los desaparecidos," meant to sustain international pressure on the regime and keep criminal accusations against it alive.[128]

Schmucler disagreed entirely with this line of action. In *Controversia* he called the Madres "pathetic" and accused those who were fighting for greater accountability from the regime and to secure the release of the disappeared to be more interested in defending their own entrenched positions than in the dead.[129] He considered the memory of the dead to be an important element of political action going forward, but not the fight to secure information about the disappeared and press for their liberation. Many *Controversia* readers wrote in to respond to Schmucler and set the record straight on this point. Author Mempo Giardinelli, along with the Solidarity Commission for Family Members Imprisoned, Killed and Disappeared for Political Reasons (Comisión de Solidaridad de Familiares Presos, Muertos y Desaparecidos por Razones Políticas, COSOFAM) in Spain, as well as others, explained to Schmucler the political importance of continuing to apply pressure on the regime to release information about the disappeared and pointed out that disappearances were still happening.[130] Meanwhile, Schmucler also used evidence from the testimonies to criticize the Montoneros organization for being a hierarchical and dogmatic "machine" whose militants had already lost the taste for struggle before they fell into the military's hands, and to argue that the weakness, internal contradictions, and authoritarian structures of militant organizations were factors in their defeat.[131] Giardinelli accused him of exonerating the junta by shifting blame to the guerrillas.[132]

Mercado's take on this debate, twenty-five years later, does not address the questions of political tactic that these testimonies had given rise to, that is, whether to keep pressing for the liberation of disappeared political prisoners or shift to other demands and whether to engage in a critique of revolutionary militants or focus exclusively on the military government. Instead, she calls attention to how human rights groups, especially the Madres, silenced the survivors' speech. This censorship happened because the CADHU and Amnesty International testimonies provided witness statements about the now infamous "traslados" or "transfers," a euphemism for "murder" or "execution" that circulated in the Argentine camps, and suggested that prisoners were being drugged and thrown out of airplanes alive.[133] In discussing this, the survivors were partially confirming the military junta's official statements. To accept as true the testimony of the survivors, who recounted that their comrades had been murdered by the military, was therefore seen in a negative light by the Madres and other groups, as a betrayal of the human rights movement and as becoming complicit with the junta's politics of forgetting.

A key point in these debates concerned the empirical and moral reliability of the witnesses. Empirically there was the question of whether detainees could know for certain the fate of their comrades. COSOFAM's statement against the presumption of death focused on the "subjective" and partial nature of the testimonies, which did not provide sufficient proof that most detainees were dead.[134] Even the three survivors who wrote in to contradict Schmucler's account took up this approach, saying that it would be wrong to generalize any broad conclusions from these testimonies because they reflected the individual experiences of the prisoners.[135] Giardinelli echoed COSOFAM on the question of proof, holding that the survivors' accounts of the dead were ultimately unreliable because they had not been in a position to unequivocally confirm that "traslados" meant death.[136] But he took his questioning of the survivors' reliability a step farther by insisting on the possibility that some of them were collaborators with, if not outright agents of, the regime.[137] All of these statements, by COSOFAM, the survivors, and Giardinelli, undermined the possibility that the survivors might be witnesses to anything but their own most individual circumstances. COSOFAM and Giardinelli also minimized the testimonies' ultimate importance. COSOFAM referred to the testimonies as "so-called 'survivor testimonies'" ("los llamados 'testimonios de los sobrevivientes'"), while Giardinelli urged his readers "to pay less attention to the 'testimonies of the survivors' and more attention to the 'survivors of the testimonies.' That is, the disappeared."[138]

Mercado, writing in 2002 about these debates, explains that she refused to call into doubt the veracity and moral standing of the survivors as their putative allies had done. She recounts an interesting anecdote from those years. She had been in Spain when one of the survivors testified to the CADHU about the La Perla camp. Within hours Mercado was given a transcript of the testimony, which she brought back to Mexico. But the next day she received a call from the witness herself, asking Mercado to destroy that first transcript. When the second version of the transcript appeared, all references to "traslados" had been redacted from it. The survivor's original words had been changed, with her consent, so that her testimony would support the tactics of the Madres and other human rights group calling for "aparición con vida" ("return alive of the disappeared").[139] Mercado says that she did not question openly the command to destroy the original testimony, but she was unable to carry it out. For Mercado, this "no to testimony" was akin to death: "The erased and censored word, the images covered up, were a second death, an excess death" ("sobremuerte").[140]

In this reference to the silenced word as a form of death, Mercado is not making a straightforward comparison between the death of a person and censorship of words and images. What has been killed, so to speak, is the affirmative potential of the testimonial situation that she discovered in her encounter with an Auschwitz survivor, its action of liberating memory to trouble the world with the disturbing knowledge it carries. "Eva's story opened the box of my memory," she notes, and it "held zones of pain that demanded to be spoken and liberated."[141] This is why she said of the Argentine survivor testimonies that they "were narratives like the ones written by the survivors of the Nazi camps."[142] Mónica Szurmuk has written of Mercado that she "socializes memory,"[143] and indeed, this is what her interviews with Holocaust survivors sought to convey—testimony as a shared event, memory brought into a shared world. The censoring of the La Perla testimony banished it, locked it away, turned it into a nonevent.

Mercado's valorization of testimony carries a charge similar to Pacheco's in the second edition of *Morirás lejos*—it responds to censorship. Except that here, in the situation that Mercado describes, it is not just state terror that is responsible for the silencing of testimonial voices, but also the left and the human rights movement, especially the Madres, who censored one of the most exhaustive testimonies of the moment.[144] It was a discouraging turn of events. We might be tempted to use this story of censorship by the left to reinforce for us the liberal frame whereby the dogmatism of the left mirrors the authoritarianism of the right, both of which require superseding by the democratic pluralism of the kind represented by the Alfonsín presidency. Indeed, when the state created its own testimonial situation for the CONADEP report, it seemed to inscribe the very possibility of testimony within that double rejection of right and left, as if only in the absence of ideological commitment could the voices of the witnesses carry the weight of truth.[145] But it would be a serious mistake to interpret Mercado's take on the controversy over survivor testimony as advocating an approach to victim testimony that is innocent of politics. Mercado has been vocal in opposing the "two demons theory" that positions Argentine civil society as the apolitical victim of militant politics on the right and the left, a view that suggests a false equivalence between these two vastly unequal opponents. She has remained remarkably consistent in her approach to the testimonial situation as one whose action in the present has the potential to open the future to thought, even when the testimony itself describes a past of abject defeat and destruction. Her memory work injects a sense of contingency, of an open horizon, into political imaginaries that might otherwise become frozen by past losses and mistakes or by the demands of political immediacy.

The critique that Mercado offers of the left for its mistakes might also at first glance appear similar to the critique of the 1970s left offered by Nicolás Casullo that I discussed in Chapter 2, because both involve an element of Holocaust consciousness. Casullo, like Mercado, looks back at *Controversia* and old debates about loaded words. Specifically, he reconsiders the debate sparked by Lilia Walsh in 1980 when she spoke of her husband Rodolfo as "dead" rather than as a "political prisoner."[146] Casullo turned to German-language philosophers whose fears about the contamination of German by Nazism and their suspicion of language as itself a part of the problem allowed him to think about "the debacle of language in Argentine society," which requires "a word that doesn't 'speak'" in order to confront the past more authentically.[147] Casullo's is a kind of anti-testimony manifesto. But Mercado's Holocaust archive is totally different from Casullo's, and though she confronts the same events as Casullo, it leads her to different conclusions about the left's defeat. She invokes the work of the murdered ghetto scribes Simon Dubnow and Emmanuel Ringelblum, noting: "To do history [hacer la historia] was a militant decision for those heroes."[148] Their words "summarize the complete utopia of writing as resistance."[149] She turns to the testimonies of the direct witnesses and to their commitment to speak about what they saw: Dubnow's "schreibn un farshreibn," to write and to record;[150] Dunia Wasserstrom's need "to write, to speak . . . to shout out in the name of those who are gone."[151] Casullo's thinking operates by paradox and self-deconstruction and, following Canetti, searches for a pure language that he knows cannot be found. Mercado's is affirmative, inscriptive, open to contingency and hope, and unconcerned by fears of linguistic contamination. Notice how her language is laden with the political words of the vanquished 1970s—"militant," "utopia," "resistance." As Szurmuk has noted in reference to Mercado's writing, "the language is the key."[152] In Mercado's work, testimony and memory are offered not to break with the leftist past, not to leave it behind as so many archaic shards, but to make cloth from its fragments.

Conclusion

Pacheco's work with testimony follows a more oblique and difficult path than Mercado's. A short time before the first edition of *Morirás lejos* appeared, Pacheco reflected on Adorno's famous words about the barbarity of writing poetry after Auschwitz.[153] Pacheco debates with himself as to the possibility of his own writing if language has become complicit in the violent system it seeks to criticize: "Since the only way to not be complicit in our era is by passive resistance, silence can be a mode of protest against contemporary injustice and abjection. But this nihilism today is a profoundly reactionary attitude: it is necessary to write, precisely because it has become an impossible activity."[154] Pacheco's comments seem both to recognize and to refuse the abyss that Adorno identified in his comments. Adorno eventually revised his views on the matter. Ten years after his first statement, he insisted: "I refuse to soften my statement that it is barbaric to write poetry after Auschwitz." But he added: "Suffering—what Hegel called the awareness of affliction—also demands the continued existence of the very art it forbids."[155] *Morirás lejos* rehearses these debates across its pages. Although here I have sought to highlight a greater commitment to testimony from the first version to the second, it would be erroneous to call either version simply "pro-testimony" and ignore the novel's profound doubts about the potential of memory and history to illuminate the past and find a measure of redemption for past crimes. In this novel, the righteous are guilty too, and the evils of history weigh over everyone. But it is no exaggeration to say that above and beyond these doubts, we can perceive a need to tell of the crimes and remember them as such.

Pacheco turns fiction into a particular form of testimony, one whose validity extends beyond the literary realm narrowly conceived. In a piece published in 1983, Pacheco muses on the "oblique testimony" that fiction provides and highlights again the intertwined scenarios of the Argentine dictatorship and the Holocaust:

> There is a *truth* to literature that is distinct from the *truth* of documents. . . . The science of historiography bases its rigor on its slavery to the document. Five years ago, German historians debated the scientific impossibility of holding Hitler responsible for the Holocaust: no one has ever found a written text that gives the order for genocide. Kafka wrote about totalitarianism and the concentrationary universe without having seen them.

> In *Artificial Respiration* [a 1980 Argentine novel], without one direct allusion to it and by means of a supposed "literary game," Ricardo Piglia gives us an oblique testimony—but from within—of what Argentina has lived through during these past years.[156]

This piece refers to David Irving's book about Hitler, which Pacheco had already condemned in an earlier essay.[157] Here, denialism provokes new reflection on the testimonial value of literature in cases in which the existing documentation about state crimes does not meet legal standards of evidence and in which, in any event, the political openings for judicial proceedings against perpetrators do not (yet) exist.

If for Pacheco the question first arose in relation to Holocaust memory in the age of Holocaust denialism, it gained a renewed significance in Mexico in the age of Tlatelolco and the Argentine dictatorship. In both his work and Mercado's, Holocaust testimony is a catalyst for unleashing political memories of dictatorship in Latin America. Both authors helped circulate Holocaust testimony in 1970s Mexico and bring into focus the Latin American affinity for a reparative approach to the Holocaust to meet the demands emanating from a defeated, exiled, and fractious left.

Chapter Four

Demetrio Cojtí Cuxil's "Maya Holocaust"

Victims and Vanquished in Post-genocide Guatemala[1]

Yeqanataj ri qach'alal xekäm ruma rutikik rutzeqelb'exik, runimirisaxik ri Maya' na'oj. / En memoria de los miembros del Movimiento Maya abatidos durante el tercer holocausto Maya. (In memory of the members of the Maya Movement struck down during the third Maya holocaust.)[2]

A pesar de 500 años . . . ¡estamos presentes! (Despite five hundred years . . . we are still here!)[3]

The Guatemalan Civil War lasted thirty-six years, from 1960 to 1996. Within that long period, the years 1981–1983 stand out because of the kind and number of atrocities suffered by unarmed civilians. During those years, the Guatemalan army waged a scorched-earth campaign in rural areas that directly targeted Maya villagers. The army had been trained by the United States in anti-Communist counterinsurgency techniques, which they then applied to Maya communities located near zones of guerrilla activity. Under the leadership of General Efraín Ríos Montt, the Guatemalan army systematically exterminated Mayas. The Guatemalan Commission for Historical Clarification, a truth commission administered by the United Nations, documented the kinds of extermination methods used by the army, noting "evidence of multiple ferocious acts," such as killing children by beating them against walls or throwing them into open graves to be crushed by corpses; impaling people, burning them alive as public spectacle, extracting their organs, or amputating their limbs; cutting open the bellies of pregnant women; gang rape of children and women; and the list goes on.[4] The truth commission estimated that over two hundred thousand people had been murdered or disappeared during the course of the war; 83 percent of them were Mayas.[5] It found the army to have acted with "an aggressive racist component" and deemed the army's actions against Mayas "genocidal."[6]

How has this violence been denounced and remembered, in Guatemala and abroad? What role has Holocaust consciousness played in the collective memory of the atrocities? In approaching the construction of memory in Guatemala, we note immediately the absence of anything approaching the "memory boom" that characterizes Southern Cone countries. Until very recently, the dominant narrative in Guatemala regarding the early 1980s supported the military's versions of events and downplayed or outright denied that massacres had taken place; there was a "forgetting boom" instead of a memory boom. Eduardo Galeano referred to Guatemala's history as "mutilated" because of the pressure to remain silent about the extent of the violence committed by the Guatemalan state.[7] It was not until General Ríos Montt was formally charged with genocide in 2013 that knowledge of the massacres became more widely diffused and their existence more accepted.[8] Legal scholar Lisa Laplante writes:

> Until the genocide trial, the economic and political elite of Guatemala did not have to actively promote a memory that denied the atrocity of the war; they merely relied on the existing dominant collective memory put in place as a part of the repressive design of the war, which violently eliminated contestation. The trial suddenly disturbed this hegemonic memory. All at once, the economic and political elite had to exert a concerted effort to maintain their interpretation of the past.[9]

Even now, however, and despite an initial guilty verdict against Ríos Montt, the military has continued to maintain control over the terms of the debate. Many Guatemalans seem to agree with its view that the violence against Mayas, because it was motivated politically by anti-Communism, was justifiable and should not be prosecuted.[10]

Yet there have been many attempts to combat the silence about the atrocities. The figure of "genocide" has played an important role in drawing attention to the severity of the violence, starting well before the 1999 determination by the Commission for Historical Clarification. During the events themselves, Guatemalan activists, some operating in exile, referred to "genocide" in report after report about the situation on the ground, based on direct witness testimony.[11] International solidarity activists did so as well.[12] The Permanent People's Tribunal, held in Madrid in 1983 and a successor to the 1967 Russell Tribunal, charged Ríos Montt with genocide after listening to witnesses and survivors of village massacres and to presentations by scholar-activists such as Arturo Arias and Ricardo Falla.[13]

Indigenous activists, meanwhile, had already been making the connection to genocide, starting in the 1970s. Maya thinkers and community leaders linked contemporary atrocities to the historical events of the Conquest of Guatemala by Pedro de Alvarado in 1524, considered an especially cruel and terrible endeavor, even by the bloody standards of the day. In response to the 1978 Panzos massacre of unarmed peasants by the Guatemalan army, Maya leaders used the term "genocide" to condemn the violence.[14] The 1980 Iximché Declaration, a document authored by Indigenous activists to denounce atrocities committed by the Guatemalan army in the Maya highlands, placed Cold War violence within the broader context of colonialism: "The suffering of our people has been going on for centuries, since 1524, when the murderer and criminal Pedro de Alvarado arrived on these lands."[15] Eight years later Maya survivors of the army's scorched-earth campaign testified before the United Nations and reiterated this long temporal frame: "During five hundred years we have been the victims of a colonial expansion that subjected us to a brutal genocide."[16] These connections would become more prolific as the five hundredth anniversary of Columbus's 1492 "discovery of the Americas" approached, shaping perceptions of the very recent past in Guatemala. "This situation is so disastrous," wrote Maya authors Victor Montejo and Q'anil Akab' in 1992, in reference to the 1980s massacres, "that it is comparable to the genocide committed during the invasion of these lands at the start of the sixteenth century."[17] The term "genocide" helps link the two temporal frames, colonialism and the Cold War, and has been gathering progressively wider acceptance in the post-conflict period.

The term "holocaust," in contrast, has not occupied a large role in public consciousness in Guatemala. Yet in both overt and hidden ways, the Holocaust is embedded in the archive of responses to Guatemala's terror, specifically in the archive of Maya writings about the war and its connection to colonialism. This archive has been largely hidden from view. Michael Rothberg has noted that "there is no shortage of cross-referencing between the legacies of the Holocaust and colonialism, but many of those moments of contact occur in marginalized texts or in marginal moments of well-known texts."[18] In Guatemala, the Holocaust appears textually and paratextually, in epigraphs, footnotes, and bibliographies, in scholarly asides and disagreements.

It is also carried implicitly in the term "genocide" itself. In Guatemala as elsewhere, "genocide" is a verbal palimpsest, layered with the speech of many voices. One such voice appeared in the 1960s, when unofficial international tribunals, modeling themselves on the Nuremberg tribunal, made connections between the Holocaust and the atrocities committed against anti-colonial insurgents. As we will see, tribunal participants called on the memory of the Holocaust and drew on the United Nations Convention for the Prevention and Punishment of the Crime of Genocide to argue that these atrocities were "genocidal" because they targeted groups seeking national self-determination. When Maya and other activists speak of genocide in Guatemala, we hear an echo of the voice that subtly links Holocaust memory to the cause of Indigenous anti-colonial self-determination. To say of the army massacres, "This is a holocaust," or, "We are victims of genocide," is also to say, "We exist as a people—a 'we' exists here, and we refuse to disappear."

"No living word relates to its object in a singular way," writes Mikhail Bakhtin. "Between the word and its object," he continues, "between the word and the speaking subject, there exists an elastic environment of other, alien words about the same object, the same theme."[19] So it is with "genocide" and "holocaust." This chapter considers the layered meanings of these words in Guatemala, developed across transnational "elastic environments" in the post-WWII era. It focuses specifically on use of the term "Maya holocaust," an emblematic moment in Guatemalan memory debates in which these separate events and their disparate time lines—the discovery and conquest of the Americas and its commemoration five hundred years later, the Guatemalan genocide of the 1980s, the Jewish Holocaust and its diverse legacies—came into contact with one another.

The term "Maya holocaust" was introduced into the postwar environment in the 1990s by a prominent Maya scholar and activist, Demetrio Cojtí Cuxil. Dr. Cojtí was one of the most prolific spokespeople for the Maya Movement in Guatemala.[20] He was a leading participant in many Maya activist and intellectual organizations and is the author of numerous books and articles. In the 1990s he was one of the main authors published by Cholsamaj Press, a venue for influential Maya thinkers. In his scholarly work, journalism, and public speeches, Cojtí advocated recognition of a distinct "Maya People" possessed of collective cultural and political rights. He has been a fierce critic of racism in Guatemala and of the country's long-standing situation of internal colonialism, and in the 1990s he gave voice to some of the Maya Movement's most radical demands in the areas of territorial and political autonomy and linguistic and other cultural rights.

The contemporary Maya Movement is an influential political and cultural phenomenon in the struggle for Maya self-determination in Guatemala. Its roots lie in the 1970s, and it gained energy in the early 1990s, due in part to international initiatives marking the five hundredth anniversary of 1492, including the awarding of the Nobel Peace Prize to Rigoberta Menchú in 1992 and the UN's proclamation of the "International Decade of the World's Indigenous Peoples" (1995–2004). Also important to its development were initiatives in Guatemala with respect to the evolving peace process between the government and the guerrillas.[21] The Maya Movement made its voice heard in national and international forums. Maya scholar-activists participated in discussions about greater Maya electoral participation, about the Peace Accords, and about the return of Maya refugees, and for a few years the Maya Movement became a defining presence on Guatemala's political scene.[22]

Cojtí's decision to use the name "holocaust" and thereby link Guatemalan historical coordinates to the Jewish catastrophe did not gain a wide audience in the broader public, but it intensified a set of fears among scholars about how we name and remember the victims of Guatemala's civil war. The terms "holocaust" and "genocide" bring to mind images of defenseless victims defined by their belonging to a single ethnic group, and the terms are often seen to imply a clear division between the perpetrators of violence and the victims of violence. The concern is that such terms will therefore paint a misleading portrait of Guatemala's Cold War history, especially in the period of the 1960–1996 armed conflict, by focusing attention away from the fact that many of the war's victims were non-Indigenous and that many, both Indigenous and other, belonged to insurgent groups, armed and unarmed.

What I will show here is that the intellectual genealogy behind Cojtí's "Maya holocaust" owes more to national liberation movements around the globe than to the human rights framework we now associate with the concept of "genocide." These points of reference to Third World anti-colonial struggles can easily be missed, leading to a misinterpretation of Cojtí's usage. What has gone unremarked about Cojtí's overt declaration of a Holocaust connection to Guatemala is that it carries those less perceptible layerings that "genocide" has accrued since its 1948 origins. The Guatemalan case I discuss here is therefore symptomatic of the complex overlap between "holocaust" and "genocide" as historical concepts, which may carry unspoken connotations of political resistance that are no longer as transparent as they might have been a few decades ago. This chapter is centrally concerned with these semantics of "holocaust" and "genocide" in Guatemala. But it is also concerned with the missing terms "conquest" and "colonialism," which must be returned to the conversation if we are to understand Cojtí's invocation of a "Maya holocaust."

Victims and Vanquished in Cold War Historiography

In approaching the semantics of state violence in Guatemala, especially use of the term "holocaust," it is important to understand that until quite recently much of it developed not in the Guatemalan public sphere itself but in a kind of parallel plane to the north. Scholars and activists in the United States, as well as other international actors, have played an important role in providing the "social framework" for creating a collective memory in Guatemala that involves a Holocaust element.[23] This happened in two distinct waves: first in the 1980s, in writings by human rights and solidarity activists in the United States, Mexico, and Canada, and second in the 1990s, in academic scholarship on Guatemala produced in the United States. There is a far greater presence of Holocaust references in works on the Guatemalan atrocity published in the United States, whether by Guatemalan or U.S. scholars, than in works published in Guatemala. We can therefore infer that the saturation of U.S. public consciousness by Holocaust images plays a role in Guatemalan memory scholarship.

The concern as regards Guatemala arises among scholars who worry about the misuse of human rights discourses for regressive political ends. Critics offer two related objections to the Holocaust and human rights discourses as interpretive frames: one, that these frames simplify history and lead to a distorted understanding of the conflict as one between Indigenous people and their ladino oppressors (the term "ladino" refers to "mestizo" and "white" Guatemalans), whereas in fact ladinos were also victims; two, that they disempower citizens by viewing them as passive sufferers of abuse. The circulation of the terms "genocide" and "holocaust" may therefore play into the hands of neoliberal governments that adopt the language of human rights superficially, in order to divert attention away from enduring structures of inequality or pursue a dependence on international aid. Geographer Elizabeth Oglesby asks: "In the strains of *nunca más* (never again) that echo across Latin America, one might also hear efforts at a parallel refrain: never again to genocide, yes, but what about the simultaneous silencing of the histories of collective, contestatory politics?"[24]

Whether Holocaust comparisons are "analytically appropriate" in understanding the Guatemalan genocide hinges on the question of whether those who were targets of state terror in Latin America can be considered "victims" in the same way as the Jewish victims of Nazism.[25] Contemporary Holocaust consciousness in Latin America has been largely shaped as a response to the atrocities committed by states that invoked a "Doctrine of National Security" to launch anti-Communist counterinsurgency wars against their own populations. But were those whom the state targeted in these campaigns innocent civilians or partisan activists? Were they Indigenous people or labor and peasant organizers? I pose these questions in stark either-or dichotomies because such polarities mark the debate about Maya political activism and its relationship to the various projects of Guatemala's multifaceted social and political movements. Historian Greg Grandin wonders: "Does labeling the massacres genocide overshadow the fact that the state was being challenged by a powerful, multiethnic coalition demanding economic and political reform? . . . Does it deny Indigenous participation in the popular movement and reduce the repression to a simplified tale of ladino violence heaped on defenseless Indians?"[26] To be clear, neither Grandin nor Oglesby denies that a genocide took place; quite the contrary.[27] But both would insist that the semantics of genocide cannot be dismissed as a merely superficial question; the terms we give to these events play a fundamental role in how we understand political violence in Guatemala.

These concerns anticipate more recent discussions about the post-WWII memory cultures of Europe and the United States. Enzo Traverso has criticized the focus on the "victims" of European fascism while forgetting the "vanquished" of the same period. These two figures, victims and vanquished, represent for him two distinct ways of remembering the twentieth century. Traverso argues that the dominant trend is to see it as "an age of war and genocides" populated by victims and epitomized by the Holocaust.[28] The problem with this, he proposes, is that the history of left-wing political struggle in the name of utopia and revolution has been eclipsed. The figure of the victim has displaced the figure of the "vanquished," whose hopes, struggles, and defeats have consequently been lost to memory while the memory of the victims has been sacralized.[29] Scholars of Latin America's Cold War have been voicing similar reservations about the language of victimhood since the 1990s.

This debate happens within progressive circles, not between the right and left wing. In Guatemala, the conversation takes place among those who agree that the army's massacres of innocent civilians did indeed occur, and who agree that those responsible for them should be tried in criminal court. Where they differ is on the weight or emphasis that the idea of genocide should be given in understanding Guatemala's civil war. The question is posed not on legal terrain, not concerning the judicial application of the category "genocide" to Guatemala, but rather on the terrain of historical analysis. Here we see a concern with how to name and describe past atrocity and those who suffer it. The response to Cojtí's usage of the term "holocaust" revolves around his semantic choice and against the backdrop of ever more frequent uses of the term "genocide" to describe the violence.

What happens to our understanding of multiethnic political activists and armed insurgents if we term their extermination by the state a "holocaust" or a "genocide"? The languages of international human rights and of criminal justice frameworks for approaching the atrocities have also been criticized for promoting too passive a view of Indigenous people.

Anthropologist Edward Fischer refers to this as the "virtual victimization" of Maya peoples in postwar Guatemala—"the representational and symbolic violence done to them by the application of categories of victimhood and the models of victimization."[30] Such concerns can be found across the scholarship on Guatemalan memory practices in the post-genocide era, and the language of victimization has generated semantic pushback on several fronts.[31]

Oglesby warns about what happens when the connotation of "victim" becomes linked too closely to the idea of "passivity":

> It's especially important to adopt a critical posture vis-a-vis the current concept of "victim." A person can be a victim of human rights violations or other kind of injustice, but that doesn't mean that their identity is restricted to that category. The simple notion of "victim," when it is synonymous with passivity, gets us stuck in the history of death without trying to untangle the diverse social actors who have pushed the history of the country forward in one way or another.[32]

For Oglesby, writing with respect to Guatemala in the early 2000s, the problem is similar to that faced in post-dictatorship Argentina. She cites Argentine memory scholars, such as Elizabeth Jelin, who express caution about the human rights framework for understanding history because it can lead to a decontextualized view of state violence, one that centers on individualized, passive victims rather than understanding them as social actors or revealing the existence of underlying systems and structures of political subordination: "State violence is recognized, but ultimately reified, as its targets are drained of their identities as historical protagonists."[33] Indeed, historian Betsy Konefal notes more recently that in Guatemala, "genocide in the public imagination seem[s] to require an apolitical victim."[34]

Nevertheless, the past two decades have shown that attempts to "depoliticize" the victims of Cold War atrocities, attempts that were initially undertaken to make state violence in Latin America fit into the framework of international human rights practices and legal categories and that more recently appear linked to neoliberal forms of governance intent on quashing dissent, have not been entirely successful.[35] The either-or structure of the debate—either victims or vanquished—thus sheds only limited light. This is because the figure of the victim cannot easily be disentangled from the figure of the vanquished, in Guatemala as elsewhere in Latin America. Victimhood or "the victim" is quite often a politicized subject category, one that links the memory of past suffering to present-day grassroots activism in the name of social justice or to other forms of exercising active citizenship.[36] In a way that those of us steeped in American-style Holocaust remembrance might have a hard time recognizing, Holocaust consciousness in Guatemala, as in other parts of Latin America, does not necessarily or inherently detract from an activist, social justice impulse.

The "Maya Holocaust" under Debate

Within Guatemala and for a Guatemalan audience, Cojtí's may be the first use of the phrase "Maya holocaust" to refer to the atrocities of the 1980s. Starting in 1994, Cojtí began using it in his essays to reference both the Conquest and the 1980s. The phrase constitutes a small piece of Cojtí's overall scholarly contribution and has been taken up infrequently by other Maya intellectuals in their published works.[37] If we look at the textual history of the idea, its presence in words across his work, we see that it starts out as a body paragraph in one document, becomes a long scholarly footnote in three subsequent texts, and is dramatically shortened into a brief dedication in another.[38] The dedication reads: "Yeqanataj ri qach'alal xekäm ruma rutikik rutzeqelb'exik, runimirisaxik ri Maya' na'oj. / En memoria de los miembros del Movimiento Maya abatidos durante el tercer holocausto

Maya. [In memory of the members of the Maya Movement struck down during the third Maya holocaust]."

Cojtí's invocation of a "third Maya holocaust" has been criticized by two scholars in particular. One is Greg Grandin, a U.S. historian of Guatemala; the other is Edgar Esquit, a Maya historian and social anthropologist at Guatemala's University of San Carlos. Both have published significant pieces about memory politics in contemporary Guatemala.[39] These scholars take issue with the dedication quoted above, rather than the more extended scholarly references found in Cojtí's other texts. This is Cojtí's briefest, most epigraphic statement about a Maya holocaust. Because Grandin and Esquit respond only to the most truncated version of the idea, they miss some important elements of its context and significance.

Before examining Cojtí's work more closely, let us look at the three principal reasons for Grandin's and Esquit's criticisms of Cojtí's phrase. First, they hold that to speak of a "Maya holocaust" to refer to the state's campaign of terror during the civil war creates a simplistic view of history. "Maya holocaust" suggests that Indigenous people were the principal victims of state repression. But Grandin reminds us that this was true only of the period beginning in 1981. In the twenty years prior to that, it had been ladinos who were most targeted—non-Indigenous "students, peasants, union organizers, politicians and revolutionaries"—and ladinos continued to be killed during the scorched-earth campaign that devastated rural Maya communities.[40] To frame the violence as a "Maya holocaust" is therefore too schematic, says Esquit.[41] Grandin likewise argues that "scholars and activists need to be particularly careful about understanding history, conflict and violence in simple, dichotomous terms."[42] He notes that the repression should be remembered "as directed against a multiethnic popular movement" rather than as directed principally against Mayas. His research is part of a larger trend that seeks to advance a clearer picture of rural life before and during the era of army massacres so that a more nuanced image of the victims emerges.[43] This nuancing work effectively criticizes the idea of a "Maya holocaust" for presenting an incomplete or distorted view of social mobilization in the countryside.

Second, Grandin believes that the idea of a "Maya holocaust" lends support to a common bias against Indigenous people, namely, that they are the passive objects of historical action rather than active subjects of it. The subtext here is that Cojtí may be reinforcing the controversial thesis of U.S. anthropologist David Stoll's 1993 book *Between Two Armies in the Ixil Towns of Guatemala*.[44] Stoll claimed that it was the leftist guerrillas, not the state, who were ultimately responsible for the atrocities committed against rural Mayas because of the way the guerrillas conducted their insurgency strategy. He argued that, after becoming allies with Maya villagers, the guerrillas abandoned them to the military's campaign of terror, and that the guerrillas knew full well that making contact with Maya villagers effectively turned the villagers into targets of the counterinsurgency war, from which the guerrillas would be unable to defend them.[45] For Grandin and many other scholars, this view of Indigenous people as "caught between two armies," as passive victims of external forces, is historically false and perpetuates a negative stereotype. "The role Mayan Indians played in the unfolding of Guatemalan history has to be recovered," writes Grandin.[46]

Finally, Esquit and Grandin hold that to paint the violence as a "Maya holocaust" distorts Maya history itself. Esquit argues that it takes as given and therefore idealizes the existence of a unified Maya identity rather than understanding this as a historical construct.[47] Grandin suggests that historians may need to subject Maya collective memory to critical scrutiny.[48] Both scholars point to the underlying tension between collective memory and scholarly history. Cojtí, through the phrase "Maya holocaust," centers the significance of state terror of the 1980s in the collective experience and memory of the Maya people, whereas Grandin and Esquit ask that we deconstruct that very notion of a collective experience or a collective memory and seek the significance of the atrocities somewhere else, in the complex unfolding of political events.

It is not a coincidence that elsewhere Grandin has turned to Holocaust historian Arno Mayer to intervene in the Cold War historiography of Latin America and make a case for a critical, historical approach to political violence. Such an approach would not give undue weight to the testimony of survivors.[49] Mayer's book *Why Did the Heavens Not Darken? The "Final Solution" in History* positioned itself explicitly as a corrective to an overreliance on memory in Holocaust studies. Mayer writes:

> It may well be that only survivors who actually passed through the fiery ordeal of the [Nazi] killing sites, ghettos, and camps are in a position to speak to it. . . . Such eyewitness accounts are indispensable for any interpretative reading of the Judeocide. It is not to depreciate their historical value to insist, however, that they are neither complete nor in themselves sufficient. . . . The embryonic creed of "the Holocaust," which has become an *idée-force*, has taken the reflective and transparent remembrances of

survivors and woven them into a collective prescriptive "memory" unconducive to critical and contextual thinking about the Jewish calamity. . . . At the core of the modern idea of history is the axiom that historical praxis and interpretation are neither static nor consensual. . . . Whereas the voice of memory is univocal and uncontested, that of history is polyphonic and open to debate. Memory tends to rigidify over time, while history calls for revision.[50]

When Grandin and Esquit ask us to be suspicious of Cojtí's "third Maya holocaust," it is in the spirit of these disquisitions by Arno Mayer, in favor of an analysis of political violence that views it as "contingent" and "indeterminate."[51]

To summarize, then, we see that Cojtí's "third Maya holocaust" gives rise to concerns about the erasure of non-Maya victims of state terror, about the erasure of Maya participation in revolutionary organizations, and about scholarly overreliance on Maya collective memory. These issues are connected in turn to broader concerns about the increasing dominance of the human rights framework to understand the Cold War in Guatemala. Cojtí's usage, in other words, is taken as a sign for a kind of "nunca más" approach to Guatemala and as the expression of an uncritical, mythologizing memory. My argument is that some of these concerns have been misapplied to Cojtí, and that although they may be well founded in general, they constitute a misinterpretation of the significance that Cojtí attributes to the Holocaust. Let us return to Cojtí and the Maya Movement and examine his usage more closely.

The Complex Textual History of the "Maya Holocaust"

In the years leading up to 1992, Maya scholars and activists mobilized to counter the Hispanophilic celebrations of 1492 and correct the record with a Maya-centric view of history. These efforts led Mayas to participate, if marginally, in the peace process between the Guatemalan government and the guerrillas that would culminate in 1996 with the historic Accord for a Lasting and Durable Peace. Diverse social groups campaigned to have their voices heard during the peace negotiations, resulting in the creation of an umbrella group called the Civil Society Assembly (Asamblea de la Sociedad Civil, ASC), which debated key points of the proposed peace accords. Maya activists were a part of this Civil Society Assembly. In May 1994, they asked that the Assembly approve a document in favor of Maya rights that could be put forward in the peace negotiations.[52] Their proposal affirmed that a distinct Maya people had existed for thousands of years and constituted the demographic majority in Guatemala and that Maya lifeways had survived five hundred years of colonial oppression.[53] The proposal listed the cultural, linguistic, economic, civil, and territorial rights that Mayas demanded in order to rectify centuries of racial discrimination.[54]

The proposal is significant for my purposes because it contains references to "Maya holocausts." The authors used the phrase to describe the discrimination, racism, genocide, and economic exploitation the Maya had faced in Guatemala over the centuries. Part of "our reality as a Maya People," the authors stated, was that "we are the survivors of three holocausts that signified massacres, scorched earth policies, deportation, uprooting, and concentration of the population."[55] The three holocausts were, first, the invasion of Guatemala by the Spanish and the barbarous actions of Pedro de Alvarado; second, the nineteenth-century implantation of liberal capitalism in Guatemala; and finally, the 1980s program of state terror, particularly the scorched-earth campaign waged by Ríos Montt against highland Maya communities.[56]

When the proposal was presented to the Civil Society Assembly for discussion, it generated tremendous controversy around the question of territorial rights, in large part because the Maya were essentially declaring a right to a limited form of political autonomy.[57] But the Assembly did eventually approve a condensed version of the proposal, one in which claims to political autonomy had been removed.[58] All references to a Maya holocaust also disappeared in this new consensus version, which eventually served as the basis for the historic Agreement on the Identity and Rights of Indigenous Peoples that was incorporated into the peace accords.[59] The idea of a Maya holocaust thus first appeared in 1994 as part of a draft document meant for internal debate in the Civil Society Assembly but was revised out as the proposal was discussed.

The textual fate of the original proposal, the process of debate and revision that it experienced, is perhaps symptomatic of the broader process of Indigenous "movements of social insubordination" in Latin America. I use Sergio Tischler's "movements of social insubordination" rather than the more common "social movements" so as to more forcefully stress their rebellious nature.[60] As the Maya Movement sought out and negotiated with political allies on the national stage, its more radical proposals were pushed into the background—but not forgotten by the leaders who had proposed them originally.

The original proposal continued to be significant even after it had been abandoned by the Assembly. A month later Cojtí published a book under his own name that included elements of the original proposal, as if desirous of preserving those elements of Maya thinking that had not survived the politicking of the ASC.[61] The book, comprising a single long essay, in turn gained a U.S. audience when it was published in an English translation as part of a volume of academic articles about the Maya Movement, and it appeared again in a subsequent Spanish-language version when that academic volume was published in Guatemala.[62] The description of the "three Maya holocausts" was relegated to a long footnote in these expanded versions. Meanwhile, in a separate book about the Maya Movement, Cojtí included the same phrase in the book's dedication: "To the members of the Maya Movement struck down during the third Maya holocaust."[63]

A close analysis of the original 1994 proposal shows that its authors adopted a narrative of Maya history that had been put forward a few years earlier by ethnohistorian George Lovell. Although they did not directly reference his work in this document, it is clear that Lovell's 1988 article "Surviving Conquest: The Maya of Guatemala in Historical Perspective" was a source for their work. Lovell wrote about three "cycles of conquest" endured by the Maya since the sixteenth century, cycles which they have survived despite heavy losses.[64] The three cycles he identified are the same as those identified in the Assembly proposal: conquest by Spain in the sixteenth century, conquest by capitalism in the nineteenth century, conquest by state terror in the twentieth century.[65] Lovell's emphasis, as his title suggests, was on "surviving conquest" and on the continuing legacy of colonialism into the present. His article presents a Maya-centric view of Guatemalan history and expresses how Mayas have experienced the major moments in national history as catastrophic events of intense destruction. It is the repetition of these catastrophes that marks their history, he proposes, and he directly compares sixteenth-century atrocities to the ones committed by the army in the present day.[66] Such comparisons, originating in the years surrounding the atrocities of 1981–1983, began to circulate more frequently in the 1990s. Indeed, as we have seen, among Guatemalan authors the sixteenth century is the most prevalent historical referent for twentieth-century atrocities.

For the Maya authors of the 1994 document presented to the Assembly, Lovell's work provided a scholarly, ethnohistorical framework for how Maya culture had survived across time in the face of brutal assaults. But when they translated and transposed Lovell's words, these authors made a significant substitution: instead of three "cycles of conquest," they referred to three "cycles of holocaust." The subsequent expanded versions of the text, which were published under Cojtí's name, are different from the original proposal in that these texts do explicitly cite Lovell's work; these are scholarly works, not political proposals. Yet Cojtí also makes the same substitution, using "holocaust" instead of "conquest" to describe these historical events.

Why "holocaust"? To understand this rhetorical act requires that we keep in mind Maya thinkers' conscious erasure of the term "conquest" that Lovell had used in his 1988 article. That erasure is important if we are to recognize how the intention behind the term "Maya holocaust" involves resisting the discourse of victimization, not reinforcing it. "Holocaust" instead of "conquest" involves semantic work that connects the two words but also differentiates them. This connecting-differentiating work merits close examination. What are the connotations that Cojtí associated with "holocaust" that make it similar yet preferable to "conquest"?

The Semantics of Genocide, Holocaust, Conquest

The first step in reconstructing the semantic chain connecting the two terms is to identify the term "genocide" as the missing link between them. The concept of genocide has been linked to the Holocaust since its origins and has circulated in Guatemala since the late 1970s. It is very likely, then, that Maya thinkers turned to the less-common "holocaust" because of its universal association with the well-known "genocide." The term "genocide" was coined by Polish Jewish jurist Raphael Lemkin, who developed the concept in the 1920s and 1930s; it began to circulate in 1944 as a result of his writings and activism.[67] The term was originally a legal one; it describes "acts committed with intent to destroy, in whole or in part, a national, ethnical, racial or religious group"[68] The focus is on "the murder of a group as a group"[69] and on atrocities committed in peacetime as well as war.[70]

In developing these ideas, Lemkin used instances of genocide from the ancient and early modern world, especially the destruction of Indigenous peoples of the Americas.[71] By the time of his definitive 1944 book on the subject, the term had become attached to the extermination of the Jews by the Nazis.[72] It became a part of international law in 1948 with the adoption of the UN Convention on the Prevention and Punishment of the Crime of Genocide, which recognized that the attempted destruction of a group constitutes a particular kind of crime against humanity. The 1961 trial against Adolf Eichmann was the first to use it, though not in so many words;[73] subsequent legal prosecutions for genocide did not occur until the trials on Rwanda and Yugoslavia in the 1990s by the International Criminal Tribunal.

In other words, the term "genocide," already in circulation in the 1980s to describe Guatemalan state violence, brings those events into the same semantic neighborhood as the Holocaust. Indeed, one term almost inevitably calls up the other. It is true that, although the term "genocide" entered global consciousness to describe the Nazi crimes, the UN genocide convention itself does not mention this historical event. The terms are linked historically, not legally. Until 1994, that is, forty-six years after the adoption of the UN genocide convention, the Nazi Holocaust was the only genocide to have been legally prosecuted as such, excepting the proceedings by the Russell Tribunal, which I will discuss below. The legal term "genocide" simply had no referent other than the Holocaust.[74] Any reference to genocide constituted an allusion to the Nazi Holocaust. Historian Pierre Vidal-Naquet confirms this when he writes about the early 1960s in France, during the Algerian War and following the October 1961 pogrom of Algerians in Paris: "In those days . . . the word genocide often was heard . . . and everyone saw in it an allusion to the genocide of the Jews."[75] It is perhaps not a coincidence that the term "genocide" as a description of the Paris pogrom circulated in the months following the Eichmann trial.

Between the Eichmann trial in 1961 and the establishment of the International Criminal Tribunal for Rwanda in 1994, there were no genocide trials. Was the concept of genocide therefore dormant during that period? Emphatically not. Between 1961 and 1994 the term was actively circulating and accruing new valences beyond the field of formal law. Thanks to the Russell Tribunal of 1967, convened by British philosopher Bertrand Russell and composed of Jean-Paul Sartre, Simone de Beauvoir, Lázaro Cárdenas, and many notable figures linked to global struggles of national self-determination, "genocide" in the age of the Cuban Revolution and the Vietnam War became invested with connotations relating to struggles for national self-determination.

The Russell Tribunal considered whether the United States was guilty of genocide in Vietnam, ultimately determining that it was. The tribunal was tasked with considering genocide "in the most exact juridical sense of the term," and it based its deliberations on the idea of the "national group" outlined in the UN Convention, which defines "genocide" as "acts committed with intent to destroy, in whole or in part, a national, ethnical, racial or religious group."⁷⁶ Some members explicitly compared the Vietnamese to the Jewish victims of Nazism—not to underscore their defenselessness but to underscore the justness of their armed resistance. In the opening sessions of the tribunal, Ralph Schoenman responded to those who accused the tribunal of not considering the crimes of the Vietcong by explaining, "We would no more regard the Vietnamese resistance a crime than we would the rising of the Warsaw Ghetto."⁷⁷ Sartre brought in the memory of the Holocaust to buttress his case: "Hitler killed the Jews because they were Jews. The armed forces of the United States torture and kill men, women and children in Vietnam merely *because they are Vietnamese*. Whatever lies or euphemisms the government may think up, the spirit of genocide is in the minds of the soldiers."⁷⁸

It is in this sense of the term—genocide committed against a nation rising up against colonial oppression—that we can understand the frequency with which Latin American thinkers turned to the figure of genocide to describe Cold War atrocities. It explains why in Argentina in the first year of the dictatorship, clandestine political groups named the terror "genocidal"; why a few years later Argentine writer Tununa Mercado lamented that her fellow political exiles in Mexico decided to "expel" terms like "genocide" and "annihilation" from their denunciations of the regime in order to depoliticize their own language—the terms were *too* political, they thought, in sharp distinction to today, and made it possible to argue that atrocities committed against insurgents were still atrocities; and why the Permanent Peoples Tribunal on Guatemala that was held in Madrid in 1983, an offshoot of the original Russell Tribunal, viewed the genocide committed against Mayas as part of the imposition of a broader economic program that demanded "the prevention of any sociocultural form of popular resistance."⁷⁹

These accusations of genocide were not uttered in a competitive frame, did not take the UN Convention as the only arbiter of the question, and did not seek to portray the victims of genocide as helpless or hapless civilians. The point, in these instances, was not just to draw attention to the atrocities committed by a military dictatorship but also to reframe the context in which they took place. The state termed this a "war against subversion." The term "genocide" made it into a struggle for self-determination against the forces of injustice. Although the term was used to call attention to the extremity and gravity of the atrocities suffered by the victims, that was not its sole purpose. It was a call to action that affirmed the victims' involvement in a fight to achieve just ends. Their extermination by the state was unjust not solely because it violated their individual and collective rights as defined by the United Nations but also because it represented the violation of their right as a national group to resist oppression. Bertrand Russell, in his comments to the tribunal panel, posed the question of genocide in terms that never ceased to remind his listeners that it was being committed against a people resisting oppression in order to cow them into submission to an unjust world order.[80]

In the present day, this context of national liberation and revolutionary consciousness that animated "genocide" with partisan political meanings is apt to be misrecognized as something else. Some scholars dismiss these Cold War rhetorical usages of the term "genocide" as cynical moves in a competition game for victim status on the world stage and believe those who wield the term to be ignorant of the legal definitions of genocide. Legal historians have been somewhat hostile to its widespread use beyond the legal setting or have expressed disbelief when activists insist on genocide prosecutions even when these are legally far-fetched.[81] Recently, however, there have been discussions, in both the Argentine and Guatemalan contexts, about the need to revisit the legal interpretations of "genocide" and open it up to these more expansive, more politically engaged perspectives. For instance, sociologist Sergio Palencia-Frener has called for using the conceptual category of genocide in Guatemala to advance an anti-capitalist critique by incorporating into the analysis of genocide an examination of the role of the landed oligarchy in supporting the army's actions and benefiting economically from the destruction of Maya villages.[82] We can hear this anti-capitalist critique implicit in the usage of "genocide" by Maya political leader Rosalina Tuyuc in a recent presentation. The "last holocaust" the Maya have experienced, she says, was the genocide of the 1980s; the first genocide was colonization, and the second was in 1954, when the Guatemalan oligarchy, in an attempt to stop a land reform program, brought down the presidency of Jacobo Arbenz in a CIA-sponsored coup d'état.[83]

Returning to Guatemala in the early 1990s and to the "Maya holocausts" found in the Maya proposal to the ASC and in Cojtí's work, we can see how these authors, steeped in a consciousness of the genocidal nature of both colonialism and Cold War violence, might have made a leap from the word "genocide" to the word "holocaust" to describe these events. In so doing, they carried over to "holocaust" some of the more militant critiques of genocide forged in the prior decades.

Another important aspect of the semantic work that led Maya thinkers to the word "holocaust" is that they used it to replace "conquest" in Lovell's article. Why was this word preferable to "conquest"? The answer lies in the years surrounding the 1992 commemorations, when we see an extended intellectual experiment with words and names, with substituting and replacing mystifying words with clarifying words. Indigenous and other scholars took up a sustained intellectual effort to show the folly of "celebrating" the 1492 event. Guatemala's "Continental Campaign: 500 Years of Indigenous and Popular Resistance" denounced "the festive character" of the commemorations.[84] Others criticized the word "discovery" for whitewashing history. Cojtí, in an article published on the anniversary date itself, October 12, 1992, resemanticized the discovery as an "ethnocide."[85] Maya thinkers used the opportunity provided by the 1992 commemorations to reflect further on the Conquest as a genocidal process, much as Lemkin had when he originally coined the term "genocide." "If the word 'genocide' has ever been used with exactitude," notes Luis Enrique Sam Colop, "it is in regard to this situation."[86] They also subjected the term "conquest" to scrutiny.

Cojtí notes, in describing his thinking at the time, that in his work regarding the 1992 anniversary, even the word "conquest," though preferable to the word "discovery," required semantic undoing.[87] He explains that "conquest" implies defeat, whereas he and other Mayas meant to stress survival. This sentiment is summed up in the phrase "a pesar de 500 años . . . ¡estamos presentes!" (Despite five hundred years . . . we are still here!), a refrain of sorts for the Cholsamaj publishing house and the various coalitions of Maya thinkers and activists that emerged in the early 1990s.[88] Cojtí also notes that "conquest" is a military event, whereas he wanted to signal the fact of a longer process of colonization that involved nonmilitary forms of devastation, such as disease and slavery.[89] Finally, he notes that "conquest" as a term tells us nothing of the ideologies involved; he wanted to bring in an element of the racism that was necessary for the Spanish to accomplish what they did, which the term "holocaust," in the post-Nazi world, conveys.[90]

The story of semantic unsettling in the wake of 1992 that Cojtí recounts is itself a chapter in the longer story of Third World decolonization and national liberation movements. These were influential precursors for the Maya intellectuals who emerged in the post-genocide period, a fact that will eventually bring us back to the Russell Tribunal. In his scholarly work Cojtí views Guatemalan modernity through the lens of internal colonialism, a concept that recurs throughout his publications. Cojtí's work emerges in dialogue with a seminal book for Guatemalan anti-colonial thought, Carlos Guzmán Böckler and Jean-Loup Herbert's 1970 *Guatemala: A Social-Historical Interpretation*. Authored by two sociologists, it lays the groundwork for an understanding of modern Guatemala as an essentially colonial society.

They argue that existing histories of Guatemala, whether Marxist, liberal, or reactionary, remain trapped by colonial and racist modes of thought and that the dominant version of national history has been an "instrument of ideological domination" rather than national liberation, and they view Indigenous identity as a fetishized construct, one that does not exist except in dialectical relationship to its ladino antagonist, thereby seeming to suggest that a nonalienated, anti-colonial thought would abandon it altogether.[91] Cojtí explicitly rejects this last point, but in other respects he builds on Guzmán Böckler and Herbert's work.[92] He turns to thinkers of African decolonization, such as Frantz Fanon and Albert Memmi, to develop his critique of racism in Guatemala and his analysis of the existential elements of colonialism, such as Mayas' internalized racism.[93] Cojtí's political views in the 1990s were similar to those of other anti-colonial nationalisms. He and many other Maya thinkers affirmed the existence of a Maya People endowed with a unique historical trajectory who therefore constituted a collective legal subject with the right to self-determination.[94]

The semantic experimentation of the early 1990s around the words "discovery" and "conquest" is a crucial component of this Maya anti-colonial thought. The Maya Movement generated an alternative national historical consciousness by placing Indigenous voices at its center, especially through the study of Maya chronicles and the Maya language itself, seen as the carrier of collective memory. The point was to rewrite Guatemalan history from the perspective of its Indigenous peoples to promote an understanding of the colonial-era social structures and attitudes that persisted to the present day. Perhaps most importantly, it reiterated that in all this time the Maya had never ceased to affirm their identity as a distinct people.[95] Cojtí cites the 1989 International Labor Organization (ILO) Convention 169 as a foundational document for this element of the Maya Movement's demands, as many Indigenous movements do around the world.[96] Cojtí also cites the Second Russell Tribunal (1974), "On Repression in Brazil, Chile and Latin America," and the resulting 1976 Algiers Charter proclaiming the Universal Declaration of the Rights of Peoples.[97] The Second Russell Tribunal, it bears noting, was the immediate successor to Russell's 1967 International War Crimes Tribunal. It was convened by Italian lawyer Lelio Basso to confront repression in Latin America, and members of its jury included Gabriel García Márquez and Julio Cortázar.[98]

Returning to the controversial "Maya holocaust," Cojtí recounts a searching and experimental intellectual mode, one that involves expansive, connective thinking rather than semantic conflation and draws on decades of decolonizing political thought. His critics understood Cojtí to be speaking of Maya victims in the passive sense. But in invoking a holocaust, he is most emphatically *not* framing the Maya as passive victims. On the contrary, his is a demand that they occupy the center of Guatemalan history and society and that they recognize and claim for themselves an identity as resisters and survivors. If anything, the term "Maya holocaust," when he inserted it into documents proclaiming the existence of a Maya people with territorial and political rights, reads as militant, empowered, and radical.

Needless to say, this unconventional set of semantic connotations has not survived into the new millennium, even as, or perhaps *because*, the Maya genocide has received greater attention in the Guatemalan and international legal arenas as some of its perpetrators have faced criminal charges. As the more victim-centric connotations of "holocaust" take stronger hold in Guatemala, due to the success of legal efforts to prosecute perpetrators as well as the increased presence of Shoah institutions from the United States, Europe, and Israel, what will become of Cojtí's more militant and unconventional usage inspired by the debates surrounding 1992?

Conclusion

The memory debates discussed here are part of the broader landscape of repair in the post-genocide environment. Liselotte Viaene clarifies the semantic distinction in Guatemala between "resarcir," which signifies economic reparation, and "reparación," which "denotes the conjunction of the search for justice, truth-seeking efforts (such as exhumations of clandestine graves for forcibly disappeared people) and initiatives to recover historical memory."[99] Repair in this context therefore needs to be taken in an ample sense, beyond a monetary consideration and beyond, too, the sense of individual or collective psychological healing that the idea of the "reparative" might connote in English. The Holocaust has been woven into this fabric of repair in subtle ways. As an instance of the globalization of the Holocaust, this Guatemalan interweaving provokes questions about the circulation of particular Holocaust models or paradigms and their translation and transposition to specific contexts. But if we think in terms of cocreation rather than transposition, we notice far more clearly the integration of Holocaust consciousness into a demand for a social justice beyond criminal justice. This demand has been anchored, by Maya thinkers in the case of Guatemala, to a narrative about historical injustice and collective resistance that stretches back to the Conquest and draws on the global currents of anti-colonial thinking of the 1960s and 1970s. For Cojtí in the 1990s, to recover historical memory meant exposing, and giving more language to, the violence of long-term systemic injustice, not just of specific events of state terror. In other words, reparative work in this ample sense includes a reflection on colonialism.

In *Left-Wing Melancholia*, Traverso argues that the Holocaust paradigm of memory has contributed to severing the link between memory and redemption that animated revolutionary politics. He argues that the memory of those who died in political struggle points to the future, to a possible redemption, in the vein of Walter Benjamin's famous concept of "weak messianism" in his Second Thesis on History.[100] Such a memory, writes Traverso, "perceives the tragedies and the lost battles of the past as a burden and a debt, which are also a promise of redemption";[101] whereas the memory of those who died in genocide, and who are epitomized by the victims of the Holocaust, points only to the ruins of the past, with memory now a "duty," "a cult object," rather than being incorporated into political struggles for a better future.[102] Even a summary revision of the discussions I have analyzed here, however, demonstrates that this pattern of thought does not do justice to the memories constructed by Maya authors in postwar Guatemala. There the genocide of the 1980s has been written by some of its victims into the longer history of colonial oppression and exploitation, as its latest chapter.

For scholars of Guatemala, most elements of the story I have presented here are already well known. The point has been to reframe this history for Holocaust scholars who are likely unaware of the particular resonance that "holocaust" holds in the Guatemalan case and who may be focused exclusively on determining whether comparing the Guatemalan genocide to the Nazi Holocaust is morally correct or historically accurate. The moral critique, framed in U.S. terms, might view Cojtí's "Maya holocaust" as an unjust appropriation of Jewish moral capital by non-Jewish victims of atrocity, or as an instance of "competing catastrophes," as has happened with regard to debates about the Native American genocide in the United States.[103] The critique on historical grounds, meanwhile, can rightly point out the obvious differences in scale (the Guatemalan atrocities involve absolute numbers so much smaller than those of the Nazi Holocaust that a quantitative comparison is patently absurd) as well as any number of other historical differences that would seem to render the comparison inoperative.

In response to these possible critiques, two salient points bear reiteration. First, Holocaust comparisons in Guatemala have generated their own debates about the appropriateness of the analogy and are the fruit of historical analysis and semantic experimentation rather than blind application. Second, the contours of these debates do not always turn on the same questions as do similar debates in the United States and Europe, particularly because they are so intimately bound up with the counterinsurgency campaigns of the Cold War. If we are to understand exactly how Holocaust consciousness has spread globally, then we must listen to these voices on their own terms.

The Holocaust frame has acquired more purchase in Guatemala in the past decade. In this most recent period we see significant activities in Guatemala by international Holocaust institutions. As will be discussed in Chapter 5, the Shoah Foundation Institute for Visual History and Education at the University of Southern California began a project in 2015 to collect visual testimony by Guatemalan genocide survivors. It has partnered with Guatemala's Forensic Anthropology Foundation (FAFG), which exhumes mass graves at the sites of genocide in the Maya highlands and seeks to identify the victims. As part of its activities and with technical support by the Shoah Foundation, the FAFG has begun to record visual testimony of the genocide by witnesses and survivors.[104] Also in 2015, the Guatemalan Ministry of Education, with support from the Guatemalan Jewish Community Association, Yad Vashem, UNESCO, and the United States Holocaust Memorial Museum, began implementing a required Holocaust module in the national K–12 curriculum, the first such module to be required in Latin America and one expressly designed to "invite analogy" with the Guatemalan context.[105] January 2016 saw the opening of a Holocaust Museum in Guatemala, sponsored by the French foundation Yahad–In Unum.[106] The mission of this group focuses on the "Holocaust by Bullets" or "genocide by bullets" committed by the Einsatzgruppen and other Nazi units against Jews, Roma, and others in the Soviet territories invaded by Germany; the foundation sponsors the excavation of mass graves and promotes greater awareness of this element of the Shoah.[107] As Holocaust institutions begin to be more active in Guatemala and perhaps generate new and greater Holocaust consciousness there, it is worth asking what the Holocaust has symbolized up until now in debates about the atrocities.

Chapter Five

Holocaust Testimony and Maya Testimony between the U.S. and Guatemala

There is no territorial border between the U.S. and Guatemala, but the two countries are geopolitical neighbors nonetheless. Neither country would be what it is today if the United States had not identified Guatemala as a hinterland of raw materials for U.S. consumers, if the United Fruit Company had not "amassed coffee and fruit / in ships which put to sea like overloaded trays with the treasures / from our sunken lands." Pablo Neruda's haunting poem continues:

> Meanwhile, in the seaports'
> sugary abysses,
> Indians collapsed, buried
> in the morning mist:
> a body rolls down, a nameless
> thing, a fallen number,
> a bunch of lifeless fruit
> dumped on the rubbish heap.[1]

In 1954, not long after Neruda's poem appeared, the CIA organized a coup against President Jacobo Arbenz and, with the backing of Guatemalan business interests and their allies in the military, turned the country into the first of the U.S. "backyards" in the war against Communism. Generations of Guatemalans have rebelled against these attempts to reduce them to disposable labor.

Is it surprising that Holocaust testimony circulates through this calamitous U.S.-Guatemala relation? Yes, considering that Holocaust consciousness in Guatemala is an extremely scarce phenomenon. Although there have been increasing efforts to promote Holocaust education by the Guatemalan Jewish community and by international organizations, it is hardly a usual point of reference in Guatemala. But then again, no, it is not all that surprising, for two reasons. First, because the massacres of Maya villagers in the early 1980s by the Guatemalan army have been deemed "genocidal" according to the legal definition of genocide put forth in the UN Convention. The concept of "genocide" therefore provides a common historical-legal framework linking Guatemala to the Holocaust, as I discussed in the previous chapter. Second, like so many other elements of U.S. culture, U.S. forms of Holocaust consciousness have had an impact in Guatemala. Americans have been primed to view questions of victimhood and state atrocity through the lens of the Holocaust. As we will see, this "Americanization" of the Holocaust has influenced approaches to Guatemala that are critical of U.S. Cold War policies and their aftermath.

Since the end of the civil war in 1996, the voices of Holocaust survivors and of Holocaust scholars have played a role in how Maya testimony about the war is shaped inside Guatemala and heard outside it. This chapter examines two distinct moments of convergence between Holocaust testimony and Maya testimony in post-genocide Guatemala. The first concerns debates about Rigoberta Menchú's 1983 *testimonio* book, *I, Rigoberta Menchú: An Indian Woman in Guatemala*, which were provoked in the 1990s by anthropologist David Stoll's accusations that she had fabricated parts of her story.[2] Holocaust testimony became a feature of the ensuing polemics. Several of the U.S. academics who came to Menchú's defense, or who disagreed with Stoll's methods and aims if not his findings, turned to scholarship about the Holocaust survivor testimonies collected in the Fortunoff Video Archive for Holocaust Testimony at Yale University to support their arguments, pointing to the parallels between the Stoll-Menchú case and Holocaust denialism. The second, a more recent moment, concerns the partnership inaugurated in 2015 between the Shoah Foundation Institute for Visual History and Education at the University of Southern California and the Guatemalan Forensic Anthropology Foundation (Fundación de Antropología Forense de Guatemala, FAFG) to produce audiovisual testimony about the Guatemalan genocide. The FAFG exhumes clandestine gravesites in the Maya highlands in order to identify the victims, return the remains to their families, and provide evidence for judicial proceedings against alleged perpetrators. As part of its activities and with technical support from the Shoah Foundation, the FAFG has expanded its mission to include recording audiovisual testimony by witnesses and survivors of human rights atrocities.[3] These video testimonies are housed at the Shoah Foundation alongside video testimony from the European Holocaust and other genocides.

Both of these engagements taking place between the U.S. and Guatemala—the Stoll-Menchú debate and the Shoah-FAFG partnership—involve attempts to place Maya voices at the center of national narratives of the past. The presence of Maya testimonies is not exceptional in postwar Guatemala, an environment "saturated with testimonial forms of truth-telling," as anthropologist Carlota McAllister has noted.[4] But both also involve a dialogue with Holocaust testimony, and in this sense they *are* exceptional. Across the many archives of survivor testimony collected during and since the civil war, direct references to Holocaust testimony figure little, even if, as I have described in Chapter 4, a Holocaust metanarrative of victimization runs through debates about how to frame or name the violence of the civil war. In the two cases examined here, two archives of Holocaust survivor testimony created in the United States, the Fortunoff Video Archive for Holocaust Testimony at Yale University and the Shoah Foundation's Institute for Visual History and Education, are brought directly to bear on testimony by Maya survivors.

The first part of this chapter addresses the controversy sparked by Stoll's accusations against Menchú. The debate concerned the authenticity of her witness statements and the complexities of her experience as a victim who was also an active resister with links to the armed insurgency. Menchú spoke out against oppression, adopted the radical tenets of liberation theology, became a grassroots peasant organizer, joined an armed rebel group, survived a genocidal extermination process, and went on to lead an international campaign against human rights abuses.

On the face of it, her testimony would seem to offer few parallels with testimony by Holocaust survivors. Holocaust testimony and the Latin American *testimonio* genre, to which Menchú's narrative belongs, represent two different kinds of witness narrative. They have distinct histories of emergence and circulation, are studied in separate scholarly fields, and generated different interpretive paradigms and debates—until the responses to Stoll's accusations brought them together. Facing a situation of genocide denial, scholars activated the latent similarities between the two forms of memoir. Those academics who defended the validity of Menchú's words turned to studies of Holocaust testimony to show that, much like Holocaust survivors,

Menchú was testifying to a historical truth involving elements that were not verifiable and that had as much to do with her personal efforts at resisting trauma as it did with the historical events she described. What standards of evidence should therefore apply to her testimony—courtroom evidence? scholarly and scientific evidence? journalistic evidence? or evidence of some entirely other kind? On the basis of their forays into Holocaust testimony, some scholars argued that Stoll's focus on the empirical facts of Menchú's story led to a decontextualized and distorted understanding of her experience and that of other Maya during the war. Adopting Holocaust testimony as a point of reference for Menchú's *testimonio*, these scholars highlighted Jewish and Maya survivors' narrative acts as testifying to a nonempirical truth, namely, their ability as survivors to reclaim dignity for themselves and a measure of self-determination.

The second part of the chapter considers the efforts of the FAFG in the realm of audiovisual testimony. It analyzes some of the testimonies it has produced to date in collaboration with technical staff from the USC Shoah Foundation. At first glance the partnership between the Shoah Foundation and the FAFG is an odd one, given their divergent orientations. The FAFG is an on-the-ground human rights organization that supports grassroots community activism by survivors of mass atrocity and is directly engaged in the criminal prosecution of perpetrators. Its memory work has taken shape in the delicate, often dangerous legal and political landscape of the post-conflict period. The Shoah Foundation is a product of Hollywood, and its struggle has been against time—to collect as many testimonies as possible from an aging witness population—not against entrenched countervailing economic and political interests. It is an archive with an educational mission and is far removed from political or legal activism. It is true that both the Shoah Foundation and the FAFG are human rights institutions. Both are memory optimists; they understand memory as a force for good. But the FAFG's memory work is more immediately and more politically consequential than the Shoah Foundation's Holocaust memory work.

The Shoah-FAFG partnership therefore raises questions about the circulation of Holocaust memory between the U.S. and Guatemala. How closely are the testimonies collected through the Shoah-FAFG partnership modeled on the Shoah Foundation's Holocaust survivor testimonies? The Shoah Foundation's Holocaust testimonies follow a set template that was applied internationally en masse, a necessary step if it wanted to fulfill its ambition to be one of the largest repositories of audiovisual Holocaust testimonies in the world.[5] To what extent have the Shoah-FAFG testimonies adopted the template offered by the Shoah Foundation's Holocaust testimonies? How does the Shoah-FAFG form of Maya testimony compare with prior forms collected in the 1980s and 1990s as part of other human rights activities—do they generate a different *content* of memory? In contemplating the Shoah-FAFG partnership, one can legitimately wonder: Has the FAFG, by harnessing itself to the Shoah Foundation's apolitical educational mission, constrained its confrontational memory politics, which seek to disrupt the postwar status quo in Guatemala? What impact has the partnership had on the FAFG's activist, social justice orientation toward the memory of genocide? What kind of dialogue between the memory of the Holocaust and the memory of the Guatemalan genocide does this partnership create?

In these two cases—the Holocaust as a reference point in the Stoll-Menchú debate and in the Shoah-FAFG testimonies—my approach addresses concerns about the dilution of politicized Latin American modes of testimony into a globalized American-style Holocaust memory. The question of trauma, of trauma as the event to which survivors bear witness, is at the center of these considerations. McAllister, in her work on the complex ecosystem of Guatemalan testimonial practices, wonders how we might recover facets of Guatemalan history "different than the one of helpless victimization and compassionate rescue that humanitarianism privileges."[6] The idea is that the trauma framework is in a sense a colonizing discursive form that has taken over and subsumed other forms of talking about violence. It has been imposed by global humanitarianism, and while trauma is undoubtedly one way to describe the experience of McAllister's Maya informants, it is also limiting, silencing in its own way.[7]

One of the surprising findings from my analysis of these cases of Holocaust testimony and Maya testimony that meet between the U.S. and Guatemala is that both involve a break with the trauma frame. In the Menchú case, U.S. scholars turn to Holocaust testimony to underscore genocide survivors' resistance to traumatized silence. In the Shoah-FAFG testimonies, one hears in them the revolutionary and activist commitments of the victims, who thereby testify to something other than helplessness and trauma. Both instances therefore involve an emphasis on the empowered victim. Each case, it bears noting, emerges at a moment of heightened genocide awareness in Guatemala, as we will see. Accusations that the army had committed genocide and other crimes against humanity, by the UN's Commission on Historical Clarification (1999) and by a Guatemalan court in its conviction of General Efraín Ríos Montt (2013), led to a backlash of military repression and judicial corruption. Menchú's defenders and the

Shoah-FAFG partnership each wield Holocaust testimony to buttress the case for genocide. They establish parallels between Holocaust survivors and Maya survivors that emphasize not only their shared experience of victimization but also their shared experience of empowerment through testimony—limited as it might be, this is the power to shape the stories people tell about their suffering.

Revisiting Stoll-Menchú: Holocaust Testimony and "Nontransparent Truths"

In 1998, U.S. anthropologist David Stoll published *Rigoberta Menchú and the Story of All Poor Guatemalans*, a book attacking the credibility of Rigoberta Menchú Tum. Menchú is the winner of the 1992 Nobel Peace Prize and was best known, before that, for her 1983 testimonio *Me llamo Rigoberta Menchú y así me nació la conciencia*.[8] She produced the testimonio in collaboration with anthropologist Elisabeth Burgos-Debray, and it was instrumental in helping to publicize to the world the atrocities then taking place in the Maya highlands. Her testimonio recounted her life as a Maya villager, focused on Maya lifeways and on her political activism and that of her family, which suffered harsh repression under the army's scorched-earth campaign; her father, mother, and brother were all murdered by the army because of their political activity. The book was immensely popular outside Guatemala and had an immediate impact in bringing wider international attention to the crimes committed by the state against the Maya.

I, Rigoberta Menchú and the 1992 peace prize turned Menchú into a global symbol for Indigenous survival and resistance. This is one of the reasons Stoll wanted to focus his attention on her. Stoll had discovered inconsistencies in her story while working on a book about the Maya experience of the war. He encountered informants who questioned elements of Menchú's account in *I, Rigoberta Menchú*, and he considered it suspicious that in her book she had not been more open about her ties to a leftist guerrilla group, the Ejército Guerrillero de los Pobres (Guerrilla Army of the Poor, hereafter EGP). Stoll believed that Menchú's claims to be a victim of state terror were essentially false because she was affiliated with a group that was itself a perpetrator of violence, though Menchú herself was not an armed combatant, and indeed Stoll in an earlier work had held groups like the EGP responsible—morally, not criminally—for the violence suffered by Maya villagers at the hands of the Guatemalan army.[9] Stoll began circulating his findings about Menchú in the early 1990s at conferences and in academic journals, and then in 1998 he published *Rigoberta Menchú and the Story of All Poor Guatemalans*, a book devoted entirely to questioning Menchú's testimony and showing it to be a misleading portrait of rural Maya life in the years before and during the scorched-earth campaign launched by the Guatemalan army.

Stoll's aims were various: one, to correct "misapprehensions about the problems facing peasants" that Menchú's book had promoted to its international audience; two, to debunk Menchú's authority and undermine the power granted to her by scholars and activists who perceived her as an icon of Indigenous peasant resistance; three, to return that authority to those wielding social-scientific standards of evidence.[10] Stoll's target was not just Menchú but the U.S. scholars and political progressives who had supported her cause and who had helped strengthen her symbolic power on college campuses. He was also pursuing a point from his previous book and taking aim at the "voice of revolutionary commitment" that she had come to embody, that is, taking issue with how leftist guerrillas explained the causes of the violence suffered by highland Mayas during the early 1980s.[11] Stoll did not call Menchú a liar, but that is how many perceived his accusations in the U.S. and Guatemala.[12] Stoll's claims were amplified by journalist Larry Rohter's follow-up article in the *New York Times*, which sparked a media firestorm in the United States and fueled a right-wing offensive in the "culture wars" of the 1990s.[13]

The empirical, methodological, and ethical merits of Stoll's case against Menchú, and of its repercussions in the "culture wars" in the United States, have been amply discussed by scholars from diverse fields.[14] Most agree that while many of Stoll's accusations lack merit, there are indeed some factual discrepancies between what Menchú says and the established historical record. For example, Stoll charged that contrary to what Menchú claimed, she had not been an eyewitness to the public torture and murder of her brother by the Guatemalan army and that her brother had not been killed by being burned alive but by being shot.[15]

But most U.S. critics and scholars who have engaged in this debate believe that this narrow discussion of whether Menchú's testimony matches the established facts on all counts can hardly do justice to the broader ethical and empirical implications of the case. The reception of Stoll's book by the media and by right-wing commentators was couched in such a way as to call into doubt the fact that the army had massacred Maya villagers. Stoll's book did not, in fact, question this fact (although Stoll would later argue that Ríos Montt should not be found guilty of genocide), but in its zeal to tear down Menchú as symbol, it offered powerful ammunition for those who did.[16]

Many commentators saw in Stoll's work the shadow of Holocaust denialism. Like the "revisionist" historians who pioneered scholarly Holocaust denial, Stoll found inconsistencies in a story by a direct witness to atrocity and used these to accuse her of falsifying her experience. "Her story . . . is not the eyewitness account it purports to be," Stoll writes.[17] Stoll's approach opened the door to a deeper questioning of the veracity of the entire historical event. U.S.-based Guatemalan scholar Arturo Arias noted in this regard: "It becomes the basis for undermining the credibility of what happened—genocide, massacres, personal losses for many people. It becomes a whitewashing of history that is similar to discourses that deny the Holocaust."[18] He echoed claims made earlier by Guatemalan critic and novelist Dante Liano:

> What we have is a classic campaign to rewrite history. It calls to mind the technique used to attack the veracity of Holocaust survivors: "but you just said you were in that camp, whereas the documents prove you were in another camp; and if that concentration camp did not exist, perhaps no concentration camps ever existed at all." The strategy is simple: humiliate the witness, make him stammer, cast the shadow of doubt on his testimony, so shame itself can be questioned.[19]

Liano paraphrases here some of the more infamous statements by French scholar Robert Faurisson, a leading Holocaust denier whose specialty consisted in using testimony by Nazi death camp survivors to call into question the existence of the gas chambers and therefore the genocide of the Jews, all in the name of "historical truth."[20]

Faurisson makes several unnamed appearances in the work of those who respond to Stoll, generally by way of Jean-François Lyotard's book *The Differend* (1983), which used the debates provoked by Faurisson's work to illustrate his speculations on a language problem emerging from a limit situation. Lyotard posed the problem by asking us to imagine the following: "Human beings endowed with language were placed in a situation such that none of them is now able to tell about it. Most of them disappeared then, and the survivors rarely speak about it. When they do speak about it, their testimony bears only upon a minute part of this situation. How can you know that the situation itself existed?"[21] This is not only an abstract situation. It refers to the concrete language problems confronting the survivors of Nazi death camps, problems created by Holocaust deniers like Faurisson, whom Lyotard cites.[22] Lyotard infers the following perverse logic from Faurisson's skepticism about whether gas chambers existed and were used to exterminate Jews: that one would have to have been inside the gas chamber to have seen it operate and thus testify to its existence, but since to have been inside it would mean being killed by it, there is no logical way for the direct witness to testify about it. Ergo, the victim of this wrong cannot bear witness to it without then losing their status as a victim of it, thereby canceling it out as a wrong. As constructed by the Holocaust denier, the wrong is such that it cannot be borne witness to.[23] Lyotard expanded on this beyond the specifics of Holocaust denial to argue for the difficulty of communicating the truth of limit events; the term "differend" refers to this difficulty. It is a moment in language "wherein something which must be able to be put into phrases cannot yet be."[24]

Critic Doris Sommer used Lyotard in her intervention in the Menchú controversy to reflect on how Stoll's accusations had a doubly pernicious effect. First, she notes, Stoll questions Menchú's status as a victim, that is, as someone against whom a wrong has been committed, based on her affiliation to a guerrilla group, a fact about which she was cagey in her *testimonio*, and because some of the events she described, such as the death of her brother, though bad, were not as bad as she had described them. Second, Sommer continues, he questions Menchú's status as a "plaintiff" seeking redress—that is, he blocks her ability to denounce her victimization and thereby to cease being a victim in the existential sense of the word. Sommer asks: "What exactly is Stoll demanding of Rigoberta's story, and is the demand fair?" She answers the question by way of Lyotard and Holocaust denial: "Do we dismiss testimony of genocidal holocaust in World War II because of controvertible details, when the incontrovertible fact of genocide is in the balance?" "Some revisionist historians do just that," continues Sommer," bringing in Lyotard's *The Differend*: "Referring to the Holocaust, Lyotard asks how a survivor can testify to what should have killed him."[25] Critic Elzbieta Sklodowska amplified these points taken from Lyotard by analyzing the dilemmas faced by survivors, who are caught between testifying to the limit event they did not witness (i.e., death inside the gas chamber) and remaining silent.[26]

Even commentators who believed Stoll's work had merit worried that his work looked a lot like Holocaust denialism. Hal Cohen's 1999 article on the Menchú controversy is a good example. Cohen overall was sympathetic to Stoll, yet he too questioned Stoll's motives by pointing to the parallels between Stoll's claims and those of Holocaust deniers. This passage is worth citing at length because it exemplifies a tendency in the criticism to place Menchú alongside Holocaust survivors and to derive a lesson from their proximity:

> Unlikely as it may seem, Holocaust studies may provide a useful counterpoint to the Guatemalan case. An entire subfield of academic criticism has emerged in the last decade or so that focuses on the construction of memory in Holocaust testimonies. Discussing Holocaust survivors, Primo Levi wrote in *The Drowned and the Saved*: "The greater part of the witnesses . . . have ever more blurred and stylized memories, often, unbeknownst to them, influenced by information gained from later readings or the stories of others." Few, if any, mainstream Holocaust scholars find such arguments threatening, because none of these critics questions the basic facts of the Holocaust (just as Stoll does not question the basic facts of the Guatemalan violence). If, however, someone were to devote years of research to finding factual lapses in the iconic Holocaust survival narrative of, say, an Elie Wiesel, the controversy would be considerable. . . . Is Stoll offering objective context to subjective memory to understand better what took place, or is he gratuitously smearing an essential symbol of terrible crimes?[27]

Although Stoll never doubted the broader fact of the army's massacres, as Cohen makes clear, his work was used by those who did. And although Stoll attempted to distance himself from them by accusing them in turn of "the Central American equivalent of Holocaust denial," it is his own work that is most open to the charge of operating insidiously as a form of genocide denial.[28] It not only displaced attention away from those with criminal and moral responsibility for the genocide, both in the United States and in Guatemala, but assisted them in their continued efforts to evade it.

Under pressure from genocide denialism, then, Holocaust references had a role to play in these debates, bringing Menchú's situation into close enough proximity to the situation of Holocaust testimony that the two became mirrors. Menchú herself did not do this, counter to critic Ron Robin's claims that she was involved in purveying Holocaust analogies in her own defense; and these mirrorings were not a case of pandering to a simplistic mass-media sensibility, as he also claimed.[29] On the contrary, the vast majority of Holocaust references in the Stoll controversy involved academic scrutiny of scholarly norms and how these negotiate the tension between the authority of the witness and the authority of the researcher.

Stoll has argued that he more than others has listened to Maya voices to formulate his analyses of their experience during the civil war. In his earlier book, the 1993 *Between Two Armies in the Ixil Towns of Guatemala*, he explained that he had arrived at his conclusions based on what his Maya informants had told him, which is that the guerrillas had exerted a "coercive pressure" on them to become allies and then deceived them, abandoning them to their fate at the hands of the army. He took these sentiments "at face value": "So many Ixils seemed open about their feelings that it convinced me to take their express condemnation of both sides at face value."[30] But others have charged him with downplaying the fact that his informants were embedded in situations that likely affected the content of the stories they told him.

Three scholars, anthropologist Beatriz Manz, geographer Elizabeth Oglesby, and public health researcher José García Noval, addressed these issues in a volume published in Guatemala in 1999 that focuses on the relationship between social scientists and their witness-informants. As Manz puts it, it's not a question of lies versus truth but "what is said and what is not said."[31] A thread of Holocaust references runs throughout this slim volume. Manz cites Primo Levi's *The Drowned and the Saved* about the tendency of witness-survivors to construct a "convenient reality" that avoids the more troubling aspects of their limit experiences.[32] García Noval cites Daniel Goldhagen's *Hitler's Willing Executioners* to rebut Stoll's argument that the guerrillas should have "predicted" the genocidal counteroffensive that the army launched against Maya villagers; they could no more have predicted the extreme brutality of the army than social scientists in the 1930s could have predicted the Nazi Holocaust.[33] Meanwhile, the book takes for an epigraph the famous lines from the Auschwitz Museum: "Olvidar es repetir. (Leyenda en la entrada del actual museo de Auschwitz [ex campo de concentración nazi])." The line is a condensed version of George Santayana's famous words: "Those who forget the past are condemned to repeat it." In this context, it suggests that Stoll's form of listening to the past is actually a form of forgetting it, and that Stoll's decision to take witness statements "at face value" constitutes naive or irresponsible scholarship that distorts the past. In other words, these scholars suggest that in both his first and his second books, Stoll arrives at determinations about the relative truth value of Maya testimonies without sufficient attention to the realities of the testimonial situation. His listening to Maya voices is so decontextualized that it amounts to a silencing of their voices.

Anthropologist Victoria Stanford has also argued for a more nuanced understanding of the victims' voices, and she too has turned to scholarship on Holocaust testimony in her interventions in the Menchú case. Citing work by historian Dominick LaCapra and literary critic Lawrence Langer, she observes that "discrepancies encountered in testimonies taken in the field should not be taken to indicate faulty memory, invention, or deception" but should lead us rather to examine how survivors and witnesses make meaning of these facts.[34] In a sense, this is what Stoll had set out to do in his first book: examine different perspectives on the significance of the Guatemalan army's massacres of Maya villagers. But in his second book the stakes got confused: he put Menchú on trial in the court of public opinion to call attention to the crimes of liberal academia, in the process relativizing and obfuscating the crimes of the Guatemalan army.

One final illuminating example from the debate is the work of critic John Beverley. If we examine two of his key essays on the *testimonio* genre, one published before the controversy and one after, we get a sense of the historicity of these Holocaust references. We see how the Holocaust became relevant to *testimonio* debates as a direct result of Stoll's accusations and also how its appearance correlates to the end of the Cold War and to a period of rethinking the significance of *testimonio* after the defeat of the revolutionary projects that had animated it. Beverley, in his foundational 1989 article "The Margin at the Center," defined *testimonio* as, in part, a literary and cultural form that reflects national liberation and other social movements of the 1960s and 1970s. Its roots are far older than this, he points out, but its current canonization, as represented by the prize in this category that Casa de las Americas began to award in 1970, gives a new platform to those involved in the struggle against exploitation in Latin America.[35] In 1995, in subsequent reflections on Menchú's *testimonio*, Beverley does not abandon the framework of this anti-colonial and anti-imperialist political praxis that gave *testimonio* much of its significance when it first became a recognized genre. But because he now seeks to address Stoll's accusations against Menchú, he also turns to a scholarly work that had addressed similar accusations regarding Holocaust testimony, Shoshana Felman and Dori Laub's 1992 book *Testimony: Crises of Witnessing in Literature, Psychoanalysis and History*.[36]

Laub's research addressed the insidious effects of Holocaust denialism. Laub had been working with Holocaust survivors through the Fortunoff Video

Archive for Holocaust Testimony at Yale University, which he cofounded, and through his clinical practice as a psychiatrist and psychoanalyst. On the basis of that research he addressed the tension that existed between historians and victim-witnesses over who had the more authoritative voice when it came to accurately portraying the events of the genocide. Historians had become fearful that witness statements by death camp survivors, whose narratives of the events were by their very nature subjective, fragmentary, and marked by the passage of time, might inadvertently provide ammunition for Holocaust deniers, who could exploit inconsistencies in those stories to cast doubt on the very fact of the genocide. Laub sought to explain how these testimonies are true but in a way that might fall outside the norms of scholarly historical inquiry. What Laub discovered in his work with survivors is that the content of Holocaust testimony reveals something of the resistance strategies of the survivor. In a section on "Testimony and Historical Truth," he explores the disconnect between the historians' approach to testimony and his own.[37] Laub recounts a lengthy anecdote about the testimony provided by a Holocaust survivor who was present at the Auschwitz uprising of 1944. Her testimony caused concern among historians because she claimed to have seen four crematoria chimneys burst into flame during the uprising, when in fact only one chimney had burned, leading to doubts about her reliability and fears that the discrepancies in her testimony might lend fuel to Holocaust deniers.[38] Laub found the historians' concern with the factual record misplaced in this instance. He writes that the survivor was testifying not to "empirical historical facts" but to a "historical truth," namely, "the very secret of survival and of resistance to extermination."[39] In other words, "not to the number of the chimneys blown up, but to something else more radical, more crucial: the reality of an unimaginable occurrence. . . . The number mattered less than the fact of the occurrence."[40] Laub provides a compelling account of why a narrow focus on the factual elements of Holocaust survivor testimony misses the larger historical truths that the testimony conveys and that are concentrated in the figure of the victim-witness herself. This is an element of testimony that "the historians could not hear."[41]

Beverley's rebuttal to Stoll cites extensively from this portion of Laub's essay. Stoll is like the historians in Laub's anecdote, Beverley implies, because he misses the larger point of Menchú's testimony by focusing exclusively on the factual record and by attempting to dismiss her voice from accounts of the violence. Beverley writes against those who, like Stoll, "grant testimonial narrators like Rigoberta Menchú only the possibility of being witnesses, but not the power to create their own narrative authority and negotiate its conditions of truth and representativity."[42]

Indeed, Beverley underscores the power of Menchú's voice when he compares a moment in her text to a moment from the film *Schindler's List* and suggests that Menchú's storytelling skills are similar to Spielberg's. He observes, "Something of the experience of the body in pain or hunger or danger inheres in *testimonio*," and he describes his response to Menchú's account of the torture of her brother—the very passage questioned by Stoll as factually incorrect. Beverley writes:

> At the climax of the massacre, [Menchú] describes how the witnesses experience an almost involuntary shudder of revulsion and anger, which the soldiers sense and which puts them on their guard. Reading this passage, you also experience this revulsion—and the possibility of defiance even in the face of the threat of death—through a mechanism of identification, just as you do at the most intense moments of *Schindler's List*—for example, when the women in the concentration camp, who have been congratulating each other on surviving the selection process, suddenly realize that their children have been rounded up in the meantime and are being taken to the gas chambers in trucks. These are instances . . . where the experience of the Real breaks through the repetitive passivity of witnessing imposed by the repression itself.[43]

Here we see the mirroring effects between Holocaust witnessing and Maya witnessing. Beverley's juxtaposition of the two allows us to see the traumatic element of Menchú's narrative more clearly, now that we perceive it through its reflection in *Schindler's List*.

This mirroring also allows us to see more clearly Menchú's skills as a narrator. Beverley is not exactly comparing the two events, the Guatemalan army's extermination of guerrilla fighters with the Nazi extermination of Jewish children. He is comparing, rather, Menchú's narrative skill to Spielberg's in conveying the horror of these atrocities—the use of which does not detract from the truth but on the contrary brings it home more forcefully by showing us how those present were shocked out of their "passive witnessing." The witnessing in question is twofold. It is ours, that of the readers/viewers who have been hit by a wave of horror and cannot retain our composure as passive consumers of atrocity. But even more so it refers to the Maya villagers and Jewish women depicted in these scenes, who were forced, by Nazi and Guatemalan perpetrators, to become involuntary witnesses to the extermination of their families and were able to respond actively to it with rage and revulsion. Beverley puts these scenes from *Schindler's List* and *I, Rigoberta Menchú* together to underscore the power of Menchú's testimonial voice, the agency she has found for herself in the art of narrative.

One of the interesting points about Laub's approach to the Holocaust survivor's agency, to the "secret of survival and resistance to extermination" that her testimony reveals, is that it is based on a concept of traumatic silence. Laub postulates that the stories the survivors tell about themselves, about their experiences in the camps or in hiding, allowed them to develop inner resources to survive their ordeals. But these resistance strategies often involve forms of not-knowing on the part of the survivor, of repressed or inaccessible knowledge, that is, of silences that represent knowledge that is so traumatic that it would overwhelm or undermine their survival strategies. He acknowledges that the historians' job may be to break those silences, to impose the missing pieces of the story on the survivor, so as to restore that repressed knowledge back to the historical record.[44] But that is not Laub's job. He writes: "The listener . . . must listen to and hear the silence," must respect the limits of the survivor's knowledge:

> My attempt as interviewer and as listener was precisely to respect—not to upset, not to trespass—the subtle balance between what the woman [an Auschwitz survivor] *knew* and what she *did not*, or *could not, know*. It was only as the price of this respect, I felt, this respect of the constraints and of the boundaries of silence, that what the woman *did know* in a way that none of us did—what she came to testify about—could come forth and could receive, indeed, a hearing.[45]

What the survivor does not know about her own situation, far from disqualifying her from testifying about it, as the historians in his account would have it, worried as they are by the power of Holocaust deniers and conscious perhaps of their more public role compared to that of the psychoanalyst, is on the contrary the very thing that makes her able to testify to it in a way that only she can.

Beverley's appropriation of Laub's work, however, is emphatically not based on a concept of silence as agency. In Beverley's work, speech is agency, integral to political struggle. Menchú is "an agent of a transformative project that aspires to become hegemonic in its own right," a "'protagonist of history,'" as she says of herself and other Mayas.⁴⁶ She insists on being seen as the author of her own story. Why then would Beverley turn to Laub's radically distinct understanding of resistance, to which silence, not speech, testifies? Has he rewritten Menchú's story of heroic resistance to extermination, with its future-oriented framework of revolutionary politics and its ideologically motivated, conscious, and strategic use of silence, into a far more ambivalent story of traumatized resistance, whose silences are unconscious to the witness, known to the clinician and historian but not to herself?⁴⁷

The proximity of *Me llamo Rigoberta Menchú* to *Schindler's List* does bring into greater focus the traumatic elements of Menchú's narrative, which are many. But however effective Beverley's operation of juxtaposition might be, trauma as an event, trauma as a story that needs telling, is not ultimately what Beverley is after when he turns the Auschwitz survivor's testimony into a mirror for Menchú's testimony. What Beverley is interested in is the model that Laub provides for how witnesses "break the frame" of situations of extreme powerlessness and degradation by orienting themselves to a liberated future.⁴⁸

Even though "liberation" means something very different for Menchú in 1983 than it does for Laub's survivors as they remember the Holocaust, the two meanings achieve a kind of powerful coalescence when they are juxtaposed. Both Laub and Beverley are speaking about resistance, after all, and claiming for it—resistance, not trauma—the status of a historical event. True, the differences between these two must not be effaced. We recognize that Menchú was involved in a resistance movement that dignified suffering, a concept with little purchase in Auschwitz testimony, and we recognize that trauma remains, for Laub's Auschwitz survivor, the most fundamental truth of the history she recounts, no matter how much resistance to it she displays. Even so, there are common lessons that we can infer from the mirroring of these two radically different testimonial situations, speaking to radically different historical moments, involving a radically different scale of destruction. These lessons have to do with being able to recognize the witness as an author in her own right, one who is intent on surviving the degradation she has suffered and who wields the narrative power of her testimony to her own ends. Although the words of the witness-author do not wield the same kind of authority as the words of the historian, hers too belong at the center of the story the West tells about itself. Across the many differences separating Menchú from the Auschwitz survivor, each has been recognized as holding a particular kind of dignity and as offering a particular kind of challenge to the extraordinary violence she faced. This challenge is anchored in the testimony she constructs and constitutes, in fact, that testimony's deeper, "nontransparent" truth, which is an unverifiable truth.[49]

The Shoah-FAFG Testimonies

Let us now turn to the partnership between the USC Shoah Foundation and the Fundación de Antropología Forense de Guatemala (FAFG). Here I will discuss the two organizations in the partnership, analyze how the FAFG adopts and adapts the Shoah Foundation's model of Holocaust testimonies, then ask: Does the transposition of the Shoah Foundation's model of Holocaust testimony to Guatemala depoliticize Cold War history? Close examination of the FAFG testimonies suggests alternative approaches to thinking about the dialogue between Holocaust testimony and Maya testimony in contemporary Guatemala.

The FAFG was founded in 1992, originally named the Equipo de Antropología Forense de Guatemala (EAFG). It became one of the most active groups dedicated to the victims of human rights abuses and was modeled on and trained by Argentina's pioneering post-dictatorship Equipo Argentino de Antropología Forense. Its early work focused on exhumations of mass graves in the Rabinal area, where local civilian "patrulleros," organized and supported by the Army, had committed massacres in the communities of Río Negro, Plan de Sánchez, and Chichupac. It was appointed court investigator in these cases, and its work was crucial to the eventual prosecutions of the perpetrators.[50]

Since its founding, the FAFG has also been a militant human rights organization. It has condemned the counterinsurgency campaign, rejected the ideology behind it, and labeled the military and paramilitary perpetrators criminals. Its forensic work has been undertaken in collaboration with the affected communities and in order to support the activism of victim aid organizations. It has complemented that forensic work with scholarly analysis of the causes of the violence and its effects on the population. The EAFG's 1995 book *Las masacres en Rabinal* included systemic and structural analysis of the violence—that is, explanatory historical and sociological accounts that drew on the work of Marxist, liberation theology, and anti-colonial authors and activists. The book offered a path-breaking narrative reconstruction of the events based on its own extensive gathering of victim testimonies as well as on published guerrilla testimonies and unpublished army documents. It labeled the massacres of Maya villagers in Rabinal and other locations "genocidal" several years before the report authored by the UN-sponsored Commission on Historical Clarification would do so.[51]

Today the FAFG is more circumspect and avoids the term "genocide."[52] Now that trials for genocide and other crimes against humanity have become a feature of the Guatemalan political landscape, the term is more partisan and polemical than ever. Yet the FAFG has continued to operate as both a human rights organization and an authoritative court investigator. Its forensic findings have been used in multiple cases. It has worked with family activists to return the remains of the victims to their home communities for proper burial. Its exhumations and inhumations have become fertile sites of community activism and Maya revival and are at the heart of the process of constructing rural memories of the war.[53] Since 2004, it has extended the reach of its forensic investigative work to include cases of *desaparecidos*; this includes those who were disappeared during the war by state security forces as well as those who have disappeared, more recently, on their way north to the United States.

The FAFG has collected witness and victim testimony since its inception. Testimony is part of its arsenal of forensic tools, essential for enabling forensic scientists to locate unmarked graves. It has relied on family members for vital information about the events leading up to specific acts of disappearance, murder, and massacre. But as Fredy Peccerelli, the organization's director, recounts, FAFG staff realized that these testimonies were constrained by the forensic framework; family members and surviving victims had more to say about their experiences. The FAFG reached out to the Shoah Foundation because it had come to understand memory work as an end or a good in itself, beyond the needs of forensic science—"not to flee from the past," as one FAFG staffer put it when I visited. The FAFG staffer noted that the topic of the war "causes problems" and that there are efforts to silence it when it is brought up in schools. The FAFG's priority, she continued, is that the audiovisual testimony contribute to fostering awareness about Guatemala's recent past.[54] Therefore, starting in 2015, the FAFG expanded its mission. It began recording nonforensic audiovisual testimony by witnesses and survivors of Guatemala's human rights atrocities. This is where the Shoah Foundation enters the picture.

The Shoah Foundation was founded by director Steven Spielberg following the success of the film *Schindler's List*. Its original mission was to produce audiovisual testimony by as many survivors of the Holocaust as possible.[55] The foundation implemented measures to distance itself from Spielberg and from his films so as to avoid a potentially damning association between Holocaust survivor testimonies and Hollywood-style feature (i.e., fictional) films.[56] Yet as film scholar Noah Shenker argues, the connections between Hollywood filmmaking and the Shoah Foundation's testimonies run deep. He sees *Schindler's List* "as a source narrative" for the Holocaust testimonies archived by the Shoah Foundation and argues that its approach to these testimonies is guided by several core ideas related to its Hollywood origins.[57] These include its belief in the power of storytelling and in the visual image and its emphasis on "lessons of healing and forgiveness" rather than on "the darker, more traumatic aftershocks of the Holocaust."[58] Furthermore, despite the project's conscious attempts to distance itself from Hollywood, it is closely associated with Spielberg in the public eye, a fact that generated both benefits and drawbacks when it came to gathering testimony, as sociologist Alejandro Baer has pointed out.[59]

Beyond the relative influence of Hollywood, the form and content of these Holocaust testimonies are determined by a desire to be relevant to historians and to combat Holocaust denialism. The point is not only to tell a powerful story that inspires future generations; it is also important that the testimonies support the research efforts of historians and provide evidence to buttress claims that the crimes did in fact occur. Because the individual, subjective memories of survivors are easy targets for deniers, the Shoah Foundation directly addresses concerns about the survivors' "veracity" and takes steps to demonstrate and preserve the integrity of the testimonies.[60] It does this through protocols regarding access to and use of the testimonies that are designed to protect them from tampering and to maintain them as the intellectual property of the Shoah Foundation. It also does this through the production format of the video testimonies. Videographers are instructed not to move the camera at all once filming has started, because camera movement can be interpreted as a kind of editorial intervention by the Shoah Foundation that then becomes part of the "message" of the testimony transmitted to viewers.[61] Furthermore, the testimonies are unedited—evidence that the materials have not been manipulated during their production. Videographers are instructed to avoid all cuts except those necessary for technical reasons—that is, for changing the videotape or the camera battery. The idea is to shield against accusations that the footage has been selectively edited or otherwise tampered with by the foundation.[62]

The content of the testimonies, too, reflects concern about the question of historical reliability. Shenker notes that interviewers are trained to ask questions developed "to verify and anchor subjective memories, thus grounding them in established historical and sociological data," and to elicit concrete and specific details from the witness about times, places, settings, and so forth, "not only to reconstruct the events, but also to establish the veracity of memory by cross-referencing it against more empirically objective information mentioned in other testimonies or in historical documents."[63] The Shoah Foundation therefore seeks to make survivor testimony a reliable and verifiable source of knowledge about the past that is useful for scholarly historical inquiry. The Shoah Foundation insists that its interviewers press the survivors to elicit historically verifiable descriptions of their experiences, using closed questions alongside open ones.[64]

The Visual History Archive (VHA) contains about fifty-five thousand testimonies by survivors of genocide; of these, fifty-two thousand are from Holocaust survivors, collected during the period 1994–2005.[65] Before the merger of the VHA's collection of Holocaust audiovisual testimony with the collection at the U.S. Holocaust Memorial Museum, it was the largest Holocaust audiovisual testimony archive in the world, a status it consciously sought to achieve.[66] Starting in 2009, the Shoah Foundation's Institute for Visual History and Education, which houses the VHA, decided to expand its holdings to include audiovisual testimonies by survivors of genocides other than the Holocaust: Armenia, Nanjing, Cambodia, Rwanda, Guatemala, and others.

What is the thinking behind this Holocaust institution's decision to promote the memory of other historical events as part of its mission? As Shenker notes, this is part of its efforts to create a sustainable model for its archival project and to become relevant "beyond the Holocaust."[67] This transition reflects the foundation's understanding of testimony as an instrument that fosters humanistic values such as hope, empathy, understanding, and "the possibilities for every individual to counter hatred."[68] Spielberg told the *New York Times* in 2018, "The Holocaust cannot stand alone. . . . We're expanding our scope to counter many forms of hate."[69] Another paradigm that serves to gather these various events under one roof is "genocide" as a historical and sociological concept. The foundation's Center for Advanced Genocide Research opened in 2014, marking its interest in genocide as an area of comparative scholarly analysis and generating a series of new research initiatives along these lines.

With respect to the Guatemalan genocide, the Shoah Foundation's Center for Advanced Genocide Research has promoted important research initiatives focusing on the events and their aftermath. In Guatemala itself, meanwhile, the Shoah Foundation provides technical support for the FAFG on how to produce survivor testimonies and houses the testimonies on its website and controls access to them there. The Shoah Foundation–FAFG partnership has so far generated over five hundred audiovisual testimonies, of which thirty-two can be viewed through the Visual History Archive as of this writing. Of these, five are in K'iche', the rest in Spanish.[70]

In many respects, the Shoah-FAFG testimonies constitute a direct transposition of a Holocaust template onto the Guatemalan situation. Relying on Alejandro Baer and Noah Shenker's respective syntheses of the main features of this template, we can identify several elements of the FAFG testimonies that clearly follow the Shoah Foundation's template:

1. The FAFG tries to give a three-act structure to the testimonies, with a beginning (prewar), middle (war), and end (postwar).

2. The testimonial situation takes place in or around the survivor's home rather than in an institutional setting.

3. At the end of the testimony, the witness is invited to show family photographs.

4. The testimony is guided by one interviewer who does not participate in the storytelling process but limits themselves to asking questions.

5. The interviewer asks a mix of open and closed questions; the closed questions seek to elicit empirical and verifiable facts about the events, the pursuit of which can lead interviewers to frequently interrupt the witness's testimony.

6. The camera position remains stable and fixed over the course of the interview, and an attempt is made to limit the number of breaks or cuts in the filming.

With respect to each of these elements, the Shoah Foundation template is visible. Yet in most instances it has been visibly either modified or adapted by the FAFG. Furthermore, its use in Guatemala is guided by reasons that overlap yet are not identical to those underlying the Shoah Foundation's use, reasons that respond to the particular circumstances of the post-conflict period in Guatemala. In other words, beneath an apparently simple case of transposition lies a more complex situation in which the actions are similar but the meanings behind them are different.

Let us start by analyzing the three-act structure of the testimonies. Shenker links the tripartite structure explicitly to Hollywood notions of effective storytelling. He suggests that the Shoah Foundation's preference for coherent, well-structured narrative lines mirrors the preferences of producers of conventional Hollywood scripts and that its interest in testimonies that cover "before, during and after" reproduces the three-act structure of commercial movies.[71] Baer offers different motives for why the Shoah Foundation implemented the three-part structure: one, to streamline and standardize the process of recording the testimonies, which it wanted to keep within a two-hour limit; two, out of respect for the survivors, to show that listeners are interested in more than the survivor's encounter with death.[72] For the FAFG, the decision to ask survivors about their lives before and after the genocidal events is motivated by reasons similar to those suggested by Baer, but also holds further significance: the "before" and "after" questions allow the FAFG to differentiate these testimonies from the forensic and legal testimonies it has also collected, creating a different optic or framework for its memory efforts. Peccerelli, the FAFG director, explains that the partnership with the Shoah Foundation involved retraining the FAFG's investigators to ask different kinds of questions, not only "what happened, who's the victim, what did you see, but also what's your first memory? How was growing up in your town? What did you eat?" He comments: "The part that's new for us is the part that happened before. It might not be the most interesting to scholars but for me what happened, the life before, is my favorite, because I've never seen them smile in an interview or remember good things." Investigators following the new guidelines might be the first to have asked witnesses about themselves: "No one asked them about themselves, not the truth commission, the Church commission, the trial judge, no one asked who they are."[73] This method of eliciting and presenting those memories bears the Shoah Foundation's imprint, but the FAFG's desire to record memories unconnected to human rights atrocities predates the partnership and responds to the local ecology of testimonial practices.

From the start, the FAFG's video testimony project was meant to operate outside the frame of legal prosecutions. It is worth noting that the FAFG consciously chose this path, in contrast to other Guatemalan human rights projects involving witness testimony, which were obligated by political necessity to operate outside the prosecutorial frame. Let us consider the two most important human rights reports to have emerged in Guatemala in the 1990s: the so-called REMHI report emitted by the Human Rights Office of the Guatemalan Archdiocese, also known as *Guatemala: Nunca más*, in

1998; and the UN-sponsored Commission on Historical Clarification report "Guatemala: Memory of Silence," released in 1999 (subsequent references to these reports will be to the "REMHI," for "Recuperación de la Memoria Histórica," and the "CEH," for "Comisión de Esclarecimiento Histórico"). The office putting forth the REMHI report decided that it would be better able to fulfill its aim of airing stories about the violence if participants were freed from being involved with questions of criminal liability. The witnesses it interviewed included victims, perpetrators, and victim-perpetrators (e.g., conscripted civilian militias), all of them anonymous, and without including any names of those allegedly responsible for the atrocities; only the dead and disappeared were named in its report. It was cognizant of the climate of fear in which it conducted its work, with both victims and perpetrators wary of facing reprisals from military higher-ups.[74] For its part, the CEH was legally prohibited, under the terms of the UN-brokered 1996 Peace Accords between the government and the rebels, from using any of its findings in any potential future legal prosecutions. Although this in some sense limited the report's ultimate political relevance, it significantly enhanced its historiographical relevance, as historian Greg Grandin has persuasively argued—the CEH could focus on the work of "historical clarification" without having to worry about folding the unpalatable truths it uncovered into a broader political project of reconciliation.[75] In both cases, it was a complex political calculus, factoring in the real dangers of leveling legally relevant accusations against the Guatemalan army, that led these two reports to become marginal to criminal proceedings. We remember that in the REMHI case, this was not enough to shield its lead author, Monsignor Juan Gerardi, from reprisals; he was assassinated two days after he released the report.[76]

The Shoah-FAFG testimonies are, like the REMHI and CEH reports, explicitly divorced from the legal realm. But this was not a calculus based on (justifiable) fear of making criminal accusations; the FAFG's primary mission, forensic in nature, is intrinsically connected to the enforcement of statutes in criminal law. Rather, its decision to create its own visual history archive responds to a desire to focus on testimonial memory work as meaningful for reasons beyond the law. The FAFG consciously chose to follow a nonforensic path. Its witness-centric approach further means that it provides no overarching expert or explanatory frameworks beyond the implicit frameworks embedded in the interviewers' questions.

It is thanks to this decision that the FAFG's video testimonies contain a wealth of information that is too personal to contribute to a factual reconstruction of events yet contributes immeasurably to our understanding of the witnesses' experience. Some survivors recount prophetic visions or dreams. For example, Pedro Pacheco Bop, a witness to the 1982 Chel massacre by the Guatemalan army in the Ixil region and one of its few survivors, remembers that his father had a dream sometime before the massacre. The lead-in to this portion of the testimony is significant. The interviewer had asked Pacheco Bop to talk about the day of the massacre itself: "What was that day like, what was that massacre here in Chel? What do you remember?" Pacheco Bop does not answer directly. Instead, as if setting the stage for his father's prophetic dream, he talks about the climate of knowing and not-knowing in the village, mentioning that some villagers would spend nights in hiding, out in the forest: "They knew that something was going to happen." In the pause that follows this statement, the interviewer asks: "Did you live here with your whole family?" This is how Pacheco Bop answers:

> Yes, with my whole family. One time—I have another story to tell you—one time, before my father's death, my father, who saw in his dream, at dawn, my father began to recount it. "Do you know what my dream means?" he asked me. "I went, they brought me to a city. I was able to see good houses, good houses," he said. "So then, there, when they showed me, these are the rooms," he told me. "A man told me," my father told me. "Places for everyone are already ready, they told me. And then he ordered me, now go back," he told me. "So who knows? What this means," my father told me, surrounded by the whole family now. Because there were nine people living at home. So we didn't realize. Who knows.[77]

As Pacheco Bop tells the story of his father recounting the dream, his voice gets rougher and starts to break. We remember that Pacheco Bop's father was murdered in the massacre, along with his mother, grandfather, great-grandfather, and five younger siblings. But he collects himself and finishes the story, then begins another. This one is about how his great-grandfather also foresaw the violence:

> They hadn't yet massacred everyone yet. He saw something directly. God gave him wisdom or knowledge. And he called me over. . . . "I know you are not going to die," he told me. "I know you are not going to die. You are going to get out of this," he said. I stood there listening to him, just listening.

"Whereas we," he told me, "we are not going to get out of this. We are going to die. Because we will not suffer hunger, thirst, cold, insect bites in the jungle. That's why we will die. Whereas you, yes, you will get out of this," he told me. I just looked at him. Not answering.[78]

These stories and the dream-visions they describe are intensely intimate, glimpses into the inner lives of the victims. Loaded with a significance that remains enigmatic, this section of Pacheco Bop's testimony is utterly unrelated to the factual reconstruction of human rights abuses. What it does instead is establish and record a Maya frame of reference for the war.

Others witnesses recount minor events in minute detail. Sandra Patricia García Paredes, a member of the EGP who was raped and tortured by the military when she was fifteen, tells a story about her journey back to Guatemala in 1995, after she had spent years living in exile in Nicaragua and Cuba. The main event of the story is that she got on the wrong bus, leading her down a circuitous path that involved unexpected roads and encounters[79]—not a useful story from a prosecutorial standpoint and not connected to a specific act of human rights abuse. Yet whether taken literally or figuratively—the scene calls to mind the hero's return home after a long odyssey—it illuminates a facet of the rebels' postwar lives.

It is in part because of the FAFG's interest in these less formal, less institutionally codified and institutionally useful forms of testimony that it follows the Shoah Foundation template and conducts interviews in the survivors' home spaces rather than in institutional spaces. But here too we find difference beneath the apparent similarity. The home space was chosen by the Shoah Foundation for the Holocaust testimonies in order to contribute to the spectator's experience of intimate access to the survivor. However, the rigidity of the Shoah Foundation's staging makes it clear that this is not a normal domestic scene; the home space appears like a stage backdrop that signifies "home" but doesn't feel particularly homey or intimate. In Guatemala, in contrast, the home space feels more authentically domestic. It has been difficult for the FAFG production team to resignify "home" into a backdrop for the testimonial situation because the interview frame is often broken during the filming by real "home" sounds off camera, such as chicken clucks, rooster crows, car motors, babies crying, the voices of other people; occasionally, children wander into the camera's field of vision. In one case, the entire crew leaves the survivor's home at the end of the interview and follows him through town to visit sites of atrocity and memorialization—in this case, the bridge at Chel where the 1982 massacre took place. The overall effect is to enhance the experience of intimacy and immediacy, the sense that we are watching a story unfold in real time and in proximity to the events.

Although the Shoah-FAFG testimonies are not meant to be used in legal proceedings, the testimonies repeatedly gesture toward the forensic reality characteristic of a post-genocide situation and adopt those features of the Shoah Foundation's Holocaust testimonies that were designed to guard against genocide denial. This reflects a convergence between the two institutions with respect to justifiable fears about genocide denial. Indeed, the FAFG faces this reality far more immediately than the Shoah Foundation, because genocide denial in Guatemala is the dominant discourse and enjoys the explicit support of many sectors of the government, and because impunity for genocidal crimes remains a real possibility for many Guatemalan perpetrators. For this reason, FAFG testimonies reveal a strong concern with ensuring the historical veracity of the testimonies.

Regarding the interview footage, most Shoah-FAFG testimonies contain several cuts, whether in response to an emotional breakdown on the part of the witness or to a technical problem like a power outage, or for reasons that remain unexplained. Yet even though the FAFG doesn't follow the Shoah Foundation's protocol in presenting seamless footage of the witnesses, interviewers seem conscious of the need to avoid the appearance of selective editing; interviewers announce the cuts formally, using similar phrasing across all the testimonies: "Now we'll take a break" or "We'll take a short break."

Furthermore, like the Shoah Foundation's Holocaust interviewers, the Guatemalan interviewers seek to elicit verifiable information from the survivors about the atrocities they witnessed. Survivors may be pressed repeatedly by interviewers to clarify details about the events they describe: "What was the place you were captured?" "Where was the place you were tortured?" Was the assault "in a house or on the street?"[80] Many FAFG interviewers show a preference for closed questions that elicit precise quantitative and historical information. Repeatedly, the forensic reality intrudes into the testimonies to shape the narrative arc.

A particularly marked instance of this can be found in this exchange with Pacheco Bop. At Chel, the Guatemalan army murdered close to a hundred people—many of them children and the elderly—by striking them with machetes and throwing them over a bridge into a river. Afterward, Pacheco Bop and a handful of other survivors emerged from their hiding places and brought some of the bodies up from the river to bury them in the cemetery. In this testimony, the FAFG interviewer plays a key role in structuring Pacheco Bop's narrative of that moment, using questions that help us visualize what he experienced. Here is one sequence of questions, with the answers omitted so to as to better convey the pattern of closed questioning:

> FAFG: How did you carry them? [referring to the bodies of the massacre victims]
>
> FAFG: How long did you carry them like that?
>
> FAFG: To bury them?
>
> FAFG: Your little brothers, were you able to recover them?
>
> FAFG: How old were you when this happened?
>
> FAFG: And the people who helped you, were they part of the community?

These are important questions, yet FAFG interviewers can be dogged in their pursuit of answers, as if the testimonial situation were a courtroom. Closed questions, such as those asking for a numerical answer, prevent the witness from proceeding at their own pace, or constitute a missed opportunity to follow up with questions that respond to the emotional content of the testimony. As the exchange continues, Pacheco Bop's interviewer pursues an answer for the historical record that the witness seems hesitant to state aloud:

> FAFG: From your household, no one survived?
>
> PACHECO: Mm-hmm.
>
> FAFG: Of the people who lived with you, none . . . ?
>
> PACHECO: [Makes a sound as if to speak]
>
> FAFG: Other than you?
>
> PACHECO: Yes?

FAFG: No one survived the massacre?

PACHECO: Mm-hmm, no.

FAFG: Just you.

PACHECO: Just me. [Nods in assent]

FAFG: [Sighs audibly][81]

The interviewer practically forces Pacheco Bop to state that he is the sole survivor of a large family group, even though he has implied this clearly several times earlier in the testimony. It is interesting to note that Pacheco Bop was one of the witnesses for the prosecution in the 2013 trial of General Efraín Ríos Montt for genocide—meaning that he had already provided legal testimony about the Chel massacre. In pressing Pacheco Bop to state what he has already repeatedly communicated, is the interviewer motivated by the fact that the guilty verdict against Ríos Montt was overturned by a corrupt appeals court? Like the Shoah Foundation's Holocaust testimonies, the FAFG testimonies display a concern with historical verifiability that can have determinative, structuring effects on the content of the testimony.

Perhaps the most significant Shoah Foundation imprint concerns the camera and continuity. Even with interruptions by the interviewer, the intrusion of outside noises, and breaks in the filming, each FAFG testimony is centered squarely on the witness and their story. The camera remains on the witness across the entire time of the testimony, which can last from one to five hours. In the world of first-person Holocaust narratives, this practically unwavering attention to the witness is common in both print and audiovisual sources. The same is not true in Guatemala. The choice to follow this model therefore holds a symbolic importance that can perhaps be best appreciated if we again compare and contrast the Shoah-FAFG testimonies to other human rights endeavors in postwar Guatemala that collect and rely on witness testimony. The various criminal proceedings for human rights violations that have taken place in Guatemala, along with the human rights reports emitted by the Catholic Church, the UN, and other institutions, also hold a commitment to combating silence about the past and upholding narrative accounts of the past. They too involve a concerted effort to give the victims a voice and to record their speech, in recognition that these practices hold symbolic reparative and emancipatory potential beyond the specific legal or historiographical ramifications also entailed. But in all of these other endeavors, in contrast to the Shoah-FAFG project, victim testimony has been cut into digestible fragments and integrated into another narrative. The witnesses are not just testifying to their own experience but also serving as informants for a larger project that subsumes individual voices under its own aims. Consider the following short excerpt from the REMHI report, in the subsection "Altered Grieving Process." Note that the italics denote quotations from victim testimony and the regular font denotes the voice of the "narrator" of the report, who in these sections appears to be a psychologist:

> All cultures have rituals, customs, and expressions of grief that emanate from their particular beliefs about life and death. In Mayan culture, death is not understood as the absence of life, and relationships with the ancestors are part of daily life.
>
> *It was necessary to leave the ancestors behind, the dead were far away, the sacred sites too. Case 569, Cobán, Alta Verapaz, 1981.*
>
> In situations of extreme sociopolitical violence and displacement, mourning also becomes a means of confronting many other losses, and it involves a sense of community. People have not only lost friends and family members but also may feel a loss of respect for the victims and survivors.
>
> *We saw how they killed people, young people, young women. So many people were left grieving—wives for their husbands; people who were poor and couldn't provide for their children. We grieved for all of those things. Case 2230 (massacre), Jolomhuitz, Huehuetenango, 1981.*
>
> The meaning of grief is broader than the loss of the loved ones. There is mourning for the destruction of the quintessential family purpose. Grief often had significant political and economic ramifications, loss of status, and loss of the land and the feeling of connection to it. The destruction of corn and nature represented more than deprivation or the loss of food; it was an assault on community identity.[82]

The authors of the REMHI report adopt the role of narrator, using victim testimony to demonstrate their points and breaking it down into short, illustrative fragments. In contrast, in the Shoah-FAFG initiative, the victim testimonies remain whole and the victims retain their status as the primary narrators of the project. Thus, because the Shoah-FAFG testimonies are practically unedited and contain only a few cuts; because the face of the witness remains always at their center; and because the witness remains the primary narrator, these testimonies do far more to "rewrite" Guatemalan history from the perspective of the victim-survivors than do other postwar human rights projects.

We can see the extent to which the Shoah-FAFG testimonies have adopted the Shoah Foundation template for Holocaust testimonies. The concern with historical verifiability; with creating a coherent narrative arc; with generating a personal story that is not limited to the events of the genocide; and with maintaining a continuous and stable focus on the witness are all features of the Shoah Foundation's approach to Holocaust testimony; some of these are unique to it, whereas others are shared across other Holocaust audiovisual testimony initiatives. But the FAFG's adoption of these features involves significant modifications; it is not a wholesale import. Furthermore, the FAFG finds these features important for reasons that do not always overlap with the Shoah Foundation's reasons but respond instead to Guatemalan circumstances and to its own evolving mission as a human rights organization.

An excellent example of this flexible approach to the template can be found in the Shoah-FAFG's treatment of testimony by Maya victims who are memory activists and/or current or former members of left-wing political organizations, including guerrilla groups. In adopting and adapting the Shoah Foundation's model of Holocaust audiovisual testimony, including some elements of its Hollywood style and its focus on genocide as a crime of hate, the FAFG testimonies, we might think, depoliticize Guatemala's Cold War history, erasing the ideological conflicts that motivated the war and that concerned basic questions about what kind of country Guatemala should be. The question is especially pertinent with regard to the war's Maya victims, who have often been represented as passive victims caught "between two armies," as anthropologist David Stoll famously proposed, unconcerned with big-picture questions about the future; their ideological commitments to the left continue to run the risk of being erased from the historical record.[83]

Do the Shoah-FAFG testimonies contribute to that erasure when they adopt the American-style approach to genocide exemplified by U.S.

Holocaust consciousness and embodied by the Shoah Foundation? Despite my initial fears about this, my conclusion is that no, they don't. Yes, some of the Maya who provide testimony expressly self-identify as nonideological victims of military repression.[84] But others are former guerrillas who explain and defend their decisions to join armed groups.[85] Others are former residents of the "Comunidades de Pueblos en Resistencia," groups of Maya villagers who fled into the forest to escape army repression and who received support from the EGP.[86] Others are victim- and memory-activists fighting against the judicial impunity enjoyed by army forces.[87] In at least one case, that of Rosalina Tuyuc, the witness has been included in this archive because of their activism on behalf of the families of those massacred or disappeared; Tuyuc was not a direct witness to human rights atrocities. In other words, Maya activism as such is a valued piece of the historical experience that the Shoah-FAFG partnership seeks to reveal. One hears in these testimonies the revolutionary and activist commitments of the victims, who thereby testify to something other than helplessness and trauma.

As I mentioned above, the Shoah-FAFG testimonies are largely unedited and have few cuts. What is especially significant about this practically unbroken attention to the witness is that in Guatemala it has previously been limited to only one testimonial genre: the revolutionary *testimonio*. Rigoberta Menchú's 1983 *Me llamo Rigoberta Menchú* is the best-known example. Although these narrative accounts are mediated and dialogical, the witness is the sole focus of attention. Furthermore, many of the Shoah-FAFG testimonies adopt the narrative arc that characterizes Menchú's story—the survivors recount the process of consciousness-raising that led them to become political militants or memory activists. These testimonies therefore reveal an unexpected kinship with revolutionary *testimonio*. Ironically, it would seem that the Spielberg-style "redemptive" approach to the Holocaust in fact meshes with the future-oriented approach to the genocidal past developed by generations of Guatemalans and espoused by today's Maya activists.

Early in the twenty-first century Andreas Huyssen expressed concern that Holocaust memory in Latin America might become a screen that blocks access to local memory.[88] We might say that the Shoah Foundation does indeed provide FAFG with a kind of screen—but a screen not in the "obstacle" sense meant by Huyssen but in the sense of "political cover" meant by Emeterio Toj Medrano, a Maya rebel leader within the EGP whose lengthy video testimony is one of the highlights of the Shoah-FAFG collection. Toj Medrano tells us that, since he was a political operative for an underground guerrilla organization, he and his family would adopt "screen" identities, known as "pantallas," fictive personas that hid their real identity so that they might adapt to local circumstances and carry out their political work clandestinely.

Toj Medrano recounts in his testimony that one of the "screen names" he chose was "Julián Aj Pop," a name that carries metaphorical significance in reference to his Maya heritage:

FAFG: What name did you use?

Toj: Pedro.

FAFG: Last name?

Toj: Aj Pop. Then I changed it to Julián Aj Pop. What was behind "Julián," no, I don't think it was symbolic. "Aj Pop," yes. It meant, or means, a lot for Maya culture.

FAFG: Can you tell us what it means?

Toj: Well, it's like the people who sit on the *pop*, the mat, to hold session, to think, to orient others, but most of all, to think. To think. It's not that back then I considered myself an adviser. But I thought, I'm going to give myself this name in honor of the ancestors who created this Maya civilization.[89]

We might think of the Shoah-FAFG partnership as this kind of "pantalla," a way to smuggle in, to honor and dignify, a consciousness-raising work that has been deemed subversive, destabilizing. Memory work around the Guatemalan genocide remains contested; remembering and studying the events is considered by many to constitute a dangerous or subversive act. The need for this screen is therefore an acknowledgment that, in Guatemala itself, the climate is not propitious for the narrative knowledge carried by the victims of the Guatemalan Civil War, whatever their ideological beliefs might be. The existence of the Shoah Foundation–FAFG partnership therefore suggests a kind of solidarity or asylum politics between Holocaust memory and Maya memory, where the Holocaust becomes a screen that does not block local memory but provides it the cover it needs to do its work.

But we might legitimately wonder whether this "screen" effect constitutes a true form of Holocaust consciousness in Guatemala. Has Holocaust consciousness shaped the consciousness of Guatemala's Cold War history through this partnership? The testimonies themselves contain no Holocaust "content." The survivors who present their stories do not allude to the role of the Shoah Foundation in making these videos possible. Nevertheless, because the Shoah Foundation houses the FAFG testimonies on its website and because the FAFG adopted and adapted the Shoah Foundation's Holocaust template, these Guatemalan testimonies form a part of the larger universe of Holocaust education and are indeed at least partially a product of it. They join an increasingly complex constellation of genocidal events that are connected to and partially subsumed by a Holocaust "template" yet remain separate from it as well. We might speak therefore of a Holocaust unconscious at work here, one that is embedded in the situation and that helps bring that situation into being but is not brought to awareness by its protagonists.

Indeed, the fact that this project involves institutional connections that are not immediately transparent to the participants raises some concerns about the unequal balance of power between the witnesses and the organization that houses their testimonies. The Shoah Foundation's channeling of resources from "the global North" to "the global South" follows the routes laid out by decades of policies surrounding U.S. aid to Latin America. Regardless of its good intentions, the Shoah Foundation occupies the position of other U.S. philanthropic and government aid agencies, which by the very structure of their endeavor perpetuate neocolonial relations. It exports technological know-how to support the postwar development of a society whose impoverishment and insecurity, seen in historical and hemispheric perspective, result from policies designed to make Americans wealthy and secure. There is also a corollary to this that is worth mentioning: many of Latin America's primary historical sources are held in U.S. and European archives, constituting an active colonial legacy with a negative impact on the ability of Latin American scholars to conduct research into their own societies. These facts must be acknowledged, but it would be a mistake to allow them to overshadow our understanding of the Shoah Foundation's work in Guatemala. The partnership advances the FAFG's goals. Regarding the fact that the Shoah Foundation archives the testimonies in the United States, this is seen by the FAFG as a net benefit, at least for now, because it shields the testimonies from the instabilities of Guatemalan politics.[90]

In analyzing the partnership, I have focused on how the Shoah Foundation's Holocaust consciousness impacts these Guatemalan accounts of the war. It is also worth asking the question in reverse: How does Guatemalan consciousness of Cold War atrocities reach back across the space between the two countries to shape America's Holocaust consciousness? On the U.S. side, the Shoah-FAFG partnership is significant because of what it tells us about the evolving "Americanization" of the Holocaust. The Shoah Foundation represents in some ways the pinnacle of an Americanized Holocaust consciousness. Emerging out of the film *Schindler's List*, its origins are inextricably tied to the commercialization of the Holocaust, and its preferences overlap with Hollywood's preference for stories of healing and hope.[91] But in another very important respect, the Shoah Foundation goes against the grain of an Americanized approach to the Holocaust because it prefers what Michael Rothberg has termed "multidirectional memory" instead of the "competitive memory" framework characteristic of memory cultures in the United States. "Competitive memory" operates on the principal that "the remembrance of one history erase[s] others from view."[92] "Multidirectional memory," in contrast, emerges through dialogue, cross-referencing, and borrowing.[93] In the United States, the competitive-memory approach to the Holocaust has been dominant for the past forty-odd years.[94] However, the Shoah Foundation's decision to expand its mission beyond the Holocaust to encompass genocide and to promote the value of testimony more generally suggests that this "competitive" approach might be on the wane. To be clear, nowhere does the foundation use or acknowledge "multidirectional memory" as an operating principle. Yet it exemplifies this principle in its recent work. Rothberg writes: "Far from blocking other historical memories from view in a competitive struggle for recognition, the emergence of Holocaust memory on a global scale has contributed to the articulation of other histories."[95] Holocaust testimonies, in other words, have served to catalyze and support testimonies of the Guatemalan genocide—even if, it bears repeating, such testimonies were already in circulation long before the Shoah-FAFG partnership. One can equally imagine a reverse pathway: a student interested in the Guatemalan genocide logs on to the VHA and eventually follows the path of the FAFG testimonies to the Holocaust testimonies, virtual close neighbors.

Conclusion

In responding to Stoll's work, the critics discussed here brought Maya testimony into closer affinity with Holocaust testimony around the questions of what it is possible for survivors to say about genocidal atrocities, where it is said and to whom, how we receive their words, and what we do with them. Because Stoll's accusations ignited reflections on whether victim-witness testimony is a reliable source of historical evidence, they led Latin Americanist scholars to draw on work on Holocaust testimony that responds to similar questions about how Holocaust memory and victim testimony relate to other modes of historical understanding and are constructed through particular testimonial situations whose circumstances warrant scrutiny. Lyotard, LaCapra, Langer, Levi, Laub, and Felman have nothing to say about the Cold War context of revolutionary politics and counterinsurgent anti-Communist repression that frames the Maya testimonies at issue here, but they become quite useful in identifying the existence of a particularly fraught communicative situation surrounding witness testimony about genocide. They explain how and why this kind of testimony carries a "nontransparent" truth that a "just-the-facts" approach cannot convey.[96]

In the court of public opinion, there was another link between Menchú's testimony and Holocaust testimony. In 1998, the same year Stoll's *Rigoberta Menchú and the Story of All Poor Guatemalans* appeared, accusations were launched against Binjamin Wilkomirski, author of a childhood Holocaust memoir, *Fragments* (1995), for having entirely invented his story.[97] There is wide consensus that these charges were correct: Wilkomirski was not a Holocaust survivor, was not Jewish, and was not even named Wilkomirski. His autobiography was a work of fiction—unlike Menchú's. Yet it is a measure of Stoll's success that despite the many differences in the degree and kind of falsification, these two were seen by some academics and at least one mainstream media source as parallel instances of fraudulent self-presentation, with damaging consequences for the cause of memory and justice that each was taken to represent. The academics who defended Wilkomirski and Menchú, meanwhile, were charged with being dismissive of the truth.[98]

How to explain to a sound-bite culture that Menchú was not a liar? The ways by which we arrive at an accepted truth about a past event, whether through legal proceedings or through historical inquiry, are complex and arduous. In the case of a narrative like Menchú's, they involve submitting the revolutionary and Christian frameworks of her testimony, or of the testimonies that circulate in Guatemala today, to standards of evidence that do some violence to these narratives, rendering them anachronistic or unreliable or quirky and pushing them to the margins. To refract the case through the Holocaust, as the Latin Americanist scholars examined here did, offers an interesting alternative, one that relies on popular consensus in the U.S. about the truth of the Jewish Holocaust. These scholars showed that, inconsistencies in Menchú's *testimonio* notwithstanding, she was no more "lying" about the events she described than was the Auschwitz survivor who testified to having seen four chimneys of the crematoria explode when historians know that only one did.

This defense of Holocaust witness testimony might seem self-evident now, a facile move in a context in which the facts of the Holocaust have come to constitute a near-unassailable truth and have largely moved out of the courts. One might think it hardly matters to the overall endeavor of Holocaust consciousness if one survivor's testimony fails to meet legal or historical standards of evidence, or if a "Wilkomirski" arrives on the scene to perpetrate a hoax. But we should not be so confident. Genocide denialism is alive and well and remains a powerful weapon of anti-Semitism and racism. Today as much as thirty years ago, it remains important to explain why and how survivor testimony can be true and valid.

Conclusion

Recuerda, mi nombre y Uruguay
(Remember, my name and Uruguay)[1]

Latin American writers, community leaders, and political activists facing state repression have seen themselves reflected in Holocaust histories and in the voices of Holocaust survivors. They have used Holocaust terms to describe the atrocities that happened in their own countries. In Argentina during the military dictatorship, the use of the Holocaust to mark the intensity of state brutality was at first limited to clandestine oppositional writings. Soon it became a feature of the Argentine Jewish community's mixed response to authoritarian rule, sparked by Jacobo Timerman's direct comparisons between Argentina's Jewish community leaders and the Judenrat of Nazi Europe. This led to intense debate in the Jewish community about whether Holocaust comparisons were historically or morally justified. In the early 1980s, still under dictatorship, Holocaust consciousness expanded outward beyond the Jewish community to other sectors, becoming a piece of human rights and anti-authoritarian discourse. Holocaust references became common in the following years, inside and outside the Jewish community. Especially during the years of the so-called "memory boom," starting in 1995, Holocaust consciousness became woven into the fabric of post-dictatorship thought.

Meanwhile, in the 1970s and at the crossroads of Argentina and Mexico, Holocaust testimonies by Jewish victims helped José Emilio Pacheco and Tununa Mercado develop their commitment to memory as resistance against state repression. Both of these writers made it easier to access testimonial accounts of the Nazi ghettos and death camps. In his novel *Morirás lejos* and in other writings, Pacheco drew the Mexican public's attention to the problem of Holocaust deniers and implied—between the lines—a connection between denial of the Holocaust and the silence surrounding the crimes of the Mexican and Argentine governments. Mercado's essays brought into focus the "testimonial situation," the time and place of speaking and being heard, to show the power of this historical moment that speaks beyond its moment.

In Guatemala, the Cold War was intricately connected to Latin America's colonial legacies, and both have at times been refracted through the Holocaust. Maya scholar Demetrio Cojtí Cuxil, in his work on the occasion of the 1992 commemorations of Columbus and with the genocidal counterinsurgency campaigns of the 1980s in mind, invoked the Holocaust as a mirror for Maya history. The Holocaust became material for a platform of Indigenous self-determination that connects the extermination of sixteenth-century Maya resisters to the extermination of twentieth-century Maya villagers. More recently, the concept of "genocide" to describe the atrocities of the military's "scorched earth" campaign has gained more legal traction in Guatemala and has become, therefore, ever more controversial in a media environment dominated by business interests and a "business-as-usual" mentality. The partnership between the USC Shoah Foundation and the Fundación de Antropología Forense de Guatemala to produce audiovisual testimony by Maya survivors illustrates how the Holocaust has been adapted to this new scenario.

These are not simple transpositions, even if they might occasionally seem so. They require creative literary and intellectual activity and are the result of diverse encounters and dialogues among people and texts that circulate in unexpected ways. The role of Jewish Latin Americans, and of Holocaust survivors who settled in Latin America, is crucial. Peruvian novelist Isaac Goldemberg suggests that Jewish immigrants in the Americas have forged an especially protean memory. He writes that "memory is not a return to the past but rather the adaptation of past events to the circumstances of the present; it reorganizes and gives new meaning to what has been lost."[2] Saúl Sosnowski similarly asserts that the meaning given to the losses of the Holocaust by Jewish Latin Americans has been forged in dialogue with more local, "closer events."[3]

Let us go back, briefly, to the 1940s and an early example of how colonial atrocities, some of those "closer events," were perceived through the Holocaust. I refer to the work of Boleslao Lewin, a Polish Jew from Lodz who in the 1930s immigrated to Latin America, first to Uruguay, then to Argentina.[4] He was an active contributor to the Yiddish-language press in Argentina and became an esteemed professor of history at the universities in Rosario and La Plata, a recognized expert in two areas of Latin American history. One of these was Jewish life in Latin America, on which he published widely. The other was the Tupac Amaru rebellion of 1780–1782, an early movement for political independence that took place in what is now highland Peru and Bolivia. Tupac Amaru was the name of its leader, a mestizo mule driver who modeled himself on the last Inca king of the sixteenth century. He led a massive uprising of mestizo and native peoples in a campaign to expel Spanish rulers; after some important military successes, the movement was brutally repressed and Tupac Amaru was beheaded. Lewin's book *Tupac Amaru el Rebelde* was a pioneering work that inspired generations of scholars.

We can see these interests converge in the short preface to Lewin's book about Tupac Amaru, which first appeared in 1943. There, "with deep pain," he noted a connection between his own "catastrophic epoch" and that of late eighteenth-century Peru.[5] Years later, in the book's second edition, from 1957, he made a second statement of parallelism between the genocide of the European Jews and the Indigenous genocide of the colonial Americas, this one clearly anchored in his own subjective vision:

> Now, a personal clarification. I am often asked why I, a European, devote myself to a topic that is so authentically American. I must confess that in my opinion there are no topics that belong exclusively to anyone. There are only topics that find a resonance in the spirit of the author. I believe that I would study, with the same disinterested dedication, the admirable figure of fray Bartolomé de las Casas and the uprising of the Jews of the Warsaw Ghetto, incomparable in its heroic grandeur, practically a suicide battle by tens of thousands of men made desperate by the indifference of the world. Despite all their differences, seeming and real, there is in each case a common denominator: the struggle for the dignity of the human being.[6]

Lewin looked back at the struggles of rebels and thinkers against Spanish colonial rule and saw in them a shadow of the Jewish experience during the Nazi Holocaust. That distant time and place become a not-so-distant mirror for his own time and place.

The idea of a "distant mirror" belongs to historian Barbara Tuchman. In her work on medieval Europe, she was drawn to the "calamitous 14th century" for the lessons it might provide her about human survival in the calamitous twentieth century. She noted the work of an earlier historian, Edouard Perroy, who had contemplated medieval Europe with the same intention. As Tuchman notes, he wrote "a book on the Hundred Years' War while dodging the Gestapo during World War II," and he arrived at an awareness of what he called the "mutual light" that one period throws on the other.[7] A not-so-distant world away, also in the early 1940s, Lewin reached a similar awareness when he refracted a colonial war for independence through the lens of the Nazi destruction of the European Jews. His reference to the Jewish Holocaust, like Cojtí's forty years later, constitutes a refusal to normalize atrocities against Indigenous insurgents.

For Lewin, the events in Warsaw in 1943 were taken as emblematic of Nazi horrors at the time. This fact is significant for how the Holocaust is remembered in Latin America, and especially for how it comes to be connected to Indigenous struggles against genocide. As I discussed in Chapter 1, throughout the 1950s and 1960s the concept of "Shoah uGevurah" (Holocaust and heroism) dominated practices of Holocaust memorialization. The Warsaw ghetto uprising was foundational to this concept, which was centered on the figure of the Jewish rebel and partisan. In the language of the day, the Warsaw resisters, unlike the vast majority of Jews, refused to go "like sheep to the slaughter"—in Spanish the slogan is "¡Judíos, no vayamos como rebaño al degollador!"

As historian Peter Novick points out, the Warsaw ghetto uprising was exceptional when compared to the experiences of most Jewish communities under Nazism; it is not a historically accurate emblem of the times.[8] But if we look at this event through the lens of the historian who sees their own time reflected through the distant or not-so-distant mirror of the past, then the uprising as emblem makes more sense. It resonates with struggles for national liberation that marked the decades after World War II—Jewish, anti-colonial, anti-imperial, Indigenous—and unites these diverse struggles for self-determination under a shared model of resistance to oppression. But that same reflection casts a harsh light on other kinds of victims, those who resist in less tangible or visible ways.

In Argentina, commemorative events in honor of the uprising continued to be central into the early 1980s and were often venues for expressing human rights discourses that were critical of the military dictatorship. Here too we see debate about the wisdom of the transposition—it sparked protest by a Holocaust survivor at the 1983 commemoration who felt that the two events should be kept separate.[9] It was not until the post-dictatorship period that, in Argentina, the emblematic images of death camp victims came to stand in for the Holocaust, much as Dachau, a concentration camp that housed many political prisoners and that had emblematized Nazi repression, would eventually be replaced by Auschwitz and the gas chambers as the main symbol of the catastrophe. The predominant tendencies in Latin American Holocaust consciousness that I have examined here have in a sense attempted to mediate this symbolic transition, creating a palimpsest of sorts such that the older image of the victim whose resistance is visible to all the world is not effaced by the newer image, that of the victim whose resistance remains unperceived or imperceptible and whose dehumanization by the machinery of death would appear to be total. How to secure the line to the Holocaust's rebellious victims when one drops into "the darkest and deepest abyss" of Auschwitz, Treblinka, Chelmo, Belzec, the victims who are killed "like cattle, like matter, like things that had neither body nor soul"?[10]

Some of the Holocaust references described in this book emerge in a state of crisis, others in its aftermath. Whether living through one or the other of these situations, the thinkers I have discussed wield the voices of the Holocaust to criticize state violence in the Cold War era. These uses have been subject to much questioning and debate, guided by the ever-present threat of denialism. In most of the cases seen here, the point is to work *against* denialism, to denaturalize the violence, to refuse the "national security" fears that normalize it, to spark our nobler senses and make us see and feel and hear otherwise. Does this intention succeed? It faces many obstacles, not least because the voices of the Holocaust do not speak in unison and the senses are easily dulled.

I remember one of my earliest and most poignant encounters with one of these attempts to refocus the senses, Mauricio Rosencof's novel-memoir *Las cartas que no llegaron* (The Letters That Never Came), published in 2000. Rosencof offers an intimate vision of the necessity and difficulty of describing one experience of suffering through another. In the 1960s he was a leader of the Movimiento de Liberación Nacional in Uruguay, the Tupamaros. Arrested in 1972 by the military, in 1973 he became a hostage in their war against subversives. As he describes in his book, for eleven years he was repeatedly tortured and kept in a hole in the ground in a state of almost total isolation. Rosencof later told his biographer that he and the other hostages were so emaciated that, on a rare occasion when they were brought together in the light of day, one hostage confessed that the other reminded him of "a Jew from a concentration camp."[11]

Rosencof was a well-known playwright in the 1960s, before his imprisonment. Since his release in 1985, he has written numerous narrative accounts of his captivity. *The Letters That Never Came* is striking among these because of its strong Holocaust themes. The title of the memoir refers to the letters that Rosencof's father Isaac never received from the family he had left behind in Poland, who were all exterminated by the Nazis. It refers as well to a letter Rosencof writes to his father in the present, after his father has died. And it also refers to the letters that Rosencof wrote to his father from prison, words "escritas en el aire" (written in the air) like those of Pedro Rojas, the fallen Spanish Republican fighter invented and memorialized by the poet César Vallejo:

> He used to write with his big finger in the air
> "Long live all combanions! Pedro Rojas"[12]

These unread, unwritten, or unreceived letters establish a string of broken transmissions that Rosencof brings into analogical alignment over the course of the story: the abyss between Isaac in Uruguay and his extended family in Poland; between Isaac and his captive son; between the son and his dead father; between suffering and the speaking or writing of it.

Rosencof's memoir is, in part, a melancholy meditation on loss and lack. "I'm not sure why I'm writing you all this today, *Viejo*," Rosencof muses.

> Maybe it's so you'll know what I remember but especially, so you'll know what I remember and realize how little I know. I want to know more, Papa, I want more memories, more of your memories.[13]

He recounts a trip to Auschwitz and his father's shtetl in Poland, where he is unable to find a single trace of his father's former life or family. It is a futile compensatory gesture.

There is, nevertheless, a powerful reparative moment that sifts through the multitemporal layers and creates a link between the Holocaust, the national liberation movement, the dictatorship, and the present day. The link is a memory of his childhood, an image of his parent's patio in Montevideo, where a strange couple is seated, number tattoos on their arms, carrying the words of a family member from beyond the grave:

> And in the middle of that jungle, the patio set, made of cheap wood, you painted and varnished it so it looked really good, were two single chairs, both with armrests, plus a two-seater where

that couple once sat, they didn't speak Spanish and wanted to learn, they had picked up a thing or two, a word here and there, because they were from the Old Country, they had been with our family, with all the relatives, or maybe just one who talked to them before going to the ovens—"Remember, my name and Uruguay, come on, repeat it"—and they were sitting there, and I was a young boy.[14]

What moves me when I read this scene? That there would be an injunction to remember on the way to the gas chambers? That it would be heard and followed, reaching its destination? That the child would not understand the pathos of this until much, much later? That the patio furniture would be realer to him than this? That part of what he finally understands is how much he still doesn't understand? That the story is factually incorrect but historically and emotionally true, because although no one went off to their deaths in the crematoria ovens, the injunction to "remember, my name and Uruguay," resonates with the spirit of Rosencof's times? That however improbably, somewhere near the ovens, Uruguay waves like a banner, signifying freedom? That this significance is now a thing of the past? That Holocaust imagery would allow me to grasp the destruction of that national idea and the people who carried it?

Inevitably, stories like this demonstrate that a reparative approach to the Holocaust requires one to listen only to parts of the Holocaust experience, those parts from which we can come back with our sense of futurity more or less intact. Geoffrey Hartman writes that the Shoah "cannot . . . be taken into mind without a severe disturbance."[15] In many of the instances of Holocaust consciousness I have described in this book, that disturbance has subsided, or has been made to subside. Does this mean that the Holocaust has not really been "taken into mind"? Perhaps. I have wondered this myself over the course of writing, coming down on one or the other side of the question, depending on the day. A lesson of this book is that there are different ways of grasping the Holocaust, some more reparative than others.

Notes

Notes to the Introduction

1. Joseph, "What We Now Know," 26, 27–28.
2. I take the word "crusade" from Grandin, *The Last Colonial Massacre*, xii. For more on the ideology of "national security," see Feierstein, "National Security Doctrines," 492.
3. I do not touch here on the many non-print sources, such as museums, memorials, and the visual arts, where Holocaust consciousness becomes intertwined with reflections on state violence in Latin America. See Huyssen, *Present Pasts*; Aizenberg, "Nation and Holocaust Narration."
4. Rabe, *The Killing Zone*. I thank Diana Wang for her comments about "consciousness" as a sign of an "internalized" awareness.
5. Huyssen, *Present Pasts*, 13–14.
6. Baer and Sznaider, *Memory and Forgetting*, 12.
7. For an overview, see Milgram, *Entre la aceptación y el rechazo*. For individual countries, see Senkman, *Argentina, la Segunda Guerra Mundial*; Chinski, "La representación del 'horror nazi'"; Kahan and Lvovich, "Los usos del Holocausto"; Gleizer, *El exilio incómodo*; Avni, "Cárdenas, México"; Bokser Liwerant et al., "Claves conceptuales y metodológicas"; Lesser, *Welcoming the Undesirables*.
8. Avni, "Los países," 15.
9. Aizenberg, *On the Edge of the Holocaust*; Szurmuk, *Una vocación desmesurada*; Sitman, "Counter Discourse in Argentina"; Schwertfeger, "Simultaneity of Past and Present."
10. Spitzer, *Hotel Bolivia*; Zaga Mograbi and Cohen Cohen, *El rostro de la verdad*; Kaplan, *Dominican Haven*; Wells, *Tropical Zion*; Chavarria, "Archival Memory Systems." See also the journal *Cuadernos de la Shoá*, published since 2010 by Argentina's Sherit Hapleita (Jewish Association in Argentina of Survivors of Nazi Persecution); the 2017 research initiative Memories of Mobility, Migration and Integration, on Holocaust testimony by Latin American Jews, sponsored by the USC Shoah Foundation–The Institute for Visual History and Education (https://sfi.usc.edu/

video/memories-mobility-migration-and-integration); and the Red Latinoamericana para la Enseñanza de la Shoá (https://www.facebook.com/LAESred). Other studies include this topic within the broader topic of Jewish immigrant experience, as is the case with these studies of Jewish communities in Cuba and Mexico: Levine, *Tropical Diaspora*; Levinson, *The Jewish Community of Cuba*; Bejarano, *The Jewish Community of Cuba*; Cimet, *Ashkenazi Jews in Mexico*. The descendants of Holocaust survivors have received some limited attention: Wang, *Hijos de la guerra*; Zaretsky, "Child Survivors of the Shoah."

11. Chinski, "Ilustrar la memoria." The "letters that never arrived" is the title of a novel by Uruguayan Mauricio Rosencof (*Las cartas que no llegaron*). The motif also appears in Bernardo Kucinski's *K*, a novelized account of his father's search for a daughter (the author's sister) who "disappeared" during Brazil's last military dictatorship. Kucinski, *K*, 28.

12. Agosín, *Among the Angels of Memory*; Chejfec, *Lenta biografía*; Halfon, *The Polish Boxer*; Heker, *El fin de la historia*; Laub, *Diary of the Fall*; Scliar, *The War in Bom Fim*. For scholarly analyses of these and other writers, see Agosín, *Memory, Oblivion, and Jewish Culture*; Huberman and Meter, *Memoria y representación*; Ruggiero, *The Jewish Diaspora*; Sheinin and Baer Barr, *The Jewish Diaspora*; Stavans, "The Impact of the Holocaust in Latin America." This is only a sampling of relevant works.

13. See Novick, *The Holocaust in American Life*; Flanzbaum, *The Americanization of the Holocaust*; Rosenfeld, "The Americanization of the Holocaust."

14. See also Baer and Sznaider on this point: "People involved in memory work do not attempt necessarily to expand their audiences' knowledge of past events in their full complexity. The primary function and goal is to keep the catastrophe—not only the event in history but also the potential for its repetition—before everyone's eyes." Baer and Sznaider, *Memory and Forgetting*, 6.

15. The reference appeared in an article he wrote for the Mexican daily *El Universal*, where he had found work. Bernetti and Giardinelli, *México*, 175. This and all other translations are my own unless otherwise noted.

16. Meyer, "Escoged, pues, la vida," 12. Meyer gave his speech in Spanish: "Los argentinos hemos vivido un mini-holocausto durante los años de la dictadura militar."

17. Rarihokwats, *Guatemala*, 5.

18. Valdés, *Tejas verdes*, 6.

19. Todorov, *Les abus de la mémoire*, 30.

20. Todorov, 34, 38.

21. Todorov, 38.

22. Wiesel, "Now We Know," 165.

23. Wiesel, 166. Other commentators on the Aché genocide, in essays collected alongside Wiesel, use loaded Holocaust terms, referring to "death camps," "Nazi extermination centers," "Belsen," and "Jewish Police" (this last in reference to the

practice of making the Aché complicit in their own destruction). Arens, *Genocide*, 17, 31–32, 59, 109. The Argentine Jewish newspaper *Nueva Presencia* covered the genocide of the Aché, including an interview with Simón Wiesenthal in which he expresses concern about the involvement of Nazi war criminals in the Paraguayan genocide. Two years later historian Leonardo Senkman, also in *Nueva Presencia*, referred to it as a "final solution." Senkman, "Los indios del silencio," 8.

24. Levi, *The Drowned and the Saved*, 9.

25. Levi, 9.

26. Roskies, *Against the Apocalypse*, 4.

27. Verbitsky, *Rodolfo Walsh*.

28. These trauma and mourning approaches have been most fully and eloquently developed with respect to the Southern Cone. See, for example, Avelar, *The Untimely Present*; Jelin, *State Repression*, 60–75; Kaiser, *Postmemories of Terror*.

29. I refer here to the title of the book by Baer and Sznaider cited earlier: *Memory and Forgetting in the Post-Holocaust Era: The Ethics of Never Again*.

30. Levy and Sznaider, *The Holocaust and Memory*, 43.

31. Sanyal, *Memory and Complicity*, 3.

32. Rothberg, *Multidirectional Memory*, 2, 3. On the Holocaust and competitive memory frames in the U.S., see also Stein, "Whose Memories? Whose Victimhood?"

33. Rothberg, *Multidirectional Memory*, 3.

34. Rothberg, 6.

35. Rothberg, 22.

36. Levy and Sznaider, *The Holocaust and Memory*, 43.

37. Arendt, *Eichmann in Jerusalem*; Levy and Sznaider, *The Holocaust and Memory*, 43.

38. Jay, "Allegories of Evil," 110.

39. Jay, 111.

40. Alexander, "On the Social Construction of Moral Universals," 49, 51.

41. Levy and Sznaider, *The Holocaust and Memory*, 4.

42. The distinction between lowercase and uppercase usages is occasionally relevant, but not generally for the cases described here. See Garber and Zuckerman, "Why Do We Call the Holocaust," 197; Lang, *Genocide*, 117. See also journalist Robert Fisk's "Do You Know the Difference" for an illuminating reflection on the distinction between "Armenian holocaust" and "Armenian Holocaust" among newspaper editors.

43. Baer and Sznaider, *Memory and Forgetting*, 1.

44. Roland, "Reception and Representation"; Miles, "Third World Views."

45. Levy and Sznaider, *Holocaust and Memory*, 10–11.

46. Rothberg, *Multidirectional Memory*, 265.

47. Comparative work under the rubric of genocide studies has been especially fruitful. Levene, "Is the Holocaust Simply Another Example of Genocide?"; Millet, *The Victims of Slavery*; Moses, "Conceptual Blockages"; Bauer, "On the Holocaust

and Other Genocides." See also the essays collected by Bloxham and Moses in *The Oxford Handbook of Genocide Studies*.

48. Rosenfeld, "The Politics of Uniqueness"; Rosenbaum, *Is the Holocaust Unique?* The "uniqueness" debate had multiple dimensions but was guided by arguments offered by some U.S. scholars of the Holocaust that the Nazi extermination of the Jews constitutes the only genocide in history.

49. See Smithers, "Rethinking Genocide in North America," for an overview and sources of the controversy as well as his own nuanced intervention. The volume edited by Rosenbaum, *Is the Holocaust Unique?*, was profoundly shaped by debates over whether the destruction of Native Americans in the United States constitutes a genocide and can be called a holocaust. For a convincing if inflammatory analysis, see Churchill, *A Little Matter of Genocide*.

50. Bischoping and Kalmin, "Public Opinion about Comparisons to the Holocaust," 486.

51. Alexander, "Stealing the Holocaust"; Bauer, "Whose Holocaust?" Bauer's thinking on this topic underwent a shift over the course of his career. Compare, for example, a more recent piece by Bauer, "On the Holocaust and Other Genocides."

52. Fermaglich, *American Dreams and Nazi Nightmares*, 11. She also writes that "a number of American Jewish thinkers . . . publicly emphasized the evils of Nazi concentration camps as a means of expressing prevalent intellectual concerns with bureaucracy, alienation, and conformity and of criticizing American society from a liberal perspective." Fermaglich, 23. Sanyal makes a similar point about post-WWII France, noting that "in the immediate aftermath of World War II, literature and film from the French-speaking world repeatedly sought not to singularize the Holocaust as *the* paradigm of historical trauma, but rather to connect its memory with other memories of atrocity, often through a focus on the complicities between distinctive regimes of violence." Sanyal, *Memory and Complicity*, 2.

53. Lipstadt suggests in *The Holocaust*, 150, that "the debate about uniqueness . . . has run out of steam." This may be true in the scholarly realm but not in the public realm. See, for example, Bartov et al., "An Open Letter to the Director of the U.S. Holocaust Museum," for evidence of the 2019 controversy surrounding use of the phrase "concentration camps" to describe detention camps on the U.S. border.

54. Torpey, "Introduction," 6.

55. LaCapra, *Representing the Holocaust*, 48.

56. See, for example, comments made by the Nazi Reinhard Spitzy, a former secretary to Von Ribentrop who had lived ten years in Argentina, during a colloquium in Madrid in response to the May 1979 airing of the television miniseries *Holocaust* in Spain: "Fine, 'Holocaust' is true, but you have to talk about the other Holocausts: the 12 million Indians massacred in North America, the one and a half million Armenians by the Turks . . . To talk only about the Jewish Holocaust is to poison public opinion." Quoted in Lerner, "'Holocausto' en España," 6.

57. Vergès was not Barbie's legal representative, but he consulted on the case for the defense.

58. Vidal-Naquet, *The Assassins of Memory*, 132.

59. Vidal-Naquet, 97.

60. Vidal-Naquet, 96.

61. Vidal-Naquet, 126.

62. LaCapra, *Representing the Holocaust*, 47. Moses likewise affirms, "Uniqueness is not a useful category for historical research." Moses, "Conceptual Blockages," 457. Novick puts it in even stronger terms: "The notion of uniqueness is quite vacuous. Every historical event, including the Holocaust, in some ways resembles events to which it might be compared and differs from them in some ways." Novick, *The Holocaust in American Life*, 9.

63. Vidal-Naquet, *The Assassins of Memory*, 96.

64. Feinmann, "Pensar y escribir después de la ESMA"; Feinmann, "Adorno y el ESMA (II)."

65. Novick, *The Holocaust in American Life*, 14, original emphasis.

66. Cited in Laplante, "Memory Battle," 654. For an argument about the similarities between the negationism that circulated during the trial and Holocaust negationism, see Casaús Arzú, "La exacerbación del racismo," 171.

67. Wieviorka, *The Era of the Witness*.

68. Rein, *Argentina, Israel and the Jews*, 196–228.

69. Novick, *The Holocaust in American Life*, 133.

70. Wieviorka, *The Era of the Witness*, 56, 66.

71. Wieviorka, 88. See also Segev in *The Seventh Million*, 361, for a similar perspective on the effects of the Eichmann trial.

72. Wieviorka, *The Era of the Witness*, 84.

73. Wieviorka, 87, 88, 89.

74. Cited in Wieviorka, 103.

75. Novick, *The Holocaust in American Life*, 131.

76. Rein, *Argentina, Israel and the Jews*, 219–21.

77. Novick, *The Holocaust in American Life*, 11; Moses, "Conceptual Blockages," 449.

78. Wieviorka, *The Era of the Witness*, 132. See also Moses in "Conceptual Blockages," 449, for a similar perspective.

79. Traverso, *Left Wing Melancholia*, 19.

80. Jelin, *State Repression*, 54.

81. Stern and Straus, "Introduction," 8.

82. McAllister, "Testimonial Truths and Revolutionary Mysteries," 97.

83. The idea of a "Latinamericanism after Eichmann" is modeled on Beverley, *Latinamericanism after 9/11*.

84. Traverso, *Left Wing Melancholia*, 10.

85. Rein, *Argentina, Israel and the Jews*, 217.
86. Rein, 220.
87. Jelin, *State Repression*, 141.
88. Robinson, "Human Rights History from the Ground Up," 32.
89. Calveiro, *Poder y desparición*, 128–29.
90. Calveiro, 136.
91. McAllister, "Testimonial Truths and Revolutionary Mysteries," 108, 97.
92. Levi, *Survival in Auschwitz*, 9.
93. Baer and Sznaider would be in partial agreement when they posit that the human rights ethic of "Nunca más" simultaneously conflicts with and reinforces the "No pasarán" ethic of anti-fascist struggles dating to the Spanish Civil War. Baer and Sznaider, *Memory and Forgetting*, 10.
94. Gurwitz, *Argentine Jews in the Age of Revolt*.
95. Traverso, *Left Wing Melancholia*, 13.
96. I discuss the Russell Tribunal and its decolonizing use of the concept of genocide in Chapter 4.
97. I borrow here a phrase from Visquerra's *Memoria, tiempo y sujeto*, 103.
98. Ellis, "Critical Thought and Messianic Trust," 377.
99. Avelar, *The Untimely Present*, 1.
100. See the essays collected in Corradi et al., *Fear at the Edge*.
101. Regarding the controversy surrounding this number, see Cué, "Polémica."
102. Argentina has the largest Jewish population of Latin America. In 2009 it was 182,000 (less than 0.5 percent of the total Argentine population); in 1970, it was 282,000 (almost 1 percent of the total Argentine population). After Argentina, 95,800 Jews lived in Brazil in 2009; in Mexico, 39,500; in Guatemala, 900. The total Jewish population in Latin America in 2009 was 390,600. See DellaPergola, "¿Cuántos somos hoy?," 314–15. For a broad historical overview of Jewish Latin America, see Laikin Elkin, *The Jews of Latin America*.
103. Avni, "Los países."
104. DellaPergola, "¿Cuántos somos hoy?," 314; Avni, "Los países." Note that this number does not include survivors who arrived in later years.
105. Wieviorka, *The Era of the Witness*, 82.
106. Grandin, "Politics by Other Means," 9–10; Schirmer, *Intimidades*.
107. Comisión de Esclarecimiento Histórico, *Guatemala, memoria del silencio*, 2: 318–21.
108. Guatemala's Jewish community numbers about nine hundred; the number of Holocaust survivors there has not been precisely identified. DellaPergola, "¿Cuántos somos hoy?," 314. See also Jewish Virtual Library, "Guatemala Virtual Jewish History Tour." An estimated 1,300 Jewish refugees entered Central America in the period 1933–1945. Avni, "Los países," 15.
109. Argentina's history of enabling Nazi perpetrators to settle there after the war is also a factor in its Holocaust consciousness but should not be overestimated; Chile

too enabled German Nazi immigrants, and these had close ties to Pinochet after the 1973 coup against Salvador Allende, in one case at least forming part of his machinery of torture and death, yet despite this close affiliation with Nazism, Chile has nowhere near the same level of Holocaust consciousness. See Mount, "Chile and the Nazis."

110. Novick argues that one of the reasons the Holocaust has become so important in American life is because it is a "consensual symbol," the only common denominator of Jewish identity in the U.S. in the late twentieth century. Novick, *The Holocaust in American Life*, 7.

Notes to Chapter 1

1. On the Judenrat councils, see Hilberg, *The Destruction of the European Jews*, 662–69; Trunk, *Judenrat*; Diner, "Historical Understanding," 130–37.

2. See the essays by Ignacio Klich and others in Senkman, *El antisemitismo en la Argentina*; Feitlowitz, *A Lexicon of Terror*, 89–109; Sheinin, "Deconstructing Anti-Semitism in Argentina," 72–85; Lotersztain, *Los judíos bajo el terror*; Lipis, *Zikarón*; Kahan, *Memories That Lie a Little*; Bargil, *Ni silencio ni olvido*.

3. Gurevich, *Proyecto Testimonio*; Rein, *Argentina, Israel and the Jews*, 167–74.

4. Finchelstein, *The Ideological Origins of the Dirty War*.

5. Gurwitz, *Argentine Jews in the Age of Revolt*, 89–105, 112–24.

6. Bell, "Bitter Conquest," 285–308; Rein, *Argentine Jews or Jewish Argentines?* 133–67.

7. Bell, "In the Name of the Community," 97.

8. Bell, 102.

9. This estimate of the Jewish population is from Hebrew University of Jerusalem, cited by Kaufman, "Jewish Victims of Repression."

10. In 1983 *Nueva Presencia* claimed that 20 percent of the disappeared were Jewish but provided no source for the figure. Schiller, "¿Terminó la impunidad de los criminales?," 4. Others generally offer a lower number, though the disproportion remains. The Asociación de Familiares de Desaparecidos Judíos en Argentina (AFDJA) cites 12.5 percent of the disappeared as Jewish, in addition to 15 percent of those assassinated, in COSOFAM, *La violación de los derechos humanos*, 70; according to Laikin Elkin, "Good Germans in Argentina?," 7–11, Jews constituted 15 percent of the disappeared; Ben-Dror in "Antisemitism in Argentina" puts the number at 10 percent. Kaufman in "Jewish Victims of Repression," 488–91, offers an analysis of "the quantitative dimension" that analyzes the different numbers.

11. The Argentine National Commission on the Disappearance of Persons (CONADEP) estimates nine thousand, while human-rights groups estimate thirty thousand, and neither of these numbers includes those who were assassinated outright by the regime, that is, whose deaths are known. COSOFAM, *La violación de los derechos humanos*, 69–78.

12. See Timerman, *Prisoner without a Name*, 66; "Antisemitismo" in CONADEP, *Nunca más*. See also testimony by Graciela Geuna about her detention in the La Perla concentration camp, cited in Kaufman, "Jewish Victims of Repression," 490; and by Strejilevich, *A Single, Numberless Death*.

13. The 1981 publication of Timerman's book disseminated this knowledge, but it had already circulated in Argentina and especially abroad via the testimony of those who were able to visit detention centers (such as priests and rabbis) as well as of ex-detainees who witnessed the harsh treatment accorded to Jewish prisoners and gave testimony outside Argentina. See Kaufman, "Jewish Victims of Repression"; Sabin, "Two Argentine Escapees"; "Antisemitism."

14. James Neilson, a journalist living in Buenos Aires, reported for *Hadassah Magazine*, "Jews here are often unable to decide whether anti-Semitism is rife or scarcely worth taking note of." Neilson, "An Air of Uncertainty," 19.

15. See, for example, Admiral Massera's comments in "Massera y la libertad."

16. In September 1976 the government finally closed down Editorial Milicia, one of the main publishers of Nazi literature, but it promptly reappeared under a different name (Odal) before being outlawed again; the pro-Nazi magazine *Cabildo* continued to publish, and physical assaults on Jews and Jewish institutions remained uninvestigated. "La clausura de Milicia"; "Desenmascarar a los agresores antisemitas."

17. Kahan, *Memories That Lie a Little*, 95.

18. Feitlowitz, *A Lexicon of Terror*, 106.

19. See Bauer, "Whose Holocaust?"; Alexander, "Stealing the Holocaust"; Rosenfeld, "The Politics of Uniqueness"; Rosenbaum, *Is the Holocaust Unique?*

20. See Gurwitz, *Argentine Jews in the Age of Revolt*, 127–53, for Argentina's "Third World Zionism."

21. Novick, *The Holocaust in American Life*, 138.

22. In *Fraie Schtime*, *Nueva Presencia*, and *Nueva Sión*, each year the April and/or May editions featured one or more pieces devoted to commemorating the event and reflecting on its contemporary significance. Examples include: "El Ghetto de Varsovia"; "Del Holocausto a la rebelión"; "En el 32 aniversario del levantamiento"; "El Holocausto y la rebelión"; "Gloria a los luchadores"; "Por nuestra y vuestra liberación"; "Ni olvido ni perdón" (1981); "La rebelión del gueto."

23. Bauer, "¿Es posible un nuevo Holocausto?," 1; Senkman, "En torno al mito," 20; Senkman, "Contra el racismo," 5; DAIA, *No olvidarás*.

24. Klich, "Política comunitaria," 299. The piece initially appeared in 1985, first in article form in the Jewish newspaper *Nueva Sión*, then in the first edition of the Senkman volume.

25. Cadena Informativa, "Informe #1" (December 1976), in Verbitsky, *Rodolfo Walsh*, 38; Rodolfo Walsh, "Carta abierta de un escritor a la junta militar," in Verbitsky, *Rodolfo Walsh*, 122.

26. Cadena Informativa, "Informe #4" (July 1977), in Verbitsky, *Rodolfo Walsh*, 44; ANCLA, "El general Paladino" (February 9, 1977), in Verbitsky, *Rodolfo Walsh*, 84.

27. ANCLA, "El mundo en guerra" (August 27, 1976), in Verbitsky, *Rodolfo Walsh*, 48.

28. ANCLA, "Servicio especial" (March 15, 1977), in Verbitsky, *Rodolfo Walsh*, 90.

29. Schiller, "Eichmann," 1. The phrase was "un pacífico trabajador."

30. Laura Schenquer and Eduardo Raíces analyze an interesting case involving the magazine *Humor*, which in October 1979 published a series of satirical Holocaust cartoons. Schenquer and Raíces, "Una narrativa fallida."

31. The word "genocide" appears frequently in the journal *Controversia*, published by political exiles in Mexico (discussed in Chapter 2), and it is also highlighted in work by the Comisión Argentina por los Derechos Humanos titled *Argentina: Proceso al genocidio*. See also the March 1980 document circulated by a group of Argentine political exiles living in Europe that denounced the military's plan for a "final solution" of the disappeared. "Denuncia sobre la situación de los detenidos-desaparecidos en la Argentina," March 1980, p. 2, box 17, folder "Denuncia sobre la situación de los detenidos-desaparecidos en la Argentina, marzo 1980," Marshall Meyer Papers, Duke University Library.

32. "Desaparecidos: 'Nuevo Holocausto.'"

33. Cited in Feitlowitz, *A Lexicon of Terror*, 100.

34. Waxman, "From the Congressional Record," 13.

35. Kennedy, "Human Rights Violations in Argentina," S3376.

36. Halter, "Les juifs d'Argentine," 3.

37. See Klich, "Política comunitaria," 291.

38. "Sectores nazifascistas."

39. Toker, *Papá, Mamá*, 87–89.

40. "Mensaje de Massera."

41. Copy of letter and attached papers in box 18, folder "Human Rights Correspondence 1976–1989 4 of 4," Marshall Meyer Papers, Duke University Library. The photographs are taken from one of the many multilingual books of photographs published in Poland starting in 1959 by the League of Fighters for Freedom and Democracy. Most examples contain some combination of Polish, French, German, Russian, and/or English and appear under the title *1939–1945: We Have Not Forgotten*. The photographs used by Bernardo Rus in his letter to Massera were copied from an edition of the book that contained Hebrew captions as well as Polish, Russian, English, and French. I have not been able to identify the exact edition containing these five languages. My thanks to the librarians at the U.S. Holocaust Memorial Museum for their help with this source.

42. Bernardo and Sara Rus were not the only Holocaust survivors whose children were among the Argentine detainees and disappeared. References to other families crop up in international press accounts. Stephen Kinzer's lengthy piece in the *Boston Globe Magazine* includes an interview with Bernardo Burstein, an Auschwitz survivor whose son figured among the disappeared. Kinzer, "Missing in Argentina,"

18. A 1977 opinion piece by Raymond Mckay in the English-language *Buenos Aires Herald* centers on the story of the Erlichs, Polish survivors whose daughter Margarita had been kidnapped by security forces. In describing the Erlichs' situation, McKay alludes to 1976 Nobel Laureate Saul Bellow's novel *Mr. Sammler's Planet*, about a Holocaust survivor, and closes with Hannah Arendt's phrase "the banality of evil," from her coverage of the Eichmann trial in 1962—the reference would have been highly charged, given Argentina's involvement in the Eichmann case, a matter that continued to inflame nationalist sentiment. Mckay, "Mr. Erlich's planet." See also Wang, *Los niños escondidos*, 218–23, for her interview with a Holocaust survivor (who wished to remain anonymous) who had two children who were tortured and disappeared in Argentina but eventually released; also the documentary *Atención (Achtung)!*, directed by Bernardo Kononovich. The film contains interviews with several Holocaust survivors, including Elena Marx, whose daughter was disappeared by the junta in Argentina. Video testimony by Elena Marx and Sara Rus was collected by the Shoah Foundation and includes their reflections on their disappeared children and how it relates to their experiences as survivors of the Holocaust. See Elena Marx Holocaust Testimony; Scheine Maria Sara Laskier de Rus Holocaust Testimony.

43. Wang, *Hijos de la guerra*, 217.

44. This letter was published when Bernardo Rus passed away in 1984. Rus, "Rus: El clamor," 30.

45. Arcuschin et al., "Réplica al 'Informe especial.'" Sara Rus's testimony concerning her visit to the Israeli embassy in Buenos Aires to seek assistance in her son's case is fascinating for its invocation of the Holocaust. In that testimony she states that neither she nor any of the other parents of Jewish disappeared were well received by Israeli embassy officials but that on mention of the Holocaust crematoria, they were finally given due attention: "Me puse de frente y le dije [al Sr. Shamir de la embajada israelí]: por favor nosotros tenemos tanto tiempo, y estamos buscando a nuestros hijos tanto tiempo, salí de los hornos de Auschwitz y estoy acá frente suyo, usted me va a escuchar. Y nos escuchó." See "Desaparecidos en Argentina."

46. Feitlowitz, *A Lexicon of Terror*, 106.

47. Wiesel, *Night*, 12.

48. Timerman, *Prisoner without a Name*, 46–50.

49. Timerman, 155.

50. Timerman, 157.

51. Timerman, 140.

52. Timerman, 141.

53. Timerman, 155.

54. This line does not appear in the 1981 English translation. See Timerman, *Preso sin nombre*, 161.

55. Timerman, *Prisoner without a Name*, 140.

56. Timerman, 140–41. I have made slight modifications to the published translation.

57. Jacobo Timerman, "Elie Wiesel (Direct Translation of Suggestions Made by Jacobo Timerman, Friday, 20th of July 1979)," translated by Marshall Meyer, box 20, folder "Argentina—Jacobo Timerman 1978–84, 1991, 2002, 1 of 2," Marshall T. Meyer Papers, Duke University Library.

58. Citation from Timerman's Spanish manuscript version of the *Ma'ariv* article, which appeared 15 Tevet 5740 (January 4, 1980), box 20, folder "Argentina—Jacobo Timerman 1978–84, 1991, 2002, 1 of 2," Marshall T. Meyer Papers, Duke University Library. The Judenrat line subsequently appeared in *Prisoner without a Name*, 70–71. Timerman was not the first to use this word against the DAIA—a contributor to *Fraie Schtime* had already done so in 1978 to protest attacks against fellow progressive paper *Nueva Presencia* by right-wing elements of the Jewish leadership. Brinkman, "Marginales," 2.

59. Novick, *The Holocaust in American Life*, 14.

60. Vidal-Naquet, *The Assassins of Memory*, 177n92.

61. Ofer, "Linguistic Conceptualization," 585.

62. Ofer, 586–87.

63. Hilberg, *The Destruction of the European Jews*, 662–69.

64. For a discussion on the idea of "martyrs" and other debates relating to the passage of this law, see Segev's "Holocaust and Heroism" in *The Seventh Million*, 421–45.

65. Young, *The Texture of Memory*, 246, 256.

66. Ofer, "Linguistic Conceptualization," 587; Young, *The Texture of Memory*, 274.

67. For a taste of the controversy, see the following articles in *Midstream*: Varon, "Don't Rescue Latin American Jews!"; Varon, "The Canonization of Jacobo Timerman"; "Last Word on Timerman"; Varon, "Benno Weiser Varon Responds." See also Shestack, "Jacobo Timerman"; Lerner, "Argentine Jewry."

68. Lewis, "Final Solution in Argentina"; Russell, "Living with Ghosts," 38–40; Strouse, "Holocaust of One." Russell's article includes this line: "A Jew, Timerman has evoked the image of a new Holocaust."

69. Madanes, "El caso Timerman"; Muchnik, "Las declaraciones de Jacobo Timerman"; Muchnik, "Caso Timerman"; Schiller, "Ni vergonzantes ni vendepatrias"; "Tres nuevos elementos de juicio"; Vasokie, "Timerman." For Timerman's response to the controversy he stirred up with his statements, see Timerman, "Coming Home."

70. Gorenstein, "No somos ciudadanos de segunda categoría."

71. "DAIA: El antisemitismo."

72. "DAIA: Schonfeld goza"; "¿Hay antisemitismo en la Argentina?"

73. "DAIA informó."

74. "DAIA: Etapas difíciles"; "Nos manejamos con prudencia y equilibrio"; "Formación moral y cívica"; "Diez años volcánicos."

75. Kahan, *Memories That Lie a Little*, 121–46.

76. "DAIA: Etapas difíciles," 6.

77. Comisión de Estudios sobre el Antisemitismo en la Argentina, *Actas de las ponencias*, 15.
78. "La pasividad de la víctima."
79. 1977 speech cited in Kaufman and Cymberknopf, "La dimensión judía," 245; Resnizky, "Discurso del Dr. Nehemías Resnizky." The phrase "Jews of Silence" was also likely an allusion to Wiesel, *The Jews of Silence*.
80. "Integramos lo argentino."
81. "Integramos lo argentino," 7; "Nehemías Resnizky dice su verdad."
82. Cited in Kinzer, "Missing in Argentina," 32.
83. Kinzer, 37.
84. Gorenstein, "No somos ciudadanos de segunda categoría."
85. Shandler, *While America Watches*, 164–78. *Nueva Presencia* reported on anti-Semitic attacks in Switzerland associated with the broadcast of the miniseries in "Nuevo testimonio."
86. Reboledo, "Finalizó"; Reboledo, "La repercusión."
87. "DAIA: El antisemitismo"; "DAIA: Schonfeld goza." See Kahan and Lvovich, "Los usos del Holocausto," 324–25, for an account of the behind-the-scenes negotiations that led to the airing of the show.
88. "DAIA: No buscamos."
89. "Ni olvido ni perdón" (1982).
90. Novick, *The Holocaust in American Life*, 14.
91. "¿Veremos 'Holocausto'?"
92. Sofer, "Terror in Argentina."
93. Tesch, "Jewish Group."
94. See Sheinin, "Deconstructing Anti-Semitism in Argentina," for a discussion of the activities of the ADL and other North American Jewish groups.
95. Weisbrot, "Anti-Semitism in Argentina"; Kinzer, "Missing in Argentina," 37; Neilson, "An Air of Uncertainty," 45; "Editorial," *The Jewish Week*.
96. Bono, "The Troubled Jews of Argentina"; Kinzer, "Missing in Argentina," 12.
97. Neier, "The Crime of Silence Revisited."
98. See Arcuschin et al., "Réplica al 'Informe especial,'" for the statement by families; Feitlowitz in *A Lexicon of Terror*, 89–109, offers a sustained critique of the DAIA based on her interviews with DAIA leaders and with Jewish families of the disappeared.
99. Klich, "Política comunitaria." For Resnizky's response to Klich's accusations, see Resnizky, "Réplica y testimonio." Note that since then the DAIA, through its Centro de Estudios Sociales, has made serious culpatory efforts to rectify its earlier discussions of this period in its history, and its researchers have been among the most vocal of those who sustain that the Proceso represents a clear case of genocide. In 1999 it produced a report on Jewish detainees and disappeared persons: Braylán et al., "Informe sobre la situación." In 2001 it created a commission to

study the role of the DAIA during the dictatorship, which led to the publication of an "Inventario del archivo histórico sobre el rol de la DAIA frente a la dictadura militar 1976–1983" (Centro de Estudios Sociales, 2003).

100. Meyer, "Latin America—Argentina," 1978, 1979, 1980.
101. Cited in Kinzer, "Missing in Argentina," 18.
102. Kinzer, 32.
103. Meyer, "Los judíos argentinos."
104. Kinzer, "Missing in Argentina," 32.
105. Schiller, "Otra vez."
106. Examples include "Significativas definiciones"; "Sábato: Ni terrorismo"; "Pérez Esquivel: Contra el terrorismo."
107. Vezzetti, *Pasado y presente*.
108. "No pedimos venganza"; "Las Mothers de desaparecidos."
109. "Pérez Esquivel: Contra la violencia."
110. Lerner, "Nuestras defensas."
111. "Una sesión con variaciones."
112. "Las 'Mothers de Plaza de Mayo.'"
113. "La rebelión del gueto." Note, however, that the transposition involved points of conflict; at the same Warsaw ghetto commemoration, Federico Storani of the political party Unión Cívica Radical compared the Warsaw ghetto uprising to the struggle to establish democracy in Argentina but then pressed the metaphor further to compare Nazi generals to Israeli militarism—at which point Resnizky intervened to contradict him. And, according to *Nueva Presencia*, not all of those who attended the event appreciated the links between Holocaust commemoration and contemporary Argentina, finding that it "denaturalized" the event's original purpose.
114. For the interlinking of Holocaust remembrance with other issues in the 1990s, see Goldstein, "El judaísmo argentino"; Zaretsky, "Child Survivors of the Shoah."
115. On the "dual loyalty" question, see Rein, *Argentina, Israel and the Jews*, 196–228.
116. Senkman, *El periodismo*, 49.
117. See the 1975 debate between José Itzigsohn, Marcos Aguinis, Nehemías Resnizky, and Juan Gurevich in Comisión de Estudios sobre el Antisemitismo en la Argentina, *Actas de las ponencias*, 9–37.
118. "Ser argentinos, ser judíos." See also Gurwitz, *Argentine Jews in the Age of Revolt*, 190.
119. Schiller, "Sí, claro."
120. "Judaísmo es sinónimo de justicia."
121. Meyer, "Los judíos argentinos." See also "El judaísmo no puede sobrevivir."
122. Fabián Bosoer claims the idea for the title *Nunca más* was Rabbi Meyer's. Bosoer, "Juicios, castigos y verdades." Emilio Crenzel attributes it to a

different CONADEP commissioner. Crenzel, *La historia política*, 81. On Resnizky's opposition to Meyer's Movimiento Judío por los Derechos Humanos, see "Contra el antisemitismo."

123. "Sospechosa impunidad."

124. "Meyer, "Los judíos argentinos."

125. Resnick, "American Rabbi in Argentina."

126. Hall, "The Disappeared." For Meyer on his use of these "precise words," see "Hay que limpiar."

127. "Se encuentra en el país Elie Wiesel"; Levinson, "Atisbos a la hondura de Elie Wiesel"; "Wiesel vino, vio y venció"; "Los iconoclastas"; "Conferencia del profesor Elie Wiesel."

128. Timerman, "Elie Wiesel (Direct Translation of Suggestions Made by Jacobo Timerman, Friday, 20th of July 1979)," translated by Marshall Meyer, box 20, folder "Argentina—Jacobo Timerman 1978–84, 1991, 2002, 1 of 2," Marshall T. Meyer Papers, Duke University Library.

129. "La intimidación interna."

130. "Only use the word Nazi if you are literally referring to former members of the Nazi party in Germany," cautioned his editor at the Free Press. Letter to Marshall Meyer from Laura Wolff, June 27, 1986, box 14, folder "Manuscripts 1985 April 24," Marshall Meyer Papers, Duke University Library.

131. "El judaísmo no puede sobrevivir."

132. Marshall Meyer, "Prologue," in *Confronting Injustice: An American Rabbi in Argentina* (unpublished manuscript), p. 13, box 14, folder "Manuscripts 1985 April 24," Marshall Meyer Papers, Duke University Library. Almost identical words can be found in an earlier text from Argentina, Meyer's 1983 interview with Herman Schiller. Meyer, "Los judíos argentinos."

133. Meyer, *Confronting Injustice*, 127.

134. "Rabino Marshall T. Meyer."

135. Meyer, "Escoged."

136. "La esperanza que jugó en contra"; " 'Para que no se repita jamás.' "

137. "Dramáticos testimonios"; "Estremecedora visión." The overall message was that, despite the shortcomings of television as a medium, the show was extremely valuable.

138. "Llega a nuestra TV la polémica 'Holocausto.' "

139. Mazas, " 'Holocausto' en el primer tramo del horror"; Mazas, " 'Holocausto': Con más emoción."

140. LaCapra, *Representing the Holocaust*, 48.

141. " 'Holocausto' confirma sus antecedentes"; García Venturini, "En torno a 'Holocausto.' " Why focus so much on the Jewish victims, complained one commentator, when plenty of Christians had also suffered, and why paint such a black-and-white portrait of "good Jews" and "bad Germans"? This last criticism, it bears

noting, was entirely misplaced, because in fact *Holocaust*-the-miniseries devoted at least half its focus to the moral dilemmas of German Gentiles and to the heroism of the Gentile wife (played by Meryl Streep) of one of the Jewish characters.

142. Senkman, "¿Genocidio humano u holocausto judío?"
143. "Holocausto: Opinan los argentinos."
144. Resnizky, "Es traumatizante, pero aleccionadora."
145. Morduchowicz, "Con mis propios ojos."
146. "Holocausto: Opinan los argentinos," 10.
147. "Holocausto: Opinan los argentinos," 10; "La rebelión del gueto," 1.
148. "Opina Polino."
149. "Holocausto: Opinan los argentinos," 10.
150. Cited in Feitlowitz, *A Lexicon of Terror*, 104.
151. Golub, "Después del silencio"; Golub, "¿Quién puede olvidar?"
152. Plavnick, "Por nuestra y vuestra liberación."
153. Brailovsky, "Y aquí también."
154. "Chile-Argentina."
155. "Una verdadera lluvia de adhesiones."
156. Lerner, "El cumpleaños de Mario."
157. Oz, "The Meaning of Homeland."
158. "Integramos lo argentino," 7.
159. ANCLA, "Alarma en la colectividad judía" (September 5, 1977), in Verbitsky, *Rodolfo Walsh*, 116; Bird, "Argentina: Get Out, Jews"; Weisbrot, "Anti-Semitism in Argentina."
160. Arcuschin et al., "Réplica al 'Informe especial.'"
161. Arcuschin et al. When Alejandra Jaimovich, daughter of Luis Jaimovich, president of DAIA Córdoba, was disappeared, her father resigned his post. See Ben-Dror, "Antisemitism in Argentina."
162. Liebman and Don-Yehiya, *Civil Religion in Israel*, 152–53.
163. In fact, as Ofer reports already in the 1940s, "Shoah uGevurah" had been considered by some scholars to be an evasion of the more painful elements of the catastrophe, and in its earliest incarnations involved a more expansive notion of resistance. Ofer, "Linguistic Conceptualization," 573–74.
164. Senkman, "El Holocausto y la estética de la muerte."
165. Senkman, "Bar Kojba." Not coincidentally, Bar Kochba commemorations were a staple feature of *Nueva Presencia*'s offerings.
166. Senkman, "En torno al mito," 20. Senkman here reviews Yehuda Bauer, *The Jewish Emergence from Powerlessness*.
167. Dreschler, "Judíos, escríbanlo."
168. Katz, Review of *El pan y la sangre*; Sneh, *El pan y la sangre*.
169. Perednik, "Nunca más, otra vez."
170. "Ni olvido ni perdón," (1982).

171. Abe Kowner [Abba Kovner], "¡Tate! Tate¡."
172. Ofer, "Linguistic Conceptualization," 576–77. An examination of the fragments of Kovner's speeches on this topic, reproduced by Ofer, reveals the extent to which Timerman's vision of Jewish silence matched Kovner's.
173. According to Liebman and Don-Yehiya, the phrase is associated with the poetry of Haim Nachmann Bialik and refers originally to a 1904 Russian pogrom. Liebman and Don-Yehiya, *Civil Religion in Israel*, 259n79.
174. "Por nuestra y vuestra liberación."
175. "Una rebelión de oprimidos."
176. Vezzetti, *Pasado y presente*, 119–20.
177. Novick, 279.
178. After the return to democracy, it also framed their sense of guilt at having been silent. See, for example, Laikin Elkin, "Good Germans in Argentina?"; Blum, "Argentine Jewry." Blum's piece starts with a quote from an Argentine Jew: "Through my silence, I now feel that I condoned the slaughter of Argentina's youth. Do you realize that it was people like me who permitted the Holocaust to occur in Germany?"
179. See Vezzetti, *Pasado y presente*; Calveiro, *Política y/o violencia*.

Notes to Chapter 2

1. Special thanks to Manuel Cuellar and Roberto Medina for their research assistance on this chapter.
2. Schmucler, "Nota preliminar," 12.
3. Kononovich, *Me queda la palabra*.
4. Feierstein, *El genocidio como práctica social*, 352–53.
5. Cerruti offers a periodization of memory activism by human rights groups during and after the dictatorship and identifies 1995–1996 as inaugurating a "memory boom." Cerruti, "La historia de la memoria," 11.
6. Goldberg, "'Judíos del sur.'"
7. The number of literary, intellectual, and scholarly works of the post-dictatorship period that invoke the Holocaust is virtually endless. Many corners of this vast landscape have been addressed by scholars. Regarding Jewish authors who invoke the Holocaust, see Meter, "Barbarie y memoria"; on Argentine literature more broadly, see Goldberg, "Judíos del sur"; on memorials, see Huyssen, *Present Pasts*; on the question of "genocide" and its applicability to Argentina, see Baer and Sznaider, *Memory and Forgetting*; on Argentine testimony, see Feierstein, "'A Quilt of Memory.'"
8. Vigevani, "El rol del testimonio," 217.
9. Crenzel, "Introducción," 16.
10. Feld, *Del estrado a la pantalla*, 111.

11. Masiello, *The Art of Transition*, 6, original emphasis.

12. A third line of post-Auschwitz critique taken up in Argentina involves a more maximalist interpretation of the "crisis of representation," by which the worst of the Nazi horrors escape our comprehension and cannot be depicted truly, following the line explored by the essays collected in Friedlander, *Probing the Limits*. Reati, *Nombrar lo innombrable*, exemplifies this line in Argentina. Some of the authors I'll discuss here will at times come close to this position without fully adopting it. For a useful summation and convincing refutation of those currents of post-Auschwitz philosophy that explore the limits of representation when it comes to atrocity, see Crenzel, "Introducción," 11–16.

13. Arendt, "The Image of Hell," 200.

14. Kaufman, "Notas sobre desaparecidos," 29.

15. Carlotto and Mosquera, "Editorial."

16. Dalmaroni shows that, in the case of *Punto de Vista*, the emphasis on seeing political rhetoric as inherently regressive because it is not sufficiently rational and distanced has led to some serious misreadings, on the part of the journal's contributors, of activist literature in the 1990s. Dalmaroni, "Dictaduras," 969–71.

17. The landscape of memory debates changed substantially under the presidencies of Néstor Kirchner (2003–2007) and Cristina Fernández de Kirchner (2007–2015), in part due to the human rights policies and alliances that the state pursued during their presidencies and in part due to the new legal landscape opened up by the 2004 definitive annulment of the "impunity laws" (which had shielded alleged military perpetrators from prosecution for their crimes during the dictatorship). For an in-depth analysis of the period 2001–2015, see Tandeciarz, *Citizens of Memory*.

18. Baer and Sznaider, *Memory and Forgetting*, 27–63.

19. Some of the most significant include the Madres de Plaza de Mayo, the Abuelas de Plaza de Mayo, the Asamblea Permanente por los Derechos Humanos (APDH), Servicio Paz y Justicia (SERPAJ; commonly referred to without an initial article), and the Centro de Estudios Legales y Sociales (CELS). See Veiga, *Las organizaciones*; Leis, *El movimiento*.

20. The Mothers of the Plaza de Mayo manifested serious reservations about both of these initiatives because of the kinds of political compromises these entailed. Crenzel, *La historia política*, 64; Leis, *El movimiento*, 1:37–44, 2:162–64. Divisions within the Mothers about whether to testify before the CONADEP deepened and finally resulted in a split, in 1986, into two separate groups: the Asociación Madres de Plaza de Mayo (led by Hebe de Bonafini) and the Madres de Plaza de Mayo Línea Fundadora.

21. These include the two laws enacted during the presidency of Raúl Alfonsín (the "Punto Final" law of 1986, making it legally impossible to prosecute those military personnel alleged to have committed crimes related to the disappeared who had not already been called to testify in such cases; and the "Due Obedience" law

of 1987, which nullified the legal prosecutions of lower-ranking military personnel that were ongoing at the time) as well as President Carlos Menem's acts granting pardons to military leaders (the "indultos" of 1989 and 1990, which included pardons for those who had been convicted in the 1985 Juicio de las Juntas and those who were wanted for "crimes against humanity").

22. His words had appeared in print a few weeks earlier, in February 1995, in a book by journalist Verbitsky, *El vuelo*, but as Feld argues, the televisual scene meant that these revelations reached a far larger audience and had far greater repercussions across Argentine society. Feld, *Del estrado a la pantalla*, 103–7.

23. Feld, *Del estrado a la pantalla*, 108. See http://www.hijos-capital.org.ar/.

24. Crenzel, *La historia política*, 156.

25. Jelin's work was supported by the Social Science Research Council as part of a regional initiative on Southern Cone memories of state repression. Jelin, *State Repression*, xi.

26. The conversion of the ESMA into a museum is discussed in Tandeciarz, *Citizens of Memory*, 22–35.

27. I refer to the CONADEP report that circulated as part of the newspaper *Página/12*; at seventy-five thousand copies, it constituted one of the largest ever circulations of the text. Crenzel, *La historia política*, 156–61.

28. Cited in Vezzetti, "Iniciativas políticas."

29. Bayer, "De Dachau a la ESMA"; Galeano, "The 1978 World Cup," 175; Feinmann, "Pensar y escribir después de la ESMA"; Feinman, "Adorno y el ESMA (II)"; Melchor Basterra, "Carta de un sobreviviente." Basterra refers to himself and his comrades detained at the ESMA as "sobrevivientes del holocausto."

30. Vezzetti, *Pasado y presente*, 112.

31. Vezzetti, 30.

32. Vezzetti, 18. See also Baer and Sznaider, *Memory and Forgetting*, 31–41, for an analysis of how the CONADEP's *Nunca más* report and the Trial of the Juntas embodied the Holocaust legacy; their argument is essentially identical to Vezzetti's earlier argument.

33. Wieviorka, *The Era of the Witness*.

34. On the international criminal proceedings, see "Resumen del 2000"; on the legal decision in 2001 regarding the Punto Final and Obediencia Debida laws, see Cañón, "Un antes y un después"; Yanzón, "Los juicios"; Rafecas, "La reapertura."

35. Kordon et al., *Efectos psicológicos*, 39–40, 98, 169; Bettelheim, "Behavior in Extreme Situations."

36. Sheinin, *Consent of the Damned*, 142.

37. Sheinin, 142.

38. Sheinin, 143.

39. Daniel Feierstein, in discussion with the author, Buenos Aires, May 2011.

40. Feierstein, *El genocidio como práctica social*, 350–52. See also his discussions about other such survivor encounters. Feierstein, *El genocidio como práctica social*, 289, 339–40, 362–64.

41. Calveiro, *Poder y desparición*.
42. Da Silva Catela, *No habrá flores*, 21. Pollak, *L'expérience concentrationnaire*.
43. Actis et al., *Ese infierno*, 261, 296–300. In his prologue to this book, philosopher León Rozitchner emphasizes the parallel between Germany and Argentina. Rozitchner, "Y huirá la tristeza," 17. For an extended analysis of this book, see Feierstein, "'A Quilt of Memory.'"
44. Strejilevich, "Testimony"; Partnoy, "Poetry as a Strategy." Strejilevich and Partnoy have also written literary-testimonial accounts of their experiences. Strejilevich, *A Single, Numberless Death*; Partnoy, *The Little School*.
45. Cerruti, "La historia de la memoria," 16–21.
46. Bayer, *Rebeldía y esperanza*, 115–16. This 1977 essay, "Residencia en la amada tierra enemiga," was originally published in Gelman and Bayer, *Exilio*.
47. Bayer, *Rebeldía y esperanza*, 114, 111.
48. Bayer, 136–37.
49. Bayer, "Pequeño recordatorio," 203.
50. Bayer, *Rebeldía y esperanza*, 47.
51. Bayer, 317–18.
52. In 1996–1997, Bayer organized a series of seminars at the Universidad de Buenos Aires with members of the Association of Ex-Detainees and Disappeared Persons and led discussions involving Holocaust testimonies. Feierstein, *El genocidio como práctica social*, 289. In 2010, he wrote a prologue to the testimony by Ruth Paradies de Weisz, who had escaped deportation to Auschwitz and whose son was disappeared by the junta. Bayer, "Prólogo."
53. Comisión members have included Nobel Prize winner Adolfo Pérez Esquivel from the organization Servicio Paz y Justicia; Estela Carlotto of the Grandmothers of the Plaza de Mayo; and many others from important human rights groups, including the Madres de la Plaza de Mayo, the Centro de Estudios Legales (CELS), and the Asamblea Permanente por los Derechos Humanos (APDH; www.comisionporlamemoria.org). See Tandeciarz, *Citizens of Memory*, 211–67, for an extended analysis of the CPM's activities in the sphere of youth education.
54. "Los puentes de la memoria."
55. Jelin, "Memorias en conflicto," 8.
56. Sarlo, "Una alucinación dispersa en agonía," 2; Sarlo, "El campo intelectual."
57. CONADEP, *Nunca más*; Crenzel, *La historia política*, 108.
58. There are many other examples of this view in *Punto de Vista*. A sampling from the early transition period includes: "Editorial," *Punto de Vista*; Terán, "Una polémica postergada"; Samoilovich, "Gelman."
59. Sarlo, "Política, ideología y figuración literaria," 33.
60. Sarlo, *Tiempo pasado*, 23.
61. Crenzel, *La historia política*, 81–89.
62. Sarlo, "Una alucinación dispersa en agonía," 2.
63. For more on the "show del horror," see Feld, "La representación."
64. Feld, "La representación," 28.

65. Sarlo, "Política, ideología y figuración literaria," 31.
66. Sarlo, *Tiempo pasado*, 49.
67. Sarlo, 45–46.
68. Sarlo, 56.
69. *Punto de Vista* published John Torpey's account of the debate, which had originally appeared a year earlier in *New German Critique*. Torpey, "Habermas y los historiadores"; Torpey, "Introduction." See my introduction for a brief discussion of the German historians' debate.
70. Sarlo, "La historia contra el olvido," 12.
71. On Lanzmann's views about the role of history in his film, see Felman, "In an Era of Testimony," 47–48.
72. Sarlo, "La historia contra el olvido," 11.
73. Sarlo, 12.
74. Goldstein, "El judaísmo argentino," 43.
75. Sarlo, "La historia contra el olvido," 13. Sarlo is citing Yerushalmi, "Réflexions sur l'oubli," 18.
76. Sarlo, 13.
77. Sarlo, *Tiempo presente*, 151–52.
78. Sarlo, 152.
79. Sarlo, *Tiempo pasado*, 78.
80. Sarlo, 77.
81. Sarlo, 23.
82. Sarlo, "Una alucinación dispersa en agonía," 2–3; Sarlo, "El campo intelectual," 96, 100.
83. Sarlo, "Una alucinación dispersa en agonía," 2; Sarlo, "El campo intelectual," 41.
84. Sarlo, "Una alucinación dispersa en agonía," 3; Sarlo, "El campo intelectual," 100.
85. Tandeciarz, *Citizens of Memory*, xxxi.
86. Vezzetti, *Pasado y presente*, 15, 191. See also Vezzetti, "Lecciones de memoria"; Vezzetti, "Verdad jurídica y verdad histórica."
87. Vezzetti, *Pasado y presente*, 41, original emphasis. These distinctions are found in Jaspers, *The Question of German Guilt*.
88. Vezzetti, 13.
89. Vezzetti, 49–50, 149–52, 167–68; Goldhagen, *Hitler's Willing Executioners*; Arendt, *Eichmann in Jerusalem*; Fromm, *Escape from Freedom*.
90. Vezzetti, 152–54, 176, 180–90; Bauman, *Modernity and the Holocaust*; Agamben, *Remnants of Auschwitz*; Levi, *The Drowned and the Saved*; Levi, *Survival in Auschwitz*.
91. Vezzetti, *Pasado y presente*, 151.
92. Vezzetti, 33.

93. Vezzetti, 15.
94. Vezzetti, 30.
95. Vezzetti's subsequent book, *Sobre la violencia revolucionaria: Memorias y olvidos*, is devoted entirely to a critique of the armed Left in the 1960s and 1970s and substantially expands on his work in *Pasado y presente* criticizing how former members of armed groups remember that period. Here, too, the Holocaust is crucial to the development of his critical perspective but receives substantially briefer treatment than in the former book; it repeats many of the arguments he puts forward in *Pasado y presente* about Holocaust memory, such as his discussions of Primo Levi, Jürgen Habermas, and Tzvetan Todorov.
96. Vezzetti, *Pasado y presente*, 13.
97. Sarmiento, *Facundo*.
98. Elias, *The Civilizing Process*, 118.
99. Elias, 120.
100. Vezzetti, *Pasado y presente*, 13. For a critique of Vezzetti's reliance on Norbert Elias to understand the Proceso, see Crenzel, *La historia política*, 198n16.
101. Vezzetti, *Pasado y presente*, 56, 125.
102. Vezzetti, 14.
103. Vezzetti, 15.
104. Vezzetti, 208, original emphasis.
105. Vezzetti, 232n51. Vezzetti's reference to "sanctified victims" in commercial representations of the Holocaust is from Cole, *Selling the Holocaust*.
106. Vezzetti, 192, 205–206.
107. Vezzetti, 188.
108. The journal was published initially by the Universidad de Buenos Aires. In 1998 the journal changed its name to *Pensamiento de los Confines*.
109. Pavón, *Los intelectuales*, 595.
110. Casullo, "Una crítica," 7.
111. Lyotard, "'Los judíos'"; Schmucler, "Formas del olvido"; Goldszmidt, "Fragmentos sobre (a) Paul Celan"; Forster, Review of Tzvetan Todorov; "Debate alemán."
112. Forster, Review of Tzvetan Todorov, 144.
113. "Debate alemán," 111.
114. Farias, *Heidegger and Nazism*.
115. Lyotard, *Heidegger*, 3. I cite here from the English translation of Lyotard's text. All of the passages I refer to from Lyotard appeared in the excerpt published by *Confines*. Lyotard, "'Los judíos.'"
116. Lyotard, *Heidegger*, 4.
117. Lyotard, 26.
118. Schmucler, "Formas del olvido," 51.
119. Schmucler, 51, original emphasis.

120. Schmucler, 52.

121. The dossier contained nine articles, six by *Confines* authors (Schmucler, Casullo, Kaufman, Forster, Matías Bruera, and Gregorio Kaminsky) and three by authors associated with the journal *Nombres*, published by the University of Córdoba in Argentina (only the authors' initials appear: G.C, D.T., and O.d.B.; the last is Oscar del Barco).

122. Revista *Nombres*, "Las Madres de Plaza de Mayo," 45.

123. The publication of Bonafini's 1993 biography and her controversial close affiliation with the Schoklender brothers added to the polemics. For a lucid defense of Bonafini's militancy, see Gundermann, *Actos melancólicos*.

124. Forster, "Los usos de la memoria," 58–59.

125. Kaufman, "*Desaparecidos*," 40–41.

126. Schmucler, "Ni siquiera un rostro"; Arendt, "The Image of Hell," 198. In his article Schmucler also discusses Primo Levi's testimony *Survival in Auschwitz* (*If This Be a Man*); Pierre Vidal Naquet's *The Assassins of Memory*, about Holocaust deniers; and David Rousset's *L'univers concentracionnaire*.

127. Schmucler, "Ni siquiera un rostro," 9.

128. Arendt, "The Image of Hell," 198.

129. Schmucler, "Ni siquiera un rostro," 10.

130. Schmucler, 9.

131. Walsh, "Rigor e inteligencia," 15.

132. Casullo, "Una temporada," 15.

133. Casullo, 15.

134. For a sense of the debates in the 2000s, see Vezzetti, "Verdad jurídica y verdad histórica"; Sigal, "La polémica"; Feierstein, *El genocidio como práctica social*.

135. Casullo, "Una temporada," 15.

136. Casullo, 16.

137. Casullo, 17.

138. Casullo, 26.

139. Casullo, 16.

140. Casullo, 28. Casullo's critique of the Mothers echoes an earlier critique by *Punto de Vista* contributor Oscar Terán, who had written in 1986 against the Antigone role that the Mothers adopted with respect to the dead; the Argentine situation was more complex, he noted, and the Mothers had romanticized and mythologized the disappeared. Terán, "Argentina."

141. Casullo, "Una temporada," 28.

142. Casullo, 25.

143. Casullo, 28.

144. Gallup Argentina, *Argentina: Actitudes*, 2–3. The poll was commissioned after the devastating terrorist bombing of the Jewish Community Center (AMIA) in Buenos Aires in 1994, which killed eighty-five people, and included questions

meant to elicit opinions about the value of Holocaust memory, knowledge of the Holocaust, the Jewish community in Argentina, and the AMIA bombing.

Notes to Chapter 3

1. Weiss, *The Investigation*, 86. The entire play is composed from testimony given during the Frankfurt "Auschwitz" trials, 1963–1965.

2. Roskies, "The Library," 40.

3. Pacheco, *Morirás lejos*. The novel was reissued in 2017. Pacheco already had a demonstrated interest in the Holocaust prior to this book. In 1962, he translated into Spanish the diary of David Rubinowicz, a Jewish boy living in a Polish village under Nazi occupation who was deported and killed at Treblinka in September 1942 with the remaining Jews of his community. Rubinowicz, *Diario de un niño judío*.

4. Siman and Kahan, "La memoria global," 95–98. See also Siman, "Reconstrucción y reparación," 2. In the 1960s and 1970s, the Jewish community of Mexico numbered about thirty-five thousand. DellaPergola, "¿Cuántos somos hoy?," 314.

5. Weiss, *The Investigation*, 85. A version of the play was performed in Mexico City in 1968, written and directed by Spanish Republican exile Rafael López Miarnau. Wasserstrom, *¡Nunca jamás . . . !*, 277.

6. The phrase "memory knot" is from Debarati Sanyal, Michael Rothberg, and Max Silverman, who revise Pierre Nora's well-known "sites of memory" ("lieux de mémoires") into "noeuds de mémoires" to emphasize the plural, often conflictual spaces that carry memory. Sanyal et al., "Noeuds de Mémoire," 1–2; Nora, "Between Memory and History."

7. Borges, "Pierre Menard, autor del *Quijote*," 532.

8. The novel won the Magda Donato Prize in 1968. It received an array of positive reviews. For notable examples regarding the first edition, see J. Campos, "*Morirás lejos*"; Donoso Paredes, "*Morirás lejos*"; Fuentes, *La nueva novela*, 33–35; Jitrik, "Destrucción y formas"; Oviedo, "Una hipótesis"; Peña, "José Emilio Pacheco: *Morirás lejos*"; Valdés, "*Morirás lejos*." For the second edition, see M. Campos, "*Morirás lejos*"; M. Campos, "Los mejores libros de 1978"; Flores Ramírez, Review of *Morirás lejos*; Jitrik, "Cuento de una tarde de mayo"; Rivera, "*Morirás lejos* de José Emilio Pacheco"; Pérez Gay, "*Morirás lejos*"; Solana, "*Morirás lejos*, de Pacheco." For more information about the publishing of the first edition, see Hancock, "Perfecting a Text," 15. Hancock sustains that the first edition did not receive much attention, as does Pérez de Medina in "Escritura y lectura," 16. The record shows otherwise. All of these references can be found in Verani, "Hacia la bibliografía de José Emilio Pacheco," a superb bibliographic resource on Pacheco up to 1993.

9. For perspectives on the industrial side of the Holocaust, see Levi and Rothberg, "Auschwitz and the Remains of Theory."

10. I follow the line of interpretation opened by Pérez de Medina, who signaled the importance of the age of repression in understanding the novel. Pérez de Medina, "Escritura y lectura," 16.

11. Pacheco, *Morirás lejos* (1977), 12.
12. Lespada, "Texto con hormigas," 6.
13. Pacheco, *Morirás lejos* (1977), 81.
14. Fuentes, "París."
15. Pacheco, "Raíz y razón del movimiento estudiantil."
16. Regarding the influence of Herbert Marcuse's ideas in Mexico in 1968, see Volpi, *La imaginación y el poder*, 182–208.
17. Pacheco, "Revolución contra sociedad industrial."
18. Pacheco, "Guerra contra todo autoritarismo."
19. Fuentes, "Paris," V.
20. Glantz, "*Morirás lejos*," 237.
21. Rousset, *L'univers concentrationnaire*.
22. Pacheco, *Morirás lejos* (1977), 97.
23. Pacheco, "Si los Estados Unidos," V.
24. Pacheco, IV.
25. Krauze, "Holocausto versión Hanoi"; Alemán Velasco, "1968," 13.
26. Pacheco, "José Emilio Pacheco," 261.
27. Pacheco, "Conversación entre las ruinas," 54.
28. Pacheco, "A.H. (1889–1989)," 51.
29. Pacheco, *No me preguntes cómo pasa el tiempo*, 14.
30. Jitrik, "Destrucción y formas," 138.
31. Aguilar Melantzón and Gladstein, "'El reposo del fuego,'" 87.
32. Pacheco, *Morirás lejos* (1977), 65.
33. Levi, *The Drowned and the Saved*, 147.
34. Pacheco, *Morirás lejos* (1977), 95.
35. Pacheco, 64.
36. Sergio Gómez Montero says in his review of the novel's first edition: "Pacheco's magnificent descriptions are horror stories that we've known about for a long time now, they are themes that European literature, principally, has presented to us in all their aspects; that is, Pacheco's novel says nothing new about them." Gómez Montero, "Iconografía," 9.
37. Pacheco, *Morirás lejos* (1977), 65.
38. Pacheco, 68.
39. Pacheco, 157.
40. Josephus, *The Jewish War*.
41. Pacheco's narrative includes testimony by Ludwig Hirshfeld, a Jewish witness and survivor, published in 1956. Hirszfeld, *Ludwik Hirszfeld*. It also cites from the diary of Hans Frank, the governor general of Nazi-occupied Poland; and from Heinrich Himmler's order commanding destruction of the Ghetto (https://

www.jewishvirtuallibrary.org/himmler-orders-the-destruction-of-the-warsaw-ghetto). Pacheco's technique of interspersing quotes from documentary sources imitates the narrative structure created by the editors of David Rubinowicz's *Diary of a Jewish Boy*, which Pacheco had translated a few years prior.

42. Pacheco, *Morirás lejos* (1977), 79, 81, 91, 112, 124.

43. Pacheco, 92–94, 107; Weiss, *The Investigation*, 185–94.

44. As critic Raúl Dorra puts it in his analysis of the novel, "the 'testimonial' writing and the 'literary' writing interpenetrate at different levels and refuse to be separated in many ways." Dorra, "*Morirás lejos*," 245.

45. Critics are divided over which of these two elements, the testimonial or the literary, is the dominant one. The most apt interpretations, in my view, are those that preserve the dialogical character of the novel. For instance, Julio Ortega proposes that the novel is essentially a question writ large: "How to write, through fiction, a contemporary history of fascist violence?" Ortega, "Tres notas mexicanas," 670. To get an idea of the range of opinions about this issue, see the following works: Clark D'Lugo, "Narrative and Historical Commitment"; Dorra, "*Morirás lejos*"; Fuentes, *La nueva novela*; Pérez de Medina, "Escritura y lectura"; Oquendo, "Moríras lejos," 96.

46. Glantz, "*Morirás lejos*," 234.

47. See Hancock, "Perfecting a Text," for a list of the most important changes between the two editions.

48. Pacheco, *Morirás lejos* (1977), 85.

49. Pacheco, 13.

50. Pacheco, 84.

51. Pacheco, 117–18.

52. Pacheco, 95–97.

53. Pacheco, 88.

54. Pacheco, 101.

55. Irving, *Hitler's War*.

56. Pacheco, *Morirás lejos* (1977), 101.

57. Pacheco, "¿Hitler reivindicado?," 58.

58. Poniatowska, *La noche de Tlatelolco*.

59. Jitrik, "Cuento de una tarde de mayo," 36.

60. Jitrik, 37.

61. Jitrik, 37.

62. Pacheco, "Rodolfo Walsh," 56. Pacheco spearheaded, and wrote the introduction to, a Mexican edition of Walsh's complete works that appeared in 1981, a time when his works could not circulate in Argentina because of the dictatorship. Pacheco, "Nota preliminar."

63. Rodolfo Walsh, "Carta abierta de un escritor a la junta militar," 122.

64. Volpi, *La imaginación y el poder*, 361, original emphasis.

65. Paz, "México," V.

66. For an analysis of this poetry, see Volpi, *La imaginación y el poder*, 370–93. Many of the poems written about the student movement and the October 2 massacres can be found collected in Aroche Parra, *53 poemas del 68 mexicano*, and Campos and Toledo, *Poemas y narraciones*.

67. León-Portilla, *Visión de los vencidos*.

68. For a striking analysis of the intertextual relationship between *Visión de los vencidos* and Poniatowska's text, see Abeyta, "Un cuadro sincrónico." My thanks to Mônica Gimenes Hernandez for drawing my attention to this article.

69. Pacheco, "Lectura de los 'Cantares Mexicanos' "; Bañuelos, "No consta en actas"; Montes de Oca, "El altar de los muertos."

70. Montes de Oca, "El altar de los muertos," IX.

71. Bañuelos, "No consta en actas," VII.

72. Pacheco, "Lectura de los 'Cantares Mexicanos,' " VI.

73. Revueltas, *México 68*, 280.

74. Castellanos, "Memorial de Tlatelolco," 164.

75. Pacheco, "Las voces de Tlatelolco," 54.

76. Vezzetti, *Pasado y presente*, 21–22.

77. Pacheco, *Morirás lejos* (1977), 123.

78. Pacheco, *Morirás lejos* (1967), 18; Pacheco, *Morirás lejos* (1977), 20–21.

79. Pacheco, *Morirás lejos* (1967), 53; Pacheco, *Morirás lejos* (1977), 63.

80. Pacheco, *Morirás lejos* (1967), 46; Pacheco, *Morirás lejos* (1977), 54.

81. Pacheco, *Morirás lejos* (1967), 95; Pacheco, *Morirás lejos* (1977), 117.

82. The Holocaust is a theme in her novel *Yo nunca te prometí la eternidad* (*I Never Promised You Eternity*; 2005), and it appears obliquely in her celebrated first memoir of exile, *En estado de memoria* (*In a State of Memory*; 1990). For an illuminating interpretation of the role of Holocaust images in *Yo nunca te prometí la eternidad*, see Szurmuk, "Memorias de lo íntimo"; for the same in *En estado de memoria*, see Avelar, *The Untimely Present*, 225–26.

83. Mercado, "Cuatro historias del terror nazi." The later writings appeared between 1996 and 2002, the height of Argentina's memory boom, and are collected in the volume *Narrar después*.

84. Wieviorka, *The Era of the Witness*, 82.

85. Avelar, *The Untimely Present*, 3, 217.

86. My formulation of "life outside and within history" is indebted to historian Greg Grandin's analysis of the Latin American Left during the Cold War and his approach to "the essentially contingent, indeterminate, and decidedly not inevitable nature of politics and history." He writes: "It is this open contingency, and not a fixed ideological template, that propels militants to act in an unfamiliar present." Grandin, "Living in Revolutionary Time," 20.

87. Sanyal, *Memory and Complicity*, 3.

88. Mercado, *Narrar después*, 122. This and all other translations are my own unless otherwise noted.

89. Mercado, *Narrar después*, 122–23.

90. The phrase refers to critic Edna Aizenberg's acerbic account of the response she usually gets when she talks about Latin America and the Holocaust. Aizenberg, "Didn't All the Nazis."

91. Castro Leal et al., *El libro negro del terror Nazi*. Mexico's contribution to this world history is gaining more recognition outside Latin America. See Blair, "After the Fact." Illustrations from *El libro negro del terror Nazi* were included in the exhibit *Paint the Revolution: Mexican Modernism, 1910–1950* at the Philadelphia Museum of Art, October 25, 2016, through January 8, 2017.

92. The first was the "Casa Argentina," or COSPA (Comité de Solidaridad con el Pueblo Argentino [Committee in Solidarity with the People of Argentina]), led by Montoneros and so-called "Revolutionary Peronism"; it was the more militant of the two. The other "house," the "Comisión Argentina de Solidaridad" (CAS), was also leftist but not affiliated with a single political party or organization; it was the one with which Mercado was principally affiliated (her husband Noé Jitrik was a founder and leader). It too received direct support from Luis Echeverría, who in 1977, after his term of office as president had ended, set it up in a furnished locale, with the rent paid six months in advance. Subsequent political splits within the Montoneros would lead to the creation of the "Casa Montonero," representing the faction Movimiento Peronista Montonero (MPM).

93. Mercado, *Narrar después*, 122–30.

94. Hamui, "Mexico," 141.

95. Gleizer, *El exilio incómodo*, 19. Note that this number does not include Jews who were among the anti-fascist refugees, who, even if they gained entry to Mexico thanks to the work of Jewish organizations, were not "counted" as Jews by immigration officials.

96. Palma estimates ten thousand Argentine exiles in Mexico. Palma Mora, "Destierro y encuentro." Yankelevich estimates six thousand to seven thousand in "México: Un exilio fracturado," 188. For a discussion of the difficulties of arriving at an accurate count, see Yankelevich and Jensen, "México y Cataluña," 217.

97. Bokser Liwerant et al., "Claves conceptuales y metodológicas," 274–75, 277.

98. Bernetti, a journalist, was a militant Peronist during the 1970s and worked for the Argentine minister of defense under Cristina Fernández de Kirchner. Mempo Giardinelli is a well-known novelist.

99. Bernetti and Giardinelli, *México*, 27–28.

100. Bernetti and Giardinelli, 27.

101. Mercado, *Narrar después*, 116, 119.

102. Schlosser was also interviewed for a collection of testimonies by Mexican Holocaust survivors that appeared in 1999. Zaga Mograbi and Cohen Cohen, *El rostro de la verdad*, 214–16. The book was published by Memoria y Tolerancia, a group that would subsequently found Mexico's second Holocaust museum in 2010 (www.myt.org.mx).

103. Mercado, "Cuatro historias del terror nazi," 29.
104. Mercado, 30.
105. Mercado, 31.
106. Mercado, 33.
107. Mercado, 33.
108. Mercado, 31, 34.
109. Todorov, *Facing the Extreme*, 107.
110. Todorov, 19.
111. Todorov, 31.
112. Calveiro, *Poder y desparición*, 131–32.
113. Calveiro, 132–33.
114. Wieviorka, *The Era of the Witness*, 100.
115. Levi, *The Drowned and the Saved*, 24.
116. See Chapter 2 for a discussion of the Comisión Provincial de la Memoria.
117. Mercado, "Cuatro historias del terror nazi," 29.
118. Mercado, *Narrar después*, 138.
119. Robbins, "Introduction Part I," 3.
120. Tununa Mercado, in discussion with the author, Buenos Aires, May 2011.
121. Wasserstrom, *¡Nunca jamás . . . !*, 243.
122. Weiss, *The Investigation*, 57–64, 95–107. Wasserstrom is one of the sources for Weiss's Female Witness 5 (a composite character made up of several witnesses).
123. Rubinstein, *Sobrevivir*.
124. Bernetti and Giardinelli, *México*, 64–67.
125. Amnesty International, "Argentina."
126. Schmucler, "Testimonio de los sobrevivientes," 4.
127. Rojkind, "La revista *Controversia*," 241.
128. Leis, *El movimiento*, 99–100; De Bonafini, "Conference."
129. Schmucler, "Testimonio de los sobrevivientes," 4.
130. Bernetti and Giardinelli, *Mexico*, 194–200; COSOFAM, "Sólo la verdad," 47; Aguad, "Ni olvido ni venganza," 5. Abridged documents from this debate have been collected as appendices in Bernetti and Giardinelli, *Mexico*, 189–202. Rojkind provides a full discussion, though her approach puts Schmucler in an almost entirely negative light. Rojkind, "La revista *Controversia*," 233–43.
131. Schmucler, "Testimonio de los sobrevivientes," 5.
132. Bernetti and Giardinelli, *Mexico*, 195.
133. Amnesty International, "Argentina," 2; Mercado, *Narrar después*, 103.
134. COSOFAM, "Sólo la verdad," 47.
135. Callizo et al., "Tres sobrevivientes responden," 29.
136. Bernetti and Giardinelli, *Mexico*, 197.
137. Bernetti and Giardinelli, 199.
138. COSOFAM, "Sólo la verdad," 47; Bernetti and Giardinelli, *Mexico*, 200. Schmucler's intervention both supported and undermined the survivors' authority. He argued that the testimonies provided "the only direct and believable facts that

we possess." Schmucler, "Testimonio de los sobrevivientes," 5. But he also painted a picture of the survivors that suggested that what they could most eloquently testify to was their own extreme abjection, as if the testimonies were not also a document of thought. For example, he saw in the testimonies evidence that the survivors had already been existentially destroyed by the Montonero machine before they were captured and tortured by the military, and he highlighted survivor testimony about the suffering that had reduced them to "animalitos," little animals. The three survivors who had provided testimony about the concentration camp La Perla rebutted these points, reminding him that their testimonies were also political denunciations of state violence, that they and others had been able to resist some forms of violence in the Argentine camps, even if not always or not consistently, and that they had been and continued to be reflective, thinking subjects animated by powerful ideas. Callizo et al., "Tres sobrevivientes responden," 30–31.

139. Mercado, *Narrar después*, 103–4.
140. Mercado, 104.
141. Mercado, 139.
142. Mercado, 102.
143. Szurmuk, "Memorias de lo íntimo," 214.
144. Mercado, *Narrar después*, 103.
145. CONADEP, *Nunca más*.
146. Walsh, "Rigor e inteligencia," 15.
147. Casullo, "Una temporada," 17.
148. Mercado, *Narrar después*, 148.
149. Mercado, 145.
150. Mercado, 145.
151. Mercado, "Cuatro historias del terror nazi," 29.
152. Szurmuk, "Memorias de lo íntimo," 223.
153. The phrase first appeared in Adorno, "Cultural Criticism and Society," 17–34. For a useful gloss on the phrase, its evolution in Adorno's work, and its influence on other philosophers, see Rothberg, "After Adorno."
154. Pacheco, "José Emilio Pacheco," 260.
155. Adorno, "Commitment," 251, 252.
156. Pacheco, "El Proceso, el Castillo," 47, original emphasis.
157. Pacheco, "¿Hitler reivindicado?"

Notes to Chapter 4

1. My thanks to the undergraduate research apprentices who provided assistance with this chapter.
2. Cojtí Cuxil, *Ri Maya' moloj*. The English translation is mine, as are all translations into English unless otherwise noted.
3. COMG, *Rujunamil ri Mayab' Amaq'*, original ellipsis.

4. Comisión de Esclarecimiento Histórico, *Guatemala, memoria del silencio*, 5:43–44. Subsequent references will appear as CEH.

5. CEH, 2:318–21.

6. CEH, 5:43, 5:51.

7. Cited in Wilson, "Verdades violentas," 50.

8. Ríos Montt was convicted of genocide in the case of the Maya Ixil in 2013, but the verdict was denied shortly thereafter by a higher court; the retrial on these charges was suspended in 2016 but resumed in October 2017. At the time of his death in April 2018, he was facing genocide charges in this case as well as in a second case related to the Dos Erres massacre. See www.ijmonitor.org for summaries of these trials.

9. Laplante, "Memory Battle," 649–50.

10. Marta Casaús Arzú analyzes the negative response to the genocide verdict from various sectors of Guatemalan society, including powerful business interests and middle-class urban ladinos, in "La exacerbación del racismo."

11. Statement of the Guatemalan Bishops (May 27, 1982), cited in Berryman, *The Religious Roots of Rebellion*. See also the following sources: García Borrajo, "Pre-Informe"; Partido Guatemalteco del Trabajo, *Debate Revolucionario*; Comité Pro Justicia y Paz de Guatemala, *Boletín Comité*; Comisión de Derechos Humanos de Guatemala, *Informe*.

12. Comisión Argentina de Solidariad, "A seis años"; Handy, *Gift of the Devil*; "Help Stop the War"; Comité Panameño de Solidaridad con el Pueblo de Guatemala, "Guatemala vencerá."

13. Jonas et al., *Guatemala*.

14. Konefal, *For Every Indio Who Falls*, 102.

15. "Declaración de Iximché."

16. "Mensaje de la Delegación Indígena."

17. Montejo and Q'anil Akab', *Brevísima relación*, 7. This book is modeled on Bartolomé de las Casas's famous denunciation *Brevísima relación de la destrucción de las Indias* (1542/1552), which documented the atrocities committed in the Conquest of Guatemala. There are numerous other examples, by both Maya and non-Maya scholars, that establish the parallels between the atrocities committed by the Spanish in the sixteenth century and the atrocities committed by the Guatemalan army in the twentieth century. Sources that are not elsewhere discussed here include: Stannard, *American Holocaust*; Falla, *Masacres de la selva*; Perera, *Unfinished Conquest*. Anthropologist Michelle Bellino reports that among the Maya youth she interviewed about the war, all of whom were born after 1996, many confused it with the Spanish conquest. Bellino, *Youth in Postwar Guatemala*, 153. Political scientist Jo-Marie Burt notes that the Kaji Tulam Memory Museum, sponsored by the Center for Human Rights Legal Action (CALDH), "tells the story of the Guatemalan genocide dating from its origins—the Spanish conquest—to the present." Burt, "From Heaven to Hell," 164.

18. Rothberg, *Multidirectional Memory*, 18.

19. Bakhtin, *The Dialogic Imagination*, 276.

20. Cojtí earned a doctorate at the University of Louvaine, Belgium, in social communication, and taught at various universities in Guatemala over the course of his professorial career. He served as vice minister of education during 2000–2004, a position that many criticized as a sign that he had "sold out." For more on his biography as a Mayanist, see Konefal, *For Every Indio Who Falls*, 143–46. For an insightful evaluation of Cojtí's service in government, see Hale, "Rethinking Indigenous Politics."

21. On the Maya Movement, see Arias, "Changing Indian Identity"; Bastos and Brett, *El movimiento maya*; Bastos and Camus, *Abriendo caminos*; Bastos and Camus, *Quebrando el silencio*; Cojtí Cuxil, *Ri maya' moloj*; Fischer, "Beyond Victimization"; Gálvez Borrell et al., *¿Qué sociedad queremos?*; Konefal, *For Every Indio Who Falls*; Montejo, *Maya Intellectual Renaissance*; Warren, *Indigenous Movements and Their Critics*.

22. Bastos and Camus, *Abriendo caminos*, 157.

23. The seminal work on the social construction of memory is by Halbwachs, *Les cadres sociaux de la mémoire*.

24. Oglesby, "Educating Citizens," 92. For other criticisms of human rights in Latin America, see the work of Latin American thinkers discussed in Chapter 2. Fernando Rosenberg provides a useful summary of broader critiques of human rights discourse in *After Human Rights*. For a more global critique that arrived several years after Latin American authors began to discuss the topic, see Moyn, *The Last Utopia*, and Moyn, *Not Enough*.

25. The phrase "analytically appropriate" is Greg Grandin's: "It is vital for us to critically engage with the Guatemalan genocide in analytically appropriate ways that help us understand the past and grapple with the notion of possible future justice." Grandin, "Politics by Other Means," 13.

26. Grandin, "Chronicles of a Guatemalan Genocide," 398–99.

27. Oglesby served as an expert witness for the prosecution in the genocide trial of Ríos Montt. See also Oglesby, "The Guatemalan Genocide."

28. Traverso, *Left Wing Melancholia*, 10.

29. Traverso, *Left Wing Melancholia*, xv.

30. Fischer, "Beyond Victimization," 84.

31. See Vanthuyne, *La présence d'un passé*, for a "thick" and nuanced account of the construction of the identity "innocent Maya victim of genocide" among massacre survivors in two highland towns; she analyzes the work of two Guatemalan human rights organizations that have fostered this identity yet also sought to link it to broader social justice struggles, with mixed results. Other analyses that criticize human rights discourses for oversimplifying the Guatemalan conflict and/or displacing other kinds of political activism include: Speed and Leyva Solano, "Introduction," 11; Bastos, "La política maya," 21. Some scholars are pushing against the

word "victim," arguing for the word "survivor" because it lacks the association with traumatized passivity that the word "victim" connotes. See Patterson-Markowitz et al., "Subjects of Change," 82, 95. See also, in regard to pushback against "victim" in favor of "survivor" in South Africa, Feldman, "Memory Theaters."

32. Oglesby, "Desde los cuadernos," 36.
33. Oglesby, "Educating Citizens," 92.
34. Konefal, "Maya Repression."
35. On Argentina and the process of editing victim testimony to make it conform to international human rights formulas, see Crenzel, *La historia política*, 44–48. On Guatemala and neoliberal appropriations of human rights, see Oglesby, "Educating Citizens."
36. For example, Jo-Marie Burt argues that the "victim-centric" nature of the genocide trial against Ríos Montt had empowering effects on the victims who testified. Burt, "From Heaven to Hell."
37. One exception can be found in the work of Víctor Montejo. See Montejo, *Voices from Exile*, 197; Montejo, *Maya Intellectual Renaissance*, 12. There is also the case of a book authored by a Maya Ixil pastor that uses "holocaust" twice to describe the violence inflicted on his pastoral community by leftist guerrillas. Guzaro and Jacob McComb, *Escaping the Fire*.
38. Its reputation exceeds it, as it were, because scholars are apt to give the impression that Cojtí's use of the phrase "Maya holocaust" is representative of a wider trend in Guatemala, despite little evidence for this until very recently. See, for example, Grandin, *The Blood of Guatemala*, 16; Esquit, "Movilización política," 250; Esquit, "Las rutas," 173; and multiple instances in Garrard-Burnett, *Terror in the Land of the Holy Spirit*. These authors may perhaps be referring to the presence of Holocaust references in scholarly works written in English that have not had much circulation in Guatemala. The trial of Ríos Montt in 2013 on charges of genocide has led to an increase in Holocaust references in Guatemala.
39. See Grandin, "Chronicles of a Guatemalan Genocide"; Grandin, "The Instruction of Great Catastrophe"; Esquit, "Las rutas"; Esquit, "Movilización política."
40. Grandin, *The Blood of Guatemala*, 16.
41. Esquit, "Movilización política," 250.
42. Grandin, *The Blood of Guatemala*, 16.
43. See also Hale, *Más que un indio*; McAllister, "Rural Markets"; Bastos, "Construcción de la identidad maya"; Bastos, "La política maya"; Bastos, "Violencia, memoria."
44. Stoll, *Between Two Armies*.
45. Stoll, 20, 64–91.
46. Grandin, *The Blood of Guatemala*, 17.
47. Esquit, "Las rutas," 168–69. See Warren, *Indigenous Movements and Their Critics*, 194–209, for a lengthy, nuanced discussion of debates about Mayanists' claims of Maya cultural unity and continuity over time.

48. Grandin, *The Blood of Guatemala*, 17.
49. Grandin, "Living in Revolutionary Time," 12–15.
50. Mayer, *Why Did the Heavens Not Darken?*, 15–18.
51. Grandin, "Living in Revolutionary Time," 14. Critic Neil Larsen, in his own response to how Mayer's work might be useful for understanding Latin American atrocities, finds it instructive that Mayer "forces us to reflect on Auschwitz as, on one level at least, a terrible historical contingency," as "an *event*, inseparable from the larger chain of events that lead into and flow out of it." Larsen, "Thoughts on Violence," 382.
52. The document is dated May 30, 1994, and unsigned, but it is more than likely that Cojtí was one of the document's authors. COMG, *Construyendo*, 37–52.
53. COMG, *Construyendo*, 43–45.
54. COMG, 45–51.
55. COMG, 37.
56. COMG, 37–38.
57. Bastos and Camus, *Abriendo caminos*, 63–75.
58. The consensus document was released on July 13, 1994, as "Identidad y Derechos de los Pueblos Indígenas" in COMG, *Construyendo*, 53–75.
59. See Bastos and Camus, *Abriendo caminos*, 63–75, for a detailed exposition of the discussions that took place during the Asamblea de la Sociedad Civil. On March 31, 1995, the government and the UNRG signed the "Acuerdo de Identidad y Derechos Indígenas." Maya Indians were excluded from the meetings between the two sides leading up to the signing of the Acuerdo. However, the final Acuerdo was based on the proposal adopted by the ASC the year before and recognized Guatemala as "una nación multicultural y plurilingüe," which Maya activists recognized as a valuable achievement despite its falling far short of Maya political demands. Bastos and Camus, *Abriendo caminos*, 75.
60. Tischler Visquerra, *Memoria, tiempo y sujeto*, 112.
61. Cojtí Cuxil, *Políticas para la reivindicación*. This is a book-length essay that contains some elements of the original proposal; the references to three Holocausts are now in a footnote. The book appeared in June 1994.
62. Cojtí Cuxil, "The Politics of Maya Revindication"; Cojtí Cuxil, "Políticas para la reivindicación," 1999.
63. Cojtí Cuxil, *Ri Maya' moloj*. A final reference to the "Maya holocaust" in this series can be found in Casaús Arzú, *Metamorfosis del racismo*, 7.
64. Lovell, "Surviving Conquest," 48.
65. Lovell, 27. Lovell had in turn adopted a model proposed earlier by ethnohistorian Edward Spicer in his 1962 book *Cycles of Conquest: The Impact of Spain, Mexico, and the United States on the Indians of the Southwest, 1533–1960*.
66. Lovell, "Surviving Conquest," 47.
67. Mcdonnell and Moses, "Raphael Lemkin."
68. Convention on the Prevention and Punishment of the Crime of Genocide.

69. Lang, *Genocide*, 28.
70. Schabas, "The Law and Genocide," 140.
71. Mcdonnell and Moses, "Raphael Lemkin," 502–3.
72. Lemkin, *Axis Rule in Occupied Europe*.
73. Schabas, "The Law and Genocide," 133.
74. The charge of genocide had been contemplated at the Nuremberg military trials (even before the adoption of the UN Convention on the Prevention and Punishment of the Crime of Genocide), but the charge "crimes against humanity" was pursued instead. See Lang, *Genocide*, 111; Schabas, "The Law and Genocide," 125. Eichmann's 1961 conviction for genocide was the first and only such conviction until the 1990s. Bazyler, *Holocaust, Genocide, and the Law*, 140.
75. Vidal-Naquet, *The Assassins of Memory*, 129.
76. Duffett, *Against the Crime of Silence*, 315; Convention on the Prevention and Punishment of the Crime of Genocide. See Zunino's thought-provoking analysis of how the Russell Tribunal should be seen as a precursor to, and model for, contemporary transitional justice, especially his emphasis on the importance of the fact that the Russell Tribunal "rejected legalism, questioned the state and denounced a global order that relegated socioeconomic inequality to a secondary position." Zunino, "Subversive Justice," 212.
77. Duffett, *Against the Crime of Silence*, 9.
78. Duffett, 625, original emphasis.
79. Rodolfo Walsh, "Carta abierta de un escritor a la junta militar," 122; Mercado, *En estado de memoria*, 91; Jonas et al., *Guatemala*, 251.
80. Duffett, *Against the Crime of Silence*, 313, 314.
81. Schabas, "The Genocide Mystique"; Bazyler, *Holocaust, Genocide, and the Law*, 59–65; González-Ocantos, "Mexico," 239. See, for example, González-Ocantos's criticisms of the Mexican Comité '68, composed of surviving leaders from the 1968 student movement and brutally repressed by the Mexican state, first under President Gustavo Díaz Ordaz and then under President Luis Echeverría during the Mexican "dirty war." The Comité '68 stubbornly insisted on bringing charges of genocide against both men despite compelling evidence that such a prosecution could not possibly be successful. González-Ocantos recounts: "When I asked him [a member of Comité '68] whether they had considered alternatives to the genocide charges, he categorically replied, 'It was a genocide!' This evidenced the organization's unwillingness to prioritize a viable legal strategy over one that semantically captured their political discourse about the massacre." González-Ocantos, "Mexico," 240.
82. Palencia-Frener, "Contrainsurgencia en Chimaltenango." Operating from a more legal standpoint than Palencia-Frener, Argentine sociologist Daniel Feierstein has argued that the concept should not be defined by the status of the victims as currently laid out in the UN Convention because this violates the principal of equality before the law. Feierstein argues for an expansion of the term "genocide" on historical and sociological grounds and proposes the concept of "genocidal social

practices," which describes a modern process of social reorganization that uses mass extermination of any identified group as its means. He paints a line of such practices that passes from Nazism through the counterinsurgency wars in Algeria and Vietnam and the violence associated with the imposition of "National Security Doctrines" in Latin America. Feierstein, *El genocidio como práctica social*, 43, 35–37, 313. See also Feierstein, "National Security Doctrines."

83. Tuyuc, Conference keynote address.

84. *Campaña continental*, 29.

85. Cojtí Cuxil, *Ub'anik*, 124. Cojtí's use of "etnocidio" was influenced by Guillermo Bonfil Batalla's important *América Latina: Etnodesarrollo y etnocidio*. It also echoes the early use of the term "ethnocide" by Guatemala Maya thinkers in response to the Panzos massacre of 1978. Konefal, *For Every Indio Who Falls*, 102.

86. Sam Colop, *Jub'aqtun Omay Kuchum*, 13. Sam Colop is citing here from Tzvetan Todorov's *La conquête de l'Amerique: La question de l'autre* (1982).

87. Cojtí Cuxil, in discussion with the author via Skype, November 20, 2017.

88. COMG, *Rujunamil ri Mayab' Amaq'*, n.p., original ellipsis.

89. The role of disease and malnutrition in genocide has been the subject of controversy. In the case of Holocaust historiography, historical evidence that disease and hunger were factors in the annihilation of the Jews was taken up by Holocaust deniers who sought to prove that the gas chambers did not exist. Mehlman, "Foreword," xviii. The topic has also come up in disputes about whether the Native American genocide constitutes a genocide or not, with "Holocaust uniqueness" scholar Steven Katz arguing that the spread of lethal diseases among Native American populations by Europeans was an unintended consequence of other actions and therefore does not constitute genocide. Smithers, "Rethinking Genocide in North America," 328–33.

90. Cojtí's emphasis on racial ideology suggests that he was consciously evoking the Nazi Holocaust rather than a dictionary definition of the word "holocaust."

91. Guzmán Böckler and Herbert, *Guatemala*, 186–87, 324, 50.

92. Cojtí Cuxil, *Ri maya' moloj*, 13–14. Cholsamaj Press published one of Guzmán's later books, *Cuando se quiebran los silencios*. Regarding the influence of Guzmán Böckler and Herbert on Mayanists, see Konefal, *For Every Indio Who Falls*, 53–54.

93. Cojtí Cuxil, *Políticas para la reivindicación*, 13; Cojtí Cuxil, *Ri maya' moloj*, 25; Cojtí Cuxil, *Ub'anik*, 82.

94. Cojtí Cuxil, *Ri maya' moloj*, 43, 67–68.

95. Cojtí Cuxil, *Ub'anik*, 125.

96. Cojtí Cuxil, *Ri maya' moloj*, 67. See Survival International for the full text of the law and an explanation of its continued relevance to Indigenous struggles (https://www.survivalinternational.org/law).

97. Cojtí Cuxil, *Políticas para la reivindicación*, 33–35. For the Universal Declaration of the Rights of Peoples, see http://permanentpeoplestribunal.org/algiers-charter/?lang=en.

98. Jerman, *Repression in Latin America*.
99. Viaene, "Life is Priceless," 8.
100. Benjamin, "Theses on the Philosophy of History," 253–54.
101. Traverso, *Left Wing Melancholia*, xv.
102. Traverso, 13.
103. See Smithers, "Rethinking Genocide in North America"; Rosenbaum, *Is the Holocaust Unique?*
104. "La fundación Shoah USC y FAFG"; "USC Shoah Foundation and FAFG."
105. "Lanzan plataforma virtual para el estudio del Holocausto," 5.
106. See mdh.org.gt.
107. See http://www.yahadinunum.org.

Notes to Chapter 5

1. Neruda, *Canto general*, 179.
2. Menchú, *I, Rigoberta Menchú*; Stoll, *Rigoberta Menchú*.
3. "La fundación Shoah USC y FAFG"; "USC Shoah Foundation and FAFG."
4. McAllister, "Testimonial Truths and Revolutionary Mysteries," 95.
5. Shenker, *Reframing Holocaust Testimony*, 113.
6. McAllister, "Testimonial Truths and Revolutionary Mysteries," 100.
7. For a discussion of how the human rights tendency to "code for trauma" can silence other forms of understanding past harm, see Theidon, *Intimate Enemies*, 25–33. For Guatemala, Vanthuyne has also criticized the imposition of a trauma framework. Vanthuyne, *La présence d'un passé*, 5, 178. Vanthuyne and McAllister both draw from Fassin, "The Humanitarian Politics of Testimony."
8. For an excellent short biography of Menchú up to the controversy in the late 1990s, see Arias, "Rigoberta Menchú's History."
9. Stoll, *Between Two Armies*.
10. Stoll, *Rigoberta Menchú*, 12.
11. Stoll, 10.
12. Arias, "Documents," 51.
13. Rohter, "Tarnished Laureate."
14. Arias, *The Rigoberta Menchú Controversy*; "If Truth Be Told."
15. Stoll, *Rigoberta Menchú*, 68–70.
16. Drouin, "'The Realities of Power.'"
17. Stoll, *Rigoberta Menchú*, 70.
18. Quoted in Cohen, "The Unmaking of Rigoberta Menchú," 52.
19. Liano, "The Anthropologist with the Old Hat," 123.
20. Mehlman, "Foreword."
21. Lyotard, *The Differend*, 3.

22. Lyotard relies not on Faurisson directly but on Pierre Vidal-Naquet's "A Paper Eichmann," originally published as an article in 1980 and included in Vidal-Naquet's *The Assassins of Memory*.
23. Lyotard, *The Differend*, 3–4, 5–6.
24. Lyotard, 13.
25. Sommer, "Las Casas's Lies," 238.
26. Sklodowska, "The Poetics of Remembering," 265.
27. Cohen, "The Unmaking of Rigoberta Menchú," 54.
28. Stoll, quoted in Cohen, "The Unmaking of Rigoberta Menchú," 52.
29. Robin, "The Wilful Suspension of Disbelief," 184–85. Robin uses the Stoll-Menchú controversy to call into doubt the existence of a Maya genocide. He labels it merely a "predicament," questions whether it constitutes a clear-cut case of good versus evil, and questions whether the Maya's suffering in the early 1980s belongs within "Western imageries of inhumanity." Robin, 184. To which imagery would it then belong? one wonders.
30. Stoll, *Between Two Armies*, 21.
31. Manz, "La importancia del contexto," 19.
32. Levi, *The Drowned and the Saved*, 14. Quoted in Manz, "La importancia del contexto," 17.
33. Goldhagen, *Hitler's Willing Executioners*, 5. Quoted in García Noval, "Entre dos fuegos," 54. Prudencio García, in his study of the Guatemalan army, likewise notes this similarity between Guatemalan testimony and Holocaust testimony: both testify to a reality whose horrors surpass credibility. García, *El genocidio de Guatemala*, 40–41.
34. Sanford, "Between Rigoberta Menchú and La Violencia," 40.
35. Beverley, "The Margin at the Center," 24–25.
36. Felman and Laub, *Testimony*.
37. Felman and Laub, 59–63.
38. Felman and Laub, 59–61, cited in Beverley, "The Real Thing," 275.
39. Felman and Laub, *Testimony*, 62.
40. Felman and Laub, 60, cited in Beverley, "The Real Thing," 275–76.
41. Felman and Laub, 62, cited in Beverley, 276.
42. Beverley, 276.
43. Beverley, 274. Beverley acknowledges in a footnote that the depiction of the Holocaust in *Schindler's List* has sparked criticisms. "The Real Thing," 284–85n14.
44. Felman and Laub, *Testimony*, 61.
45. Felman and Laub, 58, 61, original emphasis.
46. Beverley, "The Real Thing," 278.
47. Robinson argues in "*The Specialist* on the Eichmann Precedent" that Holocaust testimony furthers U.S. hegemony in the post-1989 period precisely in this way. The evidence I have offered here about the convergence of Holocaust testimony and activist-revolutionary testimony should be enough to nuance that assessment.

48. See my Introduction for more on McAllister's discussion of testimony and "revolutionary futurity."
49. McAllister, "Testimonial Truths and Revolutionary Mysteries," 103, 110.
50. Sanford, *Buried Secrets*, 282.
51. Equipo de Antropología Forense de Guatemala, *Las masacres en Rabinal*, 171.
52. Personal interview with FAFG staffer, Guatemala, May 4, 2018.
53. Bastos, "Violencia, memoria"; Salamanca Villamizar, "Los lugares de la memoria"; Sanford, *Buried Secrets*.
54. Personal interview with FAFG staffer, Guatemala, May 4, 2018.
55. Baer, *El testimonio audiovisual*, 176.
56. Baer, 152.
57. Shenker, *Reframing Holocaust Testimony*, 112.
58. Shenker, 117, 149.
59. Baer, *El testimonio audiovisual*, 192.
60. Baer, 189; Shenker, *Reframing Holocaust Testimony*, 117.
61. Baer, 199.
62. Baer, 195; Shenker, *Reframing Holocaust Testimony*, 124.
63. Shenker, 121. Baer's findings support these conclusions as well. Baer, *El testimonio audiovisual*, 189.
64. Baer, *El testimonio audiovisual*, 196.
65. Shenker, *Reframing Holocaust Testimony*, 117.
66. Shenker, 113.
67. Shenker, *Reframing Holocaust Testimony*, 116.
68. "About the Institute."
69. Popescu, "Steven Spielberg on Storytelling's Power."
70. Of these thirty-two, ten are accessible to anyone who registers with the VHA (registration is free); the remainder are accessible only through VHA subscriber institutions.
71. Shenker, *Reframing Holocaust Testimony*, 119.
72. Baer, *El testimonio audiovisual*, 187.
73. Peccerelli, "Guatemala." The "truth commission" to which Peccerelli refers is the UN-sponsored Comisión de Esclarecimiento Histórico (Commission on Historical Clarification), which issued the report *Guatemala, memoria del silencio* in 1999. The "Church commission" is the Proyecto Interdiocesano de Recuperación de la Memoria Histórica, sponsored by the Office of Human Rights of the Guatemalan Archdiocese, commonly known as REMHI, which published *Guatemala: Nunca más* in 1999 (originally released in 1998).
74. Proyecto Interdiocesano de Recuperación de la Memoria Histórica, *Guatemala: Nunca más*, 1:xxi.
75. Grandin, "The Instruction of Great Catastrophe."

76. For an excellent extended narrative account of this event, see Goldman, *The Art of Political Murder.*

77. Pedro Pacheco Bop Testimony, 34:18–35.53.

78. Pedro Pacheco Bop Testimony, 35:57–37:19, my ellipsis. For a discussion of the role of prophetic dreams in Maya communities in the aftermath of genocide, see Garrard, "Living with Ghosts," 183–84.

79. Sandra Patricia García Paredes Testimony, 1:29–1:30.

80. These questions are taken from Santiago Mo Yat Testimony.

81. Pedro Pacheco Bop Testimony, 54:10–54:28.

82. Human Rights Office, Archdiocese of Guatemala, *Guatemala, Never Again!* 14–15.

83. Stoll, *Between Two Armies.*

84. Examples include Pedro Pacheco Bop Testimony; Santiago Mo Yat Testimony; Genaro Guanché Lajuj Testimony.

85. Examples include Sandra Patricia García Paredes Testimony; Emeterio Toj Medrano Testimony; Diego Rivera Santiago Testimony.

86. Juliana Tun Xalín Testimony.

87. Jesús Tecú Osorio Testimony; Rosalina Tuyuc V. Testimony.

88. Huyssen, *Present Pasts*, 14.

89. Emeterio Toj Medrano Testimony, 1:32.

90. Personal interview with FAFG staffer, Guatemala, May 4, 2018.

91. Shenker, *Reframing Holocaust Testimony*, 149.

92. Rothberg, *Multidirectional Memory*, 2, 3. On the Holocaust and competitive memory frames in the U.S., see also Stein, "Whose Memories? Whose Victimhood?"

93. Rothberg, *Multidirectional Memory*, 3.

94. See Novick, *The Holocaust in American Life.* This is being increasingly questioned from within U.S. Holocaust institutions, but sotto voce; any overt challenge to the "competitive memory" approach to the Holocaust remains controversial in the United States.

95. Rothberg, *Multidirectional Memory*, 6.

96. McAllister says of Stoll: "Stoll's big thing is 'just the facts,' but he confuses people's subsequent interpretations of their experience with strictly referential statements." Quoted in Cohen, "The Unmaking of Rigoberta Menchú," 53. McAllister pursues the presence of "something other than a transparent reference to the truth" in her essay on Guatemalan testimony. McAllister, "Testimonial Truths and Revolutionary Mysteries," 110. Elizabeth Burgos, the original "author" or coauthor of Menchú's testimony, has also invoked Primo Levi in her intervention to the Stoll-Menchú controversy; she cites from Levi's *The Drowned and the Saved* to make a point about the unreliability of memory, thereby using the Holocaust to help her evade a confrontation with a difficult past. Burgos, "Memoria, transmisión e imagen del cuerpo," 23.

97. Wilkomirski, *Fragments*.
98. Suárez, "In Search of Literary 'Truth' "; Walford, "Truth, Lies and Politics."

Notes to the Conclusion

1. Rosencof, *The Letters That Never Came*, 83.
2. Goldemberg, *El gran libro de la América judía*, 13.
3. Sosnowski, "Fronteras en las letras judías-latinoamericanas," 264.
4. For biographical information, see http://yleksikon.blogspot.com/2017/05/boleslaolewin-borekh-levin-february-25.html and https://introduccionalahistoriajvg.wordpress.com/2013/04/06/%E2%9E%BB-boleslao-lewin-1908-1988/.
5. Lewin, *Tupac Amaru, el rebelde*, 7.
6. Lewin, *La rebelión de Tupac Amaru*, 13–14.
7. Tuchman, *A Distant Mirror*, xiv. My thanks to John Slocum for drawing my attention to Tuchman's book in the context of my research.
8. Novick, *The Holocaust in American Life*, 138.
9. "La rebelión del gueto."
10. Arendt, "The Image of Hell," 200.
11. Campodonico, *Las vidas de Rosencof*, 45.
12. Vallejo misspelled "companions" intentionally. Vallejo, *The Complete Posthumous Poetry*, 239.
13. Rosencof, *The Letters That Never Came*, 37–38.
14. Rosencof, 83. I have made some changes to this translation.
15. Hartman, "Introduction," 17.

Bibliography

Abeyta, Michael. "Un cuadro sincrónico del cuerpo en *La noche de Tlatelolco* y *Visión de los vencidos*." *Relaciones: Estudios de historia y sociedad* (Zamora, Mexico) 21, no. 82 (Spring 2000): 177–98. http://www.redalyc.org/articulo.oa?id=13708208.

"About the Institute." USC Shoah Foundation–The Institute for Visual History and Education. institute_onesheet_20190909_opt.pdf. Accessible at https://sfi.usc.edu/press-kit.

Actis, Munu, Cristina Aldini, Liliana Gardella, Miriam Lewin, and Elisa Tokar, eds. *Ese infierno: Conversaciones con cinco mujeres sobrevientes de la ESMA*. Prologue by León Rozitchner. Buenos Aires: Sudamericana, 2001.

Adorno, Theodor. "Commitment" (1961). In *Can One Live after Auschwitz? A Philosophical Reader*. Edited by Rolf Tiedemann. Translated by Rodney Livingstone and others. Palo Alto: Stanford University Press, 2003. 240–58.

Adorno, Theodor. "Cultural Criticism and Society" (1951). In *Prisms*. Translated by Samuel and Shierry Weber. Cambridge: MIT Press, 1983. 17–34.

Agamben, Giorgio. *Remnants of Auschwitz: The Witness and the Archive*. Translated by Daniel Heller-Roazen. New York: Zone, 1999.

Agosín, Marjorie. *Among the Angels of Memory/Entre los ángeles de la memoria*. Bilingual edition. Translated by Laura Rocha Nakazawa. San Antonio: Wings Press, 2006.

Agosín, Marjorie, ed. *Memory, Oblivion, and Jewish Culture in Latin America*. Austin: University of Texas Press, 2005.

Aguad, Susana. "Ni olvido ni venganza: JUSTICIA." *Controversia* 2, no. 6 (May 1980): 5.

Aguilar Melantzón, Ricardo, and Mimi Gladstein. " 'El reposo del fuego': A Germinal Anticipation of 'Morirás lejos.' " *Rocky Mountain Review of Language and Literature* 38, no. 1/2 (1984): 59–69. http://www.jstor.org/stable/1347157.

Aizenberg, Edna. "Didn't All the Nazis Go to Argentina? Latin American Studies and the Holocaust." *Yiddish-Modern Jewish Studies* 15, no. 4 (2009): 34–41.

Aizenberg, Edna. "Nation and Holocaust Narration: Uruguay's Memorial del Holocausto del Pueblo Judío." *Rethinking Jewish-Latin Americans*. Edited by Jeffrey Lesser and Raanan Rein. Albuquerque: University of New Mexico Press, 2008. 207–30.

Aizenberg, Edna. *On the Edge of the Holocaust: The Shoah in Latin American Literature and Culture*. Waltham: Brandeis University Press, 2016.

Alemán Velasco, Miguel. "1968: Un año bisiesto." *Siempre!* 810 (January 1, 1969): 12–13.

Alexander, Edward. "Stealing the Holocaust." *Midstream* 26, no. 9 (November 1980): 46–51.

Alexander, Jeffrey. "On the Social Construction of Moral Universals: The 'Holocaust' from War Crime to Trauma Drama." *European Journal of Social Theory* 5, no. 1 (2002): 5–85. Education Source, EBSCOhost.

Amnesty International. "Argentina: Revelador testimonio de dos sobrevivientes." *Boletín Mensual Informativo* 3 (March 1980): 1–2. www.amnesty.org/download/Documents/204000/nws210161980.en.pdf.

"Antisemitism." *Argentina Outreach: Bulletin of the Argentine Information Service Center* (Berkeley, CA) 2, no. 9 (July–August 1977): 11.

Arcuschin, Raquel de, et al. "Réplica al 'Informe especial sobre detenidos y desaparecidos judíos 1976–1983.' Publicado en 1984." Reprinted in *El antisemitismo en la Argentina*. Second edition. Edited by Leonardo Senkman. Buenos Aires: Centro Editor de América Latina, 1989. 421–31.

Arendt, Hannah. *Eichmann in Jerusalem: A Report on the Banality of Evil*. Translated by Amos Elon. New York: Penguin, 2006 [1963].

Arendt, Hannah. "The Image of Hell." In *Essays in Understanding, 1930–1954*. Edited by Jerome Kohn. New York: Harcourt Brace, 1994. 197–205.

Arens, Richard, ed. *Genocide in Paraguay*. Epilogue by Elie Wiesel. Philadelphia: Temple University Press, 1976.

Arias, Arturo. "Changing Indian Identity: Guatemala's Violent Transition to Modernity." In *Guatemalan Indians and the State, 1540–1988*. Edited by Carol A. Smith with the assistance of Marilyn M. Moors. Austin: University of Texas Press, ACLS Humanities ebook. 230–57.

Arias, Arturo. "Documents: The Public Speaks." In Arias, ed., *The Rigoberta Menchú Controversy*. Minneapolis: University of Minnesota Press, 2001. 51–57.

Arias, Arturo, ed. *The Rigoberta Menchú Controversy*. With a response by David Stoll. Minneapolis: University of Minnesota Press, 2001.

Arias, Arturo. "Rigoberta Menchú's History within the Guatemalan Context." In Arias, ed., *The Rigoberta Menchú Controversy*. Minneapolis: University of Minnesota Press, 2001.

Aroche Parra, Miguel. *53 poemas del 68 mexicano*. México: Editora y Distribuidora Nacional de Publicaciones, 1972.

Avelar, Idelber. *The Untimely Present: Postdictatorial Latin American Fiction and the Task of Mourning*. Durham: Duke University Press, 1999.

Avni, Haim. "Cárdenas, México y los refugiados, 1938–1940." *EIAL* 3, no. 1 (1992). http://eial.tau.ac.il/index.php/eial/article/view/1269/1295.

Avni, Haim. "Los países de América Latina y el Holocausto." In *Shoá: Enciclopedia del Holocausto*. Edited by Robert Rozett, Shmuel Spector, and Efraím Zadoff. Jerusalem: EDZ Nativ Ediciones/Yad Vashem, 2004. https://www.yadvashem.org/yv/es/holocaust/about/docs/latin_america_and_the_holocaust_avni.pdf.

Baer, Alejandro. *El testimonio audiovisual: Imagen y memoria del Holocausto*. Madrid: Centro de Investigaciones Sociológicas, 2005.

Baer, Alejandro, and Natan Sznaider. *Memory and Forgetting in the Post-Holocaust Era: The Ethics of Never Again*. London and New York: Routledge, 2017.

Bakhtin, M. M. *The Dialogic Imagination: Four Essays*. Edited by Michael Holquist. Translated by Caryl Emerson and Michael Holquist. Austin: University of Texas Press, 1981.

Bañuelos, Juan. "No consta en actas." *La Cultura en México* 352 (November 13, 1968): vii–ix.

Bargil, Abraham. *Ni silencio ni olvido: Testimonios judíos de los años de la dictadura en Argentina 1976–1983*. Buenos Aires: Acervo Cultural, 2015.

Bartov, Omer, Doris Bergen, et al. "An Open Letter to the Director of the U.S. Holocaust Museum." *New York Review of Books*, July 1, 2019. nybooks.com.

Bastos, Santiago. "Construcción de la identidad maya como un proceso político." In *Mayanización y vida cotidiana: Vol. 1. La ideología multicultural en la sociedad guatemalteca*. Edited by Santiago Bastos and Aura Cumes. Guatemala: FLACSO/CIRMA/Cholsamaj, 2007. 53–80.

Bastos, Santiago. "La política maya en la Guatemala posconflicto." In *El movimiento maya en la década después de la paz (1970–2010)*. Edited by Santiago Bastos and Roddy Brett. Guatemala: F&G Editores, 2010. 3–54.

Bastos, Santiago. "Violencia, memoria e identidad: El caso de Choatalum (San Martín Jilotepeque, Chimaltenango)." In *Mayanizacion y vida cotidiana: Vol. 2. Estudios de casos*. Edited by Santiago Bastos and Aura Cumes. Guatemala: FLACSO/CIRMA/Cholsamaj, 2007. 45–68.

Bastos, Santiago, and Marcela Camus. *Abriendo caminos: Las organizaciones mayas desde el Nobel hasta el Acuerdo de Derechos Indígenas*. Guatemala: FLACSO, 1995.

Bastos, Santiago, and Marcela Camus. *Quebrando el silencio: Organizaciones del pueblo Maya y sus demandas (1986–1992)*. Guatemala: FLACSO, 1996.

Bastos, Santiago, and Roddy Brett, eds. *El movimiento maya en la década después de la paz (1970–2010)*. Guatemala: F&G Editores, 2010.

Bauer, Yehuda. "¿Es posible un nuevo Holocausto?" *Fraie Schtime* 10, no. 59 (April 1977): 1.

Bauer, Yehuda. *The Jewish Emergence from Powerlessness*. Toronto: University of Toronto Press, 1979.

Bauer, Yehuda. "On the Holocaust and Other Genocides." John and Rebecca Meyerhoff Annual Lecture. Washington, DC: United States Holocaust Memorial Museum Center for Advanced Holocaust Studies, 2006.

Bauer, Yehuda. "Whose Holocaust?" *Midstream* 26, no. 9 (November 1980): 42–46.
Bauman, Zygmunt. *Modernity and the Holocaust*. Ithaca: Cornell University Press, 1989.
Bayer, Osvaldo. "De Dachau a la ESMA." In *En camino al paraíso: 1993–1998*. Buenos Aires: Javier Vergara Editor, 1999. 199–202.
Bayer, Osvaldo. "Pequeño recordatorio para un país sin memoria." In *Represión y reconstrucción de una cultura: El caso argentino*. Edited by Saúl Sosnowski. Buenos Aires: Editorial Universitaria de Buenos Aires, 1988. 203–28.
Bayer, Osvaldo. "Prólogo." In Claudia Rafael, *Ruth: Entre Auschwitz y el Olimpo*. Prologue by Osvaldo Bayer. Buenos Aires: Editorial Biblos, 2010.
Bayer, Osvaldo. *Rebeldía y esperanza*. Buenos Aires: Grupo Editorial Zeta, 1993.
Bazyler, Michael. *Holocaust, Genocide, and the Law: A Quest for Justice in a Post-Holocaust World*. New York: Oxford University Press, 2016.
Bejarano, Margalit. *The Jewish Community of Cuba: Memory and History*. Jerusalem: Hebrew University Magnes Press, 2014.
Bell, Lawrence D. "Bitter Conquest: Zionists against Progressive Jews and the Making of Post-war Jewish Politics in Argentina." *Jewish History* 17, no. 3 (2003): 285–308. http://www.jstor.org/stable/20101506.
Bell, Lawrence D. "In the Name of the Community: Populism, Ethnicity and Politics among the Jews of Argentina under Perón, 1946–55." *Hispanic American Historical Review* 86, no. 1 (2006): 93–122. Education Source, EBSCOhost.
Bellino, Michelle J. *Youth in Postwar Guatemala: Education and Civic Identity in Transition*. New Brunswick: Rutgers University Press, 2017. Project MUSE.
Ben-Dror, Graciela. "Antisemitism in Argentina: From the Military Junta to the Democratic Era." Stephen Roth Institute for the Study of Contemporary Antisemitism and Racism, 2002–2003. http://www.tau.ac.il/Anti-Semitism/asw2002-3/ben-dror.htm.
Benjamin, Walter. "Theses on the Philosophy of History." In *Illuminations*. Edited by Hannah Arendt. New York: Schocken Books, 1969. 253–64.
Bernetti, Jorge Luis, and Mempo Giardinelli. *México: El exilio que hemos vivido*. Buenos Aires: Universidad Nacional de Quilmes, 2003.
Berryman, Philip. *The Religious Roots of Rebellion: Christians in Central American Revolutions*. Maryknoll: Orbis, 1984.
Bettelheim, Bruno. "Behavior in Extreme Situations: Defenses." In *The Informed Heart: Autonomy in a Mass Age*. Glencoe, IL: Free Press, 1960. 177–235.
Beverley, John. *Latinamericanism after 9/11*. Durham: Duke University Press, 2011.
Beverley, John. "The Margin at the Center: On *Testimonio* (1989)." In *The Real Thing: Testimonial Discourse and Latin America*. Edited by Georg M. Gugelberger. Durham: Duke University Press, 1996. 23–41.
Beverley, John. "The Real Thing (1995)." In *The Real Thing: Testimonial Discourse and Latin America*. Edited by Georg M. Gugelberger. Durham: Duke University Press, 1996. 266–86.

Bird, Kai. "Argentina: Get Out, Jews." *Newsweek* (August 15, 1977): 31. Nexis.

Bischoping, Katherine, and Andrea Kalmin. "Public Opinion about Comparisons to the Holocaust." *Public Opinion Quarterly* 63, no. 4 (Winter 1999): 485–507. http://www.jstor.org/stable/3038253.

Blair, Sara. "After the Fact: *El libro negro*, Traumatic Identities, and the War on Fascism." *Journal of Jewish Identities* 5, no. 1 (2012): 111–25. https://doi.org/10.1353/jji.2012.0003.

Bloxham, Donald, and A. Dirk Moses. *The Oxford Handbook of Genocide Studies*. Oxford: Oxford University Press, 2010.

Blum, Leonor. "Argentine Jewry: Reflections on Military Rule." *Hadassah Magazine* (May 1984): 16–17, 30–33.

Bokser Liwerant, Judit, Daniela Gleizer, and Yael Siman. "Claves conceptuales y metodológicas para comprender las conexiones entre México y el Holocausto. ¿Historias independientes o interconectadas?" *Revista Mexicana de Ciencias Políticas y Sociales* 61, no. 228 (September–December 2016): 267–310. Education Source, EBSCOhost.

Bonfil Batalla, Guillermo. *América Latina: Etnodesarrollo y etnocidio*. San José, Costa Rica: FLACSO, 1982.

Bono, Agostino. "The Troubled Jews of Argentina." *Worldview* (November 1977): 13.

Borges, Jorge Luis. "Pierre Menard, autor del *Quijote*." In *Obras completas I. 1923–1949*. Third edition. Buenos Aires: Emecé, 2008. 530–38.

Bosoer, Fabián. "Juicios, castigos y verdades," *Revista Ñ* (September 8, 2014). www.revistaenie.clarin.com.

Brailovsky, Antonio Elio. "Y aquí también hubo muchos silenciosos." *Nueva Presencia* 5, no. 314 (July 8, 1983): 1.

Braylán, Marisa, Daniel Feierstein, Miguel Galante, and Adrián Jmelnizky. "Informe sobre la situación de los detenidos-desparecidos judíos durante el genocidio perpetrado en Argentina." http://www.desaparecidos.org/nuncamas/web/investiga/daia00htm.

Brett, Roddy. *The Origins and Dynamics of Genocide: Political Violence in Guatemala*. New York: Palgrave Macmillan, 2016.

Brinkman, B. "Marginales." *Fraie Schtime* 10, no. 62 (April 1978): 2.

Burgos, Elizabeth. "Memoria, transmisión e imagen del cuerpo." In *Stoll-Menchú: La invención de la memoria*. Edited by Mario Roberto Morales. Guatemala: Consucultura, 2001. 19–87.

Burt, Jo-Marie. "From Heaven to Hell in Ten Days: The Genocide Trial in Guatemala." *Journal of Genocide Research* 18, nos. 2–3 (2016): 143–69. Tandfonline. doi: 10.1080/14623528.2016.1186437.

Callizo, Liliana, Teresa Celia Meschiati, and Piero Di Monte. "Tres sobrevivientes responden." *Controversia* 2, no. 14 (August 1981): 29–31.

Calveiro, Pilar. *Poder y desparición: Los campos de concentración en Argentina*. Buenos Aires: Colihue, 2001.

Calveiro, Pilar. *Política y/o violencia: Aproximación a la guerrilla de los años 70*. Buenos Aires: Siglo XXI, 2013.
Campaña continental: 500 años de resistencia indígena y popular. Guatemala: Secretaria Operativa, 1991. World Scholar: Latin America & the Caribbean. http://worldscholar.tu.galegroup.com/tinyurl/6Av693.
Campodonico, Miguel Angel. *Las vidas de Rosencof*. Montevideo: Editorial Fin de Siglo, 2000.
Campos, Julieta. "*Morirás lejos*: Ese libro terrible de José Emilio Pacheco lo hemos escrito todos." *La Cultura en México* 315 (February 28, 1968): xi–xii.
Campos, Marco Antonio. "Los mejores libros de 1978." *Proceso* (January 8, 1979): 55–56.
Campos, Marco Antonio. "*Morirás lejos*." *Proceso* (June 5, 1978): 56–57.
Campos, Marco Antonio, and Alejandro Toledo, eds. *Poemas y narraciones sobre el movimiento estudiantil de 1968*. México: UNAM, 1998.
Cañón, Hugo. "Un antes y un después." *Puentes* 1, no. 3 (March 2001): 68–71. http://www.comisionporlamemoria.org/project/puentes/.
Carlotto, Estela, and Alejandro Mosquera. "Editorial." *Puentes* 1, no. 1 (August 2000): 3. http://www.comisionporlamemoria.org/project/puentes/.
Casaús Arzú, Marta. "La exacerbación del racismo durante el juicio por genocidio contra el General Ríos Montt." *Cultura de Guatemala* (Universidad Rafael Landívar) 35, no. 2 (July–December 2014): 167–94. Education Service, EBSCOhost.
Casaús Arzú, Marta. *Metamorfosis del racismo en Guatemala/Uk'exwachixiik ri Kaxlan Na'ooj pa Iximuleew*. Guatemala: Cholsamaj, 1998.
Castellanos, Rosario. "Memorial de Tlatelolco." In *La noche de Tlatelolco*. Second revised edition. Edited by Elena Poniatowska. México: Ediciones Era, 1998 [1971]. 163–64.
Castro Leal, Antonio, André Simone, Bodo Uhse, Juan Rejano, Anna Seghers, Ludwig Renn, and Egon Erwin Kisch, eds. *El libro negro del terror Nazi en Europa: Testimonios de escritores y artistas de 16 naciones*. Mexico: Editorial "El Libro Libre," 1943.
Casullo, Nicolás. "Una crítica para reencontrar al hombre." *Confines* 1, no. 1 (April 1995): 7–16.
Casullo, Nicolás. "Una temporada en las palabras." *Confines* 2, no. 3 (September 1996): 13–32.
Cerruti, Gabriela. "La historia de la memoria: Entre la fetichización y el duelo." *Puentes* 1, no. 3 (March 2001): 14–25. http://www.comisionporlamemoria.org/project/puentes/.
Chavarria, Christina. "Archival Memory Systems: The United States Holocaust Memorial Museum and Latin America." *EIAL* 23, no. 1 (2012): 99–112. http://eial.tau.ac.il/index.php/eial/article/view/305.
Chejfec, Sergio. *Lenta biografía*. Buenos Aires: Alfaguara, 2007.

"Chile-Argentina: Paz y derechos humanos." *Nueva Presencia* 5, no. 315 (July 15, 1983): 1.

Chinski, Malena. "Ilustrar la memoria: Las imágenes de tapa de la colección *Dos Poylishe Yidntum* (El judaísmo polaco), Buenos Aires 1946–1966." *EIAL* 23, no. 1 (2012): 11–33. http://eial.tau.ac.il/index.php/eial/article/view/301 thesis.

Chinski, Malena. "La representación del 'horror nazi' en la prensa argentina." *Revista de Estudios Sociales* 54 (2015): 120–33. doi: 10.7440/res54.2015.09.

Churchill, Ward. *A Little Matter of Genocide: Holocaust and Denial in the Americas, 1492 to the Present.* San Francisco: City Lights Books, 1997.

Cimet, Adina. *Ashkenazi Jews in Mexico: Ideologies in the Structuring of Community.* Albany: SUNY Press, 1997. https://muse.jhu.edu.

Clark D'Lugo, Carol. "Narrative and Historical Commitment in Pacheco's *Morirás lejos*." *Chasqui* 19, no. 2 (1990): 33–42.

Cohen, Hal. "The Unmaking of Rigoberta Menchú." *Lingua Franca* (July–August 1999): 52.

Cojtí Cuxil, Demetrio. *Políticas para la reivindicación de los Mayas de hoy: Fundamentos de los derechos específicos de los pueblo maya.* Guatemala: Cholsamaj/SPEM, 1994.

Cojtí Cuxil, Demetrio. "Políticas para la reivindicación de los Mayas de hoy: Fundamentos de los derechos específicos del pueblo maya." In *Rujotayixik ri Maya' b'anob'al/Activismo cultural maya.* Edited by Edward F. Fischer and R. Mckenna Brown. Guatemala: Cholsamaj, 1999. 31–82.

Cojtí Cuxil, Demetrio. "The Politics of Maya Revindication." In *Maya Cultural Activism in Guatemala.* Edited by Edward F. Fischer and R. Mckenna Brown. Austin: UT Press, 1996. 19–50.

Cojtí Cuxil, Demetrio. *Ri Maya' moloj pa Iximulew/El movimiento maya (en Guatemala).* Guatemala: Cholsamaj, 1997.

Cojtí Cuxil, Demetrio/Waq'i Q'anil. *Ub'aniik ri Una'ooj Uchomaba'al ri Maya' tinamit/Configuración del pensamiento político del pueblo maya, 2nda parte.* Guatemala: SPEM/Cholsamaj, 1995. 121–27.

Cole, Tim. *Selling the Holocaust: From Auschwitz to Schindler.* New York: Routledge, 1999.

COMG, ed. *Construyendo un futuro para nuestro pasado: Derechos del pueblo maya y el proceso de paz.* Guatemala: Cholsamaj, 1995.

COMG. *Derechos específicos del pueblo maya.* Guatemala: Cholsamaj, 1991.

Comisión Argentina de Solidaridad. "A seis años de la dictadura militar" (March 1982). In *México: El exilio que hemos vivido.* Edited by Jorge Luis Bernetti and Mempo Giardinelli. Buenos Aires: Universidad Nacional de Quilmes, 2003. 226–29.

Comisión Argentina por los Derechos Humanos. *Argentina: Proceso al genocidio.* Madrid: Elías Querejeta Ediciones, 1977.

Comisión de Derechos Humanos de Guatemala (México). *Informe sobre la situación de los derechos humanos en Guatemala.* Mexico: CDHG, 1986.

Comisión de Esclarecimiento Histórico (CEH). *Guatemala, memoria del silencio.* 12 vols. Guatemala, 1999. http://www.centrodememoriahistorica.gov.co/descargas/guatemala-memoria-silencio/guatemala-memoria-del-silencio.pdf.

Comisión de Estudios sobre el Antisemitismo en la Argentina. *Actas de las ponencias, debates y conclusiones de la convención de la DAIA sobre la situación de los judíos en Argentina (1975).* DAIA: Buenos Aires, 1987.

Comité Panameño de Solidaridad con el Pueblo de Guatemala. "Guatemala vencerá" (1982). World Scholar: Latin America & the Caribbean. http://worldscholar.tu.galegroup.com/tinyurl/68qxG2.

Comité Pro Justicia y Paz de Guatemala. *Boletín Comité Pro Justicia y Paz de Guatemala: Mujer guatemalteca, fe cristiana y liberación* (1985). World Scholar: Latin America & the Caribbean. http://worldscholar.tu.galegroup.com/tinyurl/68qyC4.

CONADEP, *Nunca más: Informe CONADEP* (September 1984). http://www.desaparecidos.org/nuncamas/web/investig/articulo/nuncamas/nmas0001.htm.

"Conferencia del profesor Elie Wiesel en la Comunidad Bet-El, lunes 3 de setiembre de 1979." *Majshavot* (1979): 5–17.

"Contra el antisemitismo y por la plena vigencia de los derechos humanos." *Nueva Presencia* 6, no. 329 (October 21, 1983): 1.

Convention on the Prevention and Punishment of the Crime of Genocide. Adopted by the General Assembly of the United Nations on 9 December 1948. https://treaties.un.org/doc/publication/unts/volume%2078/volume-78-i-1021-english.pdf.

Corradi, Juan E., Patricia Weiss Fagen, and Manuel Antonio Garretón, eds. *Fear at the Edge: State Terror and Resistance in Latin America.* Berkeley: University of California, 1992. http://ark.cdlib.org/ark:/13030/ft6489p0pq/.

COSOFAM. *La violación de los derechos humanos de argentinos judíos bajo el regimen militar (1976–1983).* Buenos Aires: Milá, 2006.

COSOFAM. "Sólo la verdad hará posible la convivencia." *Controversia* 3, nos. 11–12 (April 1981): 47.

Crenzel, Emilio. "Introducción. Memorias y representaciones de los desaparecidos en la Argentina, 1983–2008." In Crenzel, ed., *Los desaparecidos en la Argentina: Memorias, representaciones e ideas, 1983–2008.* Buenos Aires: Editorial Biblios, 2010. 11–23.

Crenzel, Emilio. *La historia política del* Nunca más*: La memoria de las desapariciones en la Argentina.* Buenos Aires: Siglo XXI Editores Argentina, 2008.

Cué, Carlos. "Polémica en Argentina por las cifras de desaparecidos de la dictadura." *El País.* January 28, 2016. https://elpais.com/internacional/2016/01/27/argentina/1453931104_458651.html.

Da Silva Catela, Ludmila. *No habrá flores en la tumba del pasado: La experiencia de la reconstrucción del mundo de los familiares de desparecidos.* La Plata: Ediciones Al Margen, 2001.

DAIA. "Inventario del archivo histórico sobre el rol de la DAIA frente a la dictadura militar 1976–1983." Buenos Aires: DAIA–Centro de Estudios Sociales, 2003.

DAIA. *No olvidarás . . . el Holocausto: Tres enfoques.* Buenos Aires: DAIA, 1982.

"DAIA: El antisemitismo no es problema exclusivo de nuestro país." *Nueva Presencia* 4, no. 205 (June 5, 1981): 21.

"DAIA: Etapas difíciles." *Nueva Presencia* 1, no. 39 (April 1, 1978): 6.

"DAIA informó sobre la reciente liberación de un grupo de médicos." *Nueva Presencia* 4, no. 214 (August 7, 1981): 22.

"DAIA: No buscamos logros espectaculares." *Nueva Presencia* 4, no. 233 (December 18, 1981): 16.

"DAIA: Schonfeld goza de la admiración de la colectividad judía." *Nueva Presencia* 4, no. 210 (July 10, 1981): 15.

Dalmaroni, Miguel. "Dictaduras, memorias y modos de narrar: *Confines, Punto de Vista, Revista de Crítica Cultural, H.I.J.O.S.*" *Revista Iberoamericana* 70, nos. 208–9 (July–December 2004): 957–81. http://revista-iberoamericana.pitt.edu/.

De Bonafini, Hebe. "Conference given by the president of the association 'Mothers of Plaza de Mayo' in Liber/Arte on July 8th, 1988."

"Debate alemán." *Confines* 1, no. 1 (April 1995): 110–40.

"Declaración de Iximché." Guatemala, February 1980. http://www.albedrio.org/htm/otrosdocs/comunicados/DeclaraciondeIximche1980.pdf.

"Del Holocausto a la rebelión." *Nueva Sión* 27, no. 580 (May 1976): 2.

DellaPergola, Sergio. "¿Cuántos somos hoy? Investigación y narrativa sobre población judía en América Latina." In *Pertenencia y alteridad: Judíos en/de América Latina: Cuarenta años de cambios.* Edited by Haim Avni, Judit Bokser Liwerant, Sergio DellaPergola, Margalit Bejarano, and Leonardo Senkman. Translated by Florinda Goldberg. Madrid and Frankfurt: Iberoamericana/Vervuert, 2011. 305–40.

"Desaparecidos: 'Nuevo Holocausto.'" *Hemisférica: Boletín de la Asociación Interamericana pro-Democracia y Libertad* (June–July 1979): 3.

"Desaparecidos en Argentina: Daniel Lázaro Rus." http://www.desaparecidos.org./arg/victimas/r/rus.

"Desenmascarar a los agresores antisemitas." *Nueva Sión* 28, no. 587 (March 1977): 2.

Diego Rivera Santiago Testimony (Interview Code 55367). 2015. Visual History Archive, USC Shoah Foundation.

"Diez años volcánicos." *Nueva Presencia* 3, no. 155 (June 20, 1980): 1.

Diner, Dan. "Historical Understanding and Counterrationality: The Judenrat as Historical Vantage." In *Beyond the Conceivable: Studies on Germany, Nazism and the Holocaust.* Berkeley: University of California Press, 2000. 130–37. https://ebookcentral.proquest.com/.

Donoso Paredes, Miguel. "*Morirás lejos.*" *El Día* (December 16 1967): 11.
Dorra, Raúl. "*Morirás lejos*: La ética de la escritura." In *La hoguera y el viento: José Emilio Pacheco ante la crítica*. Edited by Hugo J. Verani. Mexico, DF: UNAM/ Ediciones Era, 1993. 238–48.
"Dramáticos testimonios en el comienzo de 'Holocausto.'" *La Nación* (December 16, 1981): section 2, 1.
Dreschler, Nachmann. "Judíos, escríbanlo." *Fraie Schtime* 10, no. 60 (July 1977): 1.
Drouin, Mark. "'The Realities of Power': David Stoll and the Story of the 1982 Guatemalan Genocide." *Journal of Genocide Research* 18, nos. 2–3 (2016): 305–22. doi: 10.1080/14623528.2016.1186956.
Duffett, John, ed. *Against the Crime of Silence: Proceedings of the Russell International War Crimes Tribunal*. Introduction by Bertrand Russell. Foreword by Ralph Schoenman. New York: Bertrand Russell Peace Foundation, 1968.
"Editorial." *The Jewish Week and the American Examiner* (April 1, 1979): 30.
"Editorial." *Punto de Vista* 6, no. 17 (April–June 1983): 3.
"El Ghetto de Varsovia: Inclinémonos ante los héroes." *Nueva Sión* 27, no. 570 (April 1975): 1.
"El Holocausto y la rebelión, 35 años después." *Nueva Presencia* 1, no. 43 (April 29, 1978): 6–8.
"El judaísmo no puede sobrevivir en una sociedad donde no rijan derechos humanos." *Nueva Presencia* 2, no. 77 (December 22, 1978): 5.
Elena Marx Holocaust Testimony (Videotape 21918). 1996. Visual History Archive, USC Shoah Foundation.
Elias, Norbert. *The Civilizing Process: Vol. 2. State Formation and Civilization*. Translated by Edmund Jephcott. Oxford: Blackwell, 1994.
Ellis, Marc. "Critical Thought and Messianic Trust: Reflections on a Jewish Theology of Liberation." In *The Future of Liberation Theology: Essays in Honor of Gustavo Gutiérrez*. Edited by Marc Ellis and Otto Maduro. Maryknoll, NY: Orbis Books, 1989. 375–89.
Emeterio Toj Medrano Testimony (Interview Code 55281). 2015. Visual History Archive, USC Shoah Foundation.
"En el 32 aniversario del levantamiento del ghetto de Varsovia. Enfrentar el nazifascismo aquí y en todas partes." *Voz Libre* 8, nos. 51–52 (April 1975): 1.
Equipo de Antropología Forense de Guatemala. *Las masacres en Rabinal: Estudio histórico-antropológico de las masacres de Plan de Sánchez, Chichupac y Río Negro*. Guatemala: EAFG, 1997 [1995].
Esquit, Edgar. "Las rutas que nos ofrecen el pasado y el presente: Activismo político, historia y pueblo maya." In *Memorias del mestizaje: Cultura política en Centroamérica de 1920 al presente*. Edited by Dario E. Euraque, Dario E, Jeffrey L. Gould, and Charles R Hale. Guatemala: CIRMA, 2014. 167–92.
Esquit, Edgar. "Movilización política indígena en Comalapa en la era de la paz: Identidades, memorias y auto-determinación indígena en esta localidad." In

El movimiento maya en la década después de la paz (1970–2010). Edited by Santiago Bastos and Roddy Brett. Guatemala: F&G Editores, 2010. 233–52.

"Estremecedora visión del exterminio judío; 'Holocausto' y sus seis noches de horror." *La Nación* (December 21, 1981): section 3, 3.

Falla, Ricardo. *Masacres de la selva: Ixcán, Guatemala (1975–1982)*. Guatemala: Editorial Universitaria, 1992.

Farias, Victor. *Heidegger and Nazism*. Edited by Joseph Margolis and Tom Rockmore. Translated by Paul Burrell and Gabriel Ricci. Philadelphia: Temple University Press, 1989.

Fassin, Didier. "The Humanitarian Politics of Testimony: Subjectification through Trauma in the Israeli-Palestinian Conflict." *Cultural Anthropology* 23, no. 3 (August 2008): 531–58. http://www.jstor.org/stable/20484515.

Feierstein, Daniel. *El genocidio como práctica social: Entre el nazismo y la experiencia argentina*. Buenos Aires: Fondo de Cultura Económica de Argentina, 2007.

Feierstein, Daniel. "National Security Doctrines in Latin America: The Genocide Question." In *The Oxford Handbook of Genocide Studies*. Edited by Donald Bloxham and A. Dirk Moses. Oxford: Oxford University Press, 2010. 489–508.

Feierstein, Liliana Ruth. "'A Quilt of Memory': The Shoah as a Prism in the Testimony of Survivors of the Dictatorship in Argentina." *European Review* 22, no. 4 (2014): 585–93. https://www.cambridge.org/core. doi: 10.1017/S1062798714000374.

Feinmann, José Pablo. "Adorno y el ESMA (II)." *Página/12* (January 13, 2001). http://www.pagina12.com.ar/2001/01-01/01-01-13/contrata.htm.

Feinmann, José Pablo. "Pensar y escribir después de la ESMA." *Página/12* (March 25, 2000). http://www.pagina12.com.ar/2000/00-03/00-03-25/contrata.htm.

Feitlowitz, Marguerite. *A Lexicon of Terror*. New York: Oxford University Press, 1998.

Feld, Claudia. *Del estrado a la pantalla: Las imágenes del Juicio a los ex-comandantes en Argentina*. Prologue by Héctor Schmucler. Madrid: Siglo XXI/SSRC, 2002.

Feld, Claudia. "La representación de los desaparecidos en la prensa de la transición: El 'show del horror.'" In *Los desaparecidos en la Argentina: Memorias, representaciones e ideas, 1983–2008*. Edited by Emilio Crenzel. Buenos Aires: Editorial Biblos, 2010. 25–42.

Feldman, Allen. "Memory Theaters, Virtual Witnessing and the Trauma-Aesthetic." *Biography* 27, no. 1 (Winter 2004): 163–202. muse.jhu.edu.

Felman, Shoshana. "In an Era of Testimony: Claude Lanzmann's *Shoah*." *Yale French Studies* 79 (1991): 39–81. http://www.jstor.org/stable/2930246.

Felman, Shoshana, and Dori Laub. *Testimony: Crises of Witnessing in Literature, Psychoanalysis and History*. New York: Routledge, 1992.

Fermaglich, Kristen. *American Dreams and Nazi Nightmares: Early Holocaust Consciousness and Liberal America, 1957–1965*. Waltham, MA: Brandeis University Press, 2006.

Finchelstein, Federico. *The Ideological Origins of the Dirty War: Fascism, Populism, and Dictatorship in Twentieth Century Argentina*. Oxford: Oxford University Press, 2014.

Fischer, Edward. "Beyond Victimization: Maya Movements in Post-war Guatemala." In *The Struggle for Indigenous Rights in Latin America*. Edited by Nancy Grey Postero and Leon Zamosc. Brighton: Sussex Press, 2004. 81–104.

Fisk, Robert. "Do You Know the Difference between a Holocaust and a holocaust? The Armenians Do." *The Independent* (November 30, 2014). http://www.independent.co.uk.

Flanzbaum, Hilene, ed. *The Americanization of the Holocaust*. Baltimore: Johns Hopkins University Press, 1999.

Flores Ramírez, Miguel. Review of *Morirás lejos*. *El Nacional* (March 25, 1978): 15.

"Formación moral y cívica: La enseñanza laica quedó atrás." *Nueva Presencia* 3, no. 141 (March 14, 1980): 1.

Forster, Ricardo. "Los usos de la memoria." *Confines* 2, no. 3 (September 1996): 53–63.

Forster, Ricardo. Review of Tzvetan Todorov, *Frente al límite*. *Confines* 1, no. 1 (April 1995): 141–46.

Friedlander, Saul, ed. *Probing the Limits of Representation*. Cambridge, MA: Harvard University Press, 1992.

Fromm, Erich. *Escape from Freedom*. New York: Holt, Rinehart, 1969.

Fuentes, Carlos. *La nueva novela hispanoamericana*. México, DF: Joaquín Mortiz, 1969.

Fuentes, Carlos. "París: La revolución de mayo." *La Cultura en México*, 337 (July 31, 1968): II–V.

Galeano, Eduardo. "The 1978 World Cup." In *Soccer in Sun and Shadow*. Translated by Mark Fried. New York: Nation Books, 2013 [1997]. 174–76.

Gallup Argentina. *Argentina: Actitudes hacia los judíos y el Holocausto*. Buenos Aires: American Jewish Committee and AMIA, April 27–May 3, 2000.

Gálvez Borrell, Víctor, Claudia Dary Fuentes, Edgar Esquit Choy, and Isabel Rodas. *¿Qué sociedad queremos? Una mirada desde el movimiento y las organizaciones mayas*. Guatemala: FLACSO, 1997.

Garber, Zev, and Bruce Zuckerman. "Why Do We Call the Holocaust 'The Holocaust'?: An Inquiry into Psychological Labels." *Modern Judaism* 9, no. 2 (1989): 197–211. https://academic.oup.com/mj/article-abstract/9/2/197/1065579.

García, Prudencio. *El genocidio de Guatemala a la luz de la sociología militar*. Madrid: Sepha Edition, 2005.

García Borrajo, Antonio. "Pre-informe: Misión Especial a Guatemala para investigar sobre los derechos del hombre y en particular sobre las desapariciones forzadas e involuntarias." Mexico: Comisión de Derechos Humanos de Guatemala, 1983. World Scholar: Latin America & the Caribbean. http://worldscholar.tu.galegroup.com/tinyurl/68qyC4.

García Noval, José. "Entre dos fuegos: Desde el mundo de los gatos pardos." In *De la memoria a la reconstrucción histórica*. Edited by Beatriz Manz, Elizabeth Oglesby, and José García Noval. Guatemala: AVANCSO, 1999. 39–82.

García Venturini, Jorge L. "En torno a 'Holocausto.'" *La Prensa* (December 22, 1981), section 2, 1.

Garrard-Burnett, Virginia. "Living with Ghosts: Death, Exhumation and Reburial among the Maya in Guatemala." *Latin American Perspectives* 42, no. 3 (2015): 180–92.

Garrard-Burnett, Virginia. *Terror in the Land of the Holy Spirit: Guatemala under General Efraín Ríos Montt, 1982–83*. New York: Oxford University Press, 2010.

Gelman, Juan, and Osvaldo Bayer. *Exilio*. Buenos Aires: Editorial Legasa, 1984.

Genaro Guanché Lajuj Testimony (Interview Code 55286). 2015. Visual History Archive, USC Shoah Foundation.

Glantz, Margo. "*Morirás lejos*: Literatura de escisión." In *La hoguera y el viento: José Emilio Pacheco ante la crítica*. Edited by Hugo J. Verani. Mexico, DF: UNAM/Ediciones Era, 1993. 229–37.

Gleizer, Daniela. *El exilio incómodo: México y los refugiados judíos, 1933–1945*. Mexico: El Colegio de Mexico/Universidad Autónoma de México-Cuajimalpa, 2011.

"Gloria a los luchadores de los ghettos." *Fraie Schtime* 12, no. 65 (March–April 1979): 4.

Goldberg, Florinda. "'Judíos del sur': El modelo judío en la narrative de la catástrofe argentina." *EIAL* 12, no. 2 (2001): 139–52. Education Source, EBSCOhost.

Goldemberg, Isaac. *El gran libro de la América judía*. San Juan: Editorial de la Universidad de Puerto Rico, 1998.

Goldhagen, Daniel. *Hitler's Willing Executioners: Ordinary Germans and the Holocaust*. New York: Knopf, 1996.

Goldman, Francisco. *The Art of Political Murder: Who Killed the Bishop?* New York: Grove, 2007.

Goldstein, Yossi. "El judaísmo argentino de fin de siglo XX: Del olvido a la recuperación de la memoria colectiva." In *Memoria y representación: Configuraciones culturales y literarias en el imaginario judío latinoamericano*. Edited by Ariana Huberman and Alejandro Meter. Buenos Aires: Beatriz Viterbo, 2006. 41–64.

Goldszmidt, Jorge Mario. "Fragmentos sobre (a) Paul Celan." *Confines* 1, no. 1 (April 1995): 55–64.

Golub, F. "Después del silencio." *Nueva Presencia* 5, no. 298 (March 18, 1983): 19.

Golub, F. "¿Quién puede olvidar?" *Nueva Presencia* 5, no. 294 (February 18, 1983): 15.

Gómez Montero, Sergio. "Iconografía literaria del sufrimiento del pueblo judío." *El Día* (January 6, 1969): 9.

González-Ocantos, Ezequiel. "Mexico: An Untamed Judiciary and the Failure of Prosecutions." In *Shifting Legal Visions: Judicial Change and Human Rights Trials in*

Latin America. New York: Cambridge University Press, 2016. 206–68. https://www.cambridge.org/core. https://doi.org/10.1017/CBO9781316535509.005.

Gorenstein, Mario. "No somos ciudadanos de segunda categoría." *Nueva Presencia* 4, no. 182 (December 26, 1980): 8.

Grandin, Greg. *The Blood of Guatemala: A History of Race and Nation*. Durham: Duke University Press, 2000.

Grandin, Greg. "Chronicles of a Guatemalan Genocide Foretold: Violence, Trauma, and the Limits of Historical Inquiry." *Nepantla* 1, no. 2 (2000): 391–412. Project MUSE.

Grandin, Greg. "The Instruction of Great Catastrophe: Truth Commissions, National History, and State Formation in Argentina, Chile, and Guatemala." *American Historical Review* 110, no. 1 (2005): 46–67. http://www.jstor.org/stable/10.1086/531121.

Grandin, Greg. *The Last Colonial Massacre: Latin America in the Cold War*. Chicago: University of Chicago Press, 2004.

Grandin, Greg. "Living in Revolutionary Time: Coming to Terms with the Violence of Latin America's Long Cold War." In *A Century of Revolution: Insurgent and Counterinsurgent Violence During Latin America's Long Cold War*. Edited by Greg Grandin and Gilbert M. Joseph. Durham: Duke University Press, 2010. 1–42.

Grandin, Greg. "Politics by Other Means: Guatemala's Quiet Genocide." In *Quiet Genocide: Guatemala 1981–83*. Edited by Etelle Higonnet. Preface by Juan Méndez. Introduction by Greg Grandin. Translations reviewed by Marcie Mersky. New Brunswick: Transaction Publishers, 2009. 1–15.

Gundermann, Christian. *Actos melancólicos: Formas de resistencia en la posdictadura argentina*. Buenos Aires: Beatriz Viterbo, 2007.

Gurevich, Beatriz, ed. *Proyecto testimonio: Revelaciones de los archivos argentinos sobre la política oficial de la era nazi-fascista*. Buenos Aires: DAIA Centro de Estudios Sociales, 1998.

Gurwitz, Beatrice. *Argentine Jews in the Age of Revolt: Between the New World and the Third World*. Leiden: Brill, 2016.

Guzaro, Tomás, and Terri Jacob McComb. *Escaping the Fire: How an Ixil Mayan Pastor Led His People Out of a Holocaust during the Guatemalan Civil War*. Afterword by David Stoll. Austin: University of Texas Press, 2010.

Guzmán Böckler, Carlos. *Cuando se quiebran los silencios: Lo que debemos saber sobre la historia de Guatemala. Ri okel nquetamaj pa Iximulew*. Guatemala: Cholsamaj, 1996.

Guzmán Böckler, Carlos, and Jean-Loup Herbert, eds. *Guatemala: Una interpretación histórico-social*. Mexico: Siglo XXI, 1970.

Halbwachs, Maurice. *Les cadres sociaux de la mémoire*. Paris: Albin Michel, 1994 [1925].

Hale, Charles R. *Más que un indio: Racial Ambivalence and Neoliberal Multiculturalism in Guatemala*. Santa Fe, NM: School of American Research Press, 2006.
Hale, Charles R. "Rethinking Indigenous Politics in the Era of the 'Indio Permitido.'" *NACLA Report on the Americas* 38, no. 2 (2004): 16–21. Alternative Press Index.
Halfon, Eduardo. *The Polish Boxer*. Translated by Daniel Hahn et al. New York: Bellevue Literary Press, 2012.
Hall, Carla. "The Disappeared. Rabbi Marshall Meyer: The Triumph of Protest and the Legacy of the Missing." *Washington Post* (February 12, 1984): H1.
Halter, Marek. "Les juifs d'Argentine sont dans une situation dramatique." *Le Monde* (March 4, 1978): 3.
Hamui, Liz. "Mexico." In *Encyclopaedia Judaica*. Second edition, volume 14. Edited by Michael Berenbaum and Fred Skolnik. Detroit: Macmillan Reference USA, 2007). 137–46. Gale Virtual Reference Library.
Hancock, Joel. "Perfecting a Text: Authorial Revisions in José Emilio Pacheco's *Morirás lejos*." *Chasqui* 14, nos. 2–3 (1985): 15–23.
Handy, Jim. *Gift of the Devil: A History of Guatemala*. Boston: South End Press, 1984.
Hartman, Geoffrey, "Introduction: Darkness Visible." In *Holocaust Remembrance: The Shapes of Memory*. Edited by Geoffrey Hartman. Oxford: Blackwell, 1994. 1–22.
"¿Hay antisemitismo en la Argentina?" *La Voz* 1, no. 4 (June 1981): 3.
"Hay que limpiar la tierra ensangrentada castigando a los culpables." *Nueva Presencia* 6, no. 362 (June 8, 1984): 4.
"Help Stop the War against the Mayan Indians of Guatemala." *New York Times* (January 3, 1984), A9.
Heker, Liliana. *El fin de la historia*. Buenos Aires: Alfaguara, 1996.
Hilberg, Raul. *The Destruction of the European Jews*. Chicago: Quadrangle Books, 1961.
Hirszfeld, Ludwik. *Ludwik Hirszfeld: The Story of One Life*. Translated by Marta Balinska. Rochester: University of Rochester Press, 2010.
"'Holocausto' confirma sus antecedentes." *La Prensa* (December 17, 1981): section 2, 2.
"Holocausto: Opinan los argentinos." *Nueva Presencia* 4, no. 234 (December 24, 1981): 10.
Huberman, Ariana, and Alejandro Meter, eds. *Memoria y representación: Configuraciones culturales y literarias en el imaginario judío latinoamericano*. Buenos Aires: Beatriz Viterbo, 2006.
Human Rights Office, Archdiocese of Guatemala. *Guatemala, Never Again!* New York: Orbis Books/Maryknoll, 1999.
Huyssen, Andreas. *Present Pasts: Urban Palimpsests and the Politics of Memory*. Palo Alto: Stanford University Press, 2003.
"If Truth Be Told: A Forum on David Stoll's 'Rigoberta Menchú and the Story of All Poor Guatemalans,'" *Latin American Perspectives* 26, no. 6 (November 1999). http://www.jstor.org/stable/2633923.

"Integramos lo argentino con nuestra especificidad judía; el titular de DAIA esbozó la estrategia de esa instancia judeoargentina." *Nueva Presencia* 2, no. 101 (June 8, 1979): 7.

Irving, David. *Hitler's War*. New York: Viking, 1977.

Jaspers, Karl. *The Question of German Guilt*. Translated by E. B. Ashton. Introduction by Joseph W. Koterski. New York: Fordham, 2001 [1947]. ACLS Humanities ebook. http://hdl.handle.net/2027/heb.08575.0001.001.

Jay, Martin. "Allegories of Evil: A Response to Jeffrey Alexander." In *Remembering the Holocaust: A Debate*. Edited by Jeffrey C. Alexander. Oxford: Oxford University Press, 2009. 105–13.

Jelin, Elizabeth. "Memorias en conflicto." *Puentes* 1, no. 1 (August 2001): 6–13. http://www.comisionporlamemoria.org/project/puentes/.

Jelin, Elizabeth. *State Repression and the Labors of Memory*. Translated by Judy Rein and Marcial Godoy-Anativia. Minneapolis: University of Minnesota Press, 2003.

Jerman, William, ed. *Repression in Latin America: A Report on the First Session of the Second Russell Tribunal, Rome, April 1974*. Translated by William Jerman. Nottingham: Spokesman Books, 1975.

Jesús Tecú Osorio Testimony (Interview Code 54359). 2015. Visual History Archive, USC Shoah Foundation.

Jewish Virtual Library. "Guatemala Virtual Jewish History Tour." https://www.jewishvirtuallibrary.org/guatemala-virtual-jewish-history-tour.

Jitrik, Noé. "Cuento de una tarde de mayo." *Diálogos: Artes, Letras, Ciencias Humanas* 14, no. 1 (July–August 1978): 35–37.

Jitrik, Noé. "Destrucción y formas en las narraciones latinoamericanas actuales" (1973). In *Suspender toda certeza: Antología crítica (1959–1976)*. Edited by Noé Jitrik, Gonzalo Aguilar, and Gustavo Lespada. Buenos Aires: Editorial Biblos, 1997. 25–151.

Jonas, Susanne, Ed McCaughan, and Elizabeth Sutherland-Martínez, eds. *Guatemala: Tyranny on Trial: Testimony of the Permanent People's Tribunal*. Preface by George Wald. Introduction by Marlene Dixon and Susanne Jonas. Translated by Susanne Jonas. San Francisco: Synthesis, 1984.

Joseph, Gilbert M. "What We Now Know and Should Know: Bringing Latin America More Meaningfully into Cold War Studies." In *In From the Cold: Latin America's New Encounter with the Cold War*. Edited by Gilbert M. Joseph and Daniela Spenser. Durham: Duke University Press, 2008. 3–46. Education Source, EBSCOhost.

Josephus, Flavius. *The Jewish War*. Translated by Martin Hammond. Introduction and notes by Martin Goodman. Oxford: Oxford University Press, 2017.

"Judaismo es sinónimo de justicia y lucha por la dignidad humana." *Nueva Presencia* 4, no. 207 (June 19, 1981): 11.

Juliana Tun Xalín Testimony (Interview Code 55329). 2015. Visual History Archive, USC Shoah Foundation.

Kahan, Emmanuel. *Memories That Lie a Little: Jewish Experiences during the Argentine Dictatorship*. Translated by David William Foster. Leiden: Brill, 2019.

Kahan, Emmanuel, and Daniel Lvovich. "Los usos del Holocausto en Argentina: Apuntes sobre las apropiaciones y resignificaciones de la memoria del genocidio nazi." *Revista Mexicana de Ciencias Políticas y Sociales* 61, no. 228 (September–December 2016): 311–36. Education Source, EBSCOhost.

Kaiser, Susana. *Postmemories of Terror: A New Generation Copes with the Legacy of the "Dirty War."* New York: Palgrave Macmillan, 2005.

Kaplan, Marion. *Dominican Haven: The Jewish Refugee Settlement in Sosúa, 1940–45*. New York: Museum of Jewish Heritage, 2008.

Katz, R. F. Review of *El pan y la sangre* by Simja Sneh. *Fraie Schtime* 10, no. 60 (July 1977): 4.

Kaufman, Alejandro. "Desaparecidos." *Confines* 2, no. 3 (September 1996): 33–44.

Kaufman, Alejandro. "Notas sobre desaparecidos." *Confines* 3, no. 4 (July 1997): 29–34.

Kaufman, Edy. "Jewish Victims of Repression in Argentina under Military Rule (1976–1983)." *Holocaust and Genocide Studies* 4, no. 4 (1989): 479–99. HeinOnline.

Kaufman, Edy, and Beatriz Cymberknopf. "La dimensión judía en la represión durante el gobierno militar en la Argentina (1976–1983)." In *El antisemitismo en la Argentina*. Second edition. Edited by Leonardo Senkman. Buenos Aires: Centro Editor de América Latina, 1989. 235–73.

Kennedy, Edward. "Human Rights Violations in Argentina." *Congressional Record—Senate* (March 26, 1979): S3376.

Kinzer, Stephen. "Missing in Argentina: Is Anti-Semitism to Blame?" (November 29, 1981): 18

Klich, Ignacio. "Política comunitaria durante las Juntas Militares argentinas: La DAIA durante el Proceso de Reorganización Nacional." In *El antisemitismo en la Argentina*. Second edition. Edited by Leonardo Senkman. Buenos Aires: Centro Editor de América Latina, 1989. 274–309.

Kowner, Abe [Abba Kovner]. "¡Tate! Tate¡" *Fraie Schtime* 12, no. 68 (April 1980): 3.

Konefal, Betsy. *For Every Indio Who Falls: A History of Maya Activism, 1960–1990*. Albuquerque: University of New Mexico Press, 2010.

Konefal, Betsy. "Maya Repression, Resistance, and the Road to Genocide." Paper presented at A Conflict? Genocide and Resistance in Guatemala. 2016 international conference, Center for Advanced Genocide Research, USC Shoah Foundation, September 12, 2016. Video available at https://sfi.usc.edu/cagr/conferences/2016_international.

Kononovich, Bernardo. *Atención (Achtung)!* Argentina, 1993. DVD.

Kononovich, Bernardo. *Me queda la palabra*. Argentina, 2004. DVD.

Kordon, Diana, Lucía Edelman, and Equipo de Asistencia Psicológica de Madres de Plaza de Mayo. *Efectos psicológicos de la represión política*. Buenos Aires: Sudamericana/Planeta, 1986.

Krauze, Enrique. "Holocausto versión Hanoi." *Vuelta*, 3, no. 28 (March 1979): 45–46.
Kucinski, Bernardo. *K*. Translated by Sue Branford. London: Latin American Bureau Press, 2013.
"La clausura de Milicia." *Nueva Sión* 28, no. 584 (September 1976): 3.
"La esperanza que jugó en contra: Hablan los sobrevivientes." *La Nación* (December 16, 1981): section 2, 1.
"La fundación Shoah USC y FAFG lanzan proyecto juntos para arrojar luz sobre el genocidio guatemalteco." *PR Newswire, Hispanic PR Wire* (July 28, 2015). Education Source, EBSCOhost.
"La intimidación interna no logró impedir que miles de judíos y no-judíos se movilizaran para repudiar el antisemitismo." *Nueva Presencia* 6, no. 330 (October 28, 1983): 7.
"La pasividad de la víctima exacerba al agresor." *Voz Libre* 8, no. 53 (August 1975): 3.
"La rebelión del gueto y los derechos humanos." *Nueva Presencia* 5, no. 304 (April 29, 1983): 1.
LaCapra, Dominick. *Representing the Holocaust: History, Theory, Trauma*. Ithaca: Cornell University Press, 1994.
Laikin Elkin, Judith. "Good Germans in Argentina? We Knew but We Didn't Want to Know," *Jewish Frontier* (February 1985): 7–11.
Laikin Elkin, Judith. *The Jews of Latin America*. Revised Edition. Ann Arbor: University of Michigan Library, 2011.
Lang, Berel. *Genocide: The Act as Idea*. Philadelphia: University of Pennsylvania Press, 2017.
"Lanzan plataforma virtual para el estudio del Holocausto," *Mineduc Informativo*, no. 9 (17 March 17, 2017), 5. http://www.mineduc.gob.gt/dicoms/documents/boletines/MINEDUC_INFORMA-09.pdf.
Laplante, Lisa. "Memory Battle: Guatemala's Public Debates and the Genocide Trial of Jose Efraín Ríos Montt." *Quinnipiac Law Review* 32 (2014): 621–74. HeinOnline.
Larsen, Neil. "Thoughts on Violence and Modernity in Latin America." In *A Century of Revolution: Insurgent and Counterinsurgent Violence during Latin America's Long Cold War*. Edited by Greg Grandin and Gilbert M. Joseph. Durham: Duke University Press, 2010. 381–92.
"Las Mothers de desaparecidos introdujeron un tono distinto en la convención de la DAIA." *Nueva Presencia* 6, no. 328 (October 14, 1983): 2.
"Las 'Mothers de Plaza de Mayo,' Masada y los macabeos." *Nueva Presencia* 5, no. 304 (April 29, 1983): 1.
"Last Word on Timerman: Responses to Benno Weiser Varon." *Midstream* 28, no. 2 (February 1982): 34–42.
Laub, Michel. *Diary of the Fall*. Translated by Margaret Jull Costa. London: Harvill Secker, 2014.
Leis, Héctor Ricardo. *El movimiento por los derechos humanos y la política argentina*. 2 vols. Buenos Aires: Centro Editor de América Latina, 1989.

Lemkin, Raphael. *Axis Rule in Occupied Europe.* Washington, DC: Carnegie Endowment for International Peace, 1944.
León-Portilla, Miguel, ed. *Visión de los vencidos: Relaciones indígenas de la Conquista.* Introduction, selection, and notes by Miguel León-Portilla. Translated by Angel M. Garibay. Mexico: UNAM, 1959.
Lerner, Gregorio. "El cumpleaños de Mario." *Nueva Presencia* 7, no. 337 (December 16, 1983): 31.
Lerner, Gregorio. "'Holocausto' en España—un triunfo de la democracia." *Fraie Schtime* 12, no. 66 (September 1979): 6.
Lerner, Gregorio. "Nuestras defensas." *La Voz* 1, no. 3 (March 1981): 1.
Lerner, Natan. "Argentine Jewry: The Fundamental Problems." *Congress Monthly* 48, no. 7 (September–October 1981): 10–11. *Nexis.*
Lespada, Gustavo. "Texto con hormigas." In *Para leer Morirás lejos.* Edited by Gustavo Lespada and Elena Pérez de Medina. Buenos Aires: Universidad de Buenos Aires, 1999. 5–13.
Lesser, Jeffrey. *Welcoming the Undesirables: Brazil and the Jewish Question.* Berkeley: University of California Press, 1995.
Levene, Mark. "Is the Holocaust Simply Another Example of Genocide?" In *The Holocaust: A Reader.* Edited by Simone Gigliotti and Berel Lang. Malden, MA: Blackwell, 2005. 420–47.
Levi, Neil, and Michael Rothberg. "Auschwitz and the Remains of Theory: Toward an Ethics of the Borderland." *Symploke* 11, nos. 1–2 (2003): 23–38.
Levi, Primo. *The Drowned and the Saved.* Translated by Raymond Rosenthal. New York: Vintage, 1989.
Levi, Primo. *Survival in Auschwitz.* Prelude by Primo Levi. Translated by Stuart Woolf. New York: Macmillan, 1987.
Levine, Robert M. *Tropical Diaspora: The Jewish Experience in Cuba.* Gainesville: University Press of Florida, 1993.
Levinson, Jay. *The Jewish Community of Cuba: The Golden Age, 1906–1958.* Nashville: Westview, 2006.
Levinson, Luisa Mercedes. "Atisbos a la hondura de Elie Wiesel." *La Nación* (September 23, 1979): section 4a, 4.
Levy, Daniel, and Natan Sznaider. *The Holocaust and Memory in the Global Age.* Translated by Assenka Oksiloff. Philadelphia: Temple University, 2006.
Lewin, Boleslao. *La rebelión de Túpac Amaru y los orígenes de la emancipación americana.* Buenos Aires: Hachette, 1957.
Lewin, Boleslao. *Túpac Amaru, el rebelde, su época, sus luchas, y su influencia en el continente.* Buenos Aires: Editorial Claridad, 1943.
Lewis, Anthony. "Final Solution in Argentina." Review of Jacobo Timerman, *Prisoner without a Name. New York Times* (May 10, 1981), section 7, 1.
Liano, Dante. "The Anthropologist with the Old Hat." In *The Rigoberta Menchú Controversy.* Edited by Arturo Arias. Minneapolis: University of Minnesota Press, 2001. 121–24.

Liebman, Charles S., and Eliezer Don-Yehiya. *Civil Religion in Israel: Traditional Judaism and Biblical Culture in the Jewish State*. Berkeley: University of California Press, 1983.

Lipis, Guillermo. *Zikarón—Memoria: Judíos y militares bajo el terror del Plan Cóndor*. Buenos Aires: Editorial del Nuevo Extremo, 2010.

Lipstadt, Deborah. *The Holocaust: An American Understanding*. New Brunswick: Rutgers University Press, 2016.

"Llega a nuestra TV la polémica 'Holocausto.'" *La Nación* (December 12, 1981): section 2, 1.

"Los iconoclastas." *Fraie Schtime* 12, no. 66 (September 1979): 8 [reprint of an editorial from the *Buenos Aires Herald*, September 8, 1979].

"Los puentes de la memoria." *Puentes* 1, no. 1 (August 2001), 1.

Lotersztain, Gabriela. *Los judíos bajo el terror: Argentina 1976–1983*. Buenos Aires: Ejercitar la Memoria Editores, 2008.

Lovell, W. George. "Surviving Conquest: The Maya of Guatemala in Historical Perspective." *Latin American Research Review* 23, no. 2 (1988): 25–57. JSTOR. http://www.jstor.org/stable/2503234.

Lyotard, Jean-François. *The Differend: Phrases in Dispute*. Translated by Georges Van Den Abbeele. Minneapolis: University of Minnesota Press, 1988.

Lyotard, Jean-François. *Heidegger and "the Jews."* Translated by Andreas Michel and Mark S. Roberts. Foreword by David Caroll. Minneapolis: University of Minnesota Press, 1990.

Lyotard, Jean-François. "'Los judíos.'" *Confines* 1, no. 1 (April 1995): 39–50.

Madanes, Leiser. "El caso Timerman sigue suscitando discusiones." *Nueva Presencia* 2, no. 119 (October 12, 1979): 13.

Manz, Beatriz. "La importancia del contexto en la memoria." In *De la memoria a la reconstrucción histórica*. Edited by Beatriz Manz, Elizabeth Oglesby, and José García Noval. Guatemala: AVANCSO, 1999. 1–22.

Masiello, Francine. *The Art of Transition: Latin American Culture and Neoliberal Crisis*. Durham: Duke University Press, 2001.

"Massera y la libertad de Timerman," *Nueva Presencia* 2, no. 68 (October 20, 1978).

Mayer, Arno. *Why Did the Heavens Not Darken? The "Final Solution" in History*. New York: Pantheon Books, 1989.

Mazas, Luis. "'Holocausto': Con más emoción que indagación." *Clarín* (December 20, 1981): Espectáculos 3.

Mazas, Luis. "'Holocausto' en el primer tramo del horror." *Clarín* (December 17, 1981): Espectáculos 4–5.

McAllister, Carlota. "Rural Markets, Revolutionary Souls, and Rebellious Women in Guatemala." In *In From the Cold: Latin America's New Encounter with the Cold War*. Edited by Gilbert M. Joseph and Daniela Spenser. Durham: Duke University Press, 2008. 350–77. Education Source, EBSCOhost.

McAllister, Carlota. "Testimonial Truths and Revolutionary Mysteries." In *War by Other Means: Aftermath in Post-genocide Guatemala*. Edited by Carlota McAllister and Diane Nelson. Durham: Duke University Press, 2013. 93–115.

Mcdonnell, Michael A., and A. Dirk Moses. "Raphael Lemkin as Historian of Genocide in the Americas." *Journal of Genocide Research* 7, no. 4 (2005): 501–21. doi: 10.1080/14623520500349951.

Mckay, Raymond. "Mr. Erlich's planet." *Buenos Aires Herald* (May 26, 1977).

Mehlman, Jeffrey. "Foreword." In Pierre Vidal-Naquet, *The Assassins of Memory*. Translated and with a foreword by Jeffrey Mehlman. New York: Columbia University Press, 1992. ix–xxi.

Melchor Basterra, Víctor. "Carta de un sobreviviente." *Nueva Presencia* 434 (October 25, 1985), 21.

Menchú, Rigoberta. *I, Rigoberta Menchú: An Indian Woman in Guatemala*. Edited and with an introduction by Elisabeth Burgos-Debray. Translated by Anne Wright. London: Verso, 1984.

"Mensaje de la Delegación Indígena Unitaria de Guatemala ante la VI Sesión del Grupo de Trabajo de la ONU Sobre Poblaciones Indígenas." Guatemala, August 1, 1988. iihaa.usac.edu.gt/archivohemerografico/wpcontent/uploads/2017/09/12_estudios_septiembre_1989_mensaje.pdf.

"Mensaje de Massera a la colectividad por el Nuevo Año Hebreo," *La Nación* (September 14, 1977): 14.

Mercado, Tununa. "Cuatro historias del terror nazi." *Revista de Revistas* 158 (June 11, 1975): 29–33.

Mercado, Tununa. *En estado de memoria*. Buenos Aires: Emecé Editores/Seix Barral, 2008 [1990].

Mercado, Tununa. *Narrar después*. Buenos Aires: Beatriz Viterbo, 2003.

Mercado, Tununa. *Yo nunca te prometí la eternidad*. Buenos Aires: Planeta, 2005.

Meter, Alejandro. "Barbarie y memoria: El Holocausto y la dictadura en la narrativa argentina de hoy." In *Memoria y representación: Configuraciones culturales y literarias en el imaginario judío latinoamericano*. Edited by Ariana Huberman and Alejandro Meter. Buenos Aires: Beatriz Viterbo, 2006. 65–78.

Meyer, Marshall. "Escoged, pues, la vida." *Comunidad Bet El* 1, no. 1 (1984): 11–13.

Meyer, Marshall. "Los judíos argentinos y los derechos humanos." Interview by Herman Schiller. *Servicio Paz y Justicia* (October 5, 1983).

Meyer, Naomi. "Latin America—Argentina." In *The American Jewish Yearbook 1978*. Edited by Morris Fine and Milton Himmelfarb. New York: American Jewish Committee, 1978. 287–302.

Meyer, Naomi. "Latin America—Argentina." In *The American Jewish Yearbook 1979*. Edited by Morris Fine and Milton Himmelfarb. New York: American Jewish Committee, 1979. 202–15.

Meyer, Naomi. "Latin America—Argentina." In *The American Jewish Yearbook 1980*. Edited by Milton Himmelfarb and David Singer. New York: American Jewish Committee, 1980. 188–96.

Miles, William F. S. "Third World Views of the Holocaust." *Journal of Genocide Research* 6, no. 3 (September 2004): 371–93. Education Source, EBSCOhost.

Milgram, Avraham, ed. *Entre la aceptación y el rechazo: América Latina y los refugiados judíos del nazismo*. Jerusalem: Yad Vashem, 2003.

Millet, Kitty. *The Victims of Slavery, Colonization and the Holocaust: A Comparative History of Persecution*. London: Bloomsbury, 2017.

Montejo, Víctor, and Q'anil Akab'. *Brevísima relación testimonial de la continua destrucción del Mayab' (Guatemala)*. Providence, RI: Guatemala Scholars Network, 1992.

Montejo, Víctor. *Maya Intellectual Renaissance: Identity, Representation and Leadership*. Austin: University of Texas Press, 2005. Project MUSE.

Montejo, Víctor. *Voices from Exile: Violence and Survival in Modern Maya History*. Norman: University of Oklahoma Press, 1999.

Montes de Oca, Marcos Antonio. "El altar de los muertos." *La Cultura en México* 356 (December 11, 1968), IX.

Morduchowicz, Roxana. "Con mis propios ojos vi los hornos crematorios." *Nueva Presencia* 4, no. 235 (December 31, 1981): 10.

Moses, A. Dirk. "Conceptual Blockages and Definitional Dilemmas in the 'Racial Century': Genocides of Indigenous Peoples and the Holocaust." In *The Holocaust: A Reader*. Edited by Simone Gigliotti and Berel Lang. Malden, MA: Blackwell, 2005. 448–62.

Mount, Graeme S. "Chile and the Nazis." In *Memory, Oblivion and Jewish Culture in Latin America*. Edited by Marjorie Agosín. Austin: University of Texas Press, 2005. 77–89.

Moyn, Samuel. *The Last Utopia: Human Rights in History*. Cambridge: Belknap/Harvard University Press, 2010.

Moyn, Samuel. *Not Enough: Human Rights in an Unequal World*. Cambridge: Belknap/Harvard University Press, 2018.

Muchnik, Daniel. "Caso Timerman: Una nota poco edificante." *Nueva Presencia* 2, no. 120 (October 19, 1979): 11.

Muchnik, Daniel. "Las declaraciones de Jacobo Timerman." *Nueva Presencia* 2, no. 118 (October 5, 1979): 7.

"Nehemías Resnizky dice su verdad." *Nueva Presencia* 4, no. 230 (November 27, 1981): 10.

Neier, Aryeh. "The Crime of Silence Revisited." *The Nation* (June 13, 1981): 730–32.

Neilson, James. "An Air of Uncertainty: Letter from Buenos Aires." *Hadassah Magazine* (August–September 1981), 19.

Neruda, Pablo. *Canto general*. Translated by Jack Schmitt. Berkeley: University of California Press, 1991.

"Ni olvido ni perdón." *Nueva Presencia* 4, no. 200 (May 1, 1981): 1.
"Ni olvido ni perdón." *Nueva Presencia* 4, no. 251 (16 April 1982): 17.
"No pedimos venganza sino justicia." *Nueva Presencia* 5, no. 285 (December 17, 1982): 12.
Nora, Pierre. "Between Memory and History: *Les Lieux de Mémoire*." *Representations* 26 (Spring 1989): 7–25. JSTOR.
"Nos manejamos con prudencia y equilibrio." *Nueva Presencia* 2, no. 89 (March 16, 1979): 10.
Novick, Peter. *The Holocaust in American Life*. Boston: Houghton Mifflin, 1999.
"Nuevo testimonio sobre 'El ángel de la muerte.'" *Nueva Presencia* 2, no. 90 (March 24, 1979): 3.
Ofer, Dalia. "Linguistic Conceptualization of the Holocaust in Palestine and Israel, 1942–1953." *Journal of Contemporary History* 31, no. 3 (1996): 567–95. http://jch.sagepub.com/content/31/3/567.citation.
Oglesby, Elizabeth. "Desde los cuadernos de Myrna Mack: Reflexiones sobre la violencia, la memoria y la investigación social." In *De la memoria a la reconstrucción histórica*. Beatriz Manz, Elizabeth Oglesby, and José García Noval. Guatemala: AVANCSO, 1999. 23–37.
Oglesby, Elizabeth. "Educating Citizens in Postwar Guatemala: Historical Memory, Genocide and the Culture of Peace." *Radical History Review* 97 (2007): 77–98. Alternative Press Index. doi: 10.1215/01636545-2006-013.
Oglesby, Elizabeth. "The Guatemalan Genocide." *Modern Genocide: The Definitive Resource and Document Collection, Vol. 2.* Edited by Paul R. Bartrop and Steven Leonard Jacobs. Santa Barbara: ABC-CLIO, 2015. 879–82. ProQuest Ebook.
"Opina Polino." *Nueva Presencia* 4, no. 235 (December 31, 1981): 12.
Oquendo, Abelardo. "Moríras lejos." *Amaru* 6 (April–June 1968): 96.
Ortega, Julio. "Tres notas mexicanas." *Cuadernos Hispanoamericanos* 381 (March 1982): 669–771.
Oviedo, José Miguel. "Una hipótesis bajo forma narrativa." *Imagen: Quincenario de arte, literatura e información cultural* 29 (July 15–30, 1968): 4–5.
Oz, Amos. "The Meaning of Homeland." *Under This Blazing Light*. Translated by Nicholas de Lange. Cambridge: Cambridge University Press, 1979. 79–101.
Pacheco, José Emilio. "A.H. (1889–1989): Los asesinos entre nosotros." *Proceso* (July 3, 1989): 50–51.
Pacheco, José Emilio. "Conversación entre las ruinas." *Proceso* (May 29, 1978): 54.
Pacheco, José Emilio. "El Proceso, el Castillo, las alambradas." *Proceso* (July 18, 1983): 46–47.
Pacheco, José Emilio. "Guerra contra todo autoritarismo; Marcuse: El ideólogo de la revolución juvenil." *La Cultura en México*, 326 (May 15, 1968): vi–vii.
Pacheco, José Emilio. "¿Hitler reivindicado?" *Proceso* (August 15, 1977): 58.
Pacheco, José Emilio. "José Emilio Pacheco." *Los narradores ante el público, Vol. 1.* México: Joaquín Mortiz, 1966. 243–63.

Pacheco, José Emilio. "Las voces de Tlatelolco." *Proceso* (October 2, 1978): 54.
Pacheco, José Emilio. "Lectura de los 'Cantares Mexicanos.'" *La Cultura en México* 351 (November 6, 1968): VI.
Pacheco, José Emilio. *Morirás lejos*. México: Joaquín Mortiz, 1967.
Pacheco, José Emilio. *Morirás lejos*. México: Joaquín Mortiz, 1977.
Pacheco, José Emilio. *No me preguntes cómo pasa el tiempo: Poemas, 1964–1968*. México: Joaquín Mortiz, 1969.
Pacheco, José Emilio. "Nota preliminar: Rodolfo Walsh desde México." In Rodolfo Walsh, *Obra literaria completa*. Mexico: Siglo XXI, 1981.
Pacheco, José Emilio. "Raíz y razón del movimiento estudiantil." *La Cultura en México* 333 (July 3, 1968): x–xii.
Pacheco, José Emilio. "Revolución contra sociedad industrial." *La Cultura en México* 330 (June 12, 1968): ii–iii.
Pacheco, José Emilio. "Rodolfo Walsh y el genocidio argentino." *Proceso* (December 5, 1977): 56.
Pacheco, José Emilio. "Si los Estados Unidos no se retiran como perdedores tendrán que permanecer como genocidas." *La Cultura en México* 315 (February 28, 1968): iv–vi.
Palencia-Frener, Sergio. "Contrainsurgencia en Chimaltenango, 1978–1983: Comalapa, San Martín Jilotepeque y Poaquil." Paper presented at A Conflict? Genocide and Resistance in Guatemala, 2016 International Conference, Center for Advanced Genocide Research, USC Shoah Foundation, September 12, 2016. Video available at https://sfi.usc.edu/cagr/conferences/2016_international.
Palma Mora, Mónica. "Destierro y encuentro. Aproximaciones al exilio latinoamericano en México 1954–1980." *Amérique latine histoire et mémoire: Les Cahiers ALHIM*, 2003. 7. http://alhim.revues.org/index363.html.
"'Para que no se repita jamás esos años de horror': Hablan los sobrevivientes." *La Nación* (December 17, 1981): section 2, 4.
Partido Guatemalteco del Trabajo. *Debate revolucionario, Vol. 1* (1985). World Scholar: Latin America & the Caribbean. http://worldscholar.tu.galegroup.com/tinyurl/68qxT8.
Partnoy, Alicia. *The Little School: Tales of Disappearance and Survival in Argentina*. Translated by Alicia Partnoy with Lois Athey and Sandra Braunstein. Pittsburgh: Cleis Press, 1986.
Partnoy, Alicia. "Poetry as a Strategy for Resistance in the Holocaust and the Southern Cone Genocides." In *The Jewish Diaspora in Latin America and the Caribbean: Fragments of Memory*. Edited by Kristin Ruggiero. Brighton: Sussex Academic Press, 2005. 234–46.
Patterson-Markowitz, Rebecca, Sallie Marston, and Elizabeth Oglesby. "Subjects of Change: Feminist Geopolitics and Gendered Truth-Telling in Guatemala." *Journal of International Women's Studies* 13, no. 4 (September 2012): 82–99. https://search.proquest.com/docview/1041250700?accountid=14496.

Pavón, Héctor. *Los intelectuales y la política en la Argentina: El combate por las ideas, 1983–2012*. Buenos Aires: Debate, 2012.

Paz, Octavio. "México: Olimpiada de 1968." *La Cultura en México* (October 30, 1968): v.

Peccerelli, Fredy. "Guatemala: New Testimonies and the Guatemalan Genocide." Keynote address presented at A Conflict? Genocide and Resistance in Guatemala, 2016 International Conference, Center for Advanced Genocide Research, USC Shoah Foundation, September 12, 2016. Video available at https://sfi.usc.edu/cagr/conferences/2016_international.

Pedro Pacheco Bop Testimony (Interview Code 55325). 2015. Visual History Archive, USC Shoah Foundation.

Peña, Margarita. "José Emilio Pacheco: *Morirás lejos*." *Diálogos* 4, no. 1 (May–June 1968): 35–36.

Perednik, Gustavo. "Nunca más, otra vez, torrentes de sangre judía regarán el mundo impunemente." *Nueva Presencia* 4, no. 200 (May 1, 1981): 10.

Perera, Víctor. *Unfinished Conquest: The Guatemalan Tragedy*. Berkeley: University of California Press, 1993.

Pérez de Medina, Elena. "Escritura y lectura en *Morirás lejos* de José Emilio Pacheco." In *Para leer Morirás lejos*. Edited by Gustavo Lespada and Elena Pérez de Medina. Buenos Aires: Universidad de Buenos Aires, 1999. 15–37.

"Pérez Esquivel: Contra el terrorismo de izquierda y el terrorismo de derecha." *Nueva Presencia* 4, no. 173 (October 24, 1980): 2.

"Pérez Esquivel: Contra la violencia, por la paz." *Nueva Presencia* 4, no. 177 (November 21, 1980): 22.

Pérez Gay, Rafael. "*Morirás lejos*: La derrota cotidiana y el acoso de los fantasmas." *Nexos* 1, no. 10 (October 1978): 6.

Plavnick, Rabbi Baruj. "Por nuestra y vuestra liberación." *Nueva Presencia* 5, no. 311 (June 17, 1983): 18.

Pollak, Michael. *L'expérience concentrationnaire: Essai sur le mantien de l'identité sociale*. Paris: Metailie, 1990.

Poniatowska, Elena. *La noche de Tlatelolco*. Second revised edition. México: Ediciones Era, 1998 [1971].

Popescu, Adam. "Steven Spielberg on Storytelling's Power to Fight Hate." *New York Times*. December 18, 2018. https://www.nytimes.com/2018/12/18/arts/design/steven-spielberg-shoah-foundation-schindlers-list.html?searchResultPosition=1.

"Por nuestra y vuestra liberación; 37 años después sigue vigente la consigna de los rebeldes del ghetto de Varsovia." *Nueva Presencia* 3, no. 145 (April 11, 1980): 1.

Proyecto Interdiocesano de Recuperación de la Memoria Histórica. *Guatemala: Nunca más*. Oficina de Derechos Humanos del Arzobispado de Guatemala, 1999.

"Rabino Marshall T. Meyer: Es legítimo en el judaísmo en derecho a disentir." *Nueva Presencia* 5, no. 269 (August 27, 1982): 10.

Rabe, Stephen. *The Killing Zone: The United States Wages Cold War in Latin America.* New York: Oxford University Press, 2016.

Rafecas, Daniel. "La reapertura de los procesos judiciales por crímenes contra la humanidad en la Argentina." In *Juicios por crímenes de lesa humanidad en Argentina.* Edited by Gabriele Andreozzi. Buenos Aires: Atuel, 2011. 156–76.

Rarihokwats, ed. *Guatemala: The Horror and the Hope.* 4 vols. York, PA: Four Arrows Press, 1982.

Reati, Fernando. *Nombrar lo innombrable: Violencia política y novela argentina, 1975–1985.* Buenos Aires: Editorial Legasa, 1992.

Reboledo, Hector López. "Finalizó la exhibición de 'Holocausto' en Uruguay." *La Nación* (August 16, 1979): section 2, 10.

Reboledo, Héctor López. "La repercusión de 'Holocausto' en Lima," *La Nación* (August 19, 1979): section 2, 12.

Rein, Raanan. *Argentina, Israel and the Jews: Perón, the Eichmann Capture and After.* Translated by Martha Grenzeback. Bethesda: University Press of Maryland, 2003. 219–21.

Rein, Raanan. *Argentine Jews or Jewish Argentines? Essays on Ethnicity, Identity and Diaspora.* Leiden/Boston: Brill, 2010.

Resnick, Sid. "American Rabbi in Argentina to Help Investigate Disappeared Persons." *Morning Freiheit* (Sunday English edition, February 12, 1984): 1.

Resnizky, Nehemías. "Discurso del Dr. Nehemías Resnizky ante la Asamblea de la DAIA, que lo reeligió como Presidente para el bieno 1978–1980." Reprinted in *El antisemitismo en la Argentina.* Second edition. Edited by Leonardo Senkman. Buenos Aires: Centro Editor de América Latina, 1989. 399–405.

Resnizky, Nehemías. "Es traumatizante, pero aleccionadora." *Nueva Presencia* 4, no. 235 (December 31, 1981): 7.

Resnizky, Nehemías. "Réplica y testimonio del Dr. Nehemías Resnizky, ex-presidente de la DAIA, 1974–1980." Reprinted in *El antisemitismo en la Argentina.* Second edition. Edited by Leonardo Senkman. Buenos Aires: Centro Editor de América Latina, 1989. 439–60.

"Resumen del 2000: El largo brazo de la justicia." *Puentes* 1, no. 2 (December 2000): 94–95.

Revista *Nombres.* "Las Madres de Plaza de Mayo." *Confines* 2, no. 3 (September 1996): 45–52.

Revueltas, José. *México 68: Juventud y revolución.* México: Ediciones Era, 1978.

Rivera, Francisco. "*Morirás lejos* de José Emilio Pacheco." *Vuelta* 3, no. 28 (March 1979): 41–42.

Robbins, Bruce. "Introduction Part I: Actually Existing Cosmopolitanism." In *Cosmopolitics: Thinking and Feeling beyond the Nation.* Edited by Pheng Cheah and Bruce Robbins. Minneapolis: University of Minnesota Press, 1998. 1–19.

Robin, Ron. "The Wilful Suspension of Disbelief: Rigoberta Menchú and the Making of the Maya Holocaust." In *Scandals and Scoundrels: Seven Cases That*

Shook the Academy. Berkeley: University of California Press, 2004. 166–92. ebookcentral.proquest.com.

Robinson, Benjamin. "*The Specialist* on the Eichmann Precedent: Morality, Law and Military Sovereignty." *Critical Inquiry* 30 (Autumn 2003): 63–97. http://www.journals.uchicago.edu/t-and-c.

Robinson, Geoffrey. "Human Rights History from the Ground Up: The Case of East Timor." In *The Human Rights Paradox*. Edited by Steve Stern and Scott Strauss. Madison: University of Wisconsin Press, 2014. 31–60. Project MUSE. https://muse.jhu.edu/.

Rohter, Larry. "Tarnished Laureate." *New York Times* (December 15, 1998). In *The Rigoberta Menchú Controversy*. Edited by Arturo Arias. Minneapolis: University of Minnesota Press, 2001. 58–65.

Rojkind, Inés. "La revista *Controversia*: Reflexión y polémica entre los argentinos exiliados en México." In *Represión y destierro: Itinerarios del exilio argentino*. Edited by Pablo Yankelevich. La Plata, Argentina: Ediciones Al Margen, 2004. 223–51.

Roland, Joan. "Reception and Representation of the Holocaust in India." Paper presented at the forty-ninth annual conference of the Association for Jewish Studies, Washington, DC. December 19, 2017.

Rosalina Tuyuc V. Testimony (Interview Code 54363). 2015. Visual History Archive, USC Shoah Foundation.

Rosenbaum, Alan S., ed. *Is the Holocaust Unique? Perspectives on Comparative Genocide*. Third edition. Boulder: Westview, 2009.

Rosenberg, Fernando. *After Human Rights: Literature, Visual Arts, and Film in Latin America, 1990–2010*. Pittsburgh: University of Pittsburgh Press, 2016.

Rosencof, Mauricio. *The Letters That Never Came*. Translated by Louise B. Popkin. Introduction by Ilán Stavans. Albuquerque: University of New Mexico Press, 2004.

Rosenfeld, Alvin. "The Americanization of the Holocaust." *Commentary* 99, no. 6 (June 1995): 35–40.

Rosenfeld, Gavriel. "The Politics of Uniqueness: Reflections on the Recent Polemical Turn in Holocaust and Genocide Studies," *Holocaust and Genocide Studies* 13, no. 1 (1999): 28–61. HeinOnline.

Roskies, David G. *Against the Apocalypse: Response to Catastrophe in Modern Jewish Culture*. Cambridge: Harvard University Press, 1984.

Roskies, David G. "The Library of the Jewish Catastrophe." In *Holocaust Remembrance: The Shapes of Memory*. Edited by Geoffrey Hartman. Blackwell: Oxford/Cambridge, MA, 1994. 33–41.

Rothberg, Michael. "After Adorno: Culture in the Wake of Catastrophe." *New German Critique* 72 (Autumn 1997): 45–81. http://www.jstor.org/stable/488568.

Rothberg, Michael. *Multidirectional Memory: Remembering the Holocaust in the Age of Decolonization*. Palo Alto: Stanford University Press, 2009.

Rozitchner, León. "Y huirá la tristeza y el gemido." In *Ese infierno: Conversaciones con cinco mujeres sobrevientes de la ESMA*. Edited by Munu Actis, Cristina Aldini, Liliana Gardella, Miriam Lewin, and Elisa Tokar. Buenos Aires: Sudamericana, 2001. 15–20.

Rousset, David. *L'univers concentrationnaire*. Paris: Editions du Pavois, 1946.

Rubinowicz, David. *Diario de un niño judío*. Prologue by Jaroslaw Iwaszkiewicz. Epilogue by Maria Jarochowska. Notes and commentary by Adam Rutkowski. Spanish version by José Emilio Pachec, based on a literal translation from Polish by María Gitta Stein and Oscar Perlin. Mexico: Ediciones Era, 1962.

Rubinstein, Simón. *Sobrevivir*. Mexico: Author, 1970.

Ruggiero, Kristin, ed. *The Jewish Diaspora in Latin America and the Caribbean: Fragments of Memory*. Brighton: Sussex Academic Press, 2005.

Rus, Bernardo. "Rus: El clamor que Videla no escuchó." *Nueva Presencia* 6, no. 362 (June 8, 1984): 30.

Russell, George. "Living with Ghosts: The disappeared and charges of Nazism dog the military." *Time* (July 20, 1981): 38–40.

"Sábato: Ni terrorismo de izquierda ni terrorismo de derecha." *Nueva Presencia* 2, no. 115 (September 14, 1979): 9.

Sabin, Michael. "Two Argentine Escapees Tell How Police Torture Jews to Snare Others." *New York Jewish Week* (Manhattan edition, March 20, 1980). http://www.proquest.com/.

Salamanca Villamizar, Carlos Arturo. "Los lugares de la memoria y de la acción política en Guatemala. Justicia transicional, políticas del reconocimiento y ficciones de secularismo." *Revista de Estudios Sociales* no. 51 (January–March 2015): 62–75. http://dx.doi.org/10.7440/res51.2015.05.

Sam Colop, Luis Enrique. *Jub'aqtun Omay Kuchum K'aslemal. Cinco siglos de encubrimiento—a propósito de 1992*. Cuaderno 1. Guatemala: SPEM/Cholsamaj, 1991.

Samoilovich, Daniel. "Gelman: El sueño y la tragedia." *Punto de Vista* 6, no. 21 (August 1984): 39–40.

Sandra Patricia García Paredes Testimony (Interview Code 54336). 2015. Visual History Archive, USC Shoah Foundation.

Sanford, Victoria. "Between Rigoberta Menchú and La Violencia: Deconstructing David Stoll's History of Guatemala." In "If Truth Be Told: A Forum on David Stoll's 'Rigoberta Menchú and the Story of All Poor Guatemalans,'" *Latin American Perspectives* 26, no. 6 (November 1999). http://www.jstor.org/stable/2633923. 38–46.

Sanford, Victoria. *Buried Secrets: Truth and Human Rights in Guatemala*. New York: Palgrave Macmillan, 2003.

Santiago Mo Yat Testimony (Interview Code 55302). 2015. Visual History Archive, USC Shoah Foundation.

Sanyal, Debarati. *Memory and Complicity: Migrations of Holocaust Remembrance*. New York: Fordham University Press, 2015.

Sanyal, Debarati, Max Silverman, and Michael Rothberg, eds. "Noeuds de Mémoire: Multidirectional Memory in Postwar French and Francophone Culture." *Yale French Studies* nos. 118–19 (2010): 1–2.

Sarlo, Beatriz. "El campo intelectual: Un espacio doblemente fracturado." In *Represión y reconstrucción de una cultura: El caso argentino*. Edited by Saúl Sosnowski. Buenos Aires: Editorial Universitaria de Buenos Aires, 1988. 96–108.

Sarlo, Beatriz. "La historia contra el olvido." *Punto de Vista* 12, no. 36 (December 1989): 11–13.

Sarlo, Beatriz. "Política, ideología y figuración literaria." In *Ficción y política: La narrativa argentina durante el proceso militar*. Edited by Daniel Balderston, David William Foster, Tulio Halperin Donghi, Francine Masiello, Marta Morello-Frosch, and Beatriz Sarlo. Buenos Aires/Minneapolis: Alianza Editorial/Institute for the Study of Ideologies and Literature, 1987. 30–59.

Sarlo, Beatriz. *Tiempo pasado: Cultura de la memoria y giro subjetivo: Una discusión*. Buenos Aires: Siglo XXI, 2006.

Sarlo, Beatriz. *Tiempo presente: Notas sobre el cambio de una cultura*. Buenos Aires: Siglo XXI, 2001.

Sarlo, Beatriz. "Una alucinación dispersa en agonía." *Punto de Vista* 7, no. 21 (August 1984): 1–4.

Sarmiento, Domingo. *Facundo; or, Civilization and Barbarism*. Translated by Mary Mann. Introduction by Ilan Stavans. New York: Penguin, 1998 [1845].

Schabas, William A. "The Genocide Mystique." In *Unimaginable Atrocities: Justice, Politics and Rights at the War Crimes Tribunals*. Oxford: Oxford University Press, 2012. 99–124. Oxford Scholarship Online. doi: 10.1093/acprof:oso/9780199653072.003.0005.

Schabas, William A. "The Law and Genocide." *The Oxford Handbook of Genocide Studies*. Edited by Donald Bloxham and A. Dirk Moses. Oxford: Oxford University Press, 2010. 123–41.

Scheine Maria Sara Laskier de Rus Holocaust Testimony (Videotape 16736). 1996. Visual History Archive, USC Shoah Foundation.

Schenquer, Laura, and Eduardo Raíces. "Una narrativa fallida: Holocausto, humor y denuncia ante la última dictadura cívico-militar argentina." *Nuevo Mundo, Mundos Nuevos* (January 29, 2014). http://nuevomundo.revues.org/66305.

Schiller, Herman. "Eichmann y el retorno de los fantasmas." *Nueva Presencia* 3, no. 152 (May 30, 1980): 1.

Schiller, Herman. "Ni vergonzantes ni vendepatrias." *Nueva Presencia* 2, no. 118 (October 5, 1979): 7.

Schiller, Herman. "Otra vez los 'conocidos de siempre' en acción." *Nueva Presencia* 4, no. 158 (July 11, 1980): 1.

Schiller, Herman. "Sí, claro, volver a las fuentes." *Nueva Presencia* 3, no. 132 (January 11, 1980): 9.

Schiller, Herman. "¿Terminó la impunidad de los criminales?" *Nueva Presencia* 5, no. 296 (March 4, 1983): 4.

Schirmer, Jennifer. *Intimidades del proyecto politico de los militares de Guatemala.* Guatemala: FLACSO, 2001.

Schmucler, Héctor. "Formas del olvido." *Confines* 1, no. 1 (April 1995): 51–54.

Schmucler, Héctor. "Ni siquiera un rostro donde la muerte hubiera podido estampar su sello." *Confines* 2, no. 3 (September 1996): 9–12.

Schmucler, Héctor. "Nota preliminar: La pregunta incesante." In Pierre Vidal-Naquet, *Los judíos, la memoria y el presente*. Prologue by Héctor Schmucler. Translated by Daniel Zadunaisky. Buenos Aires: Fondo de Cultura Económica de Argentina, 1996). 7–13.

Schmucler, Héctor. "Testimonio de los sobrevivientes." *Controversia* 2, nos. 9–10 (December 1980): 4–5.

Schwertfeger, Ruth. "Simultaneity of Past and Present in Mexico." In *The Jewish Diaspora in Latin America and the Caribbean: Fragments of Memory.* Edited by Kristin Ruggiero. Brighton: Sussex Academic Press, 2005. 9–17.

Scliar, Moacyr. *The War in Bom Fim.* Translated by David William Foster. Lubbock: Texas Tech University Press, 2010.

"Se encuentra en el país Elie Wiesel." *La Nación* (September 1, 1979): 5.

"Sectores nazifascistas buscan como en la Alemania de Hitler la sangre del judío." *Nueva Sión* 27, no. 583 (August 1976): 3.

Segev, Tom. *The Seventh Million: The Israelis and the Holocaust.* Translated by Haim Watzman. New York: Hill and Wang, 1993.

Senkman, Leonardo. *Argentina, la Segunda Guerra Mundial y los refugiados indeseables, 1933–1945.* Buenos Aires: Centro Editor Latinoamericano, 1991.

Senkman, Leonardo, ed. *El antisemitismo en la Argentina.* Second edition. Buenos Aires: Centro Editor de América Latina, 1989.

Senkman, Leonardo. "Bar Kojba entre el mito y la realidad." *Nueva Presencia* 4, no. 204 (May 29, 1981): 6.

Senkman, Leonardo. "Contra el racismo, el antisemitismo y la violación de los derechos humanos." *Nueva Presencia* 4, no. 190 (February 20, 1981): 5.

Senkman, Leonardo. "El Holocausto y la estética de la muerte." *Nueva Presencia* 4, no. 199 (April 23, 1981): 1.

Senkman, Leonardo. *El periodismo judeo-argentino: Nueva Sión.* Buenos Aires: Centro J. N. Bialik, 1984.

Senkman, Leonardo. "En torno al mito de los judíos yendo como rebaño al matadero." *Nueva Presencia* 3, no. 149 (May 9, 1980): 20.

Senkman, Leonardo. "¿Genocidio humano u holocausto judío?" *Nueva Presencia* 4, no. 233 (December 18, 1981): 1.

Senkman, Leonardo. "Los indios del silencio." *Nueva Presencia* 3, no. 149 (May 9, 1980): 8.

"Ser argentinos, ser judíos." *Nueva Presencia* 1, no. 1 (July 9, 1977): 1.

Shandler, Jeffrey. *While America Watches: Televising the Holocaust.* Oxford: Oxford University Press, 1999.

Sheinin, David. *Consent of the Damned: Ordinary Argentineans in the "Dirty War."* Gainesville: University of Florida Press, 2012.
Sheinin, David. "Deconstructing Anti-Semitism in Argentina." In *The Jewish Diaspora in Latin America and the Caribbean: Fragments of Memory*. Edited by Kristin Ruggiero. Brighton: Sussex Academic Press, 2005. 72–85.
Sheinin, David, and Lois Baer Barr, eds. *The Jewish Diaspora in Latin America: New Studies in History and Literature*. New York: Garland Publishing, 1996.
Shenker, Noah. *Reframing Holocaust Testimony*. Bloomington: Indiana University Press, 2015.
Shestack, Jerome J. "Jacobo Timerman: The Perils of Silence." *Congress Monthly* 48, no. 7 (September–October 1981): 9–10. Nexis.
Sigal, Silvia. "La polémica sobre el genocidio." *Puentes* 2, no. 5 (October 2001): 62–65. http://www.comisionporlamemoria.org/project/puentes/.
"Significativas definiciones políticas y económicas." *Nueva Presencia* 1, no. 24 (December 17, 1977): 5.
Siman, Yael, "Reconstrucción y reparación de los inmigrantes-sobrevivientes del Holocausto en México: Una aproximación desde el testimonio." Paper presented at the symposium Díaspora y genocidio: Reparaciones, Buenos Aires, Argentina, March 14, 2018, 2.
Siman, Yael, and Emmanuel Kahan. "La memoria global en contextos nacionales: Prácticas conmemorativas en Argentina y México." *Istor* 21, no. 82 (2020): 79–109.
Sitman, Rosalie. "Counter Discourse in Argentina: Victoria Ocampo and SUR's Attitude toward the Jews during World War II." In *The Jewish Diaspora in Latin America and the Caribbean: Fragments of Memory*. Edited by Kristin Ruggiero. Brighton: Sussex Academic Press, 2005. 18–33.
Sklodowska, Elzbieta. "The Poetics of Remembering, the Politics of Forgetting: Rereading *I, Rigoberta Menchú*." In *The Rigoberta Menchú Controversy*. Edited by Arturo Arias. Minneapolis: University of Minnesota Press, 2001. 252–69.
Smithers, Gregory D. "Rethinking Genocide in North America." In *The Oxford Handbook of Genocide Studies*. Edited by Donald Bloxham and A. Dirk Moses. Oxford: Oxford University Press, 2010. 322–41.
Sneh, Simja. *El pan y la sangre*. Buenos Aires: Sudamericana, 1977.
Sofer, Eugene F. "Terror in Argentina: Jews Face New Dangers." *Present Tense* 5, no. 1 (Autumn 1977): 19–25.
Solana, Rafael. "*Morirás lejos*, de Pacheco. Esa segunda edición confirmatoria." *El Universal* (February 23, 1980): 4.
Sommer, Doris. "Las Casas's Lies and Other Language Games." In *The Rigoberta Menchú Controversy*. Edited by Arturo Arias. Minneapolis: University of Minnesota Press, 2001. 237–50.
Sosnowski, Saúl. "Fronteras en las letras judías-latinoamericanas." *Revista Iberoamericana* 66, no. 191 (April–June 2000): 263–78.

"Sospechosa impunidad." *Nueva Presencia* 4, no. 174 (October 31, 1980): 1.

Speed, Shannon, and Xochitl Leyva Solano. "Introduction." In *Human Rights in the Maya Region: Global Politics, Cultural Contentions, and Moral Engagements*. Edited by Pedro Pitarch, Shannon Speed, and Xochitl Leyva Solano. Durham: Duke University Press, 2008: 1–23.

Spitzer, Leo. *Hotel Bolivia: The Culture of Memory in a Refuge from Nazism*. New York: Hill and Wang, 1998.

Stannard, David E. *American Holocaust: The Conquest of the New World*. New York: Oxford University Press, 1992.

Stavans, Ilan. "The Impact of the Holocaust in Latin America." *Chronicle of Higher Education* 47, no. 34 (May 4, 2001): B7–B10. Education Source, EBSCOhost.

Stein, Arlene. "Whose Memories? Whose Victimhood? Contests for the Holocaust Frame in Recent Social Movement Discourse." *Sociological Perspectives* 41, no. 3 (1998): 519–40. http://www.jstor.org/stable/1389562.

Stern, Steve, and Scott Strauss. "Introduction: Embracing Paradox: Human Rights in the Global Age." In *The Human Rights Paradox*. Edited by Steve Stern and Scott Strauss. Madison: University of Wisconsin Press, 2014. 3–28. Project MUSE. https://muse.jhu.edu/.

Stoll, David. *Between Two Armies in the Ixil Towns of Guatemala*. New York: Columbia, 1993.

Stoll, David. *Rigoberta Menchú and the Story of All Poor Guatemalans*. Boulder: Westview, 1999.

Strejilevich, Nora. *A Single, Numberless Death*. Translated by Cristina del Toro. Charlottesville: University of Virginia Press, 2002.

Strejilevich, Nora. "Testimony: Beyond the Language of Truth." *Human Rights Quarterly* 28, no. 3 (2006): 701–13. JSTOR.

Strouse, Jean. "Holocaust of One." Review of Jacobo Timerman, *Prisoner without a Name*. *Newsweek* (May 18, 1981): 108. Nexis.

Suárez, Ray. "In Search of Literary 'Truth.'" *NPR Talk of the Nation* (June 10, 1999). Transcript.

Szurmuk, Mónica. "Memorias de lo íntimo." In *Sitios de la memoria: México Post 68*. Edited by Mónica Szurmuk and Maricruz Castro Ricalde. Santiago: Editorial Cuarto Propio, 2014. 209–28.

Szurmuk, Mónica. *Una vocación desmesurada: Una biografía de Alberto Gerchunoff*. Buenos Aires: Sudamericana, 2018.

Tandeciarz, Silvia. *Citizens of Memory: Affect, Representation and Human Rights in Argentina*. Lewisburg: Bucknell University Press, 2017.

Terán, Oscar. "Argentina: Tocar lo intocable." *Punto de Vista* 9, no. 28 (November 1986): 44–45.

Terán, Oscar. "Una polémica postergada: La crisis del marxismo." *Punto de Vista* 6, no. 20 (May 1984): 19–21.

Tesch, Kathleen. "Jewish Group Closes Argentine Office, Cites Threats." *New York Times* (July 8, 1977): 8.

Theidon, Kimberly. *Intimate Enemies: Violence and Reconciliation in Peru*. Philadelphia: University of Pennsylvania Press, 2012. https://muse.jhu.edu/.

Timerman, Jacobo. "Coming Home." *Congress Monthly* 47, no. 2 (February 1980): 9–10. Nexis.

Timerman, Jacobo. *Preso sin nombre, celda sin número*. Prologues by Arthur Miller and Ariel Dorfman. Madison: University of Wisconsin Press, 2000.

Timerman, Jacobo. *Prisoner without a Name, Cell without a Number*. Translated by Toby Talbot. New York: Alfred Knopf, 1981.

Tischler Visquerra, Sergio. *Memoria, tiempo y sujeto*. Puebla/Guatemala: Instituto de Ciencias Sociales y Humanidades/F&G Editores, 2005.

Todorov, Tzvetan. *Facing the Extreme: Moral Life in the Concentration Camps*. Translated by Arthur Denner and Abigail Pollak. New York: Henry Holt, 1996.

Todorov, Tzvetan. *Les abus de la mémoire*. Paris: Arléa, 1995.

Toker, Eliahu. *Papá, Mamá y otras ciudades*. Buenos Aires: Editorial Contexto, 1988.

Torpey, John. "Habermas y los historiadores." *Punto de Vista* 12, no. 36 (December 1989): 14–21.

Torpey, John. "Introduction: Habermas and the Historians." Special issue on the Historikerstreit. *New German Critique*, no. 44 (Spring–Summer 1988): 5–24. http://www.jstor.org/stable/488143.

Traverso, Enzo. *Left Wing Melancholia: Marxism, History, and Memory*. New York: Columbia University Press, 2016.

"Tres nuevos elementos de juicio." *Nueva Presencia* 2, no. 121 (October 26, 1979): 7.

Trunk, Isaiah. *Judenrat: The Jewish Councils in Eastern Europe under Nazi Occupation*. New York: Macmillan, 1972.

Tuchman, Barbara. *A Distant Mirror: The Calamitous 14th Century*. New York: Knopf, 1978.

Tuyuc V., Rosalina. Conference keynote address presented at A Conflict? Genocide and Resistance in Guatemala, 2016 International Conference, Center for Advanced Genocide Research, USC Shoah Foundation, September 12, 2016. Video available at https://sfi.usc.edu/cagr/conferences/2016_international.

"Una rebelión de oprimidos." *Nueva Presencia* 5, no. 304 (April 29, 1983): 4.

"Una sesión con variaciones." Separata especial, *Nueva Presencia* 4, no. 178 (November 28, 1980): ii.

"Una verdadera lluvia de adhesiones." *Nueva Presencia* 6, no. 330 (October 28, 1983): 7.

"USC Shoah Foundation and FAFG Co-launch Project to Shine Light on Guatemalan Genocide." USC Shoah Foundation–The Institute for Visual History and Education, July 28, 2015. https://sfi.usc.edu/news.

Valdés, Carlos. "*Morirás lejos*." *Hojas de crítica*. Supplement of the *Revista de la Universidad de México* 22, no. 10 (June 1968): 6–7.

Valdés, Hernán. *Tejas verdes: Diario de un campo de concentración en Chile*. Barcelona: Editorial Ariel, 1974.

Vallejo, César. *The Complete Posthumous Poetry*. Translated by Clayton Eshleman and José Rubia Barcia. Berkeley: University of California Press, 1978.

Vanthuyne, Karine. *La présence d'un passé de violences: Mémoires et identités autochtones dans le Guatemala de l'après génocide*. Presses de l'Université Laval, 2014.

Varon, Benno Weiser. "Benno Weiser Varon Responds." *Midstream* 28, no. 2 (February 1982): 40–42.

Varon, Benno Weiser. "The Canonization of Jacobo Timerman." *Midstream* 27, no. 7 (August–September 1981): 36–44.

Varon, Benno Weiser. "Don't Rescue Latin American Jews!" *Midstream* 26, no. 10 (December 1980): 11–16.

Vasokie, Felisa. "Timerman" (letter to the editor). *Nueva Presencia* 4, no. 221 (September 25, 1981): 23

Veiga, Raúl. *Las organizaciones de derechos humanos*. Buenos Aires: Centro Editor de América Latina, 1985.

Verani, Hugo J. "Hacia la bibliografía de José Emilio Pacheco." In *La hoguera y el viento: José Emilio Pacheco ante la crítica*. Edited by Hugo J. Verani. Mexico, DF: UNAM/Ediciones Era, 1993. 292–341.

Verbitsky, Horacio. *El vuelo*. Buenos Aires: Planeta, 1995.

"¿Veremos 'Holocausto'? Pequeña historia del árbol que no deja ver el bosque." *La Voz* 1, no. 5 (August–September 1981): 3.

Vezzetti, Hugo. "Iniciativas políticas de la memoria: El Museo en la ESMA." 2005. BazarAmericano.com.

Vezzetti, Hugo. "Lecciones de memoria. A los 25 años de la implantación del terrorismo de Estado." *Punto de Vista* no. 70 (2001): 12–18.

Vezzetti, Hugo. *Pasado y presente: Guerra, dictadura y sociedad en la Argentina*. Buenos Aires: Siglo XXI, 2002.

Verbitsky, Horacio. *Rodolfo Walsh y la prensa clandestina (1976–1978)*. Buenos Aires: Ediciones de la Urraca, 1985.

Vezzetti, Hugo. *Sobre la violencia revolucionaria: Memorias y olvidos*. Buenos Aires: Siglo XXI, 2009.

Vezzetti, Hugo. "Verdad jurídica y verdad histórica. Condiciones, usos y límites de la figura del 'genocidio.' " In *Lesa humanidad: Argentina y sudáfrica, reflexiones después del mal*. Edited by Claudia Hilb, Phillippe-Joseph Salazar, and Lucas G. Martín. Buenos Aires: Katz, 2014. 17–37.

Viaene, Liselotte. "Life Is Priceless: Mayan Q'eqchi' Voices on the Guatemalan Reparations Program." *International Journal of Transitional Justice* 4 (2010): 4–25. Oxford Journals. doi: 10.1093/ijtj//ijp024.

Vidal-Naquet, Pierre. *The Assassins of Memory*. Translated and with a foreword by Jeffrey Mehlman. New York: Columbia University Press, 1992.

Vigevani, Vera. "El rol del testimonio como instrumento de creación de un proyecto político." In *Juicios por crímenes de lesa humanidad en Argentina*. Edited by Gabriele Andreozzi. Buenos Aires: Atuel, 2011. 217–34.

Volpi, Jorge. *La imaginación y el poder: Una historia intelectual de 1968*. México: Era, 1998.
Walford, Lynn. "Truth, Lies and Politics in the Debate over Testimonial Writing: The Cases of Rigoberta Menchú and Binjamin Wilkomirski." *The Comparatist* 30 (2006): 113–21. Education Service, EBSCOhost.
Walsh, Lilia. "Rigor e inteligencia en la vida de Rodolfo Walsh," *Controversia* 4 (February 1980), 15.
Walsh, Rodolfo. "Carta abierta de un escritor a la junta militar." In *Rodolfo Walsh y la prensa clandestina (1976–1978)*. Edited by Horacio Verbitsky. Buenos Aires: Ediciones de la Urraca, 1985. 121–23.
Wang, Diana. *Hijos de la guerra: La segunda generación de sobrevivientes de la Shoá*. Buenos Aires: Marea, 2007.
Wang, Diana. *Los niños escondidos: Del holocausto a Buenos Aires*. Buenos Aires: Marea Editorial, 2004.
Warren, Kay B. *Indigenous Movements and Their Critics: Pan Maya Activism in Guatemala*. Princeton: Princeton University Press, 2008.
Wasserstrom, Dunia. *¡Nunca jamás . . . !* Prologue by Andrés Henestrosa. Mexico: Editorial Diana, 1989.
Waxman, Henry. "From the Congressional Record: Waxman Speaks Out on Argentina." *Israel Today* (May 12–25, 1978): 13.
Weisbrot, Robert. "Anti-Semitism in Argentina." *Midstream* 24, no. 5 (May 1978): 12–23.
Weiss, Peter. *The Investigation: A Play*. English version by Jon Swan and Ulu Grosbard. New York: Atheneum, 1966.
Wells, Allen. *Tropical Zion: General Trujillo, FDR and the Jews of Sosúa*. Durham: Duke University Press, 2009.
Wiesel, Elie. *The Jews of Silence: A Personal Report on Soviet Jewry*. New York: Holt, Rinehart and Winston, 1966.
Wiesel, Elie. *Night*. Translated by Marion Wiesel. New York: Hill and Wang, 2003.
Wiesel, Elie. "Now We Know." In *Genocide in Paraguay*. Edited by Richard Arens. Philadelphia: Temple University Press, 1976. 165–67.
"Wiesel vino, vio y venció." *Nueva Presencia* 3, no. 114 (September 7, 1979): 6.
Wieviorka, Annette. *The Era of the Witness*. Translated by Jared Stark. Ithaca: Cornell University Press, 2006.
Wilkomirski, Binjamin. *Fragments: Memories of a Wartime Childhood*. Translated by Carol Brown Janeway. New York: Schocken Books, 1996.
Wilson, Richard. "Verdades violentas: Las políticas de recordar el pasado en Guatemala." In *Guatemala 1983–1997: ¿Hacia dónde va la transición?* Edited by Jeremy Armon. Guatemala: FLACSO, 1998. 50–70. http://www.flacsoandes.edu.ec/libros/6617-opac.
Yankelevich, Pablo. "México: Un exilio fracturado." In *Represión y destierro: Itinerarios del exilio argentino*. Edited by Pablo Yankelevich. La Plata, Argentina: Ediciones Al Margen, 2004. 187–221.

Yankelevich, Pablo, and Silvina Jensen. "México y Cataluña: El exilio en números." In *Exilios: Destinos y experiencias bajo la dictadura militar*. Edited by Pablo Yankelevich and Silvina Jensen. Buenos Aires: Libros del Zorzal, 2007. 209–51.

Yanzón, Rodolfo. "Los juicios desde el fin de la dictadura hasta hoy." In *Juicios por crímenes de lesa humanidad en Argentina*. Edited by Gabriele Andreozzi. Buenos Aires: Atuel, 2011. 137–54.

Yerushalmi, Yosef H. "Réflexions sur l'oubli." In *Usages de l'oubli*. Edited by Yosef Hayim Yerushalmi, Nicole Loreaux, Hans Mommsen, et al. Paris: Seuil, 1988. 7–21.

Young, James E. *The Texture of Memory: Holocaust Memorials and Meaning*. New Haven: Yale University Press, 1993.

Zaga Mograbi, Sharon, and Ester Cohen Cohen, eds. *El rostro de la verdad: Testimonios de sobrevivientes del Holocausto que llegaron a México*. Mexico City: Memoria y Tolerancia, 2002.

Zaretsky, Natasha. "Child Survivors of the Shoah: Testimony, Citizenship and Survival in Jewish Buenos Aires." In *The New Jewish Argentina: Facets of Jewish Experience in the Southern Cone*. Edited by Adriana Brodsky and Raanan Rein. Leiden: Brill, 2013. 315–39.

Zunino, Marcos. "Subversive Justice: The Russell Vietnam War Crimes Tribunal and Transitional Justice." *International Journal of Transitional Justice* 10 (2016): 211–29. doi: 10.1093/ijtj/ijw007.

Index

Aché genocide (Paraguay), 7, 215n23
Adorno, Theodor, 11–12, 87, 142, 241n153
Agamben, Giorgio, 11, 93, 96
Aizenberg, Edna, 239n90
Alfonsín, Raúl, 61, 85–86, 94, 140, 229
Algeria, 2, 15, 160, 247n82
Algiers Charter (1976), 164
Allende, Salvador, 219n109
Alvarado, Pedro de, 147, 157
American Jewish Committee (AJC), 54, 106
American Jewish Yearbook, 56
Améry, Jean, 83
AMIA (Asociación Mutual Israelita Argentina), 35, 51, 59, 61, 106, 234n144
Anilevich, Mordejai, 71–72
anti-capitalist critique, 98–99, 117, 162
anti-Communism, 1, 6, 27, 97, 118, 145–46, 151, 169, 203
anti-colonial struggle, 2, 5, 11, 15, 21, 23, 72, 180, 207–208; Guatemalan, 12, 24, 147–49, 157, 161, 163–66, 185, 206. *See also* Russell Tribunal
anti-fascism, 19, 21, 130–31, 218n93, 239n95

Anti-Defamation League (ADL), 42, 51–52, 54, 224n94
anti-Semitism, 3, 123, 204; depicted in *Morirás lejos*, 118–20; Eichmann kidnapping and, 28–29; *Holocaust* miniseries and, 65, 224n85. *See also* Argentina, dictatorship
Arbenz, Jacobo, 162, 169
Arendt, Hannah, 11, 78–79, 93, 102–103, 116, 222n42
Argentina, dictatorship (Proceso de Re-organización Nacional, 1976–83): anti-Semitism during, 33, 37–39, 41, 43–44, 48–49, 51–60, 67, 220n14; clandestine press in, 9, 25, 32, 41–42, 64, 66, 69, 161, 205; civilian complicity with, 76, 78, 80, 84–85, 90, 93–94, 96–97; comparisons to Auschwitz and, 37, 52, 62, 63, 66, 84; concentration camps in, 9, 41, 44, 62, 82–83, 92, 93, 104, 124, 129, 130, 137, 220n12, 241n138; criminalization of state violence and, 75, 78, 80–81, 84, 91, 206; "double discourse" and, 38, 46, 53, 58; as genocide, 40, 41, 66, 75, 81, 92, 104, 105, 161, 205n27, 221n31, 224n99; as holocaust, 5, 8, 34, 38–39, 42,

Argentina, dictatorship *(continued)*
48, 53, 60, 62, 65–66; and Jewish
community leaders, 32–33, 40,
46–51, 67–68, 72, 73, 223n58,
228n172; Jewish victims of, 35,
38–39, 44–46, 55, 60, 68–72,
83, 219n10, 220n13, 221n42,
222n45; memory of, 9, 25, 48, 70,
71–73, 77–80, 84–107, 127, 205,
208, 225n114, 233n95; military
government compared to Nazis,
31, 32, 36, 41–43, 46, 48–49, 55,
62, 65, 67, 81, 83; normalcy of
Jewish life during, 33, 38, 51–52,
54, 55–56, 59; victims compared to
Holocaust victims, 31, 36, 45–46,
55, 81, 221n41. *See also* DAIA;
disappeared; human rights activists;
Timerman

Argentina, post-dictatorship period
(1983–2005): "dos demonios"
theory, 57, 85, 95, 140; economic
crisis of 2001, 92; human rights
activism during, 76–78, 80–85,
106; impunity laws, 80, 82–84, 92,
229n17, 229n21, 230n34; media
sensationalism and, 77, 86–87,
89–91, 96; politics of memory and,
25, 76–79, 83, 85, 88, 98–99;
prosecution of perpetrators, 20, 21,
66, 80, 92

Arias, Arturo, 147, 176
Armenian Genocide, 188, 215n42,
216n56
Asamblea de la Sociedad Civil (ASC,
Guatemala), 156–57, 158, 245n59
Asylum politics, 200
Auschwitz, 29, 71, 106, 113, 179,
210, 245n51; post-Auschwitz
thought, 11, 68, 79, 93, 99–100,
107, 142, 229n12; survivors of
in Argentina, 44–46, 83, 86–87,

130, 133–34, 135, 136, 140,
183–84, 204, 210, 221nn41–42,
222n45, 231n52; as symbol, 11,
116, 209; uprising, 181, 204.
See also Argentina, dictatorship;
ESMA; Frankfurt Trial; Laub; Levi;
Mercado; Pacheco; Sarlo; Vezzetti;
Wiesel
Ávila Camacho, Manuel, 131
Aztecs, 124–25

Bakhtin, Mikhail, 148
Bañuelos, Juan, 125–26
Bar Kochba, 69, 227n165
Barbie, Klaus, 14–15, 217n57
Basso, Lelio, 164
Bauer, Yehuda, 14, 32, 39–40, 70,
216n51
Bauman, Zygmunt, 11, 85, 93
Bayer, Oswaldo, 83–84
Bellow, Saul, 222n42
Benítez, Fernando, 116, 123
Benjamin, Walter, 98, 166
Bernetti, Jorge Luis, 5, 8, 132, 137,
239n98
Beverley, John, 180–84, 217n83
Bettelheim, Bruno, 82–83
B'nai Brith, 42
Black Book of Nazi Terror in Europe
(Mexico City 1943), 131, 239n91
Bolivia, 2, 34, 41, 207
Bonafini, Hebe de, 102, 229n20,
234n123
Borges, Jorge Luis, 112, 114
Brazil, 22, 24, 34, 164, 214n11,
218n102

Cabildo (Argentina), 69, 220n16
Calveiro, Pilar, 21–22, 83, 96, 134–35
Canetti, Elias, 79, 105–106, 141
Cárdenas, Lázaro, 131, 160
Carlotto, Estela, 78, 231n53

Casa de las Américas, 22, 180
Castellanos, Rosario, 126
Casullo, Nicolás, 26, 77, 97–107, 137, 141
censorship: of Holocaust media in Argentina, 42, 53, 140; by human rights groups, 138; of Jewish press, 43, 61, 64–65; as triggering comparisons to Holocaust, 110, 140; as triggering testimony, 114, 127, 140
Césaire, Aimé, 11
Che Guevara, 72
Chelmo, 209
Chel Massacre (1982), 192–96
Chile, 6, 24, 34, 164; and German Nazi immigrants, 218n109
Cholsamaj Publishing House, 148, 163, 247n92
CIA (Central Intelligence Agency), 162, 169
Clarín (Argentina), 64
Cojtí Cuxil, Demetrio, 12, 21, 28, 145–67, 206, 208, 243n20, 244n38, 247n85, 247n90
Cold War historiography, 13, 20, 24, 149, 151, 155, 185, 198, 238n86
Colombia, 22, 24
colonialism, 11, 147–50, 158, 162–64, 166, 206–208
Comisión Provincial de la Memoria, 84, 135
Commission on Historical Clarification (Guatemala), 146, 173, 186, 191, 250n73
CONADEP (Comisión Nacional sobre la Desaparición de Personas), 22, 37, 61–64, 80–82, 86, 140, 219n11, 225n122, 229n20, 230n27, 230n32; and Holocaust memory, 61–63, 72; report as a forum for testimony, 140; and "terrorism from the right or the left" (dos demonios), 57, 140
concentration camps: in Argentina, 9, 41, 44, 62, 82–83, 92, 93, 104, 124, 129, 130, 137, 220n12, 241n138; in Chile, 6; Nazi, 7, 8, 52, 63, 70, 82, 84, 89, 103, 109, 123, 116, 130, 133–34, 176, 182, 209, 216nn52–53
Confines (Argentina), 26, 77–79, 97–107, 233n108
Controversia (Mexico), 103, 137–38, 141, 221n31
Conquest of Guatemala, 21, 147–48, 158–59, 166, 242n17; semantics, 28, 150, 153, 159, 162–64
Conquest of Mexico, 26, 125
Corpus Christi Massacre (1971), 126, 132
Cortázar, Julio, 114, 164
counterinsurgency campaigns, 2, 6, 17, 27, 145, 151, 155, 167, 185, 203, 206, 247n82
crimes against humanity, 14, 75, 160, 173, 186, 230n21, 246n74
Cuba 2, 5, 22, 160, 193, 214n10

Dachau, 63, 113, 116, 209
DAIA (Delegación de Asociaciones Israelitas Argentinas), 8, 11, 21, 33, 35–38, 40, 46, 49–56, 58, 59, 60–61, 65, 67–69, 223n58, 224nn98–99, 227n161. *See also* Timerman
Dawidowicz, Lucy, 51, 65
de Beauvoir, Simone, 160
decolonization, 11, 21, 23, 149, 163–65, 207, 218n96
desaparecidos. *See* CONADEP; disappeared
Díaz Ordaz, Gustavo, 246n81
Die Presse (Argentina), 32

disappeared, 8, 157, 165, 186, 191, 199, 219n10; *aparición con vida*, 102, 138–40; collective memory of, 9–10, 85, 234n140; CONADEP and, 37, 61, 80; DAIA and, 35, 46, 55, 68–69, 227n161; demand not to forget, 101–102, 138, 176, 191 199, 214n11; and Holocaust testimonies, 83, 23n52; Jewish families and, 25, 37, 43–47, 66, 69, 83, 219n10, 221n42, 222n42, 222n45, 224nn98–99, 227n161, 229n161, 231n52; "memory boom" and, 25, 35–37, 55, 85, 138–39; press testimony and, 22, 47, 85; pressure on regime to release, 138; transition to democracy and, 80, 82, 146, 229n212. *See also* human rights activists

Echeverría, Luis, 131–32, 239n92, 246n81
Eichmann, Adolf, 11, 17–22, 42, 62, 66, 82, 115, 116, 129, 160, 217n71, 217n83, 222n42, 276n74
Einsatzgruppen, 122
Ejército Guerrillero de los Pobres (EGP), 174, 193, 199
El Salvador, 22, 24
Elias, Norbert, 79, 95, 233n100
ESMA (Escuela Superior Mecánica de la Armada), 44, 75, 96; as memory museum, 81, 230n26
Esquit, Edgar, 154–56
exiles: Argentine, 3, 5, 24, 26, 36, 42, 63, 84, 97, 103–104, 110–11, 124, 128–37, 143, 161, 221n31, 238n82, 239n96; Guatemalan, 147, 193; Spanish Republican, 130–32, 235n5

FAFG (Fundación de Antropología Forense de Guatemala), 28, 167, 170–74, 185–202, 206

Fanon, Frantz, 11, 12, 164
Farben, IG, 122
fascism, 29, 43, 130–31, 151, 237n45. *See also* anti-fascism
Faurisson, Robert, 176–77, 249n22
Final Solution, 7, 9, 11, 41, 50, 66, 88, 215n23, 221n31
forgetting, 20, 80, 123, 139, 170, 179; "forgetting boom," 146; Lyotard and, 99–101; memory as, 13, 20, 72, 79, 87–89, 94, 104–106, 120, 151; "Never Forget," 77, 109; policies of, 83, 98, 126
Fortunoff Video Archive for Holocaust Testimony, Yale University, 170–71, 180–81
Forster, Ricardo, 98–99, 102
1492–1992 commemorations, 21, 27, 147, 149, 156, 163, 206–207
Fraie Schtime (Argentina), 32, 40, 59, 70–71, 220n22, 223n58
Frank, Anne, 65, 72
Frankfurt Trial (1968), 111, 120, 136, 235n1
Fuentes, Carlos, 114, 116–17
Fundación de Antropología Forense de Guatemala. *See* FAFG

Galeano, Eduardo, 146
García Márquez, Gabriel, 164
genocide, 4, 6, 11–13, 15, 75, 81, 95, 146–60, 218n16, 221n31, 246n74, 247n89; of anti-colonial insurgents, 149–50, 161, 176, 182; definition and semantics, 7–8, 12, 17–18, 23, 146–48, 151, 159–62, 170, 186, 206, 208n82, 216n42, 246n8; denial, 171, 177–78, 194; and "Holocaust," 4, 23–24, 27–28, 161–65; indigenous struggles against, 207–208; as paradigm, 27, 41–49, 54–55, 64–65, 104–105, 160–62, 166–67, 186, 188, 215n56;

narrating, 119–20; in nineteenth century, 95; and Russell Tribunal (1967), 23, 160–63; and Second Russell Tribunal (1974), 164; and Tlatelolco massacre, 132, 246n81; trials, 18, 146, 176, 244n36. *See also* Argentina, dictatorship; Guatemala
"gray zone," 83, 135
Gerardi, Monsignor Juan, 191
Giardinelli, Mempo, 132, 137–39, 239n98
Goldhagen, Daniel, 93, 179
Gorenstein, Mario, 51–53, 65
Grandin, Greg, 151, 154–56, 191, 238n86, 243n25
Grandmothers of Plaza de Mayo, 61, 78–79, 82, 85, 94–97, 231n53
Guatemala, 2, 24, 27, 152; Agreement on the Identity and Rights of Indigenous Peoples 157; CIA in, 162; civil war (1960–96) 28, 145, 149, 152, 154, 170, 171, 179, 200; Civil Society Assembly (Asamblea de la Sociedad Civil, ASC) 156–57; Commission on Historical Clarification, 146, 173, 186, 191, 250n73; conquest of (1524) 147–48, 150, 153, 158–59, 162–64, 166, 242n17; counterinsurgency war in, 17, 27, 145, 155, 181, 185, 203, 206; criminal proceedings for human rights, 146, 165, 172, 174, 176, 178, 185, 191, 196, 244n36; disappearances, 145–46, 148; exhumations, 165, 170, 186; genocide in, 17, 20, 145–53, 157–70, 173–78, 186, 188, 194–203, 206; genocide denial in, 17, 28, 176–78, 194; Holocaust references in, 6, 12, 17, 21, 24, 28, 146–50, 157–67, 174–78, 244nn37–38; Jewish community in, 27, 218n102, 218n108; ladinos, 150–51, 154, 164, 242n10; liberal capitalism in, 157; Liberation Theology in, 22; peace accords, 149, 156–57, 191. *See also* Cojtí; FAFG; Maya Movement; Maya testimony; Menchú
Guatemala, memoria del silencio. *See* Commission on Historical Clarification
Guatemala: Nunca Más. *See* REMHI
guerrillas, 27, 46, 66, 82, 92, 138, 145, 149, 154–55, 158, 174–75, 177–79, 182, 198–99, 244n37; guerrilla as hero, 72, 186. *See also* Ejército Guerrillero de los Pobres (EGP); Montoneros
Guzmán Böckler, José, 163–64

Hartman, Geoffrey, 211
Heidegger, Martin, 99–101
Herbert, Jean-Loup, 163–64
HIJOS (Hijos por la Identidad y la Justicia y contra el Olvido y el Silencio), 80, 94
Hilberg, Raul, 50
Hiroshima, 8, 118
Hirshfeld, Ludwig, 236n41
Historians' Debate/*Historikerstreit*, 14–16, 87–88, 232n69
historical revisionism, 14–16, 176. *See also* Holocaust, denial of
historiography, 87–88, 92, 94, 142, 150–56, 247n89
Hitler, Adolf, 17, 118–19, 123, 142–43, 161; references in Argentina, 37, 41, 43, 47–50, 63, 64, 95
Holocaust (Jewish): Americanization of, 18, 62, 150, 151, 153, 162, 170, 173, 202, 219n110; and critique of modernity, 11, 116–17, 121, 161, 166; and critique of oppression, 24; commemoration, 39, 60, 70–73,

Holocaust (Jewish) *(continued)*
76, 110, 208–209, 230n26;
consciousness, definition of, 3–4;
denial of, 3, 14–16, 28, 64, 114–15,
122–23, 143, 171, 176–78, 181,
183, 187, 194, 206; education, 18,
29, 167; exemplarity of, 8–9, 116,
206–207; films, 32, 42, 52, 182–83;
Germans' moral complicity with,
6, 14, 16, 84, 92–93, 97, 119,
227n141, 228n178; globalization
of, 10, 12, 16–18, 22, 25, 79, 153,
165; and Heroism (*Shoah uGevurah*),
39–40, 49–50, 69, 74, 208,
227n63; human rights and, 72–85,
160–61, 172; memorialization, 39,
208; museums, 29, 120, 167, 179,
188, 1239n102; Studies, 13, 178;
uniqueness of, 6, 8, 13, 15–17, 39,
62, 116, 216n48, 217n62, 247n89;
universalization of, 11; uppercase or
lowercase, 12, 215n42

Holocaust victims (Jewish), 3, 4, 13,
45, 50, 89, 91, 129, 209, 226n141;
moral complicity of, 34, 39–40, 49,
54–59, 66–68, 72–74; as model,
18–19, 26, 123; other victims
compared to, 8, 17, 80–81, 92, 96,
97, 151, 166

Holocaust survivors: in Argentina,
25, 45, 64–65, 83, 208, 222n42,
222n45; in Guatemala, 218n108;
in Israel, 18, 69; in Mexico, 24,
26–27, 110, 129–30, 133–37, 208.
See also Holocaust testimony

Holocaust testimony: and *testimonio*, 3,
22–23, 171–72, 180–82; circulation
of, 3, 110; impact in Argentina,
21–22, 41, 70, 79, 81–91, 96–97;
in Mexico, 109–11, 133–37, 143;
impact in Guatemala (*see* FAFG;
Maya testimony; Menchú); as
imperative, 23; as model, 18, 20–23,
27–29, 80–83, 96, 110, 172, 184–
85, 189–90, 193–96, 198, 249n47;
republished in *Nueva Presencia*, 32,
60, 65–66; as resistance, 70, 109.
See also Mercado; Pacheco

*Holocaust: The Story of the Family
Weiss* (US, 1981), 3, 22, 25, 33,
53, 64–66, 135, 216n56, 224n87,
227n141

human rights: critiques of, 20–22,
77–80, 85–107; ethical principles,
23, 59, 60–61, 65–66, 71–74,
81–82, 96–97, 100, 104, 106–107,
149–50, 152–53, 156, 190, 205,
208, 218n93, 243n24, 243n31;
international, 52, 153, 244n35. *See
also* CONADEP

human rights activists, 3, 10, 20,
25–26, 58, 72, 76–86, 88, 94,
107, 130, 137–38, 150, 153,
228n5, 229n16, 242nn11–12;
Amnesty International, 137–38;
Asociación Pro-Derechos Humanos,
63; Comisión Argentina por los
Derechos Humanos, 221n31;
Comisión Provincial de la Memoria,
La Plata, 135; Jewish, 25; Jewish
Movement for Human Rights, 32,
61, 71; Servicio Paz y Justicia, 62.
See also FAFG; Mothers of the Plaza
de Mayo; Grandmothers of the Plaza
de Mayo

Human Rights Office of Guatemalan
Archdiocese, 190, 250n73

Huyssen, Andreas, 4, 85, 199

Indigenous activism. *See* Cojtí;
Guatemala; Maya Movement

Indigenous peoples, 66, 149, 150, 157,
207–208, 216n56; and Conquest,
125–27; and 1492 commemorations,
147; Holocaust and genocide of, 8,
13, 16, 66, 208, 216n16, 247n89;

Index 295

International Decade of the World's Indigenous Peoples (1995–2004), 149; self-determination of, 146, 206. *See also* Mayas; Maya Movement; Native Americans
industrialization of death, 4, 102–103, 117, 122, 128, 209
industrial modernity, 113, 116–19
Israel, 3, 18, 27, 32, 42, 46, 47, 48, 71, 73, 222n45, 224n113; Holocaust commemoration in, 15–16, 39, 49–50, 69, 73, 165
Irving, David, 123, 143
Iximché Declaration (1980), 147

Jaspers, Karl, 79, 92
Jelin, Elizabeth, 20–21, 81, 85, 152, 230n25
Jews: US, 14, 29, 216n52; Argentine, 18–19, 21, 25, 33–35, 39, 42, 44, 54, 59, 61, 73–74, 76, 205, 218n102, 235n144; as complicitous victims, 33, 34, 39–40, 47, 49, 54–59, 66–68, 72–74; Guatemalan, 27, 218n108; Latin American, 3, 4, 20, 28–29, 214n10, 218n102; Mexican, 26, 110, 214n10, 235n4; refugees, 4, 218n102; and silence, 36, 47–48, 51–53, 62–63, 67–68, 72, 224n79, 228n172; victimhood and, 19, 45, 50, 52, 68–69, 72–73, 151–53
Jitrik, Noé, 118, 123–24, 128, 239n92
Josephus, Flavius, 120
Judaism, 7; combative, 47, 52, 71; and human rights, 61–63; progressive, 55, 59–61. *See also* Jews
Judenrat, 33, 40, 49–55, 67–68, 70–72, 205, 219n1, 223n58

Kaufman, Alejandro, 78, 98, 102
Kennedy, Senator Edward, 42, 51

Kinzer, Stephen, 56, 221n42
Kirchner, Cristina Fernández de and Néstor, 25, 75, 79, 81, 229n17, 239n98
Kovadloff, Jacobo (AJC), 54
Kovner, Abba, 71, 228n172
Kraus, Karl, 105
Krupp, 122

LaCapra, Dominic, 14–16, 64, 96, 180, 203
Lanzmann, Claude, 80, 87–89, 91, 129, 232n71
Latin American Jewish Studies, 4
Latin American left, 9, 12, 13, 67, 72, 98, 125, 128–30, 143, 198, 238n86; armed, 46, 84, 154, 174–75; censorship by, 111, 140; critique of, 85, 94–95, 97, 99, 103, 105, 107, 141, 233n95; exiled, 26, 110, 239n92; Jewish, 32, 58. *See also* revolutionary movements
Latin American studies, 13
Laub, Dori, 180–81, 183–84, 203
Lemkin, Raphael, 159, 163
Leñero, Vicente, 133
León-Portilla, Miguel, 125
Levi, Primo, 7–8, 23, 79–80, 83, 87, 91, 93, 96, 119, 135, 178, 179, 203, 233n95, 234n126, 251n96
Lewin, Boleslao, 206–208
liberation movements (Latin America), 2, 5, 9, 13, 19, 21, 23, 39, 72, 138, 149, 162–64, 180, 184, 208, 210; Jewish support for, 61
Liberation Theology, 171, 185; Jewish, 24, 61; "testimonial reflection" and, 22
Lodz, 133, 206
López Miarnau, Rafael, 235n5
Luz, La (Argentina), 54
Lyotard, Jean-François, 11–12, 79, 99–101, 176–77, 203, 249n22

Marcuse, Herbert, 116, 236n16
Massera, Admiral Emilio, 44–45
Mayas, 6, 16, 118, 151, 155, 249n59; Ixils, 154–55, 179, 192, 242n8, 244n37; massacres of, 27, 145–47, 155, 162, 165 (*see also* Chel massacre); Maya-centric view of history, 156; "Maya holocaust(s)," 12, 16–17, 21, 27–28, 145–67, 153–55, 158–59, 244n37, 249n29; seen as victims, 180, 198; self-determination, 21, 149, 164, 172, 206. *See also* Cojtí; Guatemala; Menchú
Maya Movement, 24, 145, 148–49, 154, 156–58, 162–64
Maya testimony: audiovisual 170–71, 190–202, 206, 249n33; and Holocaust testimony, 170–73, 176–80, 185, 189–204, 206, 249n33; in REMHI report, 197–98. *See also* FAFG; Menchú; Pacheco Bop
Mayer, Arno, 155–56, 245n51
Memmi, Alberto, 164
memory: activists, 77, 198, 199; anti-colonial, 24; as moral obligation, 3, 39, 69, 77, 122, 126–27, 206, 214n14; as resistance, 10, 21, 84, 98, 122, 125–27, 141, 164, 166, 205; competitive, 10–11, 29, 161, 202, 215n32, 251n92; depoliticization of, 15, 72, 153; "deportation" of, 104–105; erasure of, 101–102, 162, 176; exemplary, 6–8; globalization of, 10–11, 202; history and, 3–4, 15–16, 18–19, 88, 155–56, 188; knots, 111, 235n6; linguistic approach to, 77–79, 98–106, 141, 164; multidirectional, 10–11, 202; politicization of, 39, 49, 76, 124; redemptive, 22, 85, 166, 199; reparative, 85, 127, 143, 165–66, 196, 211; Studies, 81. *See also* Argentina, dictatorship; Argentina, post-dictatorship; Guatemala; Holocaust (Jewish); Tlatelolco massacre
Menchú Tum, Rigoberta, 28, 149, 170–84, 199, 203–204, 249n29, 251n96
Menem, Carlos, 35, 87–89, 98, 101, 230n21
Mengele, Josef, 7, 115
Mercado, Tununa, 27, 110–11, 124, 128–43, 161, 205–206, 238nn82–83, 239n92
Mexico, 2, 6, 24, 26–27, 205; anti-fascism in, 131; exiles in, 5, 24, 26, 42, 103, 110–11, 124, 128–37, 143, 161, 221n31, 235n5, 239n92, 239n98; censorship of press, 114, 124; Conquest of, 26, 125, 148, 158; "dirty war," 129, 132, 246n81; Jewish community in, 26, 110, 214n10, 235n4; Holocaust commemoration in, 110; Holocaust museums in, 120, 239n102; Holocaust testimony in, 27, 129, 133–37; immigration policies, 131–32, 239nn95–96; Tlatelolco massacre, 26, 110, 112, 114, 122–28, 132, 143. *See also* Mercado; Pacheco
Meyer, Naomi, 56
Meyer, Marshall T. (Rabbi), 5, 8, 32, 33, 38, 51, 56, 58, 60–63, 68, 72, 225n12
Montes de Oca, Marcos, 126
Montoneros, 46, 94, 97, 103–105, 138, 239n92, 241n138
Morirás lejos, 26, 109–42, 205–206, 235n3, 235n8, 236n10, 236n36, 236n41, 237nn44–45
Mothers of the Plaza de Mayo (Madres de Plaza de Mayo), 57–60, 61,

68, 71, 79, 81, 84–86, 94–97, 98, 102–103, 105–106, 138–39, 140, 229nn19–20, 231n53, 234n140; Jewish members of, 38, 45
Mussolini, Benito, 47

Nagasaki, 8, 118
Native Americans, 6, 13, 16–17, 118, 125, 166, 207, 216n49, 247n89. *See also* Indigenous peoples
Nación, La (Argentina), 64, 66
National Security, 2, 27, 151, 209, 213n2, 247n82
Nazis: analogies to, 14; crimes, 10, 14–17, 23, 47, 60, 83–84, 118–19; fugitives in Latin America, 3, 34, 113, 115, 131, 218n109; ideology, 4, 13, 18, 42 105, 127, 164; literature in Argentina, 37; in *Morirás lejos*, 109, 112–13, 120, 122, 127; Aché genocide and, 215n23. *See also* Argentina, dictatorship; Germans
Neier, Aryeh, 54
neoliberalism, 78, 92, 150, 153, 244n35
Neruda, Pablo, 169
"Never Again," 11, 47, 52–53, 77, 79, 100, 150–51. *See also* "Nunca más"
Noche de Tlatelolco, La, 123, 126–27
Nueva Presencia (Argentina), 32, 219n10, 220n22, 224n85, 225n113; Aché massacre and, 215n23; anti-Semitism and, 56–60; Argentine-Jewish identity and, 61; commemoration of Warsaw Ghetto uprising, 39, 220n22; globalization of Holocaust and, 63–64, 215n24; *Holocaust* airing and, 64–65; Holocaust remembrance and, 70–71; human rights advocacy, 33, 39, 57; Mothers of the Plaza de Mayo and, 57–60; republication of Holocaust testimony, 32, 60, 65–66; Timmerman case and, 51, 56; right-wing Jewish leaders and, 223n58. *See also* Schiller
Nueva Sión (Argentina), 32, 43, 61, 220n22
Novick, Peter, 16–19, 39, 49, 54, 73, 96, 208, 217n62, 219n110
"Nunca más" slogan, 10, 53, 64, 66, 100, 150, 156, 218n93. *See also* "Never Again"
Nunca más Report (Argentina). *See* CONADEP
Nuremberg Tribunal, 66, 148, 246n74

Ofer, Dalia, 49–50, 227n163, 228n172
Oglesby, Elizabeth, 150–52, 179, 243n27
Olympic Games (1968), 124–25
Opinión, La (Argentina), 46–47
Oz, Amos, 68–69

Pacheco, José Emilio, 22, 26, 109–28, 140, 142–43, 205, 235n3, 236n36, 236n41, 237nn44–45, 237n62
Pacheco Bop, Pedro, 192–96
Paraguay, 7, 34, 41, 215n23
Partnoy, Alicia, 83, 231n44
Peccerelli, Fredy, 186, 190, 250n73
Pérez Esquivel, Adolfo, 57, 58, 66, 231n53
Peronism, 5, 9, 35, 64, 79, 97–98, 101, 103, 137, 239n92
Peru, 22, 206, 207
Pinochet, Augusto, 6, 81, 219n109
Pollak, Michael, 83
Poniatowska, Elena, 123, 126–27, 238n68
Prensa, La (Argentina), 64
Proceso de Re-organización Nacional. *See* Argentina, dictatorship

Puentes (Argentina), 84–85
Punto de Vista (Argentina), 26, 79, 85, 91, 98, 99, 229n16, 232n69, 234n140

racism, 11, 146, 148, 157, 163–64, 204
Rein, Raanan, 19, 21
reparative approach, 85, 90, 127, 143, 165–66, 196, 210–11
Resnizky, Nehemías, 52, 61–62, 65, 68–69, 225n113, 225n113, 226n122
Revista de Revistas (Mexico), 133–36
revolutionary movements (Latin America), 2, 5, 82, 95, 97, 105, 131, 137–38, 151, 154, 156, 160, 162, 173, 175, 180, 199, 203, 239n92; "revolutionary futurity," 22–23, 166, 184, 199, 250n48. See also Latin American left
Revueltas, José, 126
REMHI (Recuperación de la Memoria Histórica, Guatemala), 190–91, 197–98, 250n73
Ríos Montt, General Efraín, 17, 27, 145–47, 157, 173, 176, 196, 242n8, 243n27, 244n36, 244n38
Rosencof, Mauricio, 4, 209–11, 214n11
Rosenthal, Rabbi Morton, 42, 52
Roma people, 167
Rohter, Larry, 175
Rothberg, Michael, 10–12, 23, 147, 202
Rousset, David, 117, 234n126
Rozitchner, León, 231n43
Rubinowicz, David, 237n41
Rus, Bernardo, 43, 44–46, 221nn41–42, 222n42
Rus, Sara, 45–46, 221n42, 222n42, 222n45

Russell Tribunal, 23, 147, 160–62, 163, 218n96, 246n76; Second Russell Tribunal, 164
Rwanda, 160, 186

Sábato, Ernesto, 57
Sanyal, Debarati, 10, 12, 130, 216n52, 235n6
Sarlo, Beatriz, 26, 77, 79, 85–91, 92, 96, 97, 98, 102, 106, 107
Sarmiento, Domingo, 95
Sartre, Jean-Paul, 52, 116, 160–61
Schlosser, Salomón, 133–34, 136, 239n102
Senkman, Leonardo, 64, 69–70, 215n23
Schindler's List (Steven Spielberg, dir.), 182–84, 186–87, 202, 249n43
Schiller, Herman, 32–33, 56–61, 66, 71–72, 219n10
Scilingo, Adolfo, 80
Shmucler, Héctor, 26, 77, 98, 99–103, 137–39, 234n126, 240n130, 240n138
Shoah uGevurah, 39–40, 49–50, 69, 74, 208, 227n63
Shoah Foundation (USC), 28, 29, 167, 171–73, 185–86, 196, 213n10, 248n104; FAFG testimonies, 189–202, 206; filming techniques, 187–90, 194; Hollywood influence on, 172, 187, 190, 198; Visual History Archive (VHA), 188–89, 202, 250n70
Shoah (Claude Lanzmann, dir.), 87–91, 129
Siemens, 84, 122
Sonderkommando, 120
solidarity, 3, 10, 20, 60, 110–11, 129–38, 147, 150, 200, 239n92; Casa Argentina (COSPA) 239n92; Comisión de Solidaridad con

Familiares de Presos y Detenidos en la Argentina (COSOFAM), 37, 138–39; Comité Argentino de Solidaridad (CAS), 136, 138–39, 239n92; Comité Panameño de Solidaridad con el Pueblo de Guatemala, 242n12; in concentration camps, 129–30, 133–34, 136, 239n92; Permanent People's Tribunal, 147, 161
Spanish Civil War, 218n93; exiles in Mexico, 130–32
Spielberg, Steven, 182, 186–88, 199
SS, 122. *See also* Einsatzgruppen
Semprún, Jorge, 83
Stoll, David, 28, 154, 170–82, 198, 202–203, 249n29, 251n96
Strejilevich, Nora, 83, 231n44
student movements, 2, 26, 37, 113, 116–18, 123–26, 132, 154, 238n66, 246n81

testimony: by Argentine survivors, 82–83, 85–87, 110–11, 135, 137–40, 220nn12–13, 231n52, 241n138, 244n35; audiovisual (*see* FAFG; Shoah Foundation); Aztec, 125; Christian frames of reference of, 22, 203; debates on validity of, 19–20, 80, 110–11, 119, 130, 137–41, 155–56, 180–83, 203–204 (*see also* Sarlo, Stoll; Vezzetti); political force of, 10, 21–22, 85, 114, 174, 250n48; as resistance, 127, 142–43, 183–85; "testimonial situation," 27, 128–30, 135–36, 140–41, 180, 184, 189, 193, 195, 203, 206; *testimonio*, 3, 22, 23, 28, 47, 170–72, 174, 177, 180, 182, 187, 199, 204; of Tlatelolco massacre, 26, 110, 123–24, 125–27. *See also* Holocaust testimony; Maya testimony

testimonial poetry, 125–27
Timerman, Jacobo, 42, 65; accusations against junta, 47, 59; DAIA response to, 51–56; Judenrat accusations, 32–33, 40, 46–51, 58, 60, 67–68, 72, 73, 205, 223n58, 228n172; and Wiesel, 62. *See also* Argentina, dictatorship
Tlatelolco Massacre (Mexico City, 1968), 26, 110, 112, 114, 122, 123–26; Comité '68 and, 246n81; remembrance of, 124, 126–28, 132. *See also* memory; Mexico; testimony
Todorov, Tzvetan, 6–7, 21, 85, 99, 134, 233n95
Toj Medrano, Emeterio, 199–200
Toker, Eliahu, 43–44, 46
traslados, 138–39
Traverso, Enzo, 19–21, 85, 151, 166
trauma, 9–10, 11, 22, 85, 90–91, 96, 106, 173, 182–84, 199, 215n28, 216n52, 214n7; and Menchú, 171–73
Treblinka, 63, 127, 209, 235n3
Tupac Amaru Rebellion (1780–82), 207
Tuyuc, Rosalina, 162, 199

Uchmany, Eva Alexandra, 133–36
United Fruit Company, 169
United Nations Convention on the Prevention and Punishment of the Crime of Genocide (1948), 23, 148, 159, 160–62, 170, 246n74, 246n82
United States, 5, 6, 15, 63, 186; anti-Communist aid to Latin American militaries, 2, 5, 27, 148, 169; concern for Jewish victims in Argentina, 42, 50–51, 53, 69; Holocaust memory in, 4, 10, 13–14, 16–19, 21, 23–24, 29, 32, 39, 62, 151, 165–67, 171, 201–202,

United States *(continued)*
  216n49, 251n94 *(see also under* Holocaust [Jewish]); and memory in Guatemala, 150; Menchú debates in, 28, 175–78; and Vietnam, 23, 113, 116, 160–61. *See also* Jews
United States Holocaust Memorial Museum, 29, 167, 188
Uruguay, 205, 206, 209–11, 214n11

Valdés, Hernán, 6
Vallejo, César, 210, 252n12
Veil, Simone, 135
Vergès, Jacques, 15, 217n57
Vezzetti, Hugo, 26, 57, 72, 77, 79, 81, 77, 91–97, 98, 102, 106–107, 127, 230n32, 233n95, 233n100, 233n105
victims, representations of: beyond trauma, 23, 96, 173, 199, 244n36; complicit, 86, 90–91, 104–107; confused with perpetrators, 73, 78, 105, 115–17, 120, 128; innocent, 20–22, 34, 39, 70, 72, 74, 93, 96, 104, 140, 151–52, 243n31; passive, 20–21, 150–52, 155, 165, 198, 244n31; resistant, 161, 171, 173, 181, 208–209; sanctified, 19, 72, 233n105; and vanquished, 19, 21–23, 141, 145, 151–53; victim-centric interpretations, 13, 17–19, 85, 165, 244n36; victim-hero dichotomy, 69–73, victim-witness, 181–84. *See also* Jews; *Shoah uGevurah*
Vidal-Naquet, Pierre, 15–16, 49, 160, 249n22
Vietnam, 2, 7, 8, 17, 23, 113, 116–18, 160–61, 247n82

Vision of the Vanquished, 125
Visual History Archive (VHA), 188–89, 202, 250n70
Volpi, Jorge, 124

Walsh, Rodolfo, 41, 103–104, 141, 124, 237n62
Walsh, Lilia, 103–104, 141
Warsaw Ghetto, 7, 43; uprising, 39, 53, 112, 117, 120, 121, 127–28, 161, 207, 236n41; uprising, commemoration of, 54, 65–66, 70–71, 208, 225n113
Wasserstrom, Dunia, 133–34, 136, 141, 240n122
Weiss, Peter, 111, 136, 235n1, 235n5, 240n122
Wiesenthal, Simón, 215n23
Wiesel, Eli, 7, 8, 19, 46, 178, 214n23; and Argentina, 62, 66, 68, 224n79
Wieviorka, Annette, 17, 18–19, 27, 82, 129, 135
Wilkomirski, Binyamin, 203–204
World at War (UK, 1973–74), 41, 65
World Jewish Congress, 54, 59
World War II, 14, 44, 62, 63, 131, 133, 136, 177, 208; post-WWII, 34, 49, 98, 148, 151, 208, 216n52

Yad Vashem, 29, 49, 50, 71, 167
Yerushalmi, Yosef Hayim, 88, 232n75
Yiddish newspapers, 32, 59, 62, 206
Young, James, 50, 85
Yugoslavia, 160

Zionism, 32, 35, 47, 54
Zyklon B, 116–18

CPSIA information can be obtained
at www.ICGtesting.com
Printed in the USA
LVHW022134120922
728185LV00005B/215